Hænoch Livneh

PHARMACOLOGY FOR THE PSYCHOTHERAPIST

Myron Michael Goldenberg, Pharm.D., Ph.D.
Psychotherapist in Private Practice
Santa Monica, CA

 **ACCELERATED DEVELOPMENT INC.**
Publishers
Muncie   Indiana

PHARMACOLOGY FOR THE PSYCHOTHERAPIST

1 2 3 4 5 6 7 8 9 10

Printed in the United States of America

Technical Development: Virginia Cooper
                       Tanya Dalton
                       Delores Kellogg
                       Marguerite Mader
                       Sheila Sheward

Library of Congress Cataloging-in-Publication Data

Goldenberg, Myron Michael. 1940-
    Pharmacology for the psychotherapist / Myron Goldenberg
       p.   cm.
    Includes bibliographical references.
    ISBN 0-915202-97-2
    1. Psychotropic drugs.   2. Psychopharmacology.   I. Title
    [DNLM: 1. Psychotropic Drugs--therapeutic use.   QV 77 G618p]
    RM323.G65   1990
    615'.788--dc20
    DNLM/DLC
    for Library of Congress   89-84338
                                               CIP

LCN: 89-84338

ACCELERATED DEVELOPMENT INC.
Publishers
3400 Kilgore Avenue
Muncie, Indiana 47304-4896
Toll Free Order Number 1-800-222-1166

ACKNOWLEDGEMENTS

One of the special joys I have in completing this work is reflecting upon the many people who have touched me, helped me, encouraged me, taught me, believed in me, and loved me. The list is long, making it impossible to thank each and every one of them personally. I do want to acknowledge several people who have been very important to me and this project.

Marjorie Rand, Beverly Morse, and Jack Rosenberg for being my teachers, for their encouragement, and for their belief in me.

June Perelson for being a very special friend, for reading the chapters, and for her useful feedback.

My children, David and Lara, for their help and for being the special children they are.

Linda, for her encouragement, her belief in me, for standing by me during the long hours of work, and for being someone special to love and be loved by.

CONTENTS

LIST OF FIGURES

CHAPTER **I**

INTRODUCTION

This is a book about psychopharmacology, the study of drugs, specifically those used in the treatment of psychological disorders. It is written with the non-physician psychotherapist in mind, emphasizing information and principles that have practical application for the psychotherapist.

Western psychiatry incorporates a biochemically based orientation in the treatment of the various mental disorders. The success in the treatment of schizophrenia since the early 1950s, using the phenothiazine and phenothiazine-like drugs, has encouraged and challenged researchers to find biochemical causes and solutions for many mental disorders.

As a society in general, we tend to turn towards chemicals or drugs as solutions to our problems. This may be through the use of prescription drugs such as diazepam (Valium) for the treatment of anxiety or insomnia, through the use of legally available and socially acceptable "drugs" such as caffeine in coffee or tea, or through the use of drugs that are illegal, but highly used and abused in our society, i.e., heroin, cocaine, or marijuana. Not only is the use of drugs here to stay, but also the misuse of drugs is an epidemic problem for our society. Drugs are used because they work. This is a very important statement. Drugs do work and do have a valued place in the treatment of illness. They are effective as ways of handling the stress and anxiety found in our complex society. The use of drugs can be inexpensive, quick, and, in many cases, a desirable way of handling certain problems. If drugs did not work, we would not have the vast problem facing us today. This book discusses both the useful aspects and the undesirable effects of the psychotropic drugs.

The vast majority of our society uses drugs. Therefore, more than likely the psychotherapist's clients have tried, or are currently using drugs. Oftentimes, drugs have been used to control the "symptom" that leads the client to the psycho-therapist for treatment. Today, a large number of non-physician psychotherapists are being trained. Many of these people have little or no background in psychopharmacology. Without this knowledge, the psychotherapist is not prepared to (1) take a drug and medical history, (2) discuss drug use with the client, (3) communicate with the client's physician or psychiatrist regarding the client's drug use, and (4) recognize when substance abuse is an underlying factor in the therapy or counseling. The objectives of this book are to present the reader or workshop participant with an overview of (1) medical terminology, (2) functions of the major systems, organs, and glands of the body, (3) the different categories of psychotropic drugs, (4) the mechanism, dosing, effects, side effects, and rationale for use of these drugs, and (5) the commonly used legal and illegal drugs of abuse.

When I meet people and tell them about my two careers, that of being a pharmacist and a psychotherapist, a frequent response is that the two careers seem so far apart and different. This may seem true, but the field known as psychophar-macology is the combination of these very same areas. Therefore, to write this book was a natural for me to have chosen. But, actually, this is far from the truth. A great deal of my effort and energy for the past thirteen years has been in the direction of moving away from pharmacy. At first, choosing to research and write this book seemed like a step backwards; however, it has become a tool of completion, and at the very same time, a symbol of my new direction.

I first became interested in teaching this topic during the time I was pursuing my Master's degree in psychology. At that time, I submitted a proposal to the school I was attending to do a workshop on the subject. The idea was accepted, and I created an eight or nine page syllabus, and conducted the workshop three or four times that year. Some time later I was asked to give the class at the Integrative Body Psychotherapy Training Institute in Venice, California. I have since given workshops on psychopharmacology at various institutes.

In researching for my earlier workshops, I had the opportunity to review the available literature and had attended several lectures and classes on the subject of psychopharmacology. This became the impetus of an inner process in which I began to formulate that which was to become this work. What I didn't know at the time, however, was that it was to become the most exciting, most important, and most rewarding project or educational endeavor I had ever undertaken.

My first cognitive experiences into the world of psychology came when I was eight years old. I had found a book on hypnosis at a school paper drive. I read the book, became quite intrigued, and began, rather cautiously, to try some of what I had read, both on myself (my favorite experimental subject) and on some friends. I found that I could induce a hypnotic state, and this cultivated my curiosity further about this phenomenon. I learned to control pain and how to relax through my self-experiments. By the time I was a teenager, I had experienced two surgeries and the extraction of four wisdom teeth without having to depend upon medication for the relief of pain. When I finished pharmacy school and became a pharmacist I was sure that my destiny was to work in the same pharmacy at which I had been for some time in Westwood, own a house in the San Fernando Valley, have three or four children, and "live happily ever after." These plans were interrupted, some 18 months later, by a letter from "Uncle Sam," requesting my presence in the Army. I spent my 26th birthday at Fort Benning, Georgia, as a basic trainee, perhaps making me one of the oldest draftees in the Army. Two years of military service in Europe and a year of Vietnam, and I landed back in California. I went back to my old job. However, I quit after only a month to take a job in a hospital pharmacy. I had changed, my interests had changed; I felt a great deal of unrest, and at the same time was very certain that what I wanted to do was work more directly with people. This finally led me to enroll in graduate school, and begin, at age 35, my formal education in the field of psychotherapy.

In recalling those factors that eventually led me to the writing of this book, two types of experiences come to mind. The first, which often moves me to rage, has to do with the many people I have counseled about drugs. I am talking about those people who were given drugs by a physician and suffered severe adverse effects that could have been avoided with proper education.

Case I. A 44 year old woman made an appointment with a Glendale physician because she had a sore throat. She was kept waiting for over an hour beyond her scheduled appointment time. When the physician saw her, he told her that she was "very anxious." Paying little or no attention to her sore throat, he wrote her a prescription for 30 Valium 10mg tablets (the strongest dose). He then told her to take one at bedtime, without even telling her what she was getting. He told her to come back in two or three weeks, and said he was going to put her on Premarin. After I talked with her, she went to see another physician who tested her hormone level and said she did not need the Premarin. I also reassured her that being kept waiting over an hour was reasonable cause to become irritated and "anxious." She never filled the Valium prescription.

Case II. A 37 year old woman had become addicted to Valium prescribed by her physician. She wanted to stop taking the drug and came to see me. I recommended that she have medical supervision in her attempts to withdraw from the drug. She returned to her regular physician, and he immediately prescribed a new medication (another anti-anxiety drug) for her, telling her that she would need them. She eventually found a new physician who did help her to gradually taper off the Valium.

Case III. A 57 year old woman was given sulfasalazine (Azulfidine), a sulfonamide drug used for the treatment of ulcerative colitis. She began taking two pills four times a day as her physician directed, and shortly afterwards developed diarrhea. She went to him and reported the diarrhea. He told her that in "his 30 years of practicing medicine he had never heard a case of diarrhea from this drug." I let her read my copy of the *Physicians' Desk Reference (PDR)* (1983 p. 1587-8) and she found the following:

> "Adverse reactions have been observed in 5 to 55% of patients included in clinical studies reported in the literature . . . . . . The most common adverse reactions associated with AZULFIDINE therapy are anorexia, nausea, vomiting, and gastric distress . . . ."

The literature also recommended that she cut her daily dose to "lessen adverse gastrointestinal effects." She did this, the diarrhea stopped, and she was able to continue on the medication.

During my career as a pharmacist, as well as that of psychotherapist, I have encountered many similar experiences. I do not mean this to be an attack on physicians, as I believe that the vast majority of them are very prudent members of the health care team. I share this information because of the effect it has had on me, and because of its importance in leading me to write this book.

The second type of experience was far more personal. I have already shared some of my experiences with pain. I have also found that through the use of techniques taught in Yoga, meditation, and other relaxation and awareness training that I can achieve "highs" that are quite similar to those of using "drugs" without subjecting myself to the many adverse effects of the drugs.

One major incident in my life, above all else, contributed to the writing of this book. About seven years ago, I had what was labelled as an acute anxiety attack. During this time I experienced some very unusual symptoms which could be described as hallucinations and paranoia, or, using another model as reference, as a "spiritual awakening" process, some-times known by the name "kundalini." For whatever reason, to me clearly I needed to go through this experience. I also knew that if I took the medication normally given for such symptoms it would interrupt the cycle. This was the most profound spiritual and psychological experience that I had ever had, including several very powerful drug "experiences." I began to think that perhaps others had had similar experiences, and this lead me to read books on the subject. These personal events, along with my earlier experiences with hypnosis, pain, and healing, created a curiosity about the use of drugs that became the catalyst for my increased interest in tying together the fields of my professional careers, pharmacology and psychology.

This study is intended to cover those areas of pharmacology that are of importance and interest to the psychotherapist. The material also is developed so as to be the basis for workshops or classes for the psychotherapist. In this book are 15 chapters, including this introduction. The following is a summary and overview of the other 14 chapters.

Chapter II Principles of Pharmacology

Chapter II is an overview of pharmacology and its principles. It begins with a section on medical terminology. This is intended to demystify the vocabulary and nomenclature of the medical world. The next section deals with drug use. It includes information on drug information sources, regulations and drug standards, drug nomenclature, and some basic considerations about drugs. Following are sections on dosage forms, determination of doses, routes of administration, drug action and body response, and the journey and fate of a drug.

Chapter III Anatomy and Physiology

This chapter briefly reviews those aspects of the human body that are of primary importance to understanding the workings of psychotropic drugs. It covers the nervous system, starting with the central nervous system, then the peripheral nervous system, and finally the autonomic nervous system. The focus is upon the functioning of these systems and upon the significance of these effects to the psychotherapist.

Chapter IV The Nature of Psychopathology

Chapter IV includes a discussion of what makes up mental health. It also explores the use of classifications of mental health, looking at the view point of those for, and those against such practices. This leads into a section on the history of classifications, and finally an exploration of the current *Diagnostic and Statistical Manual of Mental Disorders, 3rd Edition* (DSM-IIIR).

Chapter V Antianxiety Drugs

Chapter V begins with a review of anxiety, not being a specific disorder itself, but a symptom. This is followed by a section covering the five categories of DSM-IIIR that are anxiety related disorders, namely: phobic disorders, anxiety states, posttraumatic stress disorder, atypical anxiety disorder, and anxiety disorders of childhood or adolescence. The chapter concludes with a discussion of the drugs used in treating anxiety.

Chapter VI Hypnotic Drugs

The use of drugs to initiate sleep is as old as humanity. This chapter focuses on sleep, sleep disorders, and the drugs used to treat these problems.

Chapter VII Antidepressant Drugs

Perhaps the greatest misuse of drugs in Western medicine comes in the treatment of depression. Depression like anxiety can be a normal and health defensive response to stimuli, or it can be a pathological condition. This chapter explores these two relatively difficult to distinguish conditions and the use of drugs in their treatment.

Chapter VIII Lithium

Lithium, an elemental substance readily found in nature, was introduced into medicine in the middle 1800s as a treatment for gout. Its use in the treatment of bipolar disorders is relatively recent. The serum level for a therapeutic level of lithium is very similar to that of a toxic level. Therefore, the management of lithium therapy is very critical. Little is known about the mechanism of lithium. I recently received a call from one of my colleagues about a client. The client had been sent to a psychiatrist for evaluation of drug therapy. The client, diagnosed as depressed, was started on an MAO inhibitor. He became too sedated. After some experimenting with other antidepressant drugs, he was put on lithium, and within a short period of time began to do much better. My colleague was confused by the use of lithium, as she believed it to be used only for mania. Even though it is not usually considered a drug of choice, in this case it was quite helpful.

Chapter IX The Antipsychotic Drugs

The discovery of the antipsychotic drugs totally changed the treatment and prognosis for the psychotic patient. Prior to the phenothiazines and their cousins, the psychotic was destined to a life of virtually no hope for any future. Mental institutions were overcrowded, dirty, dangerous and disgusting places. With the use of the antipsychotic drugs these people began to have a new outlook on life. Today the majority are treated as outpatients and can find a useful place in society. Like many of the drugs dealt with in this book, some have severe side effects that may develop with the use of antipsychotic drugs.

Chapter X Analgesic Drugs

Pain medication is not usually covered in texts on psychotropic drugs. I have included this chapter because of my own experience with pain and my belief that the information covered is useful for the psychotherapist. We are all quick to recognize the pitfalls of physical dependence, sometimes referred to as "addiction." Psychological dependence, sometimes called "compulsion" or "psychic craving," is a state wherein the person takes drugs in attempt to create a state of well-being. The inability to create a state of well-being from within is the result of an early injury for which a psychological component exists. A "pseudostate" of well-being is created through the use of drugs. Therefore, I see the use of drugs, psychologically, as a defensive tactic against "fragmentation." This chapter covers the emotional and physical components of pain, and the use of narcotic and non-narcotic analgesics.

Chapter XI Antiepileptic Drugs

Some symptoms of seizure disorders are common to certain psychological disorders. This leaves a dangerous window for misdiagnosis. The well trained psychotherapist, especially those doing any breathing or body work, should be versed in the symptoms of these disorders. For example, myoclonia, an involuntary series of clonic spasms, in which rigidity and relaxation alternate in rapid succession, may be symptomatic of a neurologic disorder, a chemical intoxication, such as in alcohol detoxification, or a viral infection. This response might occur as the result of breathing or body work; in this case it is probably indicative of a muscle that has been held with great tension and then been released. The chapter covers the traditional categories of epilepsy including grand mal, petit mal, psychomotor, and Jacksonian type seizures. The psychotherapist who incorporates breathing and/or body work into his/her practice needs to be very cautious with individuals who have any history of seizure disorders. This information can be gathered during the history-taking sessions that precede the breathing-body work. The probability is high for a client who has had seizures in the past to have one during an intense breathing-body session. Breathing-body work directly affects the autonomic nervous system while indirectly affecting the central nervous system. The psychological effect of this is increased vulnerability, decreased level of defense, and an increase in excitement. This can trigger a seizure in the susceptible individual.

Chapter XII Drugs and Sex

A 55 year old male client was referred by his physician for treatment of impotence. In the first session, the determination was that his problem was mostly iatrogenic, in that, he had been placed on clonidine (Catapres), an antihypertensive medication. Many drugs effect an individual's ability to perform sexually. This chapter reviews (1) the male and female reproductive systems, (2) the sexual dysfunctions, (3) drugs that enhance sexual function, and (4) drugs that have an adverse effect on sexual function.

Chapter XIII Substance Abuse

Substance abuse is of epidemic proportion in our society. This is creating a need for both professional and non-professional training and education in this complex area. This year, the Board of Behavioral Science Examiners in California began to require an extensive training in substance abuse for future licenses. The material covered in this book is intended to give the psychotherapist a broad view of the area of substance abuse. Much of the material herein is augmented by case studies.

Chapter XIV Legal and Illegal Drugs

This chapter divides the commonly (and sometimes not so commonly) used drugs into four categories. Using street names, these are (1) the downers or depressants, (2) the uppers or stimulants, (3) the highlighters or drugs which can highlight awareness without creating a great deal of distortion, and (4) the hallucinogens or drugs that scramble the mind.

Chapter XV Treatment of the Substance Abuser

Chapter XV is organized to present an overview of treatment possibilities for substance abusers. Medical aspects of treatment are covered. The issue of spiritual awakening or crisis is dealt with as well as a look at the role of the psychotherapist in this important work.

CHAPTER II

PRINCIPLES OF PHARMACOLOGY

To the average person, the language of the healing arts holds a mystique and complex aura. It is full of lengthy and complicated words. Many of these words sound and seem foreign and unrecognizable. In fact, this mystique and secret language is very straight-forward, well-organized, and always to the point. If one were to describe to another person an object, for example a chair, and they did not have in their language an agreed upon word for "chair," then considerable effort would be needed to clearly communicate the concept of the chair. Language is invented and utilized out of necessity. If no need for language or a specific word was present, then neither would exist. Medical terminology exists so that people can communicate about the body and disease states.

MEDICAL TERMINOLOGY

Many medical terms seem strange and bewildering. Their spelling and pronunciation can be quite confronting. This can be easily understood when one recognizes that about three-quarters of these terms are based upon either Greek or Latin. Even though many new words are being coined today, the use of Greek and Latin continues. The Greeks were the founders of rational medicine, and many of their terms still exist in present times. Latin became the universal language of medical science.

A working knowledge of neither Greek nor Latin is necessary to build a medical vocabulary. However, a useful procedure is to understand fundamentals in order to increase one's knowledge of diseases, anatomy, and physiology.

Medical vocabulary usually consists of words in three parts. The first of these parts is called the root. It is preceded by a prefix and followed by a suffix.

prefix—root—suffix

With the exception of anatomical words, most medical terms are derived from a combination of two or more roots or word elements. Take a word, for example "rhinitis". The root "rhin" comes from the Greek word "rhin" or "rhino," meaning nose. The suffix "itis" means inflammation. Therefore, rhinitis means inflammation of the nose. One then can deduct that laryngitis would mean an inflammation of the larynx and appendicitis is an inflammation of the appendix. If the suffix "ectomy" means the surgical removal of an organ, then the word appendectomy means the surgical removal of the appendix.

Some words may have more than one root. These words are referred to as compounds and are frequently found in the health care field. For example, the word "osteoarthritis" has two roots: "osteo" is a root meaning bone, "arthro" is a root meaning joint, and "itis" is a suffix meaning inflammation. When put together, the word becomes an inflammation of the bone joints.

As a general rule, the name of an organ or body part is Latin, while the disease or condition affecting it is Greek (Collin 1974). Some words have been taken from other languages. For example, "petit mal" is French, "beriberi" comes from Senegalese, and "pellagra" is an Italian word.

The *prefix* consists of one or more syllables and tells how many or where. A prefix will never be used independently. It is used to modify the root by describing how many or where.

The following is a partial list of commonly used prefixes:

a (without, lack of)
ab (away from)
ad (to, toward, near to)
ambi (both)
amphi (about, on both sides, both)
ante (before)
anti (against)
bi (twice, double)
cata (down, according to, complete)
circum (around, about)
com/con (with, together)
contra (against, opposite)
de (away from)
dia (through, apart, across, completely)
dis (reversal, apart from, separation)
e/ex (out, away from)
ec (out from)
ecto (on outer side, situated on)
endo (within)
epi (upon,on)
exo (outside, on outer side, outer layer)
extra (outside)
hyper (over, above, excessive)
hypo (under, below, deficient)
im, in (in, into)
infra (below)
inter (between)
intra (within)
meta (beyond, after, change)
para (beside, beyond)
per (through, excessive)
peri (around)
post (after, behind)
pre/pro (before, in front of)
re (back, again, contrary)
retro (backward, located behind)
sub (under)
super (above, upper, excessive)
sym, syn (together, with)
trans (across)
ultra (beyond, in excess)

(adapted from Young & Austrin, 1979)

Take as an example the words:

hyperthyroid means _____ thyroid
(over or high)

hypothyroid means _____ thyroid
(deficient)

extracellular means _____ the cell
(outside)

perianal means _____ the anus
(around)

If the root "tension" refers to blood pressure, then how would
you say:

high blood pressure   (   )tension   (hyper)

low blood pressure   (   )tension   (hypo)

The **suffix** identifies the condition, disease or disorder.
Many suffixes used in medical terminology also are used in
ordinary language. Some examples are:

ize/ate	(as in hypnotize) put into a state of hypnosis
ist/er	(as in dentist) one who practices the art of
ent	(as in recipient) one who receives
	(makes adjective or noun a verb)
sia, y	(as in anesthesia) the loss of feeling
	makes noun expressing action, process of condition
	when added to verb
	(as in therapy) the treatment of
ma, mata	(as in trauma) means injury
	add to verb to make noun expressing result of action
ible	(as in contractible ability to contract.

Many words are derived from Greek and Latin adjectives or verbs. The adjectives will be in combination with a noun or verb. Then a suffix will be added to make the word into a noun. For example: AUTO PHOBIA The root "auto means "self," when combined with "phobia," which comes from the Greek word "phobos" meaning fear. The resultant word "autophobia" becomes an abnormal dread of being alone.

In the word "neuralgia," the root "neur" comes from the Latin "neuralis" and the Greek "neuron" meaning "nerve." The suffix "algia" comes from the Greek "algos" (pain) and "ia" (condition).

The following list gives some examples of commonly found suffixes:

Root	Meaning
algia	pain
auto	self
brady	slow
dynia	pain
dys	difficult/bad
eu	well/good
iatro	physician or medicine
kino	move
logy	study
lysis	breaking up/dissolving
phas	speak
pseudo	false
tachy	fast
tomy	cut
tropho	nourish

Take the word "iatrogenic." It comes from the Greek root "iatros" (physician) and the Greek "gennen" (to produce). Therefore the word means "resulting from the activity of physicians."

The words used for colors and numbers are also derived from Latin and Greek. Colors and numbers are often used to describe body parts or appearances. The colors and numbers in the following list are found in medical terms.

Colors		Numbers	
albus	white	centi	a hundred
chloros	green	dis	Gr.; twice L.;
cirros	orange-		separate
	yellow	mono	one
cyano	blue	primus	first
erythro	red	proto	first
leuc (k)o	white	semi	one half
melano	black	sesqui	one and a half

The names given to body parts and body fluids are mostly taken from Latin, while the condition or disease affecting it is Greek. The estimate is that 50% of the general English vocabulary and 75% of the scientific vocabulary is of Latin or Greek derivation. To include lists of all of these words is beyond the scope of this book. Several excellent texts are available for the reader who wants to become familiar with these terms. A medical dictionary is an invaluable tool. In starting a reference library a medical dictionary would be a good first purchase.

DRUG USE

One need only to read the newspaper, pick up a magazine, or listen to the news on radio or television to realize the epidemic use of drugs in our society. Chemotherapy has become the common treatment for stress, anxiety, depression, pain, and insomnia. Many of the drugs are obtained with a prescription. Also a vast number of people self-medicate with legal or illegal drugs. Parry et al.(1973) reported that more than 1.4 billion prescriptions were filled for psychotherapeutic drugs. In 1970, one American in five had used a prescription psychotherapeutic drug, while one in ten had used an over-the-counter drug at least one time. Balter et al. (1974) reported that 15% of the people in the United States had used an antianxiety or sedative drug. This author conducted a survey of ten Los Angeles and Orange County pharmacies in 1985. The survey showed that 10.4% of the prescriptions filled were for psychotropic drugs. The non-medical psychotherapist is frequently confronted with clients who are concurrently taking drugs. Unfortunately little emphasis has been placed upon training these practitioners in the area of psychopharmacology.

DRUG INFORMATION SOURCES

Knowing where to find something is often more valuable than knowing it. In the field of pharmacology this is a necessity. It is a field with so much information that to remember it all would not be practical or possible. Many physicians use only a select handful of medications in their practice. The physician relies on reference material or other resources to help him/her prescribe. The following resources are chosen with the psychotherapist in mind. They are listed in order of preference, with the most desirable or easiest to use first.

Medical Dictionary. There are several good ones on the market. Most book stores or college book stores will have several from which to choose. Two popular dictionaries are *Dorland's Illustrated* and Taber's.

Drug Information Center. These are becoming more and more available. Computer technology has made it possible to have vast amounts of information available in a readily retrievable system. Some local hospitals make their information available to health professionals. Some community pharmacists are very knowledgeable, have access to accurate information, and are willing to be helpful. Both the quality of the information and the willingness to take the time to help are varied with the individual. A quite helpful procedure would be to establish a relationship with a pharmacist. Several computer software programs are available that can retrieve drug information.

Package Inserts. The law requires the manufacturer of prescription drugs to include in each package a complete package insert. These contain the essential data on the specific drug: pertinent information as to dose, desirable and adverse effects, warnings, and administration information. These inserts are approved by the Food and Drug Administration (FDA). They reflect a great deal of precautionary material, that is, they include all of the possible problems known for the particular drug. The lay reader, would more than likely not take any drug after reading the possible adversed effects and warnings. What this points out is, that taking drugs is a calculated trade off between a therapeutic effect and a group of possible side effects. Another problem with the package insert is that they are written in medical jargon. Package inserts can be obtained from many pharmacies, as one is supplied with each package of the drug, and are supplied free of cost.

The Physicians' Desk Reference (PDR). The PDR has some advantages and disadvantages over other resources. It is less expensive than most other references. It is furnished annually to physicians without charge. Therefore, it is possible to obtain the prior year's edition without charge from your physician or pharmacist. The book is divided into five sections. The first part of the book is a list of manufacturers whose products appear in the book. In Section 1 (pink) is an alphabetical index divided into two parts. First is a listing of drugs by brand name, followed by their manufacturers. Second is a list of manufacturers, with a partial list of their products. In Section 2 (blue) products are listed according to an appropriate category or drug classification. Section 3 (yellow) contains a generic and chemical name index of products described in the product information section. Section 4 can be very useful. It has color photos of many of the more commonly used products. These products are shown under company headings and are not in alphabetical order. Section 5 (white) is the product information section. It is organized alphabetically by manufacturer and then by product. The monograms listed are very similar to the drug package inserts. The problem with the PDR is that only the drugs listed are the ones for which the manufacturer pays.

Popular Guides To Prescription and Non-Prescription Drugs. The market is flooded with these. They are usually inexpensive and found at most book stores. They often are in easy to use form, however, usually organized by generic name. This may make it hard to find the drug monogram. They can be a good source of basic information. These books may not answer the questions of the psychotherapist as they are consumer oriented.

Facts and Comparisons. A quick and comprehensive reference. It is updated monthly, therefore very complete. The big disadvantage is the price. If money is no object, this book is excellent.

The Dispensatory of the United States of America. This book has comprehensive monographs on individual drugs and general information on pharmacologic classes of drugs. The information is quite complete but may be too much for the therapist's needs.

REGULATIONS AND DRUG STANDARDS

A drug's action is based upon many factors. Most drugs have different effects in different dosage amounts. Drugs can have a different availability, called bioavailability, based upon several factors. Therefore, some drugs are assayed by activity, while other drugs are assayed by weight or volume. For example, Vitamin A or Vitamin E are both prescribed in units called International Units (IU). Insulin is also manufactured and assayed in units. The assay is the technique by which the strength or potency of a drug is measured. These are generally one of two types. They may be chemical or biological. These drugs are sold and assayed according to activity. They are measured against a standard. Most drugs are manufactured and assayed in weight measurements. Valium is sold as 2 milligrams (mg), 5 milligrams, or 10 milligrams tablets. Very small amounts of the active ingredient must end up in each tablet. The need for accurate standards and uniform assay becomes obvious.

Many drugs are obtained from plants. Digitalis and opium are good examples. The strength of these substances tends to vary from plant to plant, from place to place, and time to time. Accurate dosage is essential to accomplishing a reliable effect. Thus the necessity to find standard methods of assaying drugs.

In the United State we have several standards. These books list drugs that have been designated as official by the *Federal Food, Drug,* and *Cosmetic Act.* The first book is the *Pharmacopeia of the United States of America* (U.S.P.). It was first published in 1820 and is now revised every five years. It lists approved medicinal agents presently being used. It defines the drug as to source, physical and chemical properties, tests for purity and identity, assay, method of storage, category (type of drug), and dosage (therapeutic and dosage range). The *National Formulary* (N.F.) is published by the American Pharmaceutical Association and lists currently used drugs not already listed by the U.S.P. Homeopathic drugs are listed in the *Homeopathic Pharmacopeia of the United States.* Canada and Great Britain have their own standard sources. The World Health Organization publishes a *Pharmacopoeia Internationalis* (Ph.I.) It was first published in 1951. These regulations and standards have not been around for a long time.

Not until 1906, when the *Pure Food* and *Drug Act* was passed, were the U.S.P. and the N.F. designated, and at that time they became official standards and the federal government was empowered to enforce these standards. However, no provision was made for the restriction of sale of drugs.

The *Harrison Narcotic Act* was passed in 1914. The original act regulated the importation, manufacture, sale and use of opium, its derivatives, and cocaine. Later, legislation to control marihuana and its derivatives was enacted.

The restriction of other drug sales came after more than one hundred tragic deaths, in 1937, which were caused by the use of a toxic solvent, diethylene glycol, in an elixir of sulfanilamide. No investigation has occurred of the toxicity of the solvent prior to its manufacture. This incident caused so much public pressure that the Congress enacted the *Federal Food, Drug, and Cosmetic Act* of 1938. This law made it mandatory for manufacturers to perform toxicity tests in laboratory animals before seeking FDA approval to market drugs. This law also gave the *Homeopathic Pharmacopoeia of the United States* official status. It established procedures for introducing new drugs and provided a means of recall for drugs. The FDA was given the responsibility of enforcing the new law.

The *Durham-Humphrey Amendment* of 1951 was aimed at tightening control of certain drugs by restricting the refilling of prescriptions. This amendment divided drugs into two categories, those that were safe for use without medical supervision, and those not safe. The first group was designated to be available over the counter. The second was to be labelled: "Caution: Federal law prohibits dispensing without prescription."

In 1962, the *Kefauver-Harris Drug Amendment* further changed the *Federal Food, Drug, and Cosmetic Act.* Once again, the impetus for legislation came out of a tragedy. Hundreds of pregnant women were given the drug thalidamide, which closely resembles the hypnotic glutethimide (Doriden). As a result, many children were born having serious birth defects. This "thalidomide" catastrophe did not directly affect the United States as the drug was never released here. Nevertheless, this force created the legislation. The amendment tightened control over the quality of drugs, gave the FDA power to regulate over procedures for new drugs, and stated that efficacy, as well as safety of drugs, had to be established prior to their approval. In part, the amendment authorizes the Food and Drug Administration to demand "substantial evidence that the drug will have the effect it purports or is represented to have under the conditions of use prescribed, recommended, or suggested in the proposed labeling thereof."

In 1970 Congress enacted the *Comprehensive Drug Abuse Prevention and Control Act.* It replaced the *Harrison Narcotic Act of 1914* and the *Drug Abuse Amendments of 1965.* This *Controlled Substance Act* (C.S.A.) places responsibility on a newly established *Drug Enforcement Agency* (DEA), as well as the FDA. The DEA is a branch of the Department of Justice. This legislation required the registration of all persons involved in drug production and distribution. It set up five schedules of controlled substances, based upon the potential abuse and medical usefulness of the drugs.

Schedule I	High abuse potential. No acceptable medical use. (Heroin, marijuana, LSD)
Schedule II	High abuse potential. Severe dependence. (Narcotics, barbiturates, amphetamines)

Schedule III	Less abuse potential. Moderate dependence. (Non-barbiturate sedatives, non-amphetamine stimulants, limited amounts of certain narcotics)
Schedule IV	Less abuse potential. Limited dependency. (some sedatives, antianxiety agents, non-narcotic analgesics)
Schedule V	Limited abuse potential. (Primarily small amounts of narcotics (codeine) used as antitussive or antidiarrheal. Federal law allows the sale of a certain number of these drugs without a prescription.

State laws may supercede the Federal law with an Rx caution, such as in California, where a prescription is required for Federally exempted Schedule V narcotics.

Recently, because of the "Tylenol" scare, the *Federal Trade Commission* (FTC) has played an important role in drug labeling, advertising, and packaging.

DRUG NOMENCLATURE

Not until the Drug Amendments of 1962 were the USP and NF required to provide only one official name for each drug. This, however, does not eliminate the confusion. Drugs can still be known by several names.

The **official** name is the one given by the official publication that lists the drug. Before becoming official each drug is assigned a **generic** name. This is given to the drug by the company that develops the drug. It is often a simplification of the **chemical** name. The generic name is not protected by law and is usually used throughout the world. The chemical name reflects the language of the chemist. It is a precise description of the constituents of the drug and a precise word map of the placement of each atom or atomic group. For example, the chemical name for the drug chlordiazepoxide

(Librium) is 7-chloro-2-methylamino-5-phenyl-3H-1, 4-benzo-diazepine 4 oxide hydrochloride. Many drugs are referred to by a **trademark** name or **brand** name. Librium is a trade name and chlordiazepoxide is the generic name. The law requires that when a brand name is used the generic name must be present in letters that are at least half the size of those of the brand name. In technical writing the generic name is most often used. The brand name may be given in parentheses. Some drugs, such as tetracycline have several brand names. Drugs used in psychiatry are often prescribed by their generic name. This is especially true in institutional settings.

DRUG USE: SOME BASIC CONSIDERATIONS

A **drug** may be defined as any substance or combination of substances taken or administrated (1) for the maintenance of health—vitamins, hormones, food, insulin; (2) to reverse disease process—antibiotics, digitalis; (3) to relieve symptoms—aspirin, codeine; (4) for prophylaxis—vaccines; (5) to alter normal body processes—oral contraceptives; and (6) to aid in diagnosis—barium.

Sources of Drugs

Five main sources exist from which drugs are derived. These are (1) plants, such as opium, belladonna, quinine, and digitalis; (2) animals, from which we get insulin, thyroid extract, and epinephrine; (3) minerals, such as iodine, iron, and calcium; (4) synthetic drugs created in the laboratory, most new drugs are of this type; and (5) antibiotics, substances derived from or produced by living cells having an inhibitory or lethal action on microorganisms.

Drugs Obtained From Plants. For thousands of years the majority of drugs used were obtained from plants. Healers, shaman, and medicine people would use the roots, seeds, bark, flowers, or leaves. These were either used as they occurred in nature, dried, or otherwise processed. Modern technology has allowed a more accurate extracting of the "active principles" on these plant sources. In looking at the pharmacologically active compounds of plants according to chemical and physical properties, one finds several groups of substances. These include **alkaloids, glycosides, gums, resins and balsams, tannins,** and *oils.*

Alkaloids are compounds composed of carbon, hydrogen, nitrogen, and oxygen. They are often poisonous, usually exist at room temperature as white crystalline solids, taste bitter, and are used in very small doses. Alkaloids have the letters "ine" at their end. For example, cocaine, caffeine, morphine, and atropine are alkaloids. When an alkaloid is combined with an acid a salt is formed. Cocaine Hydrochloride (Cocaine HCl) is a salt. Cocaine (free base) is the naturally occurring alkaloid.

Glycosides when hydrolysed (a process of decomposition resulting from the incorporation and splitting of water) form a carbohydrate (a sugar) and another chemical group such as an aldehyde, alcohol, or acid. These compounds contain carbon, hydrogen, and oxygen. Glucose is a common glycoside.

Gums are a mucilaginous (thick) excretion from plants. They are polysaccharides (contain more than four molecules of simple carbohydrates). Agar and psyllium seeds are examples of natural gums used as laxatives. Gums and balsams are rarely used these days. They would be used in topical preparations.

A **resin** is a crude drug obtained from the sap of certain trees. They are used as laxatives, and work by local irritation.

Oils are of two kinds obtained from natural sources. Volatile oils have an aroma, evaporate easily, and tend not to leave a greasy stain. Fixed oils are greasy and do not readily evaporate. Peppermint and clove oils are examples of the former. Castor and sesame are examples of the latter.

DOSAGE FORMS

The term **dosage form** has come to replace the terminology pharmaceutical preparation. As recent as fifty years ago the pharmacist was responsible for making a "proper preparation of the prescribed active ingredients" of a prescription. Today the pharmacist purchases almost all medications in ready to use dosage forms. The centralization of pharmaceutical manufacturing has come about due to the use of many new and complex drugs. This centralization has provided a more accurate product and has allowed the consumer to purchase the product at a lower cost.

A *drug product* contains the prescribed amount of the active ingredient and several other substances. These are incorporated in a very prescribed manner. Several important considerations are necessary in making a dosage form. For example, to make a tablet the manufacturer takes the powdered drug and adds a diluent (dextrose, lactose, starch, etc.). This is to make the tablet into a size that is convenient for the user. The tablet will be pressed into shape by large machines. In addition to the diluent manufacturer adds a binder, a lubricant, and a disintegrator. The binder is a substance that gives adhesiveness to the powder. The lubricant stops the tablet from sticking to the machines. The disintegrator (starch is often used) helps the tablet dissolve when it is in water. Many tablets are coated. This may be for identification or to enhance palatability. Some tablets have special enteric coatings that allow them to pass through the stomach before they dissolve.

Many drugs come in *sustained release* forms. This means that the active ingredient is released over an extended period of time. Advantages of these long-acting drugs include convenience, patient compliance, and possible lessening of side effects. Disadvantages include high cost and the possibility of irregular drug release causing other than desired therapeutic levels. New methodology has improved the performance of these drugs, and anticipation is that more of these will find their way to the marketplace in the future. Some of the new dosage forms include implantation and patches.

Physical States

Drugs are available in three basic physical states—solid, liquid, and gas—plus some others. Many drugs come in more than one of these states.

Solid. Solid dosage forms include three types of oral preparations. These are *tablets* (powdered substances molded or compressed), **capsules** (usually made of gelatin), and **troches** or **lozenges** (solid discs of medicinal powders that are made to dissolve slowly in the mouth). Topical preparations consist of **ointments** and **creams.** These are preparations in which the active ingredient is mixed into a vehicle to be applied to a body surface. Ointments are usually oil or alcohol soluble, and creams are water soluble. A cream can be rubbed into the skin, and an ointment will usually leave a protective layer. **Suppositories** are medicated masses molded into a convenient shape to be inserted into the rectum, vagina, or urethra. Their base is made to dissolve at body temperature, thereby releasing the active medication. **Patches** represent a new dosage form on the market. They are applied to the body and continue to release medicine over an extended period of time.

Liquid. Drugs in liquid form may be administered orally, rectally, injected, or applied topically. These dosage forms are very important because of the possibility of injecting them into the body. Injections can be made into muscle, veins, arteries, body cavities, bones, and joints. Injecting a drug has many advantages and some disadvantages. Disadvantages include pain in administration and the need for a trained person to administer the drug. Advantages include the ability to dose an unconscious person and the possibility of a quicker onset of drug action. Many people, especially children, cannot swallow pills, and liquids provide a vehicle for medicating them. The general classification of liquid preparations includes:

Solutions. These are preparations of one or more drugs dissolved in water.

Syrups. Concentrated solutions of sugar in water to which medication may be added. Simple Syrup contains 85% w/v sugar. This means that in every 100 fluid units of syrup are 85 weight units of sugar.

The w/v is a measurement of weight to volume—the dissolved substance is given in weight units and the vehicle is in volume units. For example 85 Gm of sugar in a total volume of 100 ml final solution.

Elixirs. Clear, sweetened solutions made from water, and alcohol containing aromatic substances and medication.

Tinctures. Solutions prepared from plant extracts or chemical substances dissolved in alcohol or alcohol and water.

Suspensions. Preparations in which finely divided particles of insoluble material are suspended in a liquid vehicle. These preparations need to be shaken before they are used.

Emulsions. Either water particles suspended in oil or oil particles in water that are held in suspension by an emulsifying agent. Milk is a good example of an oil in water emulsion.

Gas. Gaseous medications are of limited use. These include many of the anesthetic drugs and some respiratory drugs given by inhalation. Oxygen and carbon dioxide are also gaseous drugs used to support life.

The fourth dosage form is the aerosol. These drugs are separated from the above because of the use of a liquid or gas propellant that causes the medication to be expelled from its container. These medications are in the form of solutions, powders, and emulsions.

There are several additional pharmaceutical preparations that are worthy of being mentioned.

Powders. Powders are finely divided solid drugs or drug mixtures. They are rarely used. They would be dispensed in separate folded papers or in a gelatin capsule. They can be for internal or external use.

Liniments. Liniments are liquid emulsions or solutions of various substances in oil, alcoholic solutions of soap, use for external application. They are applied by rubbing directly to the skin. They have one or more active ingredients and are used generally for their rubefacient, counterirritant, mildy astringent, and penetrating effects.

Pastes. Pastes are ointment-like preparations that contain ingredients that make them stiff. They usually absorb secretions and are less likely to penetrate the body than an ointment.

Poultices. Poultices are soft moist preparations used to apply an active ingredient to the skin.

DETERMINATION OF DOSES

No two people seem to respond to a given drug or dose in exactly the same way. Some people show little effect when given a drug, and others will have exaggerated or unexpected effects. Possible reasons for these differences may be physiologic, pathologic, biochemical, genetic, immunologic, or psychological. Keep in mind that each person is an individual and will have a unique response to a given drug. These factors are extremely important in determining a dosage regimen for an individual.

Age

The age of the recipient will often affect the response to drugs. The extremes of life, the newborn infant and the elderly, usually require a much smaller dose than other people. In the newborn, the dose is critical because of the infant's sensitivity and the ratio of drug to body weight. For the elderly, the dose may need to be altered due to impaired ability to inactivate or excrete the drug, or some complication due to another illness. Some drugs are not tolerated by children or have adverse effects that eliminate their use with children. For example, the antibiotic tetracycline is no longer used for children or pregnant women because it was found to cause a permanent stain on the teeth of children or the undeveloped teeth of the prenatal child.

Weight

The ratio of body weight to drug dose may determine how concentrated the drug will become in the body. In certain drugs this is critical. In these cases the body weight is taken into consideration in calculating a dose regimen. In a very obese patient a dose may need to be increased and in a very lean person the dose may be lowered. The greater the person's body weight the smaller the chances of the administered dose arriving at the desired reactive target tissue. Dosages for young children may be figured on the basis of body surface area(BSA). The BSA is obtained from a chart called a nomogram.

Sex

The sex of a patient sometimes affects the response to a drug. The most obvious possibility is during pregnancy. Many drugs may have an adverse effect during pregnancy. The FDA has established five categories to indicate the potential of a drug in causing birth defects. These categories are to help establish the benefits versus the risk in taking a drug.

Category A is for drugs that have not demonstrated a risk to the fetus in the first trimester of pregnancy and no evidence of risk has been found in later trimesters.

Category B indicates that no demonstrated risk to the fetus has been shown in animal studies; however, no adequate studies are available in pregnant women.

Category C is for drugs that have shown adverse effects in animal studies and no adequate studies in humans are available.

Category D is for drugs where evidence has been found of human fetal risk; however, the potential benefits from the use of the drug in pregnant women may be acceptable despite its potential risk.

Category X is for drugs that show a potential for fetal abnormalities or adverse reactions in animal or human research. Reaction reports indicate evidence of fetal risk. The risk clearly outweighs any possible benefit.

Intramuscular injections are absorbed at different rates in women and in men. Women's muscles have a higher fat content and poorer blood supply than men's. Normally, women will absorb drugs at a slower rate than men. The effects of drugs after an IM injection will appear later and persist longer in women than in men.

Physiological Factors

Several physiological factors can alter the response a person has to a drug. The body has a normal diurnal rhythm. Giving hypnotic drugs in the morning will be less effective as a depressant than at night. Of course, in large enough doses the hypnotic effect will happen at anytime. Adrenocorticosteroid drugs are best given in the morning when the adrenal glands are normally secreting similar steroids at their maximum rate. This regimen lessens the potential of long term adverse effects.

The response to drugs will be different when the acid-base and water or electrolyte balance are distorted.

Pathological Factors

Underlying pathology can often change a person's response to a drug. Most commonly, diseases of the kidney and liver will interfere with the detoxification and excretion of drugs. This can cause ordinary doses to accumulate to toxic levels in the body. It may be dangerous to administer a drug that is metabolized and/or excreted from a damaged organ. For example, a person with a damaged liver may not be able to deactivate a barbiturate because of lack of liver enzymes that would ordinarily perform this function. Giving a barbiturate anesthesia to this patient may cause severe reactions, including unconsciousness or death from respiratory failure. Many drugs are excreted through the kidneys. Certain antibiotics that have a close therapeutic and toxic level can cause severe damage with the kidney-impaired person. These drugs may accumulate in the kidney tissue and then other organs, including the eighth cranial nerve. Continued accumulation of the unexcreted drug can cause deafness and loss of equilibrium, even though only seemingly safe doses have been injected at what was believed to be proper intervals. A person's underlying pathology is of the utmost concern when figuring out a proper dosage regimen. Patients with hyper or hypo-thyroidism, peripheral vascular disease, and low or high blood pressure may be compromised by otherwise normal drug dosage.

Genetic Factors

Some people are born without certain drug metabolizing enzymes and thus will have an unusual response, a sensitivity , or a resistance to various drugs.

Immunological Factors

Drug molecules stimulate the patient's immune mechanisms to produce protective antibodies. When a person takes the same drug at a later date, an immune reaction occurs that can result in many types of physiologic responses. These are known as allergic responses and can be anything from a skin rash to death.

Psychological Factors

The Latin word "placebo" literally means "I will please." In medicine, the word placebo is used to identify the administration of a pharmacologically inert material. Well documented is the statement that a large percentage of the population are active placebo-takers. In other words, most people will have a positive response to taking a drug, even if no pharmacologically active ingredient is in it. Pharmacology texts contain statements about a person's response as being influenced by the underlying personality structure, and by hopes, fears, or expectations. Also clear is that people have a placebo response to medication that has an active ingredient. Even in the carefully done "double blind" procedures used in drug research, difficulty is often encountered to determine what part of the desired effect is placebo induced and what part is pharmacologically induced. Consider the process of visiting a physician and having a prescription written, then being told to take the prescription to a pharmacist and have it filled. This is a very strong suggestion, coming from a person believed to have the knowledge or power to heal. The patient is being told that if he/she will do this, it will make him/her well. This is the "placebo effect." It is also very strong medicine.

A patient's personality also is a factor in determining dosage. A compliant person will do what is asked and go out of his/her way to follow directions. The defiant person is less likely to follow directions or take the drug as directed. Compliance with drug regimens is a considerable problem with which health practitioners have to deal.

Environmental Factors

Environment factors influence the effects of drugs. People taking alcohol or psychotropic drugs will respond differently when with others than when they are alone. The temperature or humidity also will have an influence on the effect of a drug. Heat tends to dilate blood vessels and can cause an increased effect when using a vasodilator. Patients taking antihypertensive drugs may experience a sharp drop in blood pressure from the usual dose when they suddenly move to a subtropical resort or a heat wave begins.

Tolerance

Tolerance is either congenital or acquired. As a person builds a tolerance to a drug, they will require a larger dose to get the same therapeutic effect. **Congenital tolerance** is usually caused by an increased capacity to inactivate drugs by hepatic and other drug metabolizing enzymes. In **acquired tolerance,** the person's body usually stimulates the synthesis of increased amounts of drug detoxifying enzymes.

Cumulation of Drugs

The presence of residues of previously administered doses of the same drug in the body will influence the effects of an administered dose. When a drug is given in several successive doses at intervals shorter than the time necessary to eliminate earlier doses, then the drug tends to accumulate in the body. The increased concentration of the drug at its site of action results in a more intense pharmacologic effect. The duration of the drug's action will be prolonged, because the body's drug metabolizing and excreting processes require a longer time to remove the accumulated drug.

Some drugs are metabolized at a steady rate. Alcohol is an example. This means that whatever amount of drug is in the body the body will only metabolize a fixed amount of drug per unit of time. With most drugs, the rate of elimination is proportional to the amount in the body. The amount of drug eliminated is not constant; instead, a constant fraction of the total amount of drug in the body at any time is being eliminated. When several doses of a drug are taken at regular intervals, causing an accumulation of the drug in the body, the amount of drug removed from the body in the intervals between doses also becomes greater. Eventually, a point is reached at which the amount of drug cleared is equal to the amount taken in. After that, the concentration of the drug in the body stays the same. The time needed for a drug to reach this **steady state** or **plateau level** depends on the rate of the processes by which it is eliminated. This is expressed in terms of the drug's biologic, or elimination, **half-life.** (t-½) The half-life is the time necessary for the amount of drug in the body to decrease by one-half of the previously attained peak. The half-life of drugs can vary widely.

In order to raise a drug's concentration in the tissues more quickly to a fully effective level, a loading dose is sometimes used. The drug is administered in doses that exceed the body's ability to eliminate it. After a steady state level is attained, then maintenance dosage can be initiated.

ROUTES OF ADMINISTRATION

The choice of a route of administration of a drug should be based upon an understanding of several factors: (1) the drug's chemical properties—this includes the drug's pH, ability to ionize, and stability in gastric juice; (2) the drug's physical properties—this includes the size of the molecule and the solubility in aqueous or oil vehicles; (3) the site of desired action; (4) the rapidity of the response desired; and (5) the patient's general condition.

Oral Administration

The most common route of administration is orally or by mouth. This is the safest, most economical, most convenient means of giving a medication. When a drug is taken into the body, it may be absorbed through any mucosal surface. The absorption may, therefore, happen or begin in the mouth. Nitroglycerine is a drug that is taken sublingually (under the tongue) and is absorbed directly into the circulatory system from the mouth. Drugs that are swallowed travel through the esophagus to the stomach. Very little absorption takes place in the stomach. The stomach is concerned with digestion and storage of food and not absorption. The time involved in the drug passing through the stomach to the mucosal tissues of the intestines depends upon how much food is in the stomach, what type of food, the age and the condition of the person. This trip may take from 20 minutes to an hour. Drugs taken orally have a slow onset of effect and a relatively long period of action.

Rectal Administration

Drugs can be administered into the digestive tract *rectally.* This is done by using a suppository or an enema. Rectal administration is advantageous when the stomach is nonretentive, when a drug's smell or taste is objectionable, when a patient is unconscious, or when irritation to the gastrointestinal tract is to be avoided. The use of rectal medication can be experienced as invasive by the patient.

Parenteral Administration

Drugs are often administered by means of a hollow needle and syringe. This form of administration is called *parenteral.* Parenteral administration may be in the form of an injection or an infusion. *Infusions* are large volume diluted solutions that are usually given into a vein; however, they may be injected into an artery or body cavity. Infusions are most often used to supply electrolyte, drugs and fluids, replace lost blood, and to relieve tissue dehydration. *Injections* are most frequently given intramuscularly. The shoulder or buttock areas are the usual sites because they offer the safest muscle mass. The drug will be absorbed into the circulatory system through the richly vascularized muscle mass. Drugs are administered intravenously and, on occasion, intraarterially. These drugs reach all parts of the body in seconds. They also are not affected by digestive processes, or muscle and liver enzymes. Injections are made *subcutaneously* (just below the outer skin layer),

intradermal (into the skin), **intraperitoneal** (into the abdominal cavity), or **intrathecal** (into the area surrounding the spinal column).

Topical Administration

Some drugs are administrated topically. This means they are applied to a surface of the skin, or mucous membrane. These drugs are used to treat a skin disorder called "dermatitis" or to be absorbed into the system. The patch is a example of this later dosage form. Patches are now available for treating motion sickness, angina (chest pain), and estrogen replacement. This dosage form will be used more in the future for other types of medications. They are very convenient, need to be changed once every twenty-four or thirty-six hours, and give a continual therapeutic dosage level of the drug. The problems with the patches are expense and skin irritation for some patients.

Inhalation Administration

Some drugs are given by inhalation, to be absorbed in the respiratory tract. The drug is absorbed through the large area of tissue available in the lungs. Smoking cigarettes or marihuana are two examples of drugs absorbed in this way. Anesthetic gases are administered through the lungs. This is a very fast route of administration and is easily controlled.

DRUG ACTION AND BODY RESPONSE

This section deals with where and how drugs act in the body. It also focuses upon the body's response to drugs. Drugs act at the surface of cells, within the structure of cells, or in the extracellular fluid of the body. The exact site of action within the cell is not known in most cases. Some drugs act at a site that is distant from the responding tissue. For example, a drug might stimulate the respiratory centers of the brain, activating the muscles involved in the respiration reaction.

Some drugs act locally and some act systemically. Drugs that act locally act at the sight of application. Many drugs that are applied to the skin fall into this category. Some drugs that are swallowed also fall into this category. These drugs are not absorbed in the intestine and only have a local action in the bowel. Neomycin Sulfate is an antibiotic that is not absorbed and is used to suppress bacteria prior to bowel surgery. When a drug is absorbed it can have systemic action. It is absorbed into the bloodstream and may be distributed to all parts of the body through circulation.

Several theories exist on how drugs actually act in the body. These are by (1) combining with cellular constituents called receptors, (2) interacting with cellular enzyme systems, or (3) affecting the physicochemical properties of the outer cell membrane and of intracellular structures.

Receptor Theory

Many drugs are believed to combine with chemical groups, within the cell or on the cell wall. These drugs will only combine with specific agents known as **receptors.** The theory is that these receptors actually attract the drug by having a molecular shape that fits with the drug. This is sometimes known as the "lock and key" theory. Think of the shape of a key that will only fit into a certain lock. When the correct shaped key and lock are matched up, then the lock can be opened. The receptor theory is much the same. A certain shaped drug molecule is attracted by a receptor site on the cell wall. When the two shapes fit or line up together, the drug acts the same way as a natural body chemical does to set off a chain of events. For example, the naturally occurring body chemical acetylcholine combines with receptors in the membranes of muscle and nerve cells that are chemically specialized to receive it. This activity starts a chain of events that results in making muscles cells contract or triggers nerve cell signals. Certain synthetic drug agents can duplicate the action of acetylcholine by combining at the cell wall. These drugs are sometimes referred to as **agonists.** Other drugs or foreign chemicals can combine or attach themselves to the cell wall site; however, they are not capable of starting the sequence of biochemical actions or events. These drugs then tie up or block the receptor site and interrupt the normal effect. Pharmacologically, this can be a very useful agent. The drug atropine, an anticholinergic agent, successfully blocks the natural sequence of events that are initiated by acetyl-choline. The *antagonist,* in this case atropine, competes for the cellular receptor site which normally accepts acetylcholine. The atropine will interfere with the normal activity, causing a powerful pharmacological effect; that is, it will eliminate the normal physiological function. Atropine is considered a strong antagonist agent and can totally tie up the available receptor sites. Some drugs are weak antagonists. These drugs will cause a partial interference of the natural chemical activity.

To review, three ways exist that a drug or drugs can act in the receptor theory. First, a drug can bind with a receptor site and produce an effect that will preclude another drug from binding to the cell. A second way would be by competitive antagonism. Here a drug binds to the same receptor site as another, thereby stopping the other drug from binding. Third, a drug can combine with a different receptor site and still block, and thereby prevent another drug from binding.

Drug-Enzyme Interactions

Enzymes are protein molecules that act as catalysts in the chemical reactions taking place in the body. A catalyst is a chemical substance that is necessary for a reaction between two or more substances. The catalyst, however, does not change during the chemical reaction, nor is it involved in the resultant products. Enzymes are very specific. Each enzyme can only facilitate one chemical or a few related chemicals. Many drugs produce their effects by inhibiting the activity of an enzyme. Thus a normal biochemical activity of the body ceases because the necessary enzyme is not available to assist in the reaction. The group of drugs called MAO inhibitors act by inhibiting the enzyme monoamine oxidase. These drugs will be discussed in the section on antidepressant drugs.

Some chemotherapeutic agents are selectively toxic to an invading pathogen, parasite, or neoplastic cell. Penicillin is an example of a drug that interferes with the cell wall synthesis of a bacterial cell; however, it will not interfere with the cell wall production of the host. Many anticancer drugs have this cell selective ability and will select out cancerous cells. Many of the adverse effects of anticancer drugs are the result of the killing of rapidly growing normal cells.

Heavy metal poisoning results when a metal, such as arsenic, binds to a chemical group that is a component of an enzyme system. The deadly chemical cyanide combines with iron atoms at the active sites of the enzyme, cytochrome oxidase, to stop the cells from utilizing the oxygen brought to them by the blood, with death coming in minutes.

Physical-Chemical Activity

Some drugs act by altering the physical properties of cells. Other drugs may act by having a chemical affinity for some specific cellular component. Little is known as to the mechanisms involved.

Systemic Action of Drugs

The following terms are introduced at this time to help the reader understand the different processes and become familiar with the terms used to describe these processes.

Stimulation. Increasing the activity of some cells. (Caffeine is an example of a stimulant of CNS activity.)

Depression. Causes some cellular process to occur at a decreased rate. (Barbiturates depress CNS activity.)

Replacement. A drug that is given when a normally functioning activity decreases or ceases to function. (Thyroid hormone is given to people who are hypothyroid.)

Irritation. An action that causes slight temporary damage to cells. Mild irritation causes increased activity of cells. Prolonged irritation can cause depression of cellular activity. Continued or marked irritation can produce inflammation or death of the tissue. (Castor oil works by irritating the intestine.)

Selective Action. Action that is generally greater on one tissue than on others.

Physiologic Action. The action of a drug on normal healthy tissue.

Therapeutic. The action of a drug on diseased tissue or in a sick person.

Side Effect. Any action of a drug other than the one for which it is administered.

Adverse Effect. A side effect that is regarded as harmful to the patient.

Cumulative Effect. The result of a drug being given faster than it can be metabolized.

Synergistic Action. Action of two or more drugs that, when administered together, produce effect greater than the effect of each component drug administered separately.

Potentiation. Effect one drug has on increasing the effect of another drug, often without causing any effect of its own.

Antagonistic Action. Action that results from administering two or more drugs, causing contrary effect in the same system or group of cells.

Teratogenic Effect. Defect in unborn child caused by drug administered to mother

Tolerance. Phenomenon in which an ever-increasing resistance often occurs to the drug's desired effects, but not always after prolonged administration. To continue the same effects, the drug has to be administered in larger and larger quantities.

Cross Tolerance. Development of tolerance, not only to one particular drug, but also to drugs chemically or pharmacologically related to it.

Hypersensitivity. Allergic or exaggerated reaction to a certain drug or drug class.

Idiosyncrasy. Abnormal or peculiar response to a certain drug in a particular individual. This could be under-response, showing abnormal tolerance, or over-response, showing abnormal susceptibility. It may be a qualitatively different effect than the usual one, or unexpected symptoms which are unexplainable.

Habituation. A psychic craving for a drug when it is withheld.

Addiction. A condition that develops after continued administration of certain drugs. It is characterized by altered physiological processes as well as psychic craving. In true addiction tolerance is manifested.

Therapeutic Index. The ratio of the toxic dose of 50% of the population divided by the effective dose of 50% of the population.

THE JOURNEY AND FATE OF A DRUG

When a drug enters the body, it begins an interesting and complex journey. This section will follow that journey. The section is divided into four areas: (1) the absorption into the body fluids from the site of its entry into the body (Absorption); (2) the transportation or distribution to different parts of the body (Distribution); (3) the detoxification, inactivation, or transformation into its breakdown products (Metabolism/Bio-transformation); and (4) the excretion or elimination from the body (Elimination).

Absorption

Oral. The routes of administration of a drug have already been discussed. What happens once the drug enters the body?

When a drug is taken orally, it passes down through the esophagus, through the stomach, and into the small intestine. On this journey the drug dissolves in the gastrointestinal tract fluids. The majority of the drug will be absorbed through the mucous membranes of the small intestine. The inner lining of the small intestine is covered with millions of villi that with their network of capillaries, offer a vast mucosal opportunity for the drug molecule to pass into the circulatory system. Capillaries are microscopic tiny blood vessels. The drug then passes into the portal vein that takes it to the liver. The drug may be destroyed in the liver by enzymatic action or it may just pass through the liver into the bile, the digestive secretion of the gall bladder. The bile is secreted into the upper small intestine, where the drug may become reabsorbed again and pass back into a capillary. A drug may end up passing back and forth through the gut to the liver. When a drug makes it through the liver, unchanged, or bypasses the liver, it can enter into the inferior vena cava. This is the largest vein in the body.

Food in the stomach will slow the drug from entering the small intestine. This can reduce gastrointestinal irritation. Sometimes a drug is partially or totally inactivated by complexing with food. Other times a drug may be inactivated due to the higher acidity of the gastric system or the activity of the peptic system. An advantage may be gained by taking certain drugs with food or after food to avoid gastric irritation. Other drugs may be unnecessarily delayed by having a full stomach.

Certain physical-chemical possibilities need to be considered. Some drugs are water soluble and some drugs are lipid or fat soluble. Mucous membranes are made up of cells that allow certain substances to pass readily through and prevent others from penetrating. As a rule, substances that are lipid soluble will be readily absorbed in the gastrointestinal tract. Small water soluble molecules also will easily pass through the mucous membrane pores. Larger water soluble molecules will diffuse through the nonporous portion of the cell membrane. This will slow down absorption or in some cases not allow a drug to be absorbed at all.

Drugs that are highly ionized (present mostly in the form of electrically charged particles) tend to be repelled by the cell membranes of the mucosa. These drugs are poorly absorbed or not absorbed at all. Drugs of this sort are usually given parenterally.

The pH is the numerical values of hydronium-ion concentration. It is calculated as the logarithm of $1/[H_3O^+]$. Acidity values increase as the number value gets smaller. Alkalinity values increase as the number gets larger. pH values go from 0 to 14. The value 7 is considered neutral, as in water. The pH can be a factor. Most drugs are weak acids or bases. Their absorption is dependent partially by the pH of the gastro-intestinal contents. The pH helps to determine the proportion of nonionized drug present. Aspirin is an example of a weak acid that stays in its nonionized form in the acid gastric juices. Some of it will be absorbed in the stomach as soon as the product dissolves. When given with an alkaline buffer, more of the aspirin will become ionized and less of it can be absorbed in the stomach. At the same time, the alkalinizing of the gastric content increases the rate at which the stomach empties into the duodenum. In the small intestine the aspirin will be rapidly absorbed. In truth, aspirin is so readily absorbed in either the stomach or small intestine that there is little difference as to how quickly a buffered or non buffered product is absorbed.

To illustrate a case where the factors that influence drug absorption can make a serious difference, take the example of a man with congestive heart failure. He has been adequately regulated with the drug digoxin. Then the person develops symptoms and signs of congestive heart failure. When the case is evaluated, no apparent reasons were immediately identified for the relapse. However, after additional study what was found was that recently he had begun to take the medication with a small amount of ice cream. The ice cream was stimulating gastric acid and mucus. This delayed gastric emptying just enough to increase the breakdown of the digoxin and to lower the levels of the drug absorption. He returned to a symptom free state when the digoxin was again taken on an empty stomach (Rodman et al., 1985).

Parenteral. A drug in aqueous solution will be absorbed in proportion to the amount of blood supply available at the injection site. Drugs will be absorbed more rapidly from muscles rich in blood supply than from skin (cutaneous) tissues. Therefore, a subcutaneous injection may be desired when slow, steady, sustained action is wanted. The drug epinephrine is given subcutaneously for the treatment of asthma. Massaging the injection point can speed the absorption of a drug by physically forcing more of the drug into the circulatory system. When a drug is injected directly into a vein, it is immediately being transported throughout the body. It is desirable to prolong the release of some drugs given parenterally. This can be done by using a lipid soluble base or by using a vehicle that will delay the release of the drug.

Inhalation. Drugs may be absorbed in the respiratory tract, beginning with the nose, with its lining of mucous membranes. The lungs provide an ideal area of drug absorption because of the immense area of tissue available.

Other. The skin, as well as the mucous membranes of the conjunctiva, vagina, and urethra, provide adequate mucous membranes and blood supplies for the absorption of many drugs.

Distribution

The body has three primary systems involved in distribution. These are the blood circulation, the lymphatic circulation, and the cerebrospinal fluid.

After a drug has been administered, it is absorbed from the site of administration into the bloodstream. Typically a drug will enter into the venous system via the capillaries. The venous system will eventually carry the drug to the heart. Where it empties into the right atrium of the heart. From here it goes through a valve into the right ventricle. It then passes into the pulmonary artery, which branches into smaller vessels, then into the capillaries of the lungs. The drug continues on its journey by passing from the lungs to the pulmonary vein into the left atrium of the heart and into the left ventricle. From here it goes into the aorta, the largest artery in the body. The drug may now travel to any part of the body through the arterial network. It may leave the arterial network through a capillary and pass into the fluid surrounding the tissue or reenter the venous network. Substances can pass in and out of capillaries through their very thin walls.

A drug may enter the lymphatic system from the fluid surrounding the cells. Lymph is basically plasma, the fluid constituent of blood. The lymphatic system is thought to have a relatively minor role in the pharmacology of a drug. The lymphatic system will eventually take the drug back into the circulatory system.

A drug may be transported into the brain through the arterial system. Just because a drug reaches the brain or the capillaries of the brain does not guarantee that the drug will be absorbed by the brain tissue. Many drugs that would readily penetrate most body tissues are repelled by what is known as the blood-brain barrier. The blood-brain barrier is a functional block provided by cells in the capillaries and other cells, called glial cells, that stops the absorption of many drugs. This is one reason that psychoactive substances must be taken in such large quantities that they cause many undesired effects. The drug may be transported to a lipid depot or to another storage site in the body. For example, vitamin B-12 is stored in the liver. Barbiturates such as thiopental are stored in the fatty tissues.

The drug and its more water soluable metabolites will accumulate at sites of metabolism or excretion. If biotransformation is to occur, the drug will likely end up in the liver. If it is to be excreted in the urine, then it will be distributed to the kidney. Drugs slated for elimination via the feces will be secreted into the liver and out through the bile.

Blood is made up of cellular and liquid components. The cellular components are red blood cells and white blood cells. The plasma component is made up of water, enzymes, various chemicals, salts, and proteins. Many drugs will become attached to plasma protein molecules, particularly plasma albumin. This protein-drug complex cannot diffuse through the capillary membranes and into the tissues. Some drug molecules are constantly being freed from their protein-binding sites. The drug produces its pharmacologic effect through the free drug, while the plasma-bound drug continues to circulate in the blood stream. Eventually all the drug will be released. The more the drug binds to plasma proteins, the longer the drug stays in the body, and the longer the drug may have a therapeutic effect.

A drug will not necessarily remain in the tissue to which it was first transported. Drugs will eventually go to areas of the body which are less rich in blood supply. They may travel to fat depots, skeletal muscles, connective tissues, skin, or bones. Most drugs make their way to these parts of the body and accumulate there. Because the drug is still present in its active form, some of it will make its way back into the blood stream for redistribution.

Many drugs have an affinity for passing the placental barrier and diffusing into the blood and tissues of an embryo or fetus. This can expose the unborn infant to considerable risk. For this reason pregnant women or women of child bearing age need to carefully consider the possible risk in taking a drug.

Many drugs will appear in mother's milk. These drugs then will be taken in by the infant and cause possible consequences.

The distribution of drugs in the body is complicated by a series of membranes. Some of these membranes are thick with many cell layers; however, the cell membrane is what offers the resistance. All cells have membranes. Chemical analysis and electron microscopic studies have shown that these membranes are made of lipid and protein material. These membranes have three functional components. First, a lipid membrane that is permeable to lipid-soluble molecules and impermeable to polar, water soluble molecules. Second, the membranes have pores that permit the passage of small water-soluble molecules such as electrolytes, alcohol, and water. Third, the membranes contain channels which can move substances after they have combined with a carrier.

The mechanism of transfer across the membrane can be passive or active. Transfer is said to be passive when the membrane need not generate energy to carry out the process. In *active transfer* energy is required to carry out the activity. *Passive transfer* includes filtration, simple diffusion, and carrier facilitated diffusion. *Filtration* is the passage of a liquid through a membrane, accomplished by a pressure difference which may be positive on the liquid or negative on the filtrate. Diffusion is the passage of a liquid through a membrane. *Carrier facilitated* diffusion is a process in which a substance combines with a carrier molecule at one membrane surface and dissociates from it at the other surface. The carrier is a protein that is specific for the transported ion or larger water-soluble molecule. Active transfer is carrier facilitated; however, it is able to move a substance against a chemical or electrical force.

Metabolism

The body has the capability to transform a drug into another chemical. This process may take an active drug molecule and render it inactive or take an inactive molecule and create an active drug substance. The mechanism required to bring about these changes has to do with the function of enzymes and enzyme systems. **Enzymes** are produced by genes. One gene is capable of producing one enzyme. Genes are found in chromosomes located in the nuclei of cells. Enzymes are found in most areas of the body. However, the liver has the most enzymes of any organ in the body. Most drugs are metabolized by the liver. The action of enzymes as catalysts has been discussed previously.

Several different biochemical reactions take place to metabolize or biotransform drugs. These include (1) oxidation, (2) reduction, (3) conjugation, (4) hydrolysis, and (5) miscellaneous.

Oxidation. This is the most common method of biotransformation. It occurs primarily in the liver microsomal system. The chemical reaction is the combining of a substance with oxygen. When a compound is oxidized, the result is the release of energy and the breakdown of the compound into small molecules. Chemically, this process leads to the formation of water (H_2O), carbon dioxide (CO_2), and a third compound.

Reduction. This is relatively uncommon. It is the adding of hydrogen or the gain of electrons. This process is used to produce an active metabolite from an inactive drug.

Conjugation. A large number of drugs are conjugated. Conjugation is a chemical process of combining one compound to a natural water soluble substance to yield a water soluble product. This product is usually inactive.

Hydrolysis. This is a common biotransformation process among various substances. It is literally the decomposition of a compound by incorporation and splitting of water. The two resulting products will divide the water, with one getting the hydroxyl group and the other the hydrogen atom.

Other Methods. Several other methods exist of biotransformation. Some of these are **methylation,** the addition of a methyl group; **desulfuration,** the replacement of sulfur with oxygen; **dehalogenation,** the removal of the halogen atom from certain chemicals. Insecticides are often halogenated chemicals.

Elimination

Some drugs are not biotransformed in the body. Other drugs are biotransformed; however, their products still remain to be eliminated. The body may eliminate a drug or its metabolites by many routes. Drugs may be excreted through the sweat glands, by the lungs, through the breath, through mother's milk, or in saliva. Drugs may show up in hair, nails, skin, tears, or practically any place.

Many drugs will be eliminated in the feces. This is especially true of drugs that are not absorbed and pass through the gastrointestinal tract to be eliminated. This will be the destiny of some drugs that are taken along with food and never get absorbed. Sometimes the ingredients in food will interfere with the absorption of a drug. Certain antibiotics are not to be taken with milk or other products containing calcium. This is because the calcium will inactivate the drug. As has been mentioned above, the liver is a primary organ in the elimination of a drug. Drugs pass through the liver and are excreted in the bile. Many drugs are eliminated in this manner. The drug and/or its metabolites is/are then removed from the body in the feces.

The kidney is the most influential site in the process of drug elimination. The kidney acts as a filtering mechanism. Some drugs will be filtered out of the system and sent to the bladder for eventual elimination in the urine. Other drugs will be reabsorbed back into the plasma. This is important in delaying the elimination of a drug. Many times the kidney will filter and keep the active compound and select the inactive metabolites for elimination. The reabsorption of a drug may be artificially slowed by injecting sodium bicarbonate into a vein. This causes the urine to become more alkaline, raising the number of ionized drug particles in the glomerular filtrate of the kidney, thereby reducing the amount of drug that returns to the blood and increasing the amount excreted by the kidneys. This procedure is used in aspirin or barbiturate poisoning.

SUMMARY

This section, *Principles of Pharmacology*, has briefly exposed the reader to several basic concepts. These concepts are important in the understanding of the use of psychotropic drugs. The use of medical terminology, with its Greek and Latin origins, makes it possible for health professionals to communicate. The use of drugs and drug therapy dates back throughout history. Drugs come from five main sources. These are plants, animals, minerals, synthetics, and antibiotics. Several factors go into determining an appropriate dosage for an individual. These include age, weight, sex, physiologic factors, pathological factors, genetic factors, immunological factors, psychological factors, environmental factors, tolerance, and cumulation of drugs. Drugs can be administered orally, rectally, parenterally, topically, and by inhalation. Many factors are involved in the choice of the optimal route of administration. Once a drug enters the body, it can act at many different sites. It may act by combining with a cellular constituents called receptors, or by interacting with cellular enzyme systems. Sometimes drugs act by affecting the physiochemical properties of the outer or inner cell. How a drug exits the body is equally important as how it gets into the body and how it functions in the body. A drug is absorbed into the body fluids from its entry site, and is distributed or transported in different parts of the body through the circulatory system, lymphatic system, and cerebrospinal fluid. Sometimes the body transforms a drug, through a biochemical reaction, into another chemical by a process called metabolism. The final fate of any drug is elimination. Drugs can be excreted through the sweat glands, the lungs, saliva the urine or the feces. Most drugs are eliminated through the urine or feces. To better understand what happens in the body anatomy and physiology of the nervous system is discussed in the next section, however the discussion will be limited to the areas most important in the understanding of psychopharmacology.

ANATOMY AND PHYSIOLOGY

NERVOUS SYSTEM

The nervous system is the body's response-stimulus mechanism. Its function is to integrate the body's response to internal and external stimuli and to maintain the body's unity or harmony called *homeostasis.* The nervous system has two basic properties. It has the capacity to respond to stimuli, this function is called *irritability.* It also has the ability to transmit stimuli; this is called *conductivity.*

Three general types of stimuli cause the nervous system to react:

1. external, from the sense organs (tactile, visual, auditory, olfactory, taste) and other external sources such as galvanic or thermal;

2. internal, a sense of body position, balance, and motion called proprioception (also pressure and chemical changes); and

3. emotional stimuli, which include all those stimuli generated in higher cerebral areas (love, hate, joy, and sorrow).

Major Components

Three principal parts make up the nervous system: the brain, spinal cord, and nerves.

Brain and Spinal Cord. The brain and spinal cord make up what we call the central nervous system. The human brain consists of three regions: the *cerebrum,* the *brain stem,* and the *cerebellum.* The tissue of the brain is enveloped by three membranes called meninges. Generally speaking the brain performs six functions including being

1. the regulator of body activities in response to internal and external stimuli;

2. the root of consciousness or awareness;

3. the center of sensations, sight, sound, smell, taste, pain, and movement;

4. the source of all voluntary actions;

5. the seat of emotions; and

6. the source of higher mental process such as thought, reason, judgment, memory and learning.

The *spinal cord* consists of thirty-one segments. Each segment gives rise to a pair of nerve roots, one containing sensory or afferent fibers, and the other, motor or efferent fibers. The principle functions of the spinal cord include (1) conducting afferent impulses from the periphery to the brain, and efferent impulses from the brain to the effector organs; and (2) serving as a reflex center. A *spinal reflex* consists of connections directly between sensory and motor nerves. A reflex can be described as an action taken prior to the brain becoming aware of the stimulus. For example the rapid jerking away a hand does when it touches something hot.

In the brain, spinal nerve fibers combine to form functional pathways called *tracts.* In the spinal cord the ascending tracts carry afferent impulses to various areas of the brain. Descending tracts carry efferent impulses from the brain.

Peripheral Nervous Systems. Nerve fibers outside of the brain or spinal cord are called *peripheral nerves.* They start or end at some gland, organ or muscle. Depending upon function, the peripheral nerve ends at either a receptor or effector site. The peripheral nervous system is discussed in more detail later in this chapter.

Autonomic Nervous System. The *autonomic nervous system* is a function, rather than an anatomical division of the nervous system. It is contained in both the central and peripheral nervous systems. The functioning of the autonomic nervous system is largely independent of conscious thought. It allows the maintenance of a relatively stable internal environment to the body, by controlling vital functions such as body temperature. The autonomic nervous system is discussed in detail later in the chapter.

Neuron

Neurons make up another important part of the nervous system. Neurons are made up of three main parts: the *cell body,* the *axon* (fiber), and the *dendrite.* Dendrite comes from the Greek word of tree. Impulses pass through the dendrite to the cell body which transmits the impulse through the axon or fiber. There is a microscopic space between two neurons called a synapse.

Components. The basic unit of the nervous system is the neuron or nerve cell. A cell consists of the following:

1. *Nucleus,* a spherically shaped, centrally located structure which contains genetic material.

2. *Cell membrane,* which holds the cell together.

3. *Mitochondria,* elongated oval structures which are scattered about the cell body, dendrites, and axons. The mitochondria carry out chemical reactions in the presence of enzymes to produce energy-rich *Adenosine Triphosphate* (ATP). ATP is important in membrane transport, synthesis of chemical substances within the cell, and mechanical work (the transporting of proteins,

neurotransmitters, and their precursors within the neuron from the cell body to the axons). Mitochondria have an enzyme **monoamine oxidase** (MAO) attached to their outer membrane. MAO is important in the metabolism of neurotransmitters and related substances.

4. **Endoplasmic Reticulum,** tubular networks in the space surrounding the nucleus. Small granular particles called **ribosomes** (consisting of RNA) are attached to the outer surface of some areas. The endoplasmic reticulum may function as a transport system and be the site of lipid (fatty substances that become part of the cell membranes) synthesis.

5. **Golgi** apparatus, pancake shaped cavities involved in the synthesis of proteins.

6. **Neurofilaments,** involved in transporting of substances within the cell.

7. **Lyosones,** consisting of enzymes involved in cell biochemistry.

The cells of the nervous system differ from other cells in that they have **neurofilaments.** Neurofilaments are long thin, thread-like structures. The other striking difference found in neurons is their shape. They have a central body that may be as large as 1 mm and many thin processes extending out.

For purpose of describing a neuron, let us use a motor neuron having its cell body in the spinal cord and one axon extending to a muscle. The cell body contains the nucleus, ribosomes, mitochondria, and several other subcellular parts. A great deal of the metabolism of the cell takes place in the nucleus. Short, branching structures, called **dendrites,** extend in all directions from the cell body. A thicker, longer single fiber, called an **axon,** extends from the spinal cord to a muscle. The axon is covered by a myelin sheath. This is an insulating material, consisting mostly of fats. The sheath is interrupted at intervals by unmyelinated sections called **nodes of Ranvier.** This combination of sheathed and unsheathed axon is very important in the rapidity of impulse conduction. The axon is attached to the cell at an area called the *axon hillock.* At the end of the axons are structures called *terminal buttons,* or *presynaptic endings.* The motor neuron receives excitation or inhibition from other cells on its dendrites. The information is transmitted to the cell body. The stimulation exceeds a threshold; it initiates an electrochemical impulse that passes down the axon to stimulate other cells.

Functions. Neurons can be classified according to function. *Afferent* or *sensory neurons* receive impulses from receptor sites. The receptor site is the point of origin of the stimuli. *Efferent neurons* transmit motor impulses from the central nervous system to the effector site. *Effector sites* include muscles, glands, and organs. Interneurons act to interconnect two or more neurons.

Types of Effector Neurons. The four types of effector neurons. include

1. *motor neurons*—the axons terminate in muscles which contract when stimulated;

2. *secretory motor neurons*—the axons end in glands which secrete when stimulated;

3. *accelerator motor neurons*—the axons end in involuntary visceral or cardiac muscles, either initiating or speeding up activity; and

4. *inhibitory motor neurons*—these act in opposition to accelerator neurons.

Characteristics. Several characteristics of neurons are worthwhile mentioning at this point. Neurons depend upon glucose as their main fuel source. They cannot use the wide variety of fuels that other cells use. Glucose is normally present in adequate amounts in the body or can be readily converted by the liver. The body can only utilize glucose if adequate supplies of thiamine (vitamin B_1) are available. The only other known usable fuels that parts of the brain can utilize are two ketone fats: acetoacetate and 3-hyroxybutyrate. These fats are consumed during starvation or when a person is on a no-carbohydrate diet.

Neurons consume energy and oxygen at a higher rate than the rest of the body. The brain utilizes about 20 % of the calorie and oxygen supply of the body. A ten second interruption of blood flow (therefore oxygen) to the brain results in unconsciousness, and can lead to irreversible brain damage or death.

Protein synthesis is greater than in other cells.

When the brain reaches maturity, no new neurons are produced, and old neurons cannot divide to replace destroyed ones. The only exceptions are olfactory and taste receptors.

Glia

The neurons and glia cells are the two major components of the nervous system. Glia comes from the Greek word meaning "glue." They are many times more numerous and much smaller than neurons. Unlike neurons they can divide to form new cells at any time. They serve several important functions. Glia cells

1. are the building material of the myelin sheaths,

2. fill the space of a dead neuron,

3. remove waste material, and

4. during fetal development, direct the migration and growth of neurons.

Nerve Impulse

The cell membrane of an unstimulated or resting neuron carries an electric charge. Positive and negative ions are concentrated on both sides of the membrane. The inside of the membrane, at rest, has a negative charge in comparison to the outside. A reversal in the charge, in the cell membrane, begins to travel along the membrane like an electric current. The local reversal is called an **impulse,** and the sudden electric change is called an **action potential.** Rapid, cyclic shifts in sodium and potassium across the cell membrane cause the electric charge.

The neurons send their messages via electrico-chemical impulses. If a neuron were to be electrically neutral when not stimulated (at rest), it would take an enormous amount of energy to start an impulse flowing. Because the neuron at rest has a resting potential, it doesn't have to overcome the forces of inertia in order to send its message. It can simply send a message by releasing electrical energy, instead of first having to create it. Some local and short neurons or neuron systems can and do function without an action potential. This happens only when the transmitting distance is very short.

To understand how a nerve impulse travels, assume that one end of a axon has been stimulated (depolarized). This makes the sodium sodium ion flow into the plasma, causing an action potential. The sodium ion (positive charge) spreads to adjacent areas, because it is attracted by the negative ions concentrated inside the membrane of the axon. This continues the chain of events by causing negative charges to be neutralized, causing depolarization, causing sodium ions to flow into these sites, and a new action potential occurs. This process is referred to as the **propagation of the action potential.** The propagation velocity of a nerve impulse is between 1 and 100 meters per second or 2 and 224 miles per hour. The wide variance of rates is due to the different diameters of the axons. The rate is proportional to the diameter of the axon. This is actually a slow rate, due to the time it takes to initiate and complete the action potentials.

Let's break this process down and follow it through.

1. Membranes are selectively permeable to the passage of chemicals.

2. Water, carbon dioxide and some other chemicals can cross the membrane readily in either direction; however, most chemicals cannot.

3. Potassium and chloride ions cross less easily than water.

4. Sodium ions cross with even more difficulty.

5. The inside of the membrane at rest is negative in relationship to the outside. This is referred to as being polarized.

6. A nerve impulse is the reversal in the charge of the nerve cell membrane, which spreads along the cell membrane forming an electrical current.

7. The sudden change in the membrane is called an action potential.

8. This sudden change in the potential comes when the potassium and sodium ions rapidly shift across the membrane.

9. Many proteins having a negative charge are inside the membrane, and because they are bonded to various structures they cannot pass outside of the membrane.

10. Because of the negative charge inside the membrane, positively charged potassium ions are attracted by the negative charge inside of the cell.

11. Negatively charged chloride and bicarbonate are repelled.

12. Sodium, with its positive charge, should be attracted to the inside of the membrane. This does not happen.

13. The mechanism that changes this is called the sodium-potassium pump (Kalat, 1984). The sodium-potassium pump plays an essential role in maintaining the negative charge inside the neuron. The cell brings in potassium ions that can readily diffuse out again more freely than the sodium ion can diffuse in again. Therefore, the pump is causing a net movement of positive ions out of the cell. Because of the negative charge inside of the neuron it would seem that chloride and potassium ions could move back and forth to neutralize the charge. This does not happen. Consider the competing forces acting on a potassium ion.

a. Potassium is drawn into the cell because of the negative charge.

b. This moves the electrical charge towards balance.

c. Potassium becomes more concentrated inside the cell.

d. Ions in nature tend to move from more concentrated to less concentrated areas.

e. The more potassium ions inside the cell, the greater the concentration gradient between the inside and outside of the cell.

f. This increases the pressure for the potassium to leave the cell.

g. Eventually, the electrical gradient cell will be balanced by the concentration gradient.

h. This will push the potassium out of the cell.

14. A myelinated nerve fiber conducts impulses more rapidly than an unmyelinated one because of the leaping effect that happens from node to node. Axons that require more rapid conduction have myelin sheaves. The myelin sheave accomplishes the task of spreading impulses in three ways.

    a. It acts as an insulation to eliminate leakage.

    b. It prevents voltage decreases by reducing the capacitor capability of the axon.

    c. The **nodes of Ranvier** act to accelerate the impulses.

15. This action is called saltatory conduction. Let us look further at this action.

    a. An action potential is initiated in a neuron with a myelinated axon.

b. The impulse is conducted in the normal way until it reaches the myelinated sheath.

c. The action potential cannot be propagated in the myelinated area.

d. The electric potential declines as it travels in the sheath; however, it will not drop below the threshold before it reaches the next node.

e. At the node, the action potential is regenerated, and the impulse is sent on through the myelinated sheath to the next node.

Synapse

The British neurophysiologist, Sir Charles Scott Sherrington, coined the word synapse. He described the major properties many years before the technology was available to measure the characterists directly. He received the Nobel Prize in 1932 for his work. The word synapse is derived from the Greek "synapto," which means "to clasp."

No anatomic connection exists between neurons. Each neuron is a separate unit. Synapses are specialized spaces between the axon ending of one cell and a dendrite, axon, or cell body of another, where communication occurs. A single axon may terminate in a few synapses or in as many as thousands. The synapse consists of a presynaptic portion, where the precursor chemical of the neurotransmitters is held prior to release at the synapse. The plasma membranes of the two adjacent cells are respectively called the **presynaptic membrane** and the **postsynaptic membrane.** The **synaptic cleft** is a very narrow gap (about one millionth of an inch) between neurons.

Virtually all neurotropic drugs exert their physiological and behavioral effects by altering the degree or duration of synaptic activity. This activity creates a model to explain the action of drugs, the side effects of drugs. It also suggests that psychopathological and some neurological diseases can be traced to abnormal synaptic function. Some drugs act in the area of the presynapse, some in the area of the presynaptic cleft, and others at the postsynaptic cleft.

The transmission of a message between one neuron and another is largely the responsibility of the axon of the presynaptic neuron. In order for a transmission to occur, several preparatory steps must occur. These include the maintenance of a resting potential, synthesis, and the uptake of the neurotransmitters by the vescicles for storage. Finally, the movement of filled vesicles into position at the presynaptic cell membrane.

When an action potential arrives at the tip or end bulb of the axon, the end bulb releases a chemical called the **neurotransmitter** into the synaptic cleft. The neurotransmitter diffuses from the presynaptic membrane across the cleft to the post synaptic membrane, where it interacts with a receptor, giving rise to a postsynaptic potential. The postsynaptic potential can be either excitatory or inhibitory in nature. A single **excitatory postsynaptic potential** (EPSP), by itself, is not enough to reach the threshold for an action potential. However, several EPSP combine to exceed the threshold and produce an action potential, thereby initiating a nerve transmission. The **inhibitory postsynaptic potential** (IPSP) actively suppresses excitation. It acts as a "brake" in stopping message transmission. The post synaptic cell will "fire" or not, based upon the combination of information in the form of EPSPs and IPSPs it receives.

Another mechanism of importance is **presynaptic inhibition.** This mechanism is usually accomplished by an axon to axon synapse. The effect of this mechanism may be to decrease further stimulation. Some drugs have a stronger effect on the presynaptic inhibitory synapses than on other ones.

The last junction between the CNS and the muscle or gland is called the **neuroeffector junction.** Functionally, these impulses lead to muscular contractions and glandular secretions.

Neurotransmitters

Neurotransmitters are the chemicals that carry an impulse across the synapse. Some of these chemicals have other functions in the body. Generally speaking, each neuron synthesizes, stores, and uses only one transmitter at all synapses formed by the branches of its axons. The belief is that some cells release one or more **peptides** (compounds containing amino acids) along with the transmitter substance.

Neurotransmitters are synthesized in one or more chemical reactions or steps regulated by an enzyme. The chemical necessary for the synthesizing of a neurotransmitter is called a **precursor.** The initial precursor is a chemical, such as an amino acid or metabolic intermediary of glucose metabolism, readily available in the body. These substances are taken into the body in the form of food. For example, choline, the precursor to acetylcholine, an important neurotransmitter, is found in egg yolks, soybeans, butter, nuts and liver. The reaction can be represented as follows:

. . . .
Acetyl coenzyme A + Choline→Acetylcholine (ACh)
. . . .

Serotonin is synthesized from tryptophan, an amino acid. Tryptophan is in competition with several amino acids for a transport protein that allows it to enter into the brain. Therefore, serotonin levels increase when dietary levels of tryptophan are increased. Serotonin is classified as an **indoleamine.** The reaction can be represented as follows:

. . . .
Tryptophan → 5 Hydroxytryptophan → Serotonin
. . . .

The group known as the **catacholamines** contains three of the most important neurotransmitters. These are dopamine, epinephrine, and norepinephrine and are synthesized as follows:

```
.........................................
Phenylalanine → Tyrosine → L-Dopa → Dopamine ↓
    Epinephrine    ←    Norepinephrine    ←
.........................................
```

The following is an example of the activity of a neuro-transmitter. This is over-simplified.

1. The precursor, or initial chemical, is taken into the body as food. It goes through the normal digestive processes and is in the blood and extracellular fluid.

2. Fluids are moving in and out of the cell membrane. The sodium-potassium exchange pump creates a resting potential.

3. As a result of the resting potential, the precursor is taken into the neuron. It is then synthesized in a series of chemical activities. This requires the presence of enzymes. The neurotransmitter is taken into a vesicle for storage.

4. The filled vesicle moves and awaits the propagation of the action potential. Calcium influxes through the divalent ion channel. (Calcium ions facilitate the release, and magnesium ions inhibit it.) The transmitter is released.

5. From here several choices are available:

   a. It moves across the synapse and binds to a receptor site and can create an EPSP or IPSP (Excitatory/inhibitory post-synaptic potential).

   b. It can become inactivated and not bind to the receptor site.

   c. It can dissociate, regenerate, bind to an inhibitory transmitter, or activate an enzyme linked site.

   d. It can be inactivated by reuptake, diffusion, enzymatic degradation. It can then bind to a presynaptic receptor.

Synaptic interactions may be either ionic or metabolic. The ionic interactions alter the postsynaptic membrane's permeability to a specific ion. This allows for the flowing or non-flowing of the specific ion at the membrane. Metabolic transmitters have long-lasting effects that closely resemble those of hormones.

Transmitters do not stay at the postsynaptic membrane for a long period of time. If they did, then they might continue to stimulate the postsynaptic neuron indefinitely. By different ways the neurotransmitters are broken down. Acetylcholine is broken down by the enzyme acetylcholinesterase. Serotonin and the catecholamines are not broken down at the membrane. They are detached, and most of them are reabsorbed by the presynaptic membrane. They are then reused. The rest are inactivated by the enzymes catechol-o-methyltransferase (COMT) or monoamine oxidase (MAO) and eventually diffuse out of the synaptic cleft and into general circulation.

CENTRAL NERVOUS SYSTEM

Brain

General Structure. The brain comprises about 98% of the central nervous system. It may be thought of as the greatly enlarged and modified part of the system. The average adult brain weighs between three and four pounds. It is surrounded by three successive membranes called meninges, and further protected and enclosed by the skull. The brain is divided into several different parts, depending upon the author. Collin (1974) suggested three divisions: the brainstem, the cerebellum, and the cerebrum. The brainstem is further broken down into the medulla oblongata, the pons, and the midbrain. Rodman, Karch, Boyd, and Smith (1985) divided the brain into three major divisions: the hindbrain, the midbrain, and the forebrain. In the *Encyclopedia Britannica* (Gardner, 1980) are stipulated five parts: the telencephalon (end brain), diencephalon (inner-brain), mesencephalon (midbrain), metencephalon (afterbrain), and myelencephalon (medulla oblongata). This points out how complex the brain is and that no across the board agreement exists in describing the brain or its parts.

The **cerebrum** consists of the **telencephalon, diencephalon,** and the **upper midbrain. The metencephalon** is divided into the **pons** and the **cerebellum.** The cerebellum and the pons are connected by bridges of nerve fibers called **cerebellar peduncles.** The telencephalon is divided into two halves called **cerebral hemispheres.** These consist of the **cerebral cortex** (the outer gray mantle), the **basal ganglia** (a mass of gray matter), and the **white matter,** located between the two gray masses. The hemispheres are connected by bands of nerve fibers called **commissures.** The **corpus callosum** is the largest commissure. The **thalamus** and **hypothalamus** are two major structures of the diencephalon. A series of cavities in the brain are called **ventricles.** These cavities are filled with **cerebrospinal fluid.**

Paul MacLean (1967) described the human brain as being three brains in one. The "reptilian brain" at the core, involved in fixed, stereotyped, ritualistic behaviors necessary for self-preservation and reproduction. The "old-mammalian brain" surrounds the "reptilian brain." It is involved in reproduction, self-preservation, emotions such as love, anger, and fear. The "new mammalian brain" surrounds the "old-mammalian brain" and is present in humans, other primates, whales, and dolphins. It is involved in rational thinking.

Membranes. The three membranes, or meninges, covering the brain are a tough outer fibrous layer, the **dura mater;** a thin web-like tissue, the **arachnoid;** and a soft, vascular inner lining, the **pia mater.**

The dura mater supplies the bone of the skull with nutrition and provides a channel for absorption and removal of blood and cerebrospinal fluid. Beneath the dura mater is the arachnoid membrane; a thin membrane; however, it is not permeable to fluids. Openings in the arachnoid membrane allow for cerebrospinal fluid to communicate between the ventricles of the brain and the subarachnoid space. Meningitis causes these openings to be obstructed, resulting in hydrocephalus; a condition in which an abnormal amount of fluid is accumulated in the cranium causing enlargement of the head, swelling of the forehead, atrophy of the brain, mental weakness, and convulsions. The pia mater is a delicate vascular membrane. The vascular system of the pia mater supplies the brain.

Ventricles. Ventricles are cavities containing fluid located within the brain. They are lined by a thin membrane. The four true ventricles are connected and contain cerebrospinal fluid. They allow cerebrospinal fluid to flow between the brain and the spinal column. The fluid acts as a mechanical support for the brain and spinal cord. It also performs some functions similar to the tissue fluid and lymph.

Blood Supply. The brain is supplied blood through two paired arteries, the *internal carotid* and *vertebral arteries.* Venous return is through the *internal jugular veins.* This is different than the organization of most of the rest of the body. Usually the arterial and venous systems are located alongside of each other.

Medulla Oblongata. The medulla oblongata lies next to the spinal cord and extends from the first cervical nerve to the inferior border of the pons. It is the most posterior part of the brain and consists of only ½% of the central nervous system. It is a highly specialized structure that mediates a number of life-preserving reflexes. These include breathing, heart rate, vomiting, salivation, coughing, sneezing, and gagging (Kalat, 1984). The medulla houses vital centers, including: (1) the respiratory center (controls the muscles of respiration), (2) the cardiac center (aids in regulating the rate and force of the heart beat), and (3) the vasomotor center (contraction of smooth muscle in the blood vessel walls). Cranial nerves IX through XII arise in the medulla. Nerve fibers coming from the spinal cord will cross over in the spine or in the medulla. The left side of the brain controls the right side of the body, and the right side of the brain controls the left side of the body.

Pons. The pons is located between the medulla and the midbrain, in front of the cerebellum. It is a link between the cerebellum and the rest of the nervous system. Pons is Latin for "bridge." It is involved in coordinating the muscles of the two sides of the body. It is also concerned with facial muscles, including the muscles of mastication and the first stages of breathing. Cranial nerves V through VIII originate in the pons.

Midbrain. The midbrain is located just below the center of the cerebrum. It forms the forward part of the brain stem. It contains the optic and auditory reflex centers. It also is involved in regulation of muscle tone, body posture, and equilibrium. The IIIrd and IVth Cranial nerves originate in the midbrain.

Cerebellum. The cerebellum is referred to as the little or small brain. It is the second largest division of the brain, made up of three parts: two lateral hemispheres and a mid-part. The outer area, like the cerebrum, is made of gray matter on the outside and white matter on the inside. It is involved in bringing balance, harmony, and coordination to the motions of the body. It acts to coordinate the voluntary muscles of the body.

Disease of the cerebellum causes muscular jerkiness and tremors. The cerebellum is involved in maintaining balance in standing, walking, sitting, as well as in more strenuous activities. It is connected with the semicircular canals of the ear that react to gravity and sudden changes, or movement of the head. Another important function of the cerebellum is the maintenance of muscle tone. It aids in keeping all muscles slightly tensed and ready to make the necessary adjustment in position, as quickly as is needed.

Diencephalon (Innerbrain). The diencephalon is located between the midbrain and the cerebrum. It includes the thalamus (from the Greek word meaning "inner chamber" or "anteroom") and the hypothalamus. Almost all sensory impulses pass through the thalamus. The *thalamus* is responsible for sorting out the impulses and directing them to the correct area of the cerebral cortex. The *hypothalamus* helps control body temperature, water balance, sleep, appetite, and some emotions. The *sympathetic* and *parasympathetic* divisions of the autonomic nervous system are under control of the hypothalamus. The pituitary gland is also controlled by the hypothalamus. Therefore, the hypothalamus influences the heart beat, the contraction and relaxation of the walls of blood vessels, hormone secretion, as well as other vital body functions.

Cerebral Cortex. The outer gray matter of the cerebral hemispheres is called the cerebral cortex. The term cortex means "covering or outer layer." The inner area is made of white matter with a large number of axons. The central core which forms the essential conducting part of a nerve fiber consists of two hemispheres, each organized to receive sensory information from the opposite side of the body. The information is communicated between hemispheres by two bundles of axons called the *corpus callosum.* The gray cortex is arranged with folds, called *gyri,* which form raised areas. Next to the folds are grooves called *sulci.* Inside the two hemispheres are two spaces called the *lateral ventricles.* These contain cerebrospinal fluid.

The cerebral cortex is the area of the brain that receives and analyzes impulses. This activity forms the basis for knowledge. The ability to recall the stored information on demand is called *memory.* The cerebral cortex is the center of thought processes such as judgment, discrimination, and association. Voluntary action and conscious deliberation are accessed also in the cerebral cortex.

Each hemisphere of the cerebral cortex is divided into four lobes. The lobes are named to correspond with the adjacent cranial bone. The brain's activities are normally a complex coordination of various areas. Various areas of the cortex influence specific functions or categories of activity. The four lobes of the cortex are as follows:

Occipital Lobe. The occipital lobe, located at the posterior (caudal) end, is the target area of receiving sensory afferent fibers from the eyes. The very posterior pole is sometimes called *area 17.* This nomenclature is the work of the German neurologist K. Brodmann. Complete destruction of area 17 will result in blindness. Partial destruction of area 17 causes loss of vision in part of the visual field. Lashley (1929) found that damage to the occipital lobe of a blind rat would impede the ability of the rat to learn a maze. Even areas of the brain that have very specific function also may be involved in other activities.

Parietal Lobe. The parietal lobes occupys the upper part of each hemisphere and is located between the occipital lobe and the central sulcus. This lobe contains the sensory area where impulses from the skin, such as touch, temperature, and pain are processed.

Frontal Lobe. The frontal lobe is larger in the human than in other organisms. It is located from the central sulcus to the anterior (front) limit of the brain. This lobe contains the motor cortex which directs body actions. The left frontal lobe of the human contains an area that specializes in language production. The operation called a *prefrontal lobotomy,* frequently performed in the 1950s, was the surgical cutting of the connections between the prefrontal areas and the rest of the brain. This was an attempt to control schizophrenia and several other "troublesome" behaviors (Kalat,1984). The operation was said to "reduce anxiety and make some wilder mental patients easier to control." The undesirable effects include "generally blunted emotions, decreased energy levels, loss of initiative and planning, and inability to suppress one habitual behavior and substitute another" (Damasio, 1979). *Broca's* area is located in the left frontal lobe and is critical for the production of speech.

Temporal Lobe. The temporal lobe lies below the lateral sulcus and folds under the hemisphere on each side. It contains the auditory area, which, in turn, receives and interprets impulses from the ear and olfactory area, which receives and interprets messages from the nasal area. *Wernicke's* area is located in the left temporal lobe in humans. It is critically involved in the comprehension of language. The temporal lobe is also connected with the limbic system; therefore, it is involved in emotions and motivation.

The ability to communicate by verbal and written means demonstrates the intricate interrelating of the various areas of the cerebral cortex. These functions and their development are related to the process of learning. Auditory areas, located in the temporal lobe, are involved in experiencing sounds from the environment, while other areas within the lobe interpret and understand the sounds. Language is learned first by auditory means.

Talking and writing are motor functions that emulate from the front of the lowest part of the motor cortex, located in the frontal lobe. The coordination of arms and hands is controlled by the written speech center in the front of the motor cortical area. Speech is controlled by the motor speech center, located in the lower part of the motor cortex. This area controls muscles of the tongue, soft palate, and the larynx.

The visual areas of the cortex are located in the occipital lobe. This allows the individual to see the printed word. The area in front of the receiving center is involved with interpretation of the image. This area coordinates the ability to read.

Memory is the mental faculty for recalling ideas. Grinder and Bandler (1976) suggested that individuals use auditory, visual, and/or kinesthetic triggers to recall images. The nature of memory is unknown. The study of the many theories of learning, as well as the many attempts to locate the site or sites of memory, is quite interesting; however, it is beyond the scope of this book.

Pyramidal System. The pyramidal tracts (so named because the cell bodies are the shape of a pyramid) are a series of nerve tissues that carry impulses down through the brain. These tracts arise in the motor cortex and cross over, then descend down into the spinal cord. The impulses will connect with the roots of the spinal nerves through connecting neurons. The spinal nerves will carry the impulse to the muscles. The contraction of the muscles will cause voluntary motion of the face, limbs, and trunk.

Extrapyramidal System. The pyramidal tracts carry impulses from the consciously controlled motor cortex. Other movement responses are not voluntary. A person normally performs many accessory motions which are not conscious. These include swinging the arms when walking, facial expressions, and other nonvoluntary movements. These movements are influenced by structures located below the cortex, known as the extrapyramidal system. These structures are a series of unrelated parts. Three main structures create the extrapyramidal system. These are fibers from the cerebral cortex, the red nucleus, and the reticular formation. Each of these sources receives input from many areas of the brain.

Reticular Formation. The reticular formation, sometimes known as the ***ascending reticular activation system*** (ARAS), is involved in arousal, wakefulness, and attention. The ARAS influences muscle control and integrates sensory input. It acts as a screen for input that may be irrelevant to the functioning of the individual. Structurally, it is a network of neurons located in the core of the brain stem. The name reticular is based on the Latin word "rete," meaning net. It suggests that the ARAS is made up of several different types of nerve cells scattered diffusely among a tangled mass of nerve processes and lacks a specific shape.

Limbic System. The limbic system in primitive animals functions mainly as a part of the olfactory system. In man, its functions include emotion, approach and avoidance, recent memory, and some control over parasympathetic and sympathetic function. The term "limbic" comes from the Latin, meaning "border." The limbic system includes the hypothalamus, the hippocampus, the amygdala, the olfactory bulb, parts of the thalamus, the temporal lobe and cingulate gyrus of the cerebral cortex. The limbic theory was introduced by J. W. Papez in 1937. He based his theory upon the following facts:

1. the cells of most of the system respond to smell, taste, and pain stimuli;

2. all three sensory modalities have slow onset, slow offset, and a vagueness of location; and

3. all three evoke a strong emotional response, ranging from disgust to joy.(Kalat, 1984)

Paul MacLean (1949, 1958, 1970) furthered the limbic system theory in his work with epileptic seizures. MacLean suggested three circuits within the limbic system:

1. the amygdala is involved in self-preservation;

2. the cingulate gyrus of the cerebral cortex, the septum, and several other structures seem to be involved in pleasure versus displeasure and are particularly important in sexual enjoyment; and

3. parts of the hypothalamus and the anterior thalamus make up the third circuit. These parts are important in cooperative social behavior and some aspects of sexuality.

The Spinal Cord

The spinal cord makes up the rest of the central nervous system. Anatomically, the spinal cord is a long tube about 45 centimeters in length. It extends from just above the first cervical vertebra at the base of the skull to the level of the first or second lumbar vertebra. Note that the spinal cord does not extend the entire length of the vertebral canal. Thirty-one (31) segments make up the spinal cord.

The spinal cord is covered by the same three meninges as the brain. A cross section of the spinal cord shows an H-shaped gray matter surrounded by white matter. The gray matter is made up of cell bodies of nerve cells. The white matter consists of nerve fibers that run parallel to the long axis of the spinal cord. These fibers ascend to the brain or descend from the brain. The white color comes from the fatty sheath that surrounds many of the fibers.

The cord's functions may be divided into three categories:

1. reflex activities, involving the transfer and integration of impulses that enter and leave the cord without having to involve the brain,

2. conduct sensory impulses from nerves up to the brain, and

3. conduct motor impulses from the brain down the cord to the corresponding nerves that connect with muscles or glands.

A reflex pathway usually involves three or more neurons. First, sensory neuron, which begins in a receptor, and its nerve fiber that leads to the cord. Second, one or more central neurons are entirely within the cord. Third, the motor neuron, which takes the impulse from a central neuron and carries it to a muscle or a gland.

Reflexes are a safety system built into the body. They eliminate the time that it would take for impulses to travel to and from the brain. They protect the body from possible injury. For example, the knee jerk reflex protects the knee joint from injury due to sudden or possible injurious movements. Other reflexes protect the person from injury due to touching a sharp or hot object.

PERIPHERAL NERVOUS SYSTEM

The peripheral nervous system consists of the cranial nerves, the spinal nerves, and the part of the autonomic nervous system that is outside of the central nervous system.

Cranial Nerves

Twelve (12) pairs of cranial nerves can be classified as part of the peripheral nervous system. The cranial nerves are numbered from I to XII according to where they connect with the brain. The first nine pairs and the twelfth pair supply structures in the head. Cranial nerves are involved in

1. special sensory impulses, such as smell, vision, and hearing;

2. general sensory impulses, such as pain, touch, temperature, pressure, vibration, and deep muscle sense;

3. somatic motor impulses that create voluntary control of skeletal muscles; and

4. visceral motor impulses that produce involuntary control of glands and involuntary muscles (cardiac and smooth).

The nuclei of the cranial nerves are located as follows:

Cranial Nerves I and II—In the olfactory bulb and the thalamus.

Cranial Nerves III and IV—In the midbrain.

Cranial Nerves V through XII—in the medulla or pons.

The medulla regulates a number of life-preserving reflexes via the cranial nerves. These include breathing, coughing, gagging, heart rate, salivation, sneezing, and vomiting. The olfactory and the optic nerves, referred to as the Ist and IInd cranial nerves, are not peripheral nerves, but tracts belonging to the central nervous system. The Ist, IInd, and VIIIth cranial nerves contain only sensory fibers. The IIIrd, IVth, VIth, and XIIth are exclusively motor, and innervate the extraocular muscles and the muscles of the tongue. The remaining, Vth, VIIth, IXth, and Xth contain both sensory and motor neurons.

I. Olfactory Nerve. It carries smell impulses from the nasal mucosa to the brain.

II. Optic Nerve. Carries visual impulses from the eye to the brain.

III. Oculomotor. Is concerned with the contraction of most of the eye muscles.

IV. Trochlear. Supplies nerve impulses to the superior oblique muscle of the eyeball.

V. Trigeminal. This is the important sensory nerve of the face. It carries pain, touch, and temperature messages from the face to the brain. Its motor function includes chewing and swallowing.

VI. Abducens. It carries sensations from the eye muscles and facilitates eye movements. It innervates the lateral rectus muscle of the eyeball.

VII. Facial. Sensory functions include taste from the anterior two-thirds of the tongue, visceral sensations from the head. Motor functions include crying, dilation of blood vessels in the head, facial expressions, and salivation. Lesions of the facial nerve produce a paralysis of facial muscles know as Bell's Palsy.

VIII. Vestibulocochler (acoustic). Contains sensory fibers for hearing and for balance from the semicircular canals of the inner ear.

IX. Glossopharyngeal. Sensory fibers from the back of the tongue and throat. Motor functions include dilation of blood vessels, salivation (fibers innervate the parotid—the largest salivary gland), and swallowing.

X. Vagus. This is the longest cranial nerve. It supplies most of the organs of the abdominal and thoracic cavities. It is involved with sensory functions of taste and sensations from the neck, chest, and abdomen. Motor functions include swallowing, control of the larynx, and parasympathetic inner-vation of the heart, viscera, and blood vessels.

XI. Accessory. It controls two muscles in the neck, the trapezius and the sternocleidomastoid. It is involved in movement of the head and shoulders.

XII. Hypoglossal. It is involved in sensations from the tongue and movement of the tongue.

Spinal Nerves

Each segment of the spinal cord has both a sensory nerve and a motor nerve on its left and right side. The thirty-one pairs of spinal nerves are numbered according to the level of the spinal cord from which they arise. From the top down, there are eight (8) *cervical nerves,* twelve (12) *thoracic nerves,* five (5) *lumbar nerves,* five (5) *sacral nerves,* and one (1) *coccygeal nerve.* Each spinal nerve innervates a limited area of the body. These areas are either patches or bands on the body. The area of the skin innervated by a sensory spinal nerve is called a dermatome. For example, the first thoracic nerve innervates the skin on the palm side of the arm between the wrist and the elbow. The third thoracic nerve innervates the area of skin above the nipples on the chest and the underarm area. An overlap occurs between dermatomes. Each nerve has two roots that attach to the spinal cord. The *dorsal* (toward the back—in the brain, the top is considered dorsal because that is its position in four-legged animals) and the *ventral* (toward the stomach side—"Vener" is Latin for belly) root. The dorsal root contains the sensory neurons. These neurons respond to a stimuli. These stimuli give rise to sensation such as pain, touch, temperature, and the location and position of body parts.

The ventral roots of the spinal nerves are a combination of motor nerve fibers supplying voluntary muscles, involuntary muscles, and glands.

The spinal nerves extend only a short distance from the spinal cord and then branch into two subdivisions, the smaller posterior (same as dorsal in humans—towards the rear) and the rather large anterior (toward the front end). The larger anterior branches become interwoven to form networks called *plexuses.* The plexuses distribute nerve branches to the body parts. The three main plexuses are

1. the *cervical plexus* which supplies motor impulses to the muscles of the neck and receives sensory impulses from the neck and the back of the head;

2. the *brachial plexus* which branches go out to the shoulders, arms, wrists, and hands; and

3. the *lumbosacral plexus* which supplies nerves to the lower extremities of the body.

AUTONOMIC NERVOUS SYSTEM (ANS)

Two men can be credited for the present view of the structure and functioning of the autonomic nervous system: Anatomist, W. H. Gaskell, (1916) who began publishing in 1885 and summarized his work in 1916; and also the Cambridge physiologist J. N. Langley (1921), who suggested the word "autonomic" in place of "involuntary" (which was used by Gaskell), and further suggested the sub-division of the autonomic nervous system into the *sympathetic* and *parasympathetic systems* (Day, 1979).

The sympathetic system is generally concerned with preparing the body for increased activity, and the parasympathetic has a conserving effect. W. B. Cannon (1929) described the effects of extreme sympathetic activation as preparing the body for flight or fight. When faced with fear or excitement, the heart-rate and force of contraction are increased, thereby increasing the blood flow to the skeletal muscles; the respiratory tract muscles are relaxed, facilitating the passage of air into the lungs; the pupils are dilated, blood glucose is increased, and body hair is erected. Other functions, which are not immediately essential for survival, such as digestion, are suppressed. The parasympathetic system is involved in digestion, sweating, urination, and defecation.

In the autonomic nervous system two neurons connect the central nervous system and end organ. The fiber of a neuron lying in the central nervous system extends to an autonomic ganglia and synapses on the dendrites or cell body of an autonomic neuron. The fiber of the second neuron passes from the ganglion to the effector to be innervated. The first fiber is the *preganglionic fiber,* and the second is the *post ganglionic fiber.* Both fibers are of approximate equal length in the sympathetic system. In the parasympathetic system, the preganglionic fibers are long, and the post ganglionic fibers are short. This is because the cell bodies are usually in the organ being innervated or in a ganglion that is close to the organ.

The parasympathetic system fibers arise from the third (to the ciliary muscle of the eye and pupillary sphincters), seventh (to lachrymal, nasal, submaxillary, and sublingual glands), ninth (to parotid gland), and tenth (to heart, lungs, esophagus, stomach, small intestine, proximal half of the colon, gallbladder, liver, and pancreas) cranial nerves and from the second, third, and fourth sacral nerves. The pelvic nerves originate from the latter three and send fibers to the pelvic plexus. From here, postganglionic fibers are sent to the viscera. Motor fibers pass to the smooth muscle of the descending colon, rectum, anus, bladder, and reproductive organs. The parasympathetic system is referred to as the craniosacral division of the autonomic nervous system.

The sympathetic ganglia originate from thoracic nerves, one through twelve, and lumbar nerves one and two. The fibers from thoracic, one through five, are distributed to the heart, lungs, and blood vessels. Fibers from thoracic, six through twelve, form the splanchnic nerves. The preganglionic fibers terminate in the *celiac ganglia* (solar plexus). The postganglionic fibers are distributed to the esophagus, liver, gallbladder, stomach, and intestine as far as the proximal colon. Fibers from lumbar one and two form the preganglionic fibers that terminate in the inferior mesenteric ganglia. The postganglionic fibers are distributed to the distal part of the colon, rectum, and genitourinary organs. This system is called the thoracolumbar division. This explains why breathing into the chest causes excitement and a "charge" (sympathetic) and breathing into the abdomen causes relaxation (parasympathetic).

Nerve fibers that release acetylcholine are called *cholinergic,* and those that release norepinephrine are known as *adrenergic.* A large group of drugs used in medicine is classified anticholinergic, this means they block the release or uptake of acetylcholine. This action is also responsible for many of the side effects of drugs. Cholinergic fibers include pre-ganglionic fibers to all ganglia, post-ganglionic parasympathetic fibers to heart, glands and smooth muscle, post-ganglionic fibers to sweat glands, and motor fibers to striated muscle. Adrenergic fibers include post-ganglionic sympathetic fibers to smooth muscle, heart, and glands. These chemicals are called neurotransmitters. Neurotransmitters are synthesized in the nerve ending from precursor chemicals. The necessary enzymes are manufactured in the cell body and migrate down the axon to the end region.

The microscopic space between two neurons, called a synapse, is very important in psychopharmacology, because it is the sight of most chemotherapy. An impulse reaching a nerve ending starts a complex set of events that will release a chemical substance at the nerve ending. This substance will migrate to an appropriate receptor site on the next neuron. This process allows the impulse to travel from neuron to neuron. Many actions and side effects of drugs come from their ability to stimulate or block the release or uptake of these neurotransmitter chemicals. Other drugs curtail their development by inhibiting the release of enzymes necessary for the production of the neurotransmitter.

In looking at the parts of the body and the effects of the parasympathetic and sympathetic systems, an important aspect to remember is that the systems are often antagonistic.

The Eye

Postganglionic sympathetic nerve fibers terminate in the smooth muscle of the pupil (dilator pupillae muscle), in the smooth muscle of the upper and lower lids (superior and inferior tarsal muscle), and in the blood vessels or the conjunctiva and retina. The parasympathetic nerves in the eyes pass through the IIIrd cranial nerve (oculomotor) coming from the Edinger-Westphal nucleus in the midbrain. The post ganglionic fibers innervate the circular muscle of the iris (constrictor pupillae muscle) and the smooth muscle of the ciliary body. Sympathetic stimulation causes dilation of the pupil (mydriasis) and retraction of the eyelids, producing a staring gaze. Blood vessels in the conjunctiva and retina are constricted. Parasympathetic stimulation contracts the muscle of the iris, reducing the diameter of the pupil (miosis). It also contracts the ciliary body causing the eye to accommodate for near vision. Pupil changes are usually parasympathetic in man. However, during emotional states such as fear and rage, sympathetically induced mydriasis can occur.

Lachrymal Glands

The lachrymal glands receive sympathetic fibers from the superior cervical ganglion. The parasympathetic nerves come from the brain stem through the VIIth cranial nerve (facial). Sympathetic fibers innervate blood supply and vasoconstriction. The parasympathetic fibers stimulate tear production.

Salivary Glands

Sympathetic postganglionic fibers arise from the superior cervical ganglion and end mainly in the blood vessels of the glands. The parasympathetic supply comes from the brain stem via the VIIth and the IXth (glossopharyngeal) nerves. Parasympathetic stimulation causes secretion of thin, watery saliva. Sympathetic stimulation causes a flow of thick saliva. This may be the indirect result of the reduction of blood flow.

Blood Vessels In The Head

Sympathetic stimulation causes vasoconstriction, and parasympathetic causes vasodilation.

Organs In The Skin

Sympathetic stimulation usually causes vasoconstriction of skin. In the face area it can cause vasodilation resulting in "blushing." Pilomotor muscles which are attached to hair follicles are contracted, causing the follicles to stand out from the skin. In man, this is usually experienced as "goose bumps." Sympathetic stimulation also increases sweat secretion by the eccrine glands. The skin structures are free of parasympathetic nerve supply.

Cardiac

Pregangliar parasympathetic neurons originate in the vagus and end in the intrinsic cardiac ganglia. Stimulation causes cardiac inhibition, slowing of the heart (bradycardia), and probably constriction of the coronary arteries. The sympathetic system produces acceleration (tachycardia) of the heart and the conduction of cardiac pain.

Pulmonary

Sympathetic preganglionic fibers arise from the upper four or five thoracic segments. Stimulation causes bronchodilation by relaxing the smooth muscle. Parasympathetic stimulation causes bronchoconstriction and increased flow of mucus from the bronchial glands.

Esophagus

Sympathetic innervation travels from the fourth to sixth thoracic segment. Stimulation causes increased tone of the cardiac sphincter, diminished tone and motility in the lower third of the organ, and augments vagal constriction in the upper third. Parasympathetic stimulation causes motility and increased tone in the upper and lower third and relaxation in the cardiac sphincter.

Stomach and Intestines

Peristaltic movement is inhibited by the sympathetic system. It increases the tone of the sphincters. Peristalsis is increased, gastric and other digestive juices are decreased by the parasympathetic.

Liver

Glucose is released by sympathetic stimulation. This may be due to stimulation of an enzyme reaction. There is no parasympathetic innervation.

Pancreas

Pancreatic juices and insulin are stimulated by parasympathetic stimulation. The sympathetic system causes vasoconstriction.

Gall Bladder

By affecting the musculature of the biliary tract, the sympathetic inhibits bile flow, while the parasympathetic stimulates bile flow by inhibiting contraction of the sphincter.

Adipose Tissue

Fat tissue receives sympathetic innervation which leads to an increase in blood level of free fatty acids.

Spleen

Sympathetic stimulation contracts the spleen, causing the flow of erythrocytes.

Kidneys

Sympathetic stimulation causes vasoconstriction which leads to decreased urine flow.

Urinary Bladder

Sympathetic stimulation causes the ureteral orifices to close and the base of the bladder to be pulled down. Parasympathetic stimulation results in a contraction of the detrusor muscle and relaxation of the sphincter thus aiding emptying of the bladder.

Sex Organs

In the male, sympathetic stimulation causes vasoconstriction and contraction of the smooth muscles of the prostate, seminal vesicles, prostatic urethra and vas deferens. Ejaculation is a sympathetic stimulated activity. The parasympathetic system causes vasodilation of the blood vessels of the cavernous tissue of the penis, promoting erection. In females, sympathetic stimulation contracts the uterus and fallopian tubes and increases secretion of mucus from the vestibular glands. Clitoral erection is caused by parasympathetic innervation.

Implications for Psychotherapists

The preceding anatomical and physiological considerations are meant to give the reader a sense of the autonomic nervous system and how it functions. This information can become quite useful to the psychotherapist. In exploring the psychological implications of the autonomic nervous system one might think of the ANS as a filter of emotional input. If one were to conceptualize the nervous system as that part of the body that connects itself to the mind and that part of the mind that connects itself to the body, then the autonomic nervous system can be identified as that part of the body-mind that links events and awareness. For the psychotherapist, this knowledge and an awareness of how to use and interpret it becomes extremely important.

In body-based psychotherapy approaches, breathing is very important. In body-based psychotherapy, clients are asked to breathe into their chests. This causes the sympathetic division of the ANS to be stimulated and helps the client to build a charge. "Intensification and expansion of the excitement in the body, coming from the free flow of energy." (Rosenberg, Rand, & Asay 1985, p. 320). This feeling or experience of aliveness can be spread over the entire body by using release techniques. The author uses a containment model and incorporates the releases to help spread the charge throughout the body. This allows for both a fuller charge and more complete release. For a more complete description of using breathing in a containment model refer to Rosenberg, Rand, and Asay (1985).

As the client breathes and builds a charge, the therapist can observe certain changes going on in the body. When these changes are discussed, keep in mind the actions and responses of the sympathetic and parasympathetic divisions of the ANS. As the client begins to breathe into the chest, he/she feels and/or reports a sensation such as tingling, or heat, in some areas of the body. The areas that he/she does not feel anything, or feels less intensity, are probably blocked by muscular tension, thereby decreasing sensitivity and awareness. The therapist can notice a change in the skin color. As the client builds a charge, the skin will become pink or red. White areas denote blockage. The client will usually feel an increase in skin temperature as he/she breathes. White or blocked areas will feel cool. Oftentimes, a client will feel cold after a release. As the client builds an even greater charge, he/she will begin to shake or vibrate. This will be visible to the therapist and felt by the client. This is evidence that blocked muscles and fixed muscular patterns are beginning to release tension (Parasympathetic). These activities correlate to both sympathetic and parasympathetic stimulation, as the excitation builds by levels.

Stomach breathing causes parasympathetic stimulation. This principle is used in many yoga practices to calm the individual. A therapist can use this knowledge of the ANS to calm a highly excited or hysterical client by having him or her do abdominal breathing.

Frequently the therapist will note that the client is holding his/her breath. This is one way that people can control feelings. A helpful procedure is for the therapist to monitor the client and note when he/she is holding his/her breath. One simple and useful technique is to remind the client to continue to breathe. Clients may be blocking positive as well as negative feelings.

Relaxation, imagery, meditation, and biofeedback are all ways that help a client to be more consciously in control of his/her ANS. It has become well known that people can lower blood pressure, heat or cool body parts, fall asleep, become calm, or excited by using these techniques (Mason, 1980). The Native Americans practiced many rituals to calm or stimulate the individual by using techniques to activate the ANS. The different dances or ceremonies they used were all carefully selected to create a "state-of-being," using ANS stimulation. Psychotherapists can incorporate many of these techniques into their practice. No matter what type of psychotherapy is being practiced, careful attention to the body clues can only help the therapist become more aware of the state in which the client is. By helping the client become aware of his/her "state of being" as reflected in the body clues, the therapist gives the client a useful tool to monitor while outside as well as in the therapy session.

Our society, more so than any other in the past, has to deal with "stress." The sympathetic division of the ANS is directly involved in preparing the individual for what is called the fight-flight syndrome (Cannon, 1929). The trained and observant therapist can evaluate the client by reading the body for signs of sympathetic stimulation by looking at the eyes, skin, breathing, and energy level.

Most drugs used for treating psychotropic disorders, as well as many other drugs, are anticholinergic. This means that they block parasympathetic stimulation. They work by interfering with the neurotransmission at the synapse. Of value for the therapist is to know what drugs the client is taking, because the side effect or effect of the drug may be causing much of the client's problem. This is often the case when the client reports a decrease in sexual energy or interest. Some chemicals that one may not think of as a drug can also cause ANS problems. Nicotine, for example, causes stimulation of autonomic ganglia in small doses and paralysis in larger doses.

By paying close attention to the client's body during a psychotherapy session, the "body-aware" psychotherapist can pick up many clues as to the emotional state of the client. These clues can come as direct observation or by the result of the client's report. The client's eyes, skin, breathing, and energetic levels can tell the trained psychotherapist many things that might be missed if attention is not paid to the body. The autonomic nervous system plays a very important role in maintaining homeostasis. Many of the effects of this balance process can be seen, felt, or heard. Even to the untrained observer, often the detection is made that something is happening. The difficulty is being able to make an accurate analysis of the factual data. A good example of this process can be cited in the police department. Many officers can accurately determine blood alcohol levels by observing an individual. These police officers have learned to interpret and assign a numeric value to their observations.

The psychotherapist, through his/her own life's experience, has learned to tune into the many clues or signs of the client's emotional and energetic status. When this information is intuited, psychotherapy is an "art." When the psychotherapist becomes conscious of his/her experience and observations, then he/she can learn to accurately interpret the data. This opens the door to a more "scientific" practice of psychotherapy. Knowledge of the autonomic nervous system, learning to read the body clues, and being able to accurately interpret these findings can open new doors in the "art and science" of psychotherapy. To assist in function and structure with the sympathic and parasympathetic basic information is supplied in Figure 3.1.

ENDOCRINE SYSTEM AND HORMONES

The endocrine system, along with the nervous system, are the controlling and coordinating mechanisms of the body. Unlike the nervous system, which responds through the use of chemical and electrical impulses, the endocrine system uses only chemical stimuli. The action of the nervous system on muscles and glands is immediate and short-term, while the effects of the endocrine system are slower, longer, and more widespread. The endocrine system also has a more generalized effect on growth, metabolism, and reproduction.

The chemical messengers of the endocrine system are called *hormones.* The glands release the hormones directly into the blood stream. They are sometimes referred to as ductless glands, as opposed to the ducted *exocrine glands* which release their secretions into body cavities, organs, or outside the body through ducts. These glands are found in the stomach, intestine, liver, pancreas, and mouth. Some of the secretions are mucus, sweat, saliva, and other digestive juices.

(Continued on page 87)

Function or Structure	Sympathetic	Parasympathetic
I. General		
A. CNS connection	Thoracolumbar	Craniosacral
B. Ganglia location	Close to CNS	Close to effector
C. Neurotransmitter	Norepinephrine[1]	Acetylcholine
D. Pharmacology	Adrenergic	Cholinergic
E. Distribution	Through body	Limited
F. Homeostatic function	Fight or flight mobilize energy	Relaxation conserve energy
II. Structure		
A. Eye 1. Iris	Pupillary dilation mydriasis	Constriction miosis
2. Ciliary muscle	no effect	contraction accommodation
3. Lachrymal gland Psych Impli[2]	little effect	stimulates secretion
	Dry eyes (Sadness)	Bright eyes (Joy)
B. Glands		
1. Salivary	scanty viscous decreased secretion	watery increased secretion
Psych Impli	dry mouth	moist mouth
2. Sweat	secretion[3]	no effect
Psych Impli	moist cool skin sweating	dry skin

[1] Sympathetic has alpha (norepinephrine—results in excitation) & beta (epinephrine—results in inhibition, except in heart) receptor. Beta-1 cardiac receptor for stimulation. Beta-2 peripheral receptor causes vasodilation and bronchodilation.

[2] Psychological implications

[3] In the sweat glands, suprarenal medulla, and some blood vessels of skeletal muscle sympathetic neuroeffector transmission is mediated by acetylcholine.

Figure 3.1. Autonomic nervous system.

Figure 3.1. Continued.

Function or Structure	Sympathetic	Parasympathetic
B. Glands (cont)		
3. G.I.	inhibition	secretion
Psych Impli		sounds
4. Suprarenal medulla	secretion	no effect
C. Cardiac		
1. Heart rate	increases	decreases
2. Force of contraction	increases	no effect
3. A V node	increase conduction	decrease or block
D. Bronchi	dilation	constriction
E. Gallbladder	relax inhibits bile flow	constrict stimulate bile flow
F. G.I. tract		
1. Sphincters	contract	relax
2. Motility	decreased peristalsis & tone	increased
Psych Impli	constipation	diarrhea
G. Urinary		
1. Detrusor	relaxation	contraction
2. Trigone & sphincters	contraction	relaxation
Psych Impli	inhibits micturition	stimulates micturition
H. Sex organs		
1. Male	ejaculation	erection
2. Female	contraction of uterine muscle dry vagina decrease blood flow	relaxation of uterine muscle moist vagina increase blood flow
Psych Impli	decrease sexual desire	increase sexual desire
I. Pilomotor muscles	contraction "goose bumps"	no effect

Figure 3.1. Continued.

Function or Structure	Sympathetic	Parasympathetic
J. Metabolism		
1. Basal	marked increase	no effect
2. Liver	glucose released	no effect
3. Blood sugar	increased	no effect
K. Mental activity	increased	no effect
L. Blood coagulation	increased	no effect
M. Blood vessels		
1. Skeletal	dilation	constriction
2. Skin	constriction	no effect
3. Respiratory	dilation	constriction
4. Digestive organs	constriction	dilation
N. Stomach & Intestines	inhibited peristalsis	increased peristalsis decreased gastric & other digestive juices
O. Skin	blushing	no effect
P. Adipose tissue	Increase free fatty acids	
Q. Pancreas	vasoconstriction	stimulation increased insulin

Hormones are transported throughout the body in the blood stream. Each hormone has an affinity to certain cells, called receptors. The two catagories of hormones are proteins and steroids.

1. **Proteins.** Most hormones are protein or related compounds made up of amino acids. Generally, protein hormones attach to the surface of the target cell and activate another substance within the cell. This substance, called the second messenger, travels within the cell to alter its activity. Protein hormones usually are involved with changes in the rate of protein manufacture in the cytoplasm.

2. **Steroids.** The hormones of the sex glands and adrenal cortex are steroids. Steroids are a group of chemicals that contain a cyclic structure resembling cholesterol. These steroid hormones can pass through the cell membrane. They enter the target cell, combine with receptors, and then enter the nucleus. Steroid hormones have a direct effect of the DNA, therefore altering the activity of the cell.

Most hormones are released on an "as needed" basis. Hormones are involved in the body's steady state called **homeostasis.** The mechanism for this activity is sometimes called a negative feedback system. It works by using feedback to reverse processes in order to bring the system back to a normal state.

A brief description of the endocrine system is included in Figure 3.2 because of the many possible implications of hormone imbalance. For example, hypoglycemia (low blood sugar) can cause fatigue, muscular weakness, excessive perspiration, nervous irritability, anxiety, insomnia, vertigo, crying spells, difficulty in concentration, unsocial or antisocial behavior, depression, phobias, blurred vision, neuroses, convulsions, and death. These symptoms will only go away if the underlying hormonal imbalance is dealt with. This may be accomplished, in this case, by nutritional control. Recent studies show that some women begin to have a decrease in estrogen levels around age thirty. This hormonal imbalance can cause symptoms that would bring someone into psychotherapy.

(Continued on page 91)

Name:	*Pituitary* (hypophysis)
Description:	A small gland with two lobes.
Location:	In the brain just behind the point where the optic nerves cross.
Hormones:	ANTERIOR LOBE

Growth hormone (GH) promotes growth of all body tissues.

Thyroid-stimulating hormone (TSH) stimulates the thyroid gland to produce thyroid hormones.

Adrenocorticotropic hormone (ACTH) stimulates the cortex of the adrenal gland to produce cortical hormones. Aids in protecting the body in stress situations such as pain or injury.

Follicle-stimulating hormone (FSH) stimulates the growth and hormonal activity of the ovarian follicles. Promotes the development of sperm cells and stimulates the growth of the testes.

Luteinizing hormone (LH) in males is called the interstitial cell-stimulating hormone (ICSH). Female: Causes development of the corpus luteum at site of ruptured ovarian follicle. Male: Stimulates the secretion of testosterone.

Prolactin (PRL) stimulates mammary glands to secrete milk.

POSTERIOR LOBE

Antidiuretic hormone (ADH) (vasopressin) promotes reabsorption of water from kidney tubules. Raises blood pressure by contracting smooth muscles of the blood vessels. *Diabetes insipidus* is a disorder caused by inadequate ADH causing excessive water loss.

Oxytocin causes contraction of uterine muscle and milk ejection from the mammary glands.

Figure 3.2. Endocrine glands and their hormones.

Figure 3.2. Continued.

Name:	***Thyroid***
Description:	The largest endocrine gland. It has two oval parts called lateral lobes and a narrow band called the isthmus.
Location:	In the neck.
Hormones:	*Thryoxin and triiodothyronine* increases the rate of metabolism for the production of heat and energy in the body tissues, influences mental and physical activities, regulates normal growth. The body requires the ingestion of iodine in order for gland to function properly.
	Calcitonin decreases calcium level in blood.
Name:	***Parathyroid***
Description:	Composed of four tiny glands.
Location:	Behind the thyroid.
Hormones:	Parathyroid hormone regulates exchange of calcium between bones and blood. Increases calcium level in blood.
Name:	***Adrenal*** (suprarenal)
Description:	Two in number, each has a medulla (inner) and a cortex (outer).
Location:	Above each kidney
Hormones:	ADRENAL CORTEX
	Glucocorticoid (cortisol) aids in metabolism of carbohydrates, fats, and proteins. Involved in stress.
	Mineralocorticoid (aldosterone) regulation of electrolytes and water balance by controlling reabsorption of sodium and the secretion of potassium in the kidney.
	Sex hormones secreted in small amount with little effect in the body. May have some influence on secondary sexual characteristics in males.

Figure 3.2. Continued.

Name:	*Pancreas*
Description:	Contains special cells called the islets of Langerhans. The rest of the pancreas is considered to be an exocrine gland (produces digestive juices, bile, and releases them through ducts).
Location:	In the abdominal cavity near duodenum.
Hormones:	*Insulin* aids in the transport of glucose into cells; required for metabolism of food; decreases blood sugar levels.
	Glucagon works with insulin to regulate blood sugar levels. Causes liver to release stored glucose into the blood, thereby raising blood sugar levels.
	Diabetes mellitus is caused when the pancreas fails to produce enough insulin, and sugar cannot be metabolized.
Name:	*Ovary*
Description:	Two in number, where the female sex cells, or ova, are formed. The ovaries are small, flattened, oval bodies.
Location:	Extended down in pelvic portion of abdomen.
Hormones:	*Estrogens* stimulate growth of primary sexual organs (uterus, etc.) and development of secondary sexual organs (breasts and pelvic changes).
	Progesterone stimulates the development of secretory parts of mammary glands; prepares the uterine lining for implantation of the fertilized ovum; aids in the maintenance of pregnancy.

SUMMARY

This section has given the reader an overview of the nervous system. The workings of the system are quite complicated. The information presented was for the purpose of familiarizing the reader with the system. Further reading or study is suggested for the individual interested in a more in-depth understanding of the nervous system. Understanding the nervous system is essential to the exploration of psychopharmacology. Most psychotropic drugs act directly upon the nervous system. In studying the system a useful procedure is to break it down into three general categories: the central nervous system, composed of the brain and spinal cord; the peripheral nervous system, composed of nerves that transport impulses to and from the central nervous system and the periphery; and the autonomic nervous system, consisting of the sympathetic and parasympathetic divisions. The nervous system is the body's response-stimulus mechanism. The brain acts to regulate the body activities and is the center of higher mental process, the seat of emotion, and the source of voluntary actions. The spinal cord connects the periphery to the brain. The autonomic nervous system usually functions independent of conscious thought. It allows the maintenance of a relatively stable internal environment to the body, called "homeostasis."

CHAPTER **IV**

NATURE OF PSYCHOPATHOLOGY

In order to understand the nature of psychopathology, we will explore first the question: What is mental health? Swonger and Constantine (1983) suggested three primary components that are essential to mental health.

1. The psychologically healthy person feels good about his/her-self as a person. The two components that enter into this are self esteem and self acceptance. This translates into the person liking his/herself under both positive and negative conditions. This does not preclude normal periods of anxiety or depression. These periods are usually situational and may last for short or prolonged times.

2. The psychologically healthy person is capable of "interpersonal flexibility." He/she can successfully conduct relationships with others, using a wide variety of skills and behaviors to meet "the slings and arrows" (Bower 1969) of interpersonal life.

3. The psychologically healthy person is capable of effectively functioning in "real social systems," requiring both the ability to be autonomous and dependent.

Swonger uses the terminology "interdependence" or "synergic autonomy" to describe the balanced mixture of dependence and independence.

The three aspects of a psychologically healthy person include the **intrapersonal** or **intrapsychic,** the **interpersonal** or **interactive,** and the **metapersonal** or **social characteristics** of an individual.

CLASSIFICATION—FOR AND AGAINST

A debate as to the use of classification has drawn strong support as well as opposition. The argument for and against the use of classifications, as Hersen, Kazdin, and Bellack (1983) pointed out, results in gains and losses for the patient. Laing (1967) stated that the diagnostic label could result in a self-fulfilling prophecy for both the patient and the labeler. The three main considerations against classification are

1. the label can not contain all the relevant information about the specific patient; therefore it functions as a stereotype and overlooks the individual;

2. a label may modify the way others see or treat the individual; and

3. treatment and prognosis may be based upon the label, and not the observed behavior of the individual.

Allbee (1970) criticized labeling as focusing on deficits instead of strengths. Korchin (1976) also pointed out that labeling emphasized weakness, and not strength. Szasz (1961) took a stand as to moral and logical bias of classifying human behavior. He called it "controlling and demeaning" to a person.

Goldenberg (1977) discussed the utility of a classification for communication, research, and understanding etiology. Spitzer and Wilson (1975) wrote "the purpose of a classification of mental disorders always involve, in the broadest sense, communication, control, and comprehension" (p. 1035).

Blashfield and Draguns (1976), in their study of classification, proposed the following functions of classification:

1. provide a nomenclature or consistent set of terms,

2. provide efficient information retrieval,

3. provide a uniform description of the classification,

4. provide a prediction of outcome, and

5. provide basic concepts.

A case can be made for or against a formal process of classification and drawbacks and pluses exist for both positions. For any practitioner to work successfully with a patient or client some sort of assessment is essential. This process may be highly formalized, very informal to the point that the therapist is not consciously aware of categorizing, or somewhere in the middle. Classification is often based upon the presenting symptoms. These may be the temporary result of an underlying disorder. Often the emphasis in practice is to treat the overt manifestation and ignore the underlying etiology. One consideration in the question of utilizing drug therapy is the possibility of eliminating the symptoms while the underlying disease is still present.

When a client/patient begins psychotherapy, he/she begins the diagnostic work by presenting a problem. "I am depressed." "I cannot fall asleep." "Something is wrong. I feel depressed, and can't seem to work any more." In essence, the client/patient begins the diagnostic procedure by presenting a problem. The elements of the presenting problem include "affect," "behavior," and "insight." Usually, the client/patient has attempted to work the problem out on his/her own. Therefore, the client/patient is also stating that he/she lacks the means for "self change" (Swonger & Constantine, 1983). The client/patient is presenting material that falls into five areas which becomes the beginning of a diagnostic procedure and the basis for a treatment plan.

These five areas include

1. the problem or the pathology,

2. the mood or feeling level (affect),

3. the functioning (behavior),

4. the insight, and

5. the inability to "self change."

The focus of the therapy depends upon the school or modality of the psychotherapist. In **behavioral therapy** or in **behavior modification,** as it is known, the focus of the treatment is on the client's/patient's behavior. Traditional **psychoanalytic therapy** places emphasis on **insight.** Other **supportive psychotherapies** focus upon **affect.** The difference in each therapy is a matter of emphasis. A truly successful therapist doubtlessly deals with all three elements directly and indirectly.

PSYCHOPATHOLOGICAL SYMPTOMS

Psychopathological symptoms fall into three categories. These categories can be separated for a theoretical discussion, however, clinical manifestations can be a complex mixture of all three. The elements are interwoven in a unique pattern for each individual. The three elements are organic, psychological, and interpersonal systemic processes.

Organic Process

This includes all physiological and anatomical factors. Examples include genetic defects and physical trauma. The diagnosis of the psychopathology of organic etiology is a subtle, complex, and often overlooked process. Small (1973) suggested the following grounds for suspecting neurologic implications:

1. birth injuries, prolonged birth, or forceps delivery, head injuries or trauma, especially in cases of loss of consciousness, high fever, prolonged anesthesia, poisonings;

2. sudden recurring (paroxysmal) symptoms involving a sensory loss, such as vertigo;

3. sudden or disturbing emotional states or changes that cannot be connected to a psychological or systemic onset;

4. impaired recall, problem with orientation, intellectual or attention disorders; and

5. gradual change in sensory or motor control.

Psychological or Personal Process

This includes factors that are of an individual nature. Examples include personal trauma and personality organization. If one thinks of the organic process as the complex electronics and wiring that make up the behavioral and emotional computer, then the psychological process is the programing that is stored in the computer.

Interpersonal Systemic Process

This includes factors of the family, social, and psychotherapy system. For example, the labeling of the client/patient by the psychotherapist.

Probably the diagnosing of clients/patients can "box them in," overlook their uniqueness, and even cause them to repeat symptomatic patterns. Equally true the psychotherapist can do a disservice by missing or overlooking symptoms of organic etiology. Many organic disorders have symptoms that includes behavioral manifestations. The exploration of this subject is beyond the scope of this text.

EARLY CLASSIFICATIONS

Attempts to classify mental disorders have their roots back in the dawn of civilization. Hippocrates (Hersen, Kazdin, & Bellack 1983) classified and described *melancholia* and *mania.* Ancient Egyptian literature (Spitzer & Wilson, 1975) mentioned hysteria and melancholia as early as 2600 B.C. Hippocrates (460 to 377 B.C.) was the first to write about the idea of treating mental illness in medicine (Hersen, Kazdin, & Bellack, 1983). He categorized mental disorders into "chronic disturbances without fever" (melancholia), acute mental disturbances with and without fear, and hysteria. Sydenham (1624 to 1663) proposed multiple disorders (Jaffe & Martin, 1980). He was the first to move away from the theory of a single pathological process for mental illness. Pinel (1745 to 1826), a French physician, came up with a simplified diagnostic system of four types of mental illness. These were mania, melancholia, dementia, and idiotism. In 1801, Pinel called for the scientific study and the categorization of mental disease. He further argued for the use of case studies, life histories, and the study of treatment methodology (Pichot 1986).

Prior to the 20th century, most attempts to classify mental illness were limited to insanity. Not until the mid 19th century were institutions established for the insane. This also lead to the specialty of medicine known as psychiatry. In 1885, the *Congress of Mental Medicine* was formed with the purpose of deriving a single system of classifying mental disorders. The Congress came up with eleven disorders. Most of the terms used are still recognizable today. The categories are dementia, organic and senile dementia, periodic insanity, progressive systematic insanity, mania, melancholia, periodic paralysis, insane neuroses, toxic insanity, moral and impulsive insanity, and idiocy.

Emil Kraepelin (1913) published a series of texts on abnormal psychology. His intention was to write textbooks on psychopathology. However, his organization, by chapters, became the basis of modern psychological nosologies (the science of the classification of diseases). Kraepelin gave concise descriptions and case histories of categories. In his sixth edition of the *Textbook of Psychiatry* (1913) he introduced the concepts of a manic-depressive disorder and dementia praecox, as distinct from paranoia. Bleuler (1950) used the name **schizophrenia** for the disorder known as dementia praecox.

CLASSIFICATION SYSTEMS—
TWENTIETH CENTURY

In the United States census of 1840, only one category of mental illness was used. By 1880, seven categories of mental illness were recognized: mania, melancholia, monomania, paresis, dementia, dipsomania, and epilepsy. The American Psychiatric Association, in 1917, adopted a system of classification based upon Kraepelin's work. This was used until 1934, when it was replaced by *The Standard Classified Nomenclature of Disease.* *The Standard* had 24 categories, 19 of which had been described in Kraepelin's textbook. World War II stimulated the need and interest for new classifications. *The Standard* dealt only with chronic inpatients. The War created a need for categorizing acute disturbance, personality disturbances, and psychosomatic disorders. As a result the Army, Navy, and the Veteran's Administration each developed their own system. The American Psychiatric Association, in order to reduce the confusion, developed the DSM-I (*Diagnostic and Statistical Manual for Mental Disorders, first edition.*) The DSM-I, published in 1952, emphasized the communication purpose of classification and was derived from the VA's classification system.

DSM-II was published in 1968 as an effort to be compatible with the newly published eighth edition of the *International Classification of Diseases* (ICD-8). Critics of the DSM-II complained of no single organizing principle, (Korchin, 1976) the need for specific symptoms of a given diagnosis, and categories that were arbitrary and subjective (Goldenberg, 1977).

In the 1970s, a group of psychiatrists, called "neo-Kraepelinian's" by Klerman (1978) set out to revise the DSM-II. They were interested in the importance of classification and research, and were opposed to the psychoanalytic perspective. Their work culminated in the publishing of DSM-III in 1980. The DSM-III was a long and complicated manual. It included 265 categories, compared to 108 in the DSM-I and 182 in the DSM-II. The ancient nosologies consisted of ten or fewer categories of severe, psychotic conditions. As Korchin (1976) stated, the tendency is towards complexity and coverage of a wider range of problems. The DSM-III used a specific diagnostic criteria, listed separate symptoms for each category, and gave specific clarification of symptoms necessary for a diagnosis.

In 1983 the American Psychiatric Association (APA) began the process of revising DSM-III. DSM-IV was not scheduled to be released until the early 1990s to coincide with the tenth revision of the *International Classification of Diseases* (ICD-10). Among the reasons cited for revising DSM-III were studies showing that some of the diagnostic criteria were inconsistent. Also, some criteria was not clear or even inconsistent between catagories. Finally, the APA was asked to work on developing parts of ICD-10. As a result, the APA published DSM-III-R in 1987. Some twenty-six committees, consisting of over two hundred members worked to revise DSM-III.

DSM-III-R

DSM-III-R can be divided into several sections. It begins with an introduction which gives a brief historical background of the DSM's, gives a description of the revising process, discusses the basic features of DSM-III-R, and makes several cautionary notes on the use of the manual. Three basic chapters are included. Following the chapters are eight appendices and two indexes.

The three chapters include a summary of the classifications in Axes I and II, directions on how to use the manual, and a description of the diagnostic categories.

Chapter 1

Chapter 1 is entitled Classification: Axes I and II Categories and Codes. Some eighteen major categories are listed—disorders Usually First Evident in Infancy, Childhood, or Adolescence. This includes various disorders that can be broken down by how they manifest. Those that are developmental in nature and effect intelligence include **Mental Retardation** which manifests a significantly subaverage general intelligence and a deficit or impairment in adaptive behavior. About 85% of these people are considered "educable" with a mild degree of severity. They have an IQ of between 50 and 70. Some 10% of the retarded population (moderate) is considered "trainable" with an IQ of 35 to 50. Three to 4% of these people are considered "severe" with an IQ of 20 to 35. The final group of "profound" mental retardees is made up of 1 to 2% of the disorder population and they have an IQ of below 20.

Disorders which characterize an impairment in development include symptomatology of impaired reciprocal social interaction, impaired communication and imaginative activity, and an impairment in activities and interest. These categories include the *Pervasive Developmental Disorders* (Autistic Disorder) and the *Specific Developmental Disorders* such as developmental reading, language, arithmetic, and articulation disorders. Other disorders that are usually first evident in infancy, childhood, or adolescence include the *Disruptive Behavior Disorders* manifesting symptoms of inappropriate inattention and impulsivity and repetitive (*Attention Deficit Disorder*) and persistent patterns of conduct in which the basic rights of others or age appropriate social norms or rules are violated (*Conduct Disorder*).

Disorders for which symptoms of separation, avoidance, over anxiety fall under the category of *Anxiety Disorders of Childhood or Adolescence.* The eating disorders include *anorexia nervosa (an intense fear of becoming obese), bulimia* (binge-eating with an awareness of the pattern), *pica* (persistent eating of a non-nutritive substance), and *rumination* (repeated regurgitation of food). DSM-III-R has changed the nomenclature of "Stereotyped movement disorders" to *Tic* (recurrent involuntary repetitive, rapid movements) Disorders. This includes "Tourette's" disorder (tics including multiple vocal tics). Other disorders with physical manifestations includes functional *encopresis* (repeated voluntary or involuntary passage of feces into non-appropriate places) and functional *enuresis* (involuntary urination during the day or night).

The *Organic Mental Disorders* include the dementias (severe loss of intellectual abilities), organic mental disorders induced by psychoactive substances, and organic mental disorders associated with physical disorders or conditions such as delirium. Alzheimer's disease is coded on Axis III as a physical disorder or condition.

Psychoactive Substance Use Disorders include the dependence and abuse of alcohol, amphetamines, cannabis, cocaine, hallucinogens, inhalants, nicotine, opioids, phencyclidine (PCP), sedative, hypnotic or anxiolytic drugs.

The **Psychotic Disorders** include "Schizophrenia," "Delusional (Paranoid) Disorder," and "Psychotic Disorders Not Elsewhere Classified."

DSM-III-R changes the terminology "Affective Disorders," found in DSM-III to **Mood Disorders.** Included under the mood disorders are the "Bipolar" disorders (what was called manic depressive disorder) and "Cyclothymia" (a chronic mood disturbance, lasting over two years, involving numerous periods of hypomanic and periods of depressed mood.

The **Anxiety Disorders,** subtitled the anxiety and phobic neuroses include panic disorder, "agoraphobia" (fear of being alone or in a place or situation for which escape is impossible), "social phobia," "obsessive compulsive disorder," "post-traumatic stress disorder," and "generalized anxiety disorder."

Somatoform Disorders include conversion (the loss of physical functioning that appears to have physical causes but is psychologically induced), somatization (recurrent and multiple conversion responses of mental experiences or states into bodily symptoms), and hypochondriasis (a preoccupation with the fear of having a serious disease which is justified by the individuals interpretation of the physical signs).

Dissociative Disorders (or Hysterical Neuroses, Dissociative Type) include multiple personality disorder, psychogenic fugue (the individual suddenly moves away from home and assumes a new identity while not able to recall the previous one) and amnesia (the inability to recall vast amounts of personal information).

Sexual Disorders include the Paraphilias, characterized by sexual arousal to objects or situations that are not normally considered sexually arousing, and Sexual dysfunctions, the inhibition of sexual activity or the psycho-physiological changes in the sexual cycle. The Paraphilias include fetishism, achieving sexual excitement using non-living objects; transvestism, cross dressing; zoophilia, using animals as the preferred method of achieving sexual excitement; pedophilia, fantasizing or engaging in sexual activity with children who haven't achieved puberty; exhibitionism, exposing of one's genitals; voyeurism, peeping at naked or disrobing persons; sexual masochism and sadism, achieving sexual excitement by humiliating, beating, bounding, or other forms of physical or psychological suffering. The psychosexual dysfunctions include premature ejaculation, vaginismus, dyspareunia, impotence, and frigidity.

The **Sleep Disorders** consist of chronic sleep disturbances that are not expected in every day life. They do not include several nights of insomnia that may be brought on by a psychosocial stressor. Sleep disorders are divided into two types: those involving a disturbance in the amount, quality, or timing of sleep; and those for which an abnormal event occurs during sleep. The nomenclature for these two types of sleep disturbance is dyssomnias and parasomnias. The dyssomnias include insomnia (inability to sleep) and hypersomnia (excessive daytime sleep). The parasomnias include dream anxiety (nightmares), sleep terror (abrupt awakening from sleep), and sleepwalking.

A group of disorders characterized by intentional manifestation of a symptom or group of symptoms is called the **Factitious Disorders.** Patients with this disorder, however, are unable to refrain from the behavior. The so called compulsive voluntary act is used to control involuntary goals.

Impulse Control Disorders include "Kleptomania" (the recurrent act of stealing objects that are of no value to the individual), "Pathological gambling," "Pyromania" (deliberate and purposeful setting of fires), and "Trichotillomania" (the pulling out of ones own hair).

The **Adjustment disorders** manifest in some maladaptive reactions to lives stresses, such as work or school. Another group of disorders covers the psychological factors affecting one's physical condition. These disorders have been referred to in the past as "psychosomatic" disorders. An example would be a headache that is judged to be psychologically induced.

The **Personality Disorders** are used to diagnose individuals who manifest long term and inflexible personality patterns that cause significant functional impairment. Included are the "Paranoid" (suspicious and mistrusting), "Schizoid" (unable to make social relationships), "Schizotypal" (patterns of thought, perception, and behavior not serious enough to be considered Schizophrenic), "Antisocial," "Borderline" (an instable self-image with difficulties in interpersonal relationships, and mood), "Histrionic" (dramatic, reactive, and intensely expression of behavior with consequential disturbances in relationships), "Narcissistic" (exaggerated sense of self importance), "Avoidant," "Dependent," Obsessive Compulsive" (inflexible and perfectionist), and "Passive Aggressive" personality disorders.

One section in the DSM-III-R is for other conditions that are not attributable to a mental disorder that may be treated in a mental health setting. For example marital problems and malingering are treated in this section. Like the ICD-9, the DSM-III-R distinguishes these classifications with **V Codes.** Therefore, they are listed with a V and then a number. For example, a marital problem that is not due to a mental disorder is given the code V61.10.

Chapter 2

In Chapter 2 are given detailed directions for the use of the manual. The DSM-III-R uses a multiaxial evaluation. "To insure that certain information may be of value in planning treatment and predicting outcome," the DSM-III-R uses a five axes diagnosis evaluation. **Axes I** and **II** include all the mental disorders. Axis II is for Personality Disorders and Specific Developmental Disorders. All the other mental disorders are assigned to Axes I. **Axis III** is for physical disorders and conditions. The DSM-III-R makes the traditional separation of behavior or psychological disorders from other manifestations, thus, it made a distinction between "mental" and "physical" disorders. **Axis IV,** the "Severity of Psychosocial Stressors," and

Axis V, the "Highest Level of Adaptive Functioning Past Year", are normally used for special clinical study or research. The official diagnoses (Axes I, II, and III) are for treatment planning and predicting outcome.

In considering significant psychosocial stressors (Axis IV), DSM-III-R lists several areas of importance. These include

1. conjugal (marital and non-marital—engagement, marriage, discord, separation, and death of a spouse;

2. parenting—becoming a parent, friction with or illness of a child;

3. other interpersonal—includes relationship with friends, neighbors, associates, and boss;

4. occupational—includes work, homemaking, school, unemployment, and retirement;

5. living circumstances—residence change, immigration, or personal threat;

6. financial—includes change in status or inadequate finances;

7. legal—arrest, jail, lawsuit, or trial;

8. developmental—any change in life cycle phase;

9. physical illness or injury—listed in Axis IV when impact is due to the interpretation of the individual and it is also listed in Axis III;

10. other psychosocial stressors—a "catch-all" to include areas not covered, e.g., natural or manmade disaster, unwanted pregnancy, or rape; and

11. family factors (children and adolescents—specific stressor considered for children in the family, e.g., overly hostile parents, inconsistent parental control, and institutional rearing.

Axis V looks at the "highest level of adaptive functioning" during the "past year." Emphasis is placed on social relations, occupational functioning, and the use of leisure time. The three areas are considered together, with social relations being given greater weight. The rating scale here is from one to seven, "superior" to "grossly impaired." The levels include (1) Superior, defined as unusually effective; (2) Very Good, better than average; (3) Good, slight impairment; (4) Fair, moderate impairment; (5) Poor, marked impairment in either social or occupational functioning; (6) Very Poor, marked impairment in both; and (7) Grossly Impaired, recognizing all areas of functioning. The notation "zero" is used to indicate "unspecified," or no information available.

Chapter 3

In Chapter 3, *The Diagnostic Categories,* the text is systematic in organization. It lists all of the categories in Axis I and Axis II. Under each diagnostic category a discussion is provided that includes information regarding essential features, associated features, age at onset, course, impairment, complications, predisposing factors, prevalence, sex ratio, familial pattern, and differential diagnosis. It does not list information about theories of etiology, management, and treatment.

Appendixes and Indexes

In the eight appendixes, the DSM-III-R contains a multitude of information, such as the discussion of the need for further study of certain categories in Appendix A. Appendix B is very important, as it is a series of five decisions trees that can be used to isolate a differential diagnosis. These trees include a list of questions, for which the answers take the practitioner through a road map toward a diagnosis. The questions approximate the diagnostic criteria of chapter three and can be very useful in making a diagnosis. The five trees isolate on 1) psychotic symptoms; 2) mood disturbance; 3) specific organic factors; 4) irrational anxiety, avoidance behavior, and increased arousal; and 5) physical complaints or anxiety about illness. Appendix C contains a glossary of technical terms used, while Appendix D gives a comparison of the listings in DSM-III and DSM-III-R. Appendix E is a historic review, classification, and glossary of ICD-9. A list of the field trial participants is found in Appendix F. Appendix G offers an alphabetic listing and Appendix H a numeric listing of the DSM-III-R diagnoses and codes. Two indexes are included. The first provides information by symptom and the second by diagnoses or diagnostic terms.

CHAPTER **V**

ANTIANXIETY DRUGS

ANXIETY

Anxiety is a symptom and not a specific disorder. It has been called a "pervasive feeling of apprehension," thought to be brought on by some unspecified future threat. Other terms used to describe anxiety include a threatened feeling, an uneasy feeling, nervousness, edginess, or jitteriness. It differs from fear in that fear is a response to an immediate and identifiable stimulus or event. The response to fear is rapid, distinct, and appropriate to the triggering circumstance. In anxiety, no specific circumstance or object generates the feeling. Anxiety may arise when a situation has no fearful or threatening qualities. The response to anxiety is often inappropriate to the precipitating event. Anxiety symptoms are seen in many psychological disorders, as well as being a component of medical or other problems.

Rahe (1979) listed five categories that are sources of stress. These are health, work, financial, home and family, personal, and social. In each of the five categories that Rahe listed are possible life-changing events that lead to stress. For example, under financial are included (1) making a major purchase, i.e., the purchase of an automobile; (2) acquiring a mortgage loan on the family home, business, or property; (3) the foreclosure of a mortgage or loan; (4) a sudden increase or decrease in income; (5) credit rating difficulties; and (6) unprofitable investments.

An important and debatable question arises in considering the treatment of anxiety. Since anxiety is a universal human experience, an important procedure for the physician or psychotherapist is to determine if drug intervention is warranted. Historically, the seeking of drug intervention, from the state of anxiety, is what has led to most of the drug abuse and dependence.

Anxiety, to keep things in perspective, has a positive side as well as a negative one. It helps people to stay alert during a stressful or threatening situation. It is also a force to help individuals to avoid adverse experiences. Anxiety can be a help or a hindrance to an individual, depending upon the degree of anxiety experienced. A certain level or amount of anxiety can stimulate an individual to participate in need-fulfilling activity, aid in developing coping skills, and aid in personal growth. Severe anxiety can get in the way of an individual's performance and promote carelessness. If the anxiety becomes extreme, it can alter a person's life style. The Latin term "anxius" means troubled in mind about something uncertain.

Anxiety can be thought of as being "situational," "traumatic, "toxic," or "free-floating." **Situational anxiety** arises from a stressful experience such as being mugged. **Traumatic anxiety** is the result of an unexpected tragic event, i.e., the death of a parent. **Toxic anxiety** is brought on by the use of a psychotropic substance, such as LSD. **Free-floating anxiety** has no distinct causative event or agent.

Generally speaking, the anxiety state includes several symptoms. **Subjective symptoms** include apprehension, rumination, edginess, tension, and worry. **Behavioral symptoms** include distractibility, insomnia, irritability, impatience, tension, excessive need for reassurance, and exaggerated self-consciousness. **Motor symptoms** include headaches, restlessness, fidgeting, shakiness, jumpiness, trembling tremor, fatigue, and furrowed brow. Symptoms that can be traced to the **Autonomic Nervous System** include increases in blood pressure and heart rate, sweating, dizziness, upset stomach, diarrhea, sense of fecal or urinary urgency, flushing, pallor, dry mouth, headache. Anxiety symptoms also can be classified by body system as shown in Figure 5.1.

CARDIOVASCULAR	palpitations
	tachycardia
	chest tightness
RESPIRATORY	breathlessness
GASTROINTESTINAL	choking feeling
	indigestion
	diarrhea
GENITOURINARY	urinary urgency
SKIN	flushing
NERVOUS SYSTEM	headache
MUSCULAR	tension
	muscle aches

Figure 5.1. Anxiety symptoms classified by body system.

The DSM-III-R (1987) lists four categories, with twelve specific diagnoses, of anxiety related disorders.

Phobic Disorders. Three subclassifications are under phobic disorder—***Agoraphobia, Social,*** and ***Simple*** phobias. Agoraphobia is the most severe. It is the fear of being alone or in a public place. "Agora" in Greek means "marketplace", or literally translated, Agoraphobia is the fear of the marketplace.

Agoraphobia is associated with depression, anxiety, rituals, and rumination. The onset of symptomatic agoraphobia usually manifests itself in the late teens or early 20s, but can happen later in life. The disorder is most frequent in women and is believed to exist in 0.5% of the population.

People with phobic disorders are usually not good candidates for antidepressant or antianxiety medication.

Anxiety States (or *Anxiety Neurosis*). These include **Panic, Generalized Anxiety,** and **Obsessive-Compulsive** disorders. A diagnosis of panic disorder requires at least three panic attacks within a three week period. These attacks must be accompanied by at least four of the following symptoms: (1) dyspnea (difficult or labored breathing), (2) palpitations, (3) chest pain, (4) choking or smothering sensations, (5) dizziness, (6) feelings of unreality, (7) paresthesia (tingling in hands or feet), (8) hot and cold flashes, (9) sweating, (10) nausea or abdominal distress, (11) trembling or shaking, (12) fear of dying, and (13) going crazy, or losing control. Panic disorder is relatively common and must be differentiated from physical disorders such as *hypoglycemia* and *hyperthyroidism.* Persons suffering from Panic disorder often had Separation Anxiety as a child.

Panic disorder is often treated with imipramine, an antidepressant drug. Supportive psychotherapy and anti-anxiety drugs are also used in treatment. A diagnosis of Generalized Anxiety can be made if symptoms are noted in three of the following categories, for at least one month's duration: (1) motor tension, (2) autonomic symptoms, (3) apprehensive expectations, and (4) vigilance and scanning. Hyperthyroidism and caffeine intoxication may show similar symptoms.

Post-traumatic Stress Disorder. This classification became popular as an outcome of the Vietnam War. It is experienced after a "markedly distressing" event that is outside of our usual experience, i.e., war or earthquake. Symptoms include a reexperiencing of the trauma, an avoidance of stimuli associated with the causative event, or an increase or decrease in arousal.

Anxiety Disorders Of Childhood or Adolescence. These include **separation anxiety disorder, avoidance disorder of childhood,** and **overanxious disorder.**

Many of the anxiety disorders are frequently treated with antianxiety (anxiolytic) agents. These agents have been known by the misnomer, tranquilizers. Drugs are not the only treatment for anxiety. Appropriate situational anxiety, a normal part of life, usually requires no therapeutic intervention. In fact, to intervene might be counterproductive in these situations, as the anxiety is an important part of the individual's coping process. Chronic to severe anxiety may be managed by psychotherapy, with or without the use of antianxiety agents. Antianxiety drugs account for about half the prescriptions filled in retail pharmacies in the United States (Balter et al., 1974). The estimate is that 15% of the population was treated with antianxiety drugs during the 1970s. The vast majority, 85%, of these prescriptions were written by non-psychiatric practitioners (Parry et al., 1973).

The exact mechanism of anxiety is unknown. What is known is that anxiety states can be induced in both normal and anxious individuals by stimulating the sympathetic division of the autonomic nervous system. This can be accomplished by using drugs such as epinephrine, ephedrine, amphetamine, or lysergic acid diethylamide. The anxiety symptoms that result are more than likely physiological rather than psychological (Lader, 1974). Greden (1974) reported that excessive doses of caffeine may mimic clinical anxiety.

Researchers believe that three systems in the brain are directly involved in the process of anxiety. These are the **reticular activating system,** the **limbic system,** and the **hypothalamus.** Emotions are triggered by internal and/or external stimuli. The reticular activating system, by regulating the degree of arousal, is involved in the determination of anxiety levels. The limbic system determines the degree of affect. The hypothalamus, through its control of the autonomic nervous system and indirect control of the endocrine system and via its control of the pituitary, regulates the physiological response (Hollister, 1978).

HISTORY OF ANTIANXIETY DRUGS

Man has sought chemical agents to modify tension, stress, anxiety, and discomfort since the dawn of history. Most of the drugs used were sedative in nature. Alcohol was probably the first drug used. Alcohol is the product of yeast activated fermentation of sugar. This process would happen naturally when crushed grapes or berries were left standing in water in a warm place. The use of alcohol is recorded as far back as 6400

B.C. Mead, a product made from honey, is regarded as the earliest known alcoholic beverage and is believed to have existed around 8000 B.C. (Blum, 1969). The advent of distillation made it possible to manufacture stronger alcoholic products.

In the early twentieth century, bromides and barbiturates were used as antianxiety drugs. By 1930, the evidence was available that bromides soon accumulate in the body and are toxic. The use of bromides dropped off; however, some preparations are still available today. After the decline of the bromides, the barbiturates were used for anxiety. In the 1950s, barbiturates were shown to create a tolerance, physical dependence, and withdrawal (Hollister, 1978).

The use of opiates (alkaloids derived from the poppy plant) dates back to early historic times. These drugs are still widely used. They produce drowsiness, changes in mood, and mental clouding. Individuals experience euphoria when given small doses. Opiates produce both tolerance and physical dependence (Feldman, & Quenzer 1984).

MEPROBAMATE

In the 1940s, chemists at Wallace Laboratories were working with a chemical disinfectant. They were hoping to make a drug that would kill bacteria and be resistant to penicillin. In their work, they came up with a chemical called mephenesin carbamate. When they tested this new drug on animals, they found that it produced muscle relaxation and a sleep-like condition. In larger doses, it produced a temporary paralysis similar to the effects of curare. The mechanism of its curare action is different than that of curare. Mephenesin carbamate was used extensively in treating psychiatric patients in the late 1940s. This practice changed with the discovery and use of reserpine, and chlorpromazine. The major problem with mephenesin carbamate was its short duration of action, caused by its rapid metabolism by the liver. The chemists at Wallace began searching for a new drug, which would have a longer therapuetic effect, by modifying the mephenesin carbamate molecule. Their work resulted in the discovery of meprobamate in 1951. Meprobamate, under the trade name Miltown, (after a town near the Wallace factory) and Equanil were at once believed to be wonder drugs. Meprobamate became widely used. Today meprobamate is rarely used. It has no advantages over the barbiturates or the benzodiazepine drugs. Its most important disadvantage is its potential for dependence.

Actions

Possible CNS effects: it is mildly tranquilizing, and has some anticonvulsant and muscle relaxant properties. It is absorbed from the GI tract, reaches a peak plasma level in 1 to 3 hours. Metabolism takes place in the liver with the small remaining amounts being excreted unchanged. Its plasma half-life ranges from 6 to 17 hours. After continual administration, the half-life may increase up to 48 hours.

Uses

Reduces mild anxiety, tension, and insomnia.

Precautions

Physical and psychological drug dependence may occur. The drug is subject to abuse.

Interactions

Meprobamate may increase the effects of antidepressants, MAO inhibitors, narcotics, sedatives, and hypnotics. Alcohol increases the effects of meprobamate.

Side effects

Nervous System. Dizziness, confusion, agitation, paradoxical excitement, over-stimulation, drowsiness, slurred speech, headache, weakness, euphoria, sedation, vertigo, and impaired visual accommodation. It may cause seizures in epileptics.

GI. Diarrhea, nausea, and vomiting.

Cardiovascular. Arrhythmias, tachycardia, palpitations, and hypotensive crises.

Hematologic. Agranulocytosis (reduced or no production of polymorphonuclear leukocytes, a type of white blood cells that destroy bacteria), aplastic anemia (deficiency of blood cell formation), and thrombocytopenic purpura (decrease in number of platelets in the blood) have been reported.

Allergic. Rash, hives, itch, and fever.

Overdose. Lethargy, stupor, coma, shock, acute intoxication, vasomotor and respiratory collapse, and death. Overdoses of as little as 12 grams of meprobamate have proven fatal. Others have survived a dose of 40 grams. When meprobamate is taken in conjunction with alcohol, CNS depressant, or psychotropic drug, the lethal dose level is lowered.

BENZODIAZEPINES

Chlordiazepoxide (Librium) was marketed in 1960, and diazepam (Valium) came along in 1963. This began the "tranquilization" of America. By 1977, sixty million prescriptions were written for Valium in the United States alone. It was the world's best selling prescription drug, resulting in retail sales of one-half billion dollars. The estimate is that 75% of its use is for the relief of anxiety. One survey showed that in a single year 20% of the females and 14% of the males in the United States used Valium (Bachmann, 1983). Bachmann (1983) reported that two-thirds of the prescriptions for Valium are written by general practitioners, gynecologists, internists, and pediatricians. Because of the marked success of these drugs, the market soon became flooded with benzodiazepines. Several of these drugs are used for sleep disorders which will be covered in the chapter on hypnotics. Others are used as anticonvulsants and will be mentioned in the chapter on antiepileptic drugs.

The development of these compounds is an interesting story. Leo H. Sternbach (1973), a chemist at Roche Laboratories, was interested in tranquilizers in the mid-fifties shortly after the first representatives of this group of drugs (meprobamate) proved to be of remarkable clinical value. The Roche people, under the leadership of Sternbach, chose to explore a group of drugs that Sternbach had synthesized, while at the University of Cracow in Poland, as part of his post doctoral research in the 1930s. The plan, according to Tinklenberg (1977), was to screen the drugs Sternbach had synthesized, some 20 years prior, for biological activity. Of the 40 compounds, all but one were pharmacologically inert. This one was never tested, because of other priorities. It sat on a shelf until May 1957, when one of Sternbach's co-workers suggested that it be tested. The Roche pharmacological team, under the leadership of Lowell O. Randall, ran a series of tests on the remaining compound and found it to have a number of clinically important properties. The drug turned out to be the compound methaminodiazepoxide, which was renamed chlordiazepoxide. Randall and his group (1960) announced they had discovered a potent sedative, muscle relaxant, taming, and anticonvulsant drug. Soon, it became clear that they had a potent antianxiety drug, and they named it Librium (derived from "equilibrium") (Randall & Kappell, 1973). Diazepam (Valium), a more potent derivative, followed within the year. Diazepam, in the body, is metabolized into desmethyldiazepam and methyloxazepam. Wyeth Laboratory, followed with oxazepam (Serax), which is an active metabolite of diazepam. Oxazepam, because it doesn't need to undergo metabolism to be therapeutically active, has a shorter half-life than either chlordiazepoxide or diazepam. Flurazepam (Dalmane) was marketed by Roche in 1970. It was found to have marked hypnotic properties. By the beginning of 1977, more than 2300 papers had been published describing the use of the benzodiazepine drugs (Feldman & Quenzer, 1984). In Figure 5.2 are listed current benzodiazepines marketed for anxiety.

Actions

The benzodiazepines are believed to affect GABAergic synapses in the CNS. GABA (gamma-amino-butyric acid) is an amino acid that displays a potent inhibitory transmitter activity in the CNS (Goodman, 1980). This unique chemical was first discovered in 1950. Kravitz, Kuffler, and Potter (1963), while working with the nerve of a crayfish, showed that GABA was the only inhibitory amino acid present. Other researchers demonstrated that GABA mediates the inhibitory action of nerves in the brain and spinal cord (Otsuka, 1973; Ryall, 1975).

Generic Name	Trade Name	Oral Dose[1]	t 1/2[2]	Onset
alprazolam	Xanax	0.75-4.0	12-15	intermed
chlordiazepoxide	Librium	15-100	5-30	intermed
chlorazepate	Tranxene	15-60	30-100	fast
Diazepam	Valium	6-40	20-50	very fast
halazepam	Paxipam	60-160	14	intermed
lorazepam	Ativan	2-6	10-18	intermed
oxazepam	Serax	30-120	5-13	slow
prazepam	Centrax	20-60	30-100	very slow

[1]Defined in milligrams (mg) per 24 hours.

[2]Half-life information varies from reference to reference.

Figure 5.2. Current benzodiazepines marketed for anxiety.

Kelly and Beart (1975) showed GABA to have inhibitory effects in the cerebral cortex.

Baraldi et al. (1979) suggested that the receptor sites for a protein known as "GABA modulin" and the receptor sites for GABA are located adjacent to each other at the neuron membrane. When the GABA modulin is attached to its receptor site, then the neighboring GABA receptor site is inactivated. Benzodiazepines also can occupy the receptor sites for the GABA modulin. When a benzodiazepine occupies the GABA modulin receptor site, the GABA receptor site is not inactivated.

The calming effect of the benzodiazepines may take place in the limbic system and reticular formation. (Kastrup, Olin, & Schwach 1986). This is done by (1) facilitating a GABA-mediated pre-synaptic inhibition in the spinal cord, (2) a presynaptic and postsynaptic inhibition in the cuneate nucleus of the brain stem, (3) enhancement of GABA-mediated depression in the cerebellum, and (4) enhancement the GABAergic inhibition in the substantia nigra of the midbrain (Bachmann, & Sherman 1983; Feldman, & Quenzer 1984).

Benzodiazepines have a large safety margin between therapeutic and toxic doses. In choosing a benzodiazepine, the *half-life* (t ½) is an important consideration. Drugs that have a metabolite which is active tend to have a longer half-life. Alprazolam, lorazepam, and oxazepam do not have active metabolites. Therefore, they have a shorter half-life. In dosing an individual, the half-life becomes an important consideration. Chlordiazepoxide has a long half-life and can be administered on a once a day basis. Diazepam and clorazepate may be given once or twice a day. Oxazepam and lorazepam may require three or four doses a day. The optimum therapeutic benefit of the benzodiazepines may not show up for nearly a week or more of continuous treatment. Adverse effects may not show up for several days, and withdrawal reactions will not show up for about a week after termination of the drug.

Indications

The benzodiazepines are used for the management of anxiety disorders or for the short term treatment of the symptoms of anxiety. The tension and anxiety brought on by everyday stress does not usually require the use of drugs. The characteristics that make benzodiazepines useful are (1) the ability to relax voluntary muscles, (2) the ability to tame aggressive behavior, (3) anticonvulsant activity, and (4) the ability to reduce anxiety. These drugs are generally safer than the barbiturates and meprobamate type antianxiety drugs, and less addictive than these other antianxiety drugs.

Precautions

Rapid withdrawal may lead to seizures. Although these drugs are safer than other antianxiety drugs, in the presence of alcohol they can lead to respiratory depression and even death. A major problem arising from the use of benzodiazepines is dependence. Prolonged use of theses drugs can lead to a true dependence in a significant number of individuals. More of a tendency for withdrawal syndrome exists with the short-acting benzodiazepines—when the drug has been taken on a regular basis for a period of 4 months or longer, when higher doses have been taken, and when the drug is abruptly withdrawn. Symptoms may show up in 3 to 10 days and last for 20 days or longer. Symptoms include increased anxiety, insomnia, irritability, nausea, palpitations, headache, muscle tension, muscle cramps, tremor, and dysphoria. A smaller percentage (20%) of cases include confusion, "psychosis" or seizures.

Interactions

The recommendation is to avoid the use of alcohol when taking benzodiazepines. These drugs can change the severity or frequency of seizures when combines with anticonvulsant drugs. The sedative effect of antihistamines, antidepressants, narcotics, and hypnotics may be potentiated. Kastrup, Olin, & Schwach (1986) reported a decreased effect of the benzodiazepines in people who smoke cigarettes. Oral contraceptives are reported to impair the metabolism of diazepam and chlordiazepoxide.

Adverse Effects

CNS. Addiction, sedation, sleepiness, lethargy, depression, increased appetite, respiratory arrest (very rare, except when combined with alcohol), ataxia (a stumbling gait), confusion, dizziness, euphoria, excitement, extrapyramidal symptoms (rare), fatigue, fever, hallucinations, headache, insomnia, irritability, increased or decreased libido, nightmares, seizures during withdrawal, vertigo, and physical and psychological dependence.

Allergic. Agranulocytosis (reduced or no production a polymorphonuclear leukocytes, a type of white blood cells that destroy bacteria), conjunctivitis, jaundice, liver damage, leukopenia, and neutropenia (decrease in a type of white blood cells).

Cardiovascular. Edema (fluid retention), bradycardia (slow heart), hypertension, hypotension, syncope (fainting) tachycardia (rapid heart), thrombosis (a clot in a blood vessel), and phlebitis (inflammation of venous walls at I.V. site).

Endocrine. Failure to ovulate, menstrual irregularities, and weight gain.

Gastrointestinal. Constipation, diarrhea, anorexia (lack or loss of appetite for food), change in appetite, difficulty in swallowing, dry mouth, nausea, and change in appetite.

Genito Urinary. Loss of bladder control, retention of urine, abnormal laboratory results for kidney functions, changes in libido, and menstrual irregularities.

EENT. Blurred vision, diplopia (double vision), auditory disturbances, depressed hearing, and nasal congestion.

Skin. Urticaria, pruritus, skin rash, and dermatitis.

OTHER ANTIANXIETY AGENTS

Buspirone HCl (BuSpar)

Buspirone is an oral antianxiety agent not chemically or pharmacologically related to the other antianxiety agents, such as barbiturates or benzodiazepines. BuSpar became available in late 1986. It does not exert anticonvulsive or muscle relaxant effects. An important asset of BuSpar is its lack of sedative effect. This makes it different than the other drugs used for anxiety. The mechanism of its actions is unknown. The most common adverse reactions are dizziness, nausea, headache, nervousness, lightheadedness and excitement. Of the 2200 individuals, participating in the premarketing trials, 10% discontinued the drug within three to four weeks due to adverse effects. Busiprone HCl (BuSpar) is supplied in 5 mg and 10 mg tablets. The dose range is from 15 mg to 60 mg per day.

Hydroxyzine (Atarax)

Hydroxyzine is an antihistamine that is useful in the treatment of anxiety related itching or dermatitis. Adverse effects include drowsiness, dry mouth, and involuntary motor activity.

Doxepin HCl (Sinequan/Adapin)

Doxepin is a tricyclic antidepressant which exhibits antianxiety effects.

SUMMARY

Anxiety is a universal experience, having both positive and negative consequences. In managing anxiety, drug intervention is not always necessary. A great deal of debate exists as to the overuse of antianxiety drugs. The majority of prescriptions are written by non-psychiatric physicians. For many cases, psychotherapy is a preferred treatment modality over drug therapy.

The benzodiazepines are no less effective, therapeutically, than either the barbiturates or meprobamate; however, they are considerably safer. The benzodiazepines are less toxic and have less of a tendency to cause physical dependency. Therefore, when treating anxiety, they are the drugs of choice.

Very little evidence exists that any of the benzodiazepines exhibit superiority in treating anxiety. Elderly individuals and individuals with severe liver disease may take longer to eliminate chlordiazepoxide and diazepam. With the exception of certain side effects and half-life considerations, all the available benzodiazepines seem to be equivalent in treating anxiety.

Buspirone HCl (BuSpar), a new antianxiety agent, lacks the sedative effect of other antianxiety drugs.

Anxiety is a symptom and not a specific disorder. The seeking of drugs for the intervention of anxiety, historically, has led to considerable drug abuse and dependence. Anxiety, according to the level, can be helpful or a hinderance to people. Anxiety symptoms can be subjective, behavioral, or physical. Meprobamate was the break through drug in the treatment of anxiety. Due to its side effects and the discovery of the benzodiazepines in the 1960s meprobamate is rarely used anymore. Today, over one-half of a dozen benzodiazepines compete in the market-place. One survey shows that 20% of the females and 14% of the males in the United States use Valium, still the most popular benzodiazepine.

CHAPTER **VI**

HYPNOTIC DRUGS

SLEEP

Hartmann (1973) defined sleep as an altered state of consciousness. Hauri (1982) said of sleep, "today it is regarded as an active and complex state...with various components" (p.6). The question that arises, beyond a definition of sleep, is, what is the function of sleep? It seems safe to assume that the alternating sleep-wake mechanisms would not have evolved if the process was not needed.

When a person does go for several days without sleep, the need to sleep grows stronger. Differing from hunger and thirst, a person can go through a sleepless night, and in the morning the need for sleep dissipates. If the individual does not sleep again the next night, he/she will feel better again in the morning. This phenomenon seems to point to the biological clock, i. e., the need for sleep is great during certain hours for the individual.

The need for sleep is not cumulative over a period of time. For example, if someone goes for three or four nights without sleep, they will only need to have the equivalent of one good night's sleep to recover.

Karadzic (1973) reported that no one has ever been reported of dying from a lack of sleep.

Two theories of sleep dominate researchers' thinking. The first, the theory of repair and restoration, suggests that sleep is a time when repairs are made to the body after the day's exertions. Many restorative processes do occur during sleep. For example, digestion and the removal of waste products from the body. Sleep may be a time for synthesizing the neurotransmitters dopamine and norepinephrine used during the day (Hartmann, 1973; Stern & Morgane, 1974). These functions do occur, to a lesser extent during waking hours.

Physical and mental activity do not seem to be factors for most people. After a high or low amount of physical or mental activity, most people do not require an unusual amount of sleep to make up for the energy expended. Hartmann (1973) found that sleep time did not correlate with activity, however it did have some correlation with personality variables. Long-sleepers showed artistic or creative talent and a tendency to be nonconformists. Short-sleepers were more energetic, more extroverted, and less prone to be nervous or worry.

The need for sleep varies with age. The very young sleep about 16 hours a day. As people move into adulthood, the need for sleep gradually declines to about 7 ½ to 8 hours a night. The literature does point out that some people exist on three hours of sleep a night. These people were reported to be in good physical and mental health (Jones & Oswald, 1968).

The second theory of the need for sleep is the evolutionary theory. This theory equates sleep to hibernation (Kleitman, 1963; Webb, 1974). The function of hibernation is to "conserve energy during a time when the environment is hostile." Sleep, according to the "evolutionary theory," is a mechanism built into animals that forces them to "conserve energy at times when they would be relatively inefficient." The real need for sleep is not denied. The theory states that "the urge and the need for sleep were built in by evolution to guarantee that energy was conserved." This theory predicts that sleep needs vary, according to life factors such as safety from predators, and the search for food. Animals that graze, spending most of their waking hours eating, sleep relatively few hours per day. Animals, such as cats and other predators that eat one short, nutritional meal a day, sleep for a longer time (Swonger & Constantine, 1983).

MECHANISMS OF SLEEP

The use of the **electroencephalograph** (EEG) has helped researchers to measure the different brain waves that occur during sleep. The EEG records the average gross-electrical potential of the fibers and cells in the part of the brain being measured. The actual measurement is done by placing electrodes at specific sites on the surface of the head. The EEG records the net average of all the neurons. Therefore, if one-half the cells increase their electrical potentials while the other one-half decreases, the EEG reading will show no change. The reading of the EEG changes only when a significant number of cells are responding in a like manner.

In order to understand the phenomenon called sleep, a necessary procedure is to consider two systems in the brain that act mutually and reciprocally. Routtenberg (1968) formulated a theory of a two system control over arousal. He hypothesized that one system was associated with the reticular formation, maintaining arousal and orientation. The other system, related to the limbic system, controlled incentive behaviors. He revised his theory by stipulating that the reticular formation was a stimulus-processing system, and the limbic and midbrain structures functioned as a response execution system (Routtenberg 1970). Deikman (1971) postulated that the human brain functions in two modes: a receptive mode for gathering and processing sensory information and an active mode in which the "environment is manipulated." Swonger and Constantine (1976) suggested that these "dual arousal systems" are "anatomically, electrophysiologically, and functionally distinct." One system, the **diffuse thalamic system** (DTS), is anatomically associated with the dorsal thalamus and interconnected with the limbic and cerebral cortical areas. Its function is equivalent with cerebral "alpha" wave activity, i.e., goal-directed behavior, internalization of attention, and stimulus-processing. The **reticular activating system** (RAS) is anatomically linked with the midbrain reticular formation. Functionally, it is equivalent with cerebral "beta" wave activity, arousal of the sympathetic nervous system, and externalization of attention and sensory-mediated behaviors.

The two systems, the DTS and RAS work together. The DTS is responsible for maintaining consciousness. The frequency of electrical activity (measured in waves), which is dictated by the thalamic pacemaker, determines the state of consciousness.

Impulses are given names according to wave length. **Alpha waves** have a wave length of 8 to 12 cycles per second (**hertz** or Hz). These waves are recorded when an individual is at rest or quiet and not actively engaged in thought process. **Beta waves** exceed 13 cycles per second and may go up to 30 cycles per second. These waves show up when the individual is awake and involved in thought. Slower waves are known as **theta waves** (3 to 7 cycles per second) and **delta waves** (frequencies of l/2 to 2 cycles per second). Theta waves are recorded at the parietal and temporal regions of the brains of children. Some adults have theta waves during emotional stress. Delta waves are recorded during sleep, surgical anesthesia, and stupor.

The relationship between the DTS and the RAS can be seen by the four possible combinations of the two systems. When the wave lengths of the DTS are around three Hz and the RAS is in an inactive state, then "delta" waves are observed by the EEG, and the behavioral state is non-dreaming sleep. If the RAS is in the active state, then the observed EEG frequency is "beta" and the behavioral state is dreaming sleep. When the wave lengths of the DTS is around ten and the RAS is in the inactive state, the observed wave lengths of the EEG is "alpha" and the behavioral state is awake, relaxed and internalized. If the RAS is active, then the observed EEG frequency is "beta," and the behavioral state is awake, externalized, and stimulus-processing (Swonger, 1983). In Figure 6.1 is shown the status among DTS, RAS, and behavior.

Sleep is characterized by stages. During "stage 1" sleep, the EEG shows waves of very low amplitude with little regularity. Usually the onset of "stage 2" comes in a few seconds or minutes. During this stage the EEG has "sleep spindles" or

Diffused Thalamic System (DTS)	Reticular Activating System (RAS)	Behavior
delta	inactive	non-dream sleep
beta	active	dream sleep
alpha	inactive	awake, relaxed, internal focus
beta	active	awake, externalized stimulus processing

Figure 6.1. Status among diffused thalamic system, reticular activating system, and behavior.

frequent bursts of larger and then smaller wave lengths. "Stage 3" comes in a few more minutes and is characterized by the appearance of delta waves. In "stage 4" slow, synchronized waves become dominant. Stage 2 through 4 sleep is known collectively as *slow-wave sleep* (SWS) The EEG waves become larger in amplitude in each succeeding stage.

Two states of sleep exist: *Slow wave sleep* (stages 2 through 4) and *REM sleep,* sometimes known as "desynchronized sleep" (D Sleep), or "paradoxical sleep." Slow wave sleep has been referred to as "deep sleep"; however, some investigators believe that REM sleep is, in part, a deeper state. REM sleep, or paradoxical sleep, is a combination of deep sleep and light sleep. Because of this controversy, most investigators avoid the terms deep and light.

Heart rate, breathing rate, and muscle activity are all lower during stage 4. Sleep begins with stage 1 and gradually progresses through stages 2 and 3 before reaching stage 4. This process can be halted by external stimuli. An individual who has been disturbed during stage 3, may upon returning to the sleep state, go back to stage 1 or 2, or return to stage 3.

After about 60 or 90 minutes, a person begins a gradual shift back through stages 3, 2, and 1. From stage 1, the person then cycles back to stage 4, then back to stage 1 again. This cycle lasts throughout the night and takes between 90 and 100 minutes. Early in the sleep process, stage 4 dominates, and as the night continues, stage 4 gets shorter and stage 1 gets longer.

The first stage 1 experience of the night is different from the others. Starting with the second stage 1 event, the EEG shows a desynchronized pattern resembling the awake stage. The heart rate and breathing rate are higher and more variable than in the other stages. Encounter is more difficult when trying to awaken a person during this stage. During this stage, males of all ages experience penis erections. The belief is that females have vaginal moistening during this stage (Kalat, 1984). Other characteristics of this sleep stage are face and finger twitching and rapid eye movements. This rapid eye movement is the reason that this stage of sleep is known as REM sleep (Aserinsky & Kleitman, 1955; Dement & Kleitman, 1957).

Rapid Eye Movement (REM) sleep is associated with dreams. Dement and Kleitman (1957) awakened volunteers during various stages of sleep. They found that people awakened during REM sleep reported dreams, right before awakening, about 80 to 90% of the time. Dreams have been reported during short wave sleep; however, the percentages are much lower and the experiences usually did not include the elaborate visual imagery. Possibly what was reported was more of a vague thought-like experience.

SLEEP DISORDERS

Insomnia, sometimes called "hyposomnia," or "disorders of initiating and maintaining sleep," is characterized by several different symptoms: the inability to fall asleep; the inability to stay asleep, an abbreviated period of sleep with premature awakening, an interrupted sleep filled with nightmares and voluntary arousals, or sleep that is not regenerating. (Hollister, 1978). Oswald (1975) reported that older people experience an increasingly fragmented and less deep sleep.

Some types of insomnia are normal. These are experienced when a person is traveling from time zone to time zone and their normal biological rhythm is thrown out of balance. Sleeping in a strange bed or new environment causes insomnia for some. A change in the environmental sound level will disrupt sleep for some.

Insomnia is a symptom of emotional distress, worry, depression, or anxiety. It may occur because of excitement. Physical disorders such as pain or cramping may lead to insomnia. Many drugs, whether prescription or over-the-counter, may interfere with normal sleep patterns. Caffeine is the most commonly used non-prescription drug that affects sleep. Caffeine induced insomnia may not occur in young people. Frequently, caffeine disturbance of sleep begins to appear during adulthood. Alcohol may enhance sleep for many, as it is a depressant. However, some heavy drinkers tend to awaken in the morning in a over-stimulated condition.

Sleep laboratory studies have made us aware of other sleep disturbances. The most common of these is drug-withdrawal insomnia, associated with the use of hypnotic drugs. Prolonged use of hypnotic drugs results in severe deprivation of REM sleep. Upon withdrawal of the drug, the individual may suffer poor quality sleep, nightmares, and frequent awakenings (Guilleminault, Eldridge, & Dement, 1973).

Sleep apnea, a situation in which the individual stops breathing momentarily, is a less frequent type of sleep disorder. Sleep apnea is a universal occurrence in young infants. The belief is that sleep apnea is caused by either a central mechanism of the respiratory center, or a peripheral mechanism causing an upper airway obstruction, or possibly both (Guillerninault, 1973). **Sleep myoclonus** (characterized by severe rigidity and spasms, especially of the legs), **sleep-walking,** and **enuresis** are other sleep disorders worthy of mention.

A rare, but important condition to mention is "narcolepsy." **Narcolepsy** is a condition in which a person falls asleep during the day (Dement, 1972). These sleep "attacks" vary from gradual to very sudden and dramatic sleep episodes.

The Association of Sleep Disorders Centers published a list of 68 sleep and arousal disorders in 1979. This included (1) disorders of initiating and maintaining sleep (insomnia), (2) disorders of excessive sleep, (3) disorders of sleep-wake schedule, and (4) dysfunctions associated with sleep, sleep stages, or partial arousals (parasomnias).

TREATING INSOMNIA

The AMA reports that one in five people in the United States complains of frequent or constant dissatisfaction with the quality or quantity of their sleep. Bachmann and Sherman (1983) reported that 30% of the United States population suffers from some form of insomnia. In 1975, only five medical institutions in the United States had developed centers devoted to the treatment and diagnosis of sleep disorders. This number had grown to seventy by 1984 (Lamberg, 1984). Today, over five hundred scientists specialize in the study of sleep disorders.

Insomnia is treated, far too often, with hypnotic drugs. Many people who complain of insomnia can be helped by addressing the underlying cause, for which insomnia is a symptom. This includes anxiety and depression. People who suffer insomnia due to underlying physical disorders, such as pain, may find their insomnia alleviated with the successful treatment of their pain. Many individuals who identify themselves as insomniacs are really not. They need less sleep than they believe. Others believe that they cannot fall asleep in a reasonable time. In sleep laboratory studies, the information obtained does not always support such statements. Frequently, these people believe that much longer time is needed to fall asleep than is really used, i.e., they report that more than one hour is needed when in reality approximately 15 minutes is needed.

The AMA lists several, non-drug ways to a better nights sleep (Lamberg 1984). They listed ten ways. (1) Keeping a regular sleep schedule. Going to bed and getting out of the bed at the same time each day will increase the quality of sleep. Napping at the same time each day is more effective than doing it at different times. (2) Paying attention to what food is eaten and when it is eaten. Some foods can promote drowsiness, and others alertness. This may differ from person to person. Coffee, tea, and cola drinks contain caffeine and may interfere with sleep. Large meals can make a person drowsy; however, for some, the discomfort experienced makes sleep difficult. (3) Regular exercise, preferably late in the afternoon, facilitates more restful sleep. (4) Sexual activity may help or hinder sleep. This is an idiosyncratic experience. (5) Creation of bedtime rituals are helpful. (6) Use the bedroom only for sleeping. (7) Create a "safe" environment for sleep. (8) Don't use smoking at bedtime to induce sleep. Nicotine is a stimulant. (9) Alcohol may be helpful for getting to sleep; however, it can create difficulties for some to stay asleep. (10) Create a dark, noise free, and comfortable place to sleep.

The most obvious problem with the use of hypnotic drugs is the tendency for abuse or overuse, complicated by a tolerance that occurs with most of the drugs. These drugs are not meant to be taken nightly and for long periods of time. The monitoring of this problem lies with the prescriber, the pharmacist, and ultimately, the user. Pressure from users causes physicians to prescribe hypnotic drugs in large quantities. Some of the responsibility lies with the pharmacist, who offers the drug at a lower price-per-pill when purchased in larger quantities. Drug control and drug education seem to have little effect in this area. Swonger and Constantine (1976) estimated that over 300 tons of barbiturates are manufactured yearly in the United States, and nearly one-half of this amount finds its way to the "black market." Barbiturate addiction may be more dangerous than opiate addiction, because of the severity of withdrawal. Barbiturates are involved in one-fifth of all suicides, with a total of 3,000 deaths each year in the United States. Three of the five most common causes of fatal drug overdosage are the sedative-hypnotic drugs: barbiturates, glutethimide, and meprobamate.

PHARMACOLOGY OF SLEEP
SEDATIVE-HYPNOTICS

The basic action of the barbiturates and other sedative-hypnotics is depression. These drugs exert depressive action at the cellular level. Oxygen consumption is decreased and energy storing is inhibited. This activity takes place at various tissue sites throughout the body; however, the activity at the central nervous system level is what is involved in the mechanism of sleep induction.

The hypnotic activity of the barbiturates is believed to center primarily at the subcortical centers of the brain. This activity is targeted at the GABA receptor sites. The barbiturate receptor site is different from that of the benzodiazepines. The barbiturates act at the pre-synapse by (1) impairing the excitatory transmission and (2) by enhancing GABA synthesis. Post-synaptic activity includes (1) enhancement of GABA binding by a process called "positive cooperativity" and (2) reduction of inhibitory post-synaptic potential (IPSP) (Swonger & Constantine 1976). The benzodiazepines (1) facilitate GABA-mediated pre-synaptic inhibition in the spinal cord, (2) cause a pre- and post-synaptic inhibition in the brain stem, (3) enhance the GABA-mediated depression in the cerebellum, and (4) enhance the GABA-ergic inhibition in the midbrain (Feldman & Quenzer, 1984; Bachmann & Sherman, 1983).

The respiratory center located in the medulla oblongata is another area of the brain that is of particular importance in reference to the hypnotic drugs. Respiratory depression is the main cause of death in cases of hypnotic drug overdose.

All of the sedative-hypnotic drugs, including alcohol, produce a cross tolerance. This means that the withdrawal symptoms of one drug can be suppressed by any other drug in this category, i.e., a barbiturate may be used by an alcoholic to maintain both dependence and to curtail or postpone withdrawal symptoms. The physical dependence associated with these drugs is a serious medical problem. Withdrawal from continual use may be quite severe. Symptoms usually begin within 24 hours, reach a peak within 72 hours, and slowly decrease. **Delirium tremens,** similar to that seen in alcoholic withdrawal, is the most severe symptom. Other symptoms that may develop include: anxiety, tremor and involuntary muscle twitches, dizziness, nausea, vomiting, insomnia, weight loss, illusions, delusions, hallucinations, paranoia, convulsive seizures, and death (Swonger & Constantine, 1976).

HYPNOTIC AGENTS

The ideal hypnotic has not been discovered. The qualities of this perfect drug would include (1) "the ability to induce sleep rapidly and thereby decrease sleep latency," (2) "increase total sleep time," (3) "decrease the number of awakenings," (4) "not interfere with normal sleep patterns," (5) "not produce after-effects," (6) "not create a tolerance," (7) "not be habituating," (8) "not be lethal if an overdose is infested," and (9) "lead to a sense of well-being during the day" (Bachmann & Sherman, 1983).

Hauri (1982) suggested five criteria of evaluating a hypnotic drug once it has been shown to be safe and non-toxic. (1) "How effective is the drug initially?" (2) "How long is the drug effective?" (3) "How are daytime performance and mood affected by treatment with the hypnotic drug?" (4) "What level of sleep results from chronic use?" (5) "What happens on withdrawal?"

Drugs used for insomnia can be divided into several categories. These are (1) chloral hydrate, (2) barbiturates, (3) barbiturate-like hypnotics, (4) benzodiazepines, (5) antihistamines, and (6) l-tryptophan. They will be discussed in the order listed.

CHLORAL HYDRATE

Chloral hydrate is amongst the oldest drugs used for its sedative or hypnotic effects. It was synthesized by Liebig in 1832. It is believed to be the first synthetic hypnotic (Krantz & Carr, 1961) and is still widely used today.

The mechanism of action of chloral hydrate is unknown; however, what is postulated is that its hypnotic effects are due to an active metabolite, trichloroethanol (Bachmann & Sherman, 1983).

Chloral hydrate has several advantages as a hypnotic. During short term use it has little effect on sleep patterns, i.e., neither rapid eye movement (REM) nor non rapid eye movement (NREM) sleep are markedly altered. Most other hypnotics cause an alteration of sleep patterns. Sleep latency decrease is short lived with chloral hydrate. Latency intervals return to pre-chloral hydrate status after one to two weeks of continuous administration. Another important attribute of chloral hydrate shows up during withdrawal. This is the lack of REM rebound found with withdrawal of other hypnotics, especially the barbiturates. REM rebound is characterized by a higher percentage of REM sleep, usually accompanied by nightmares and poor quality sleep. Chloral hydrate tends to increase the length of total sleep and decrease waking.

The use of chloral hydrate has several major drawbacks. It may leave an unpleasant aftertaste and cause nausea, vomiting, or irritation to the gastrointestinal tract. Chloral hydrate has caused occasional cases of disorientation, incoherence, and paranoid behavior. In doses ten to twenty times the therapeutic dose (500mg), it can be lethal. In combination with alcohol, the central depression of alcohol is synergistic. Tolerance develops with chloral hydrate use, and habituation and dependence are not uncommon (Kastrup, Olin, & Schwach 1986).

BARBITURATES

In 1864 Adolph von Baeyer, the founder of the Bayer (Bayer's Aspirin) chemical firm in Germany, synthesized barbituric acid. It was formed by combining the acid from apples with urea. The story goes that Baeyer visited a tavern on the day he discovered the substance. Some artillery officers were celebrating their patron saint, St. Barbara. Therefore, by combining "Barbara" and "urea" he came up with the name "barbituric acid" (Sharpless, 1970). Barbituric acid itself is not a central nervous system depressant. The active substances derived from barbituric acid, were first introduced in 1903 by Fischer and von Mering. They replaced two hydrogen atoms in the barbituric acid molecule with methyl groups. This product was called barbital, and its trade name was Veronal. The other oral barbiturates have different groups substituted in the same position as the methyl groups of barbital. Thiopental (Pentothal) and Methohexital (Brevital), both used as anesthetics, have other minor changes in the basic structure (Feldman & Quenzer, 1984).

Phenobarbital was introduced in 1912. It showed excellent sedative and anticonvulsant properties. Some 2500 different varieties of barbituric acid have been synthesized. About 50 of these were eventually marketed; however, only 5 or 6 of them became popular. A major goal in the barbiturate research was to find compounds with a shorter duration of action. This research led to the discovery of amobarbital in 1923, and pentobarbital and secobarbital in 1930. The ultra-short-acting barbiturates, hexobarbital, methohexital, and thiopental were introduced in the 1930s. These drugs, especially thiopental, are still popular as anesthetics today.

Barbiturates are effective in the short-term management of insomnia. They have a wide range of duration of action. This allows for more specific selectivity in choosing a drug. If the individual has problems falling asleep, a short or intermediate acting barbiturate may be chosen. This minimizes the possibility of carry over effects the next day. When the problem is remaining asleep, a longer acting barbiturate may be chosen.

The mechanism of action of the barbiturates is not well defined. Like other hypnotic drugs, the barbiturates depress the reticular activating system. The evidence is that the barbiturates augment the effects of GABA. This augmentation may be facilitated by an increase in the affinity between GABA and GABA receptors. Phenobarbital also seems to diminish the inhibitory calcium mediated release of GABA and norepinephrine (Bachmann & Sherman, 1983). Barbiturates have been shown to depress excitatory postsynaptic potentials (EPSPs), and at a high dose, to affect or enhance inhibitory postsynaptic potentials (IPSPs) (Feldman & Quenzer, 1984).

The barbiturates are quite effective as hypnotics for short term usage. However, continuous use can lead to many problems. Barbiturates can shorten the length of REM sleep time. After continuous use, the percentage of REM sleep time normalizes; however, the time spent in stages 3 and 4 decreases. The total sleep time diminishes. Tolerance develops, and increased doses are required to maintain the hypnotic effect. When the dose is increased, the REM time, once again, is decreased. These drugs can be very disturbing to normal sleep patterns. Upon discontinuance of the drug, the individual often experiences "REM rebound." This phenomenon is associated with increased dreaming, nightmares, and insomnia. Both secobarbital and pentobarbital lose most of their sleep inducing effects within two weeks of continuous administration. This is true, regardless of dose increases (Kastrup, Olin, & Schwach, 1986).

The use of barbiturates can affect the body's response to other drugs. Two examples are the anticoagulant drug, warfarin (Coumadin), which may require a larger dose to effectively maintain anticoagulation; and acetaminophen (Tylenol), which is more likely to have serious hepatic necrosis with the concurrent administration of a barbiturate.

Barbiturates are habituating and lead to a physical dependency. A remarkable potential exists for abuse with these drugs.

Traditionally, the barbiturates have been used as sedatives and hypnotics. They have generally been replaced by the benzodiazepines as sedatives. Since they are only effective in sleep induction and maintenance for two weeks, they can be used for the short term treatment of insomnia. Long term, or chronic insomnia, is best treated with other drugs. In Figure 6.2 is a list of barbiturates with their generic names, trade names, half lives, and hypnotic doses.

Adverse Effects

Nervous System. Somnolence (sleepiness or unnatural drowsiness) is common. Other effects include agitation, confusion, hyperkinesia, ataxia (irregularity of muscle coordination), vertigo, nightmares, depression, lethargy, residual sedation (hangover), paradoxical excitement, nervousness, psychiatric disturbances, hallucinations, insomnia, anxiety, and dizziness; in higher doses, delirium and stupor. Chronic use of phenobarbital may lead to headaches and fever.

Generic Name[1]	Trade Name	Half-life[2]	Hypnotic Dose[3]
Phenobarbital (L)	Luminal	79	100-320
Mephobarbital (L)	Mebaral	34	90-400
Amobarbital (I)	Amytal	25	65-200
Aprobarbital (I)	Alurate	24	40-160
Butabarbital (I)	Butisol	100	50-100
Talbutal (I)	Lotusate	15	120
Secobarbital (S)	Seconal	28	100
Pentobarbital (S)	Nembutal	22	100

[1] L = long acting (10 - 12 hours); I = intermediate acting (6 - 8 hours); S = short acting (3 - 4 hours).

[2] This is the mean half in hours; half-life ranges vary, i.e., the mean half-life for phenobarbital is 79 hours. The half-life range for phenobarbital is 53 to 118 hours. Half-life data is inadequate for talbutal (Kastrup, Olin, & Schwach, 1986).

[3] This is the oral does range in milligrams.

Figure 6.2. Barbituates—generic name, trade name, half-life, and hypnotic dose.

Respiratory. Hypoventilation, apnea, respiratory depression, laryngospasm, bronchospasm, and circulatory collapse.

Cardiovascular. Bradycardia and hypotension.

Gastrointestinal. Nausea, vomiting, constipation, and diarrhea. Chronic use of phenobarbital may lead to liver damage.

Allergic. Skin rashes, edema, and serum sickness.

BARBITURATE-LIKE HYPNOTICS

The drugs discussed in this section are chemically different from the barbiturates and each other. They act, pharmacologically, in a manner much the same as the barbiturates. They are mentioned together because of the similarity of their pharmacological properties. The drugs included are **Glutethimide** (Doriden), **methyprylon** (Noludar), **ethchlorvynol** (Placidyl), and **methaqualone** (Quaalude). Because of its abuse potential and ability to cause peripheral paresthesia, which some individuals find pleasant, methaqualone is no longer legally available in the United States. The three barbiturate-like drugs available are listed in Figure 6.3 together with trade names, half-life, and dosage.

Generic Name	Trade Name	Half-life	Dose
Glutethimide	Doriden	10-12 hours	500 mg
Methyprylon	Noludar	4 hours	200-400 mg
Ethchlorvynol	Placidyl	10-20 hours	500 mg

Figure 6.3. Barbiturate-like drugs—generic name, trade name, half-life, and dose.

These drugs are capable of depressing the **reticular activating system** (RAS) in the brain stem, and generally they act in a manner similar to the barbiturates. They are effective in the short-term management of insomnia. They tend, like the barbiturates, to depress REM sleep and produce REM rebound upon withdrawal. Tolerance, habituation and physical dependency can develop with long term use of these drugs. Respiratory depression may occur, when taken in combination with alcohol. They have no advantages over the barbiturates, and tend to cost more.

BENZODIAZEPINES

The benzodiazepines are believed to be as effective as hypnotics, with some important advantages over the barbiturates and the barbiturate-like drugs. The benzodiazepines do not all have the same ability to effectively induce or maintain sleep. For example, diazepam (Valium) is more effective than chlordiazepoxide (Librium) in maintaining sleep, even though both are effective in producing sleep. Generally, the benzodiazepines do not depress REM sleep. Flurazepam (Dalmane) is said to decrease sleep latency, that is, shorten the interval for sleep induction by 50 to 75% (Bachmann & Sherman, 1983). Flurazepam acts as rapidly as the short-acting barbiturates. Its effects last as long as the intermediate-acting barbiturates.

Not all the benzodiazepines are used for insomnia. Three compounds are specifically used for sleep disorders. They are flurazepam (Dalmane), Temazepam (Restoril), and triazolam (Halcion). Lorazepam (Ativan) is primarily used as a antianxiety drug, however, it has gained some popularity as a hypnotic. These drugs are listed in Figure 6.4. These drugs offer advantages over the other drugs used for insomnia. They produce little or no alterations in REM sleep, they do not promote REM rebound upon withdrawal. Tolerance to the hypnotic effect does not develop for periods up to four weeks. The benzodiazepines do not seem to alter the metabolism of other drugs, i.e., the anticoagulant, warfarin. These drugs have a wider safety margin than most other hypnotic drugs. They can, however, cause increased central nervous system depression when combined with alcohol.

Adverse Effects

Nervous System. Dizziness, drowsiness, lightheadedness, staggering, ataxia, falling, especially in older and debilitated

Generic Name	Trade Name	Half-life	Oral Dose
Flurazepam	Dalmane	50-100 hours	15-30 mg
Temazepam	Restoril	10-17 hours	15-30 mg
Triazolam	Halcion	1.5-5.4 hours	0.25-0.5 mg
Lorazepam	Ativan	10-20 hours	2-4 mg

Figure 6.4. Benzodiazepines-generic name, trade name, half-life, and dose.

people. Sedation, lethargy, disorientation, and coma are caused by drug intolerance and overdosage. Headache, nervousness, apprehension, and irritability have been reported. Other effects reported include confusion, euphoria, weakness, tremor, confusion and tinnitus.

Gastrointestinal. Heartburn, nausea, vomiting, diarrhea, constipation, pain, anorexia, and dry mouth.

Cardiovascular. Palpitations, chest pains, tachycardia, and hypotension.

Dermatological. Dermatitis, sweating, flushes, pruritus, and skin rash.

Miscellaneous. Body joint aches, GU cramps and pain, blurred vision, burning eyes, and sleep apnea.

ANTIHISTAMINES

The over-the-counter sleep aids are mostly antihistamine preparations. Little evidence, if any, is available to indicate that these products are effective in controlling insomnia. They produce drowsiness, an effect related to their anticholinergic activity (see Autonomic Nervous System). Adverse effects of these drugs include drowsiness, blurred vision, dry mouth, dizziness, and tinnitus. They have a wide margin of safety, although acute intoxication has been reported. Symptoms include hallucinations and convulsions. In Figure 6.5 is a list of over-the-counter sleep aids.

L-TRYPTOPHAN

L-tryptophan is an amino acid ingested when eating meat and fish. It has been shown to reduce sleep latencies when ingested in doses of 1 to 15 grams (Bachmann & Sherman, 1983). A normal diet in the United States contains from 1 to 2 grams of L-tryptophan. Doses up to 5 grams have been shown not to distort sleep patterns. It can be metabolized in the body into niacin, one of the B vitamins. It is also a precursor to

Active Ingredient(s)	Drug Product
Diphenhydramine 25 mg	Nervine Nighttime Sleep-Aid Nytol Sleep-Eze Sominex 2
Diphenhydramine 50 mg	Compoz Twilite
Pyrilamine 25 mg	Dormarax
Pyrilamine/Aspirin/ Acetaminophen	Quiet World
Doxylamine 25 mg	Unisom Nighttime Sleep-Aid

Figure 6.5. Over-the-counter sleep aids.

serotonin, a neurotransmitter substance which can depress the reticular activating system (RAS). Kastrup, Olin, and Schwach (1986) reported that doses of 4 to 5 grams reduced sleep latency, increased sleep time and reduced the number of awakenings; however, no well-controlled data substantiates this use. In fact, the package label of L-tryptophan says nothing about its use for insomnia. Some evidence does link a metabolite of L-tryptophan with bladder cancer, and some researchers have indicated that "therapeutic" levels of the drug may cause liver damage. More evaluation is required in order to determine the safety and effectiveness of l-tryptophan as an hypnotic agent.

SUMMARY

In Chapter VI are reviewed sleep and the hypnotic drugs. While agreement exists that sleep is a necessary function in life, the exact function of sleep remains unknown. Through the use of the electroencephalograph (EEG), measurements of brain waves have been made during waking and sleeping periods. An at rest person exhibits an alpha brain wave (8 to 12 hertz). An individual who is awake and involved in thought shows a beta wave (13 to 30 hertz). Theta waves are recorded in certain areas of children's brains and sometimes in adults during emotional stress (3 to 7 hertz). During states of sleep, surgical anesthesia, and stupor the EEG records delta waves (½ to 2 hertz). The four stages of sleep include (1) very low amplitude irregular waves, (2) frequent bursts of alternating larger and smaller waves, (3) appearance of delta waves, and (4) slow, synchronized waves which become dominant. Stages 2 through 4 are collectively known as "slow-wave sleep." The most common sleep disorder is insomnia, characterized by the inability to initiate or maintain sleep. The hypnotic drugs fall into the following categories: (1) the barbiturates, effective for short term use; (2) the barbiturate-like drugs, glutethimide (Doriden), methyprylon (Noludar), and ethchlorvynol (Placidyl), [(methaqualone (Quaalude) a drug no longer available in the United States]; (3) the benzodiazepines, as effective as the barbiturates without depressing REM sleep; (4) the antihistamines, found in the over-the-counter drugs; and L-tryptophan, an amino acid that is the precursor to serotonin.

CHAPTER **VII**

ANTIDEPRESSANT DRUGS

DEPRESSION

Dorland's Medical Dictionary (1957, p. 366) describes depression as "a lowering or decrease of functional activity" and the "absence of cheerfulness or hope: emotional dejection." Like anxiety, depression can be a healthy, normal response to a stimuli, or it can be a pathological condition. It is an important component to effective coping. For example, following the death of a loved one, the expectation would be that a state of depression would be experienced. The grieving process, as described by Elizabeth Kubler-Ross (1969), is a specific form of depression which includes fluctuating states of "denial," "anger," "bargaining," and "acceptance." To draw a line between the normal and the pathological state of depression is impossible.

Frequently, drug therapy is initiated for normal depressive responses. Whether or not this is an appropriate treatment is an arguable point. Most cases of mild, reactive depression are best left to run their course. Some of the criteria that can be evaluated in making such a decision include duration of the condition, severity, and etiology.

The literature makes several attempts to define depression. This is done through the use of selective pairs of categories. These dichotomous categories include primary vs. secondary, psychotic vs. neurotic, endogenous vs. reactive, and agitated vs. retarded. A further look at what these terms reflect may be helpful in coming to an understanding of the nature of depression.

Primary and **secondary** are terms that, theoretically, divide depression into states, based upon etiology. Primary depression occurs independently of other disorders. Depression is considered secondary, when it is related to another psychological disorder that is not related to the affective disorders, such as drug usage or an organic disorder. Many organic disorders can bring on a secondary depression. Swonger and Constantine (1983) suggested the following disorders as possible conditions for a secondary depression: hypoglycemia; liver disfunction; depletion of ions, such as calcium and potassium; and elevation of blood urea nitrogen, indicating possible renal disfunction. Drugs that may be responsible for a secondary depression include alcohol; sedative-hypnotics; antipsychotics; antianxiety drugs; antiepileptics; narcotics; anticholinergics; antihypertensives; digitalis; corticosteroids, especially when the drug is withdrawn; estrogen preparations; and immunosuppressives. The psychotherapist, by taking a medical and drug history, can be alert to these factors that may lead to secondary depression. Even when evidence is present of a primary depression, these factors may be contributing, and are best not ignored.

The terms **endogenous** and **reactive** (sometimes called exogenous) are both related to etiology and are characteristic of symptoms. Endogenous depression arises from internal causes, while reactive depression is set off by some identifiable causative stimuli at the psychological or interpersonal level. Another way of defining these terms is to say that endogenous depression arises at the organic level and reactive depression arises at the psychological or interpersonal level. The diagnosing of the reactive type depression does not rule out the possibility of an underlying endogenous depression. Symptomatically, endogenous depression tends to manifest more somatic symptoms, i.e., appetite changes and altered energy levels. The onset of endogenous depression is gradual, and the onset of reactive depression is sudden. This is because reactive depression manifests itself as the result of a causative incident or agent. In endogenous depression, functioning may be greatly impaired, while only mild impairment is experienced during reactive depression. Reactive depression tends to be brief, and endogenous depression may last for a prolonged time. In treating the two, the endogenous form is a good candidate for drug therapy, the reactive type is responsive to supportive psychotherapy and often, it simply improves with time.

When making the choice to use a drug in treating depression, an important factor is the presence or absence of psychomotor agitation. The terms *agitated* and *retarded* refer to the presence or absence of this symptom. The antidepressant drugs have a varying degree of sedative potential. The drugs with the most sedative potential are best used with agitated individuals, while non-sedative drugs may be prescribed for those who exhibit psychomotor retardation.

MOOD DISORDERS

The DSM-III (1980) classifies depression as an *Affective Disorder.* DSM-III-R (1987) changed the nomenclature to *Mood Disorders.* Mood disorders result from emotions, and consist of marked extremes of mood. The more classical terms for the mood disorders are mania and depression. *Mania* is characterized by elevated or irritable moods and hyperactivity, expressed physically, sexually, or socially. Other manifestations found in mania include excessive talking and grandiosity. The symptoms or characteristics of *depression* include a depressive mood, feelings of guilt and worthlessness, hostility, anxiety, tension, somatic complaints, sleep disturbances, bizarre thoughts and behavior, excitement, subjective uncertainty, withdrawal from social interaction, motor retardation in speech and behavior, and denial of illness (Bachmann & Sherman, 1983). Affective reactions can be traced to the neuropsychological involvement of the limbic system in the brain.

The mood disorders are classified as "unipolar" or "bipolar." The unipolar form consists of recurrent depressive episodes.

The bipolar form is characterized by both manic and depressive episodes. The more familiar nomenclature for this disorder is manic-depressive disorder.

THE BIOLOGICAL BASIS OF THE MOOD DISORDERS

Curt Richter, who performed experiments by removing or inactivating endocrine glands of rats, hypothesized that the underlying cause of manic-depressive syndrome may be an impairment in the endocrine system. Richter's hypothesis, although it never became popular, was partially correct in that most depressed and manic-depressed people do have one or more hormonal imbalances (Winokur, Amsterdam, Caroff, Snyder, & Brunswick, 1982). In the 1960's, several independent investigators hypothesized that depression could be caused by a deficiency of activity at catecholamine synapses (Kalat, 1984). Larry Stein (1968), a research psychologist, suggested that depressed people have a deficiency in the "rewards areas" of their brains due to a decreased catecholamine activity.

Several hypotheses have been advanced that attempt to show a biochemical causation of depression. The "cathecholamine" or "norepinephrine" hypothesis states that the affective disorders are related to an imbalance in the norepinephrine level at the postsynaptic receptors. The levels are low in depression and excessive in mania. Several problems make this hypothesis fall short. The most obvious, being the 10 days to 2 weeks that pass before clinical effectiveness is observed in the tricyclic antidepressants and the MAO inhibitors (Schildkraut & Kety, 1967).

A second theory, focusing attention upon the neurotransmitter serotonin, came along about the same time as the "norepinephrine" hypothesis. This theory stated that low serotonin levels coincided with depression, and high serotonin levels with mania. This theory also did not hold up (Swonger & Constantine, 1983). However, evidence is available that tryptophan (a serotonin precursor) levels are low in depressed people (DeMyer, Shea, Hendrie, & Yoshimura, 1981), and some researchers indicate that dietary supplements of tryptophan can be of benefit (Kalat, 1984). Swonger and Constantine (1983) pointed out that "elevated serotonin levels are related to depression of central nervous system (CNS) activity and the onset of sleep." (p. 292).

The inevitable followed, with researchers calling depression two different diseases. One occurring as the result of low norepinephrine, and the other as the result of low serotonin. The belief is that more than one type of depression leads to a revised hypothesis: Depression is due to a high number of receptor sites for the neurotransmitters, and not to the low concentrations of norepinephrine or serotonin. This hypothesis resolved the questions regarding the 2 to 3 week waiting period before onset of action of the antidepressant drugs. This hypothesis has problems, also.

An important and promising hypothesis explores the difference between presynaptic and postsynaptic receptors. Presynaptic and postsynaptic endings have different drug sensitivities from each other (Skirboll, Grace, & Bunney, 1979). The antidepressant drugs currently being used make the presynaptic inhibitory receptors less sensitive, an effect that develops gradually. The presynaptic decrease in activity causes an increase in stimulation of the postsynaptic receptors. Differentiating the effects on the presynaptic and postsynaptic receptors helps to bring understanding of the effects of antidepressants. Through the pharmacological understanding of drug mechanisms, researchers hope to become more knowledgable about the physiology and biochemistry of depression.

DSM-III-R

DSM-III-R lists depression under the title "Mood Disorders." The authors chose this more "descriptive" term over "Affective Disorders" and have reorganized the section into the *Bipolar Disorders* (including Bipolar Disorder and Cyclothymia) and the *Depressive Disorders* (including Major Depression and Dysthymia).

The distinction between the two categories is the presence of one or more manic episodes in the "Bipolar Disorder." The "Bipolar Disorder" is further subclassified into "Mixed," "Manic," or "Depressed." "Major Depression" has subclassifications of "Single Episode" or "Recurrent." The recurrent episode is further categorized by characteristics such as the presence or absence of psychotic features or "Melancholia." The term Melancholia is a carryover from the past. In its current usage, it describes a severe form of depression that is responsive to drug therapy.

The diagnosis of Mania requires "a distinct period of abnormally and persistently elevated, expansive, or irritable mood" (DSM-III-R). The DSM-III-R criteria for a manic episode is for three or more of the following symptoms to occur and persist during a period of one week or more: (1) inflated self-esteem or grandiosity; (2) decreased need for sleep: (3) more talkative than usual or persistent talking; (4) flight of ideas; (5) distractibility, i.e., attention being drawn to unimportant or irrelevant external stimuli; (6) excessive involvement in activities that have a high potential for painful consequences which are not recognized, such as, buying sprees, sexual indiscretions and reckless driving; (7) increase in goal-directed activity.

To diagnose a major depressive episode, five or more of the following symptoms have to be present for a period of at least two weeks: (1) significant weight loss or gain; (2) insomnia or hypersomnia; (3) psychomotor agitation or retarded activity; (4) loss of interest or pleasure in usual activities, or decrease in sexual drive; (5) loss of energy or fatigue; (6) feeling of worthlessness, self-reproach, or excessive or inappropriate guilt; (7) diminished ability to think or concentrate; (8) recurrent thoughts of death, suicidal ideation, wishes to be dead or suicide attempt; (9) depressed mood. For a diagnosis of a major depressive episode, no hallucinations, mood-incongruent delusions, or bizarre behavior can be present.

The "Bipolar Disorder" usually occurs before age 30. "Major Depression" can begin at any age. Typically, a manic episode comes on suddenly, with a rapid escalation of symptoms. The duration of an episode may be from a few days to several months. The onset of a major depressive episode is usually slow, taking from several days to weeks. According to DSM-III-R (1987) approximately twice as many females as males in the United States have a major depressive episode. "Bipolar Disorder" is equal among men and women. About 0.4% to 1.2% of the United States population have had "Bipolar Disorder." A familial predominance seems to be for the "Mood Disorders."

The classification of "Mood Disorders" includes **Cyclothymic Disorder** and **Dysthymic Disorder.** "Cyclothymic Disorder" is characterized by both manic and depressive symptoms. "Dysthymic Disorder" manifests only depressive symptoms. In both cases, the symptoms are not severe enough, nor do they meet the requirements of duration to be labelled a "Major Affective Disorder."

A diagnosis of "Cyclothymic Disorder" requires periodic symptomatic episodes of manic and depressive syndromes for a period of two years, but not sufficient to meet the requirements for a major depressive or manic episode.

Case

Jane is a thirty-four year old who came into therapy being very depressed. She was feeling inadequate, having trouble sleeping, and socially withdrawn. Just three months ago, she reported that everything was wonderful. She was "maddly" in love with her physician, who she was sure cared about her the same way, even though he did not see this yet. During that time she was "higher than a kite." She was "the first woman to be in love," described herself as a "virgin," even though she had been married. During treatment it came out that she had, over the past three years, had a series of extreme highs and lows. Her symptoms and behavior indicates that she is probably cyclothymic. The symptoms are not serious enough to be diagnosed "Bipolar," however, they have lasted longer than two years, and she has manifested a pattern of having numerous periods during which some symptoms characteristic of both the manic and depressive syndrome were present.

Dysthymic Disorder (or Depressive Neurosis) requires a duration of two years of symptoms. Depressive periods need at least three of the following symptoms: (1) insomnia or hypersomnia; (2) low energy or fatigue; (3) low self-esteem; (4) poor concentration; (5) feeling hopeless; and (6) poor appetite.

A critical problem for the psychotherapist, in dealing with depression, is estimating the severity and assessing the type (Ashcroft, 1975). The consequence of misdiagnosing suicidal depression is obvious. The psychotherapist, psychologist, or psychiatrist must make an assessment of the client based upon the client's history, symptoms, and complaints. From this assessment, the therapist establishes a treatment plan that may include the use of drugs.

ANTIDEPRESSANTS

Two general groups of drugs are used for the treatment of depression. These are the tricyclic antidepressants and the MAO inhibitors. The tricyclics are more broadly used. For several years the MAO inhibitors were considered too toxic for use by American clinicians. Recently, they have found their way back into the marketplace.

TRICYCLIC ANTIDEPRESSANTS

In the nineteenth century, a substance from the tricyclic antidepressant chemical group was synthesized. Little was done with this substance until the late 1940s. At that time, some 40 compounds of the group were synthesized for their possible use as antihistamines, sedatives, analgesics, and antiparkinsonian drugs. One of these chemicals was imipramine, a substance which resembles the phenothiazines, except for the substitution of an ethylene group for a sulfur. Kuhn (1958) found that, unlike the phenothiazines, imipramine was ineffective in quieting agitated psychotic patients. In fact, it was found to be beneficial in depressed individuals (Baldessarini, 1980).

The tricyclic antidepressant drugs are believed to act by inhibiting the uptake mechanism that normally terminates the action of the neurotransmitter. This restores monoamine levels (norepinephrine and serotonin) to the norm at the receptor sites. The tricyclics are believed to block the pumping mechanism responsible for bringing the transmittors back to the presynatic cleft, thereby preventing neuronal reuptake of norepinephrine and serotonin from the synaptic cleft. The early reuptake blockade is offset by compensatory short term adjustments, or tolerance, by the neurons. This theory explains the 2 or 3 week waiting period for therapeutic activity.

The name tricyclic refers to the three-ring molecular structure that is common to this class of drug. A new group of drugs, the tetracyclics has been developed. Initially, the belief was that these substances acted faster than the tricyclics. Recent studies question these claims (Alford, 1983).

Actions

The tricyclic antidepressants are structurally related to the phenothiazine antipsychotic drugs. The three major pharmacologic actions are (1) potentiation of the central nervous system bioamines, (2) sedation, and (3) anticholinergic activity. The tricyclics can be classified by their ability to inhibit presynaptic reuptake of norepinephrine and serotonin. Individuals with norepinephrine deficiencies are more likely to respond to imipramine and other secondary amines. Individuals with low serotonin levels respond to amitriptyline and other tertiary amines.

The two major side effects are sedation and anticholinergic activity. The extent of these is shown in Figure 7.1.

The plasma half-lives of the tricyclics is as follows: imipramine, 9-24 hours; amitriptyline, 17-40 hours; desipramine, 14-76 hours; nortriptyline, 18-93 hours; and protriptyline, 54-198 hours (Bachmann & Sherman, 1983).

Anticholinergic Effect. The autonomic side effects of the tricyclics are similar to those of the phenothiazines, only more pronounced. They include dry mouth, offset with fluid intake or artificial saliva; urinary retention, often treated with bethanechol (Urecholine); increased intraocular pressure, which may worsen glaucoma; constipation, also a symptom of depression; increased sweating; blurred vision; increased blood pressure, usually at low doses; and decreased blood pressure and postural

Tricyclic Antidepressants	Sedative Effect	Anticholinergic Effect
TERTIARY AMINES		
Amitriptyline	high	high
Imipramine	moderate	moderate
Doxepin	high	moderate
Trimipramine	high	moderate
SECONDARY AMINES		
Amoxapine	moderate	low
Nortriptyline	moderate	moderate
Desipramine	low	low
Protriptyline	low	high
TETRACYCLIC		
Maprotiline	moderate	low
TRIAZOLOPRYIDINE		
Trazodone	moderate	low
FLUOXETINE		
Prozac	high	low

Figure 7.1. Sedation and anticholinergic effects of tricyclic antidepressants. (Adapted from Kastrup et al., 1986)

hypotension, occurs at higher doses (may lead to heart failure or precipitate a myocardial infarction).

Other Adverse Reactions

Cardiovascular. Cardiovascular effects include Orthostatic hypotension, hypertension, syncope, tachycardia, palpitations, myocardial infarction, arrhythmias, heart block, congestive heart failure, stroke, and changes in ECG. Orthostatic hypotension is a lowering of blood pressure that happens when an individual changes position from supine (lying down) to erect (standing). Hypertension or high blood pressure is caused by the increase of circulating catecholamines. Syncope is the temporary loss of consciousness due to lack of blood in the brain. Tachycardia is usually caused by the anticholinergic effect on the vagus nerve. Myocardial infarction (MI), sometimes called a heart attack, refers to the heart muscle damage occurring with inadequate blood supply to the area of the heart. MI may be brought on by the tricyclics through anticholinergic blockage of the vagus nerve or by the increase in catecholamines which increases sympathetic activity. Low doses may result in arrhythmias and heart block due to vagus nerve block. In higher doses these effects are the result of a direct cardiac tissue response.

CNS. An important difference between the phenothiazines and tricyclics is that the tricyclics almost never cause extrapyramidal side effects. Central nervous effects include confusion; disturbed concentration; decrease in memory; feelings of unreality; delusions; anxiety; nervousness; restlessness; agitation; panic; insomnia; nightmares; hypomania; mania; drowsiness; dizziness; weakness; fatigue; and headaches.

Neurological. Neurological side effects include numbness; tingling; paresthesia of the extremities; incoordination; motor hyperactivity; akathisia; ataxia; tremors; peripheral neuropathy; seizures; speech blockage; and tinnitus.

Allergic. Allergic reactions include skin rash; pruritus; photosensitivity; and edema.

Hematological. Bone marrow depression, including agranulocytosis, is possible.

Gastrointestinal. The gastrointestinal effects that are most common include nausea, vomiting, and diarrhea. Other effects are increased salivation, an unusual taste, abdominal cramps, and sometimes a black tongue.

Endocrine. The female may experience breast enlargement and menstrual irregularity. The male may find swelling of the testicles. Libido may be either increased or decreased, and some individuals become impotent. Blood sugar levels may either increase or decrease.

Miscellaneous. Other adverse reactions reported include nasal congestion, excessive appetite, weight gain or loss, increased perspiration, hyperthermia, flushing, chills, urinary frequence, and alopecia (loss of hair/baldness).

Generic Name	Brand Name	Average Daily Dose
Tricyclic Antidepressants		
Amitriptyline	Elavil, Endep	75 - 300 mg
Imipramine	Tofranil	75 - 300 mg
Doxepin	Adapin, Sinequan	75 - 300 mg
Trimipramine	Surmontil	75 - 300 mg
Amoxapine	Asendin	75 - 300 mg
Desipramine	Norpramin, Pertofrane	75 - 300 mg
Protriptyline	Vivactil	10 - 60 mg
Nortriptyline	Aventyl, Pamelor	50 - 150 mg
Tetracyclic Antidepressants		
Maprotiline	Ludiomil	75 - 300 mg

Figure 7.2. Tricyclic and tetracyclic antidepressants—generic names, brand names, and average daily dosage.

Withdrawal. Rapid termination of tricyclic antidepressants may result in nausea, headache, vertigo, and nightmares. See Figure 7.2 for average daily dosages, generic names and brand names of tricyclic and tetracyclic antidepressants.

Case

Tom, a 58 year old man, was diagnosed as suffering from primary unipolar depression. He had not had an episode in several years. He was vague about his history; however, it appeared that he had experienced two or three untreated episodes over the past twenty years. He was given a bedtime dose of amitriptyline 150mg. A week later, he complained of a dry mouth and blurred vision. He was told that these were common side effects that would go away and was kept on the treatment. Another week went by and he complained of constipation and difficulty urinating. His constipation was treated with milk of magnesia. After three weeks of therapy he reported feeling better, his urinary problem persisted, but was no worse than previously noted. The side effects experienced by this patient were all due to the significant anticholinergic effects caused by the tricyclic antidepressants. The dry mouth usually, but not always, goes away. The constipation is responsive to milk of magnesia or dioctyl sodium sulfosuccinate (D.S.S.).

TRAZODONE (Desyrel)

Trazodone is an antidepressant that is in a class of its own. It is not a MAO inhibitor and is known to inhibit serotonin uptake in animals. Trazodone shows a lower incidence of anticholinergic side effects. A significant adverse effect is the occurrence of priapism (a persistent abnormal erection of the penis without sexual desire). In approximately one-third of the reported cases, surgical intervention is required. The side effects of trazodone are similar to the tricyclics.

FLUOXETINE (Prozac)

Fluoxetine was introduced during 1988. It is a new oral antidepressant agent, unrelated to the tricyclics or other antidepressant agents. Fluoxetine's action is believed to stem from its ability to block the uptake of serotonin. It has become a rather well used antidepressant. Some of its popularity may be due to a marketing strategy based upon its ability to cause weight loss. The literature reports a weight loss greater than 5% in 13% of the tested users. A comparable weight loss was reported in 3% of tricyclic users and 4% of placebo takers (Kastrup 1988).

MAO INHIBITORS

The MAO inhibitors were developed during the same time period as the tricyclics. A group of people being treated for pulmonary tuberculosis with isoniazid and its derivative, iproniazid, showed marked mood elevation. Isoniazid was too toxic to be used; however, iproniazid was found to be an effective mood elevator. Researchers discovered that iproniazid was capable of inhibiting the enzyme monoamine oxidase (MAO) (Weil-Malherbe, 1967).

Monoamine oxidase is an enzyme that is found in neuron endings throughout the body. Its function is to metabolically decompose amine compounds such as the neurotransmitters: norepinephrine, epinephrine, and serotonin. Drugs that inhibit this enzyme system, MAO inhibitors, cause an increased concentration of neurotransmitters in the storage sites of the nervous system. This increased concentration of monoamines is responsible for the antidepressant activity of the MAO inhibitor drugs. Chemically, two types exist of MAO inhibitors: the hydrazine compounds (isocarboxazid and phenelzine), that require 3 to 4 weeks for onset of activity; and the non-hydrazine compounds (tranylcypromine) that have a more rapid onset of activity of 10 days.

The MAO inhibitors are used as a second choice in the treatment of depression. They also have been used in the treatment of bulimia; however, this is not a labelled use of the drugs. The generic and brand names of MAO inhibitors and the average daily dose are shown in Figure 7.3.

MAO inhibitors can inhibit the oxidation of the amino acid tyramine by the enzyme MAO. Tyramine is present in many foods. When tyramine is not broken down in the system, the individual may experience a hypertensive crisis. This is known as the tyramine effect. Tyramine acts to liberate norepinephrine from the nerve endings. Norepinephrine, in turn, stimulates alpha adrenergic receptors. This causes a constriction of blood vessels, increases the heart rate, and makes heart muscle

Generic Name	Brand Name	Average Daily Dose
Isocarboxazid	Marplan	10 - 30 mg
Phenelzine	Nardil	15 - 90 mg
Tranylcypromine	Parnate	10 - 30 mg

Figure 7.3. MAO inhibitors—generic names, brand names, and average daily dose.

contract more strongly. Therefore, the individual experiences an increase in blood pressure.

Individuals taking MAO inhibitors are warned not to eat certain foods or take certain drugs that can cause the tyramine effect.

Tyramine Containing Foods

Cheese/Dairy Products. Most cheeses, yogurt, and sour cream.

Meat/Fish. Beef or chicken liver, meats prepared with tenderizer, fermented sausage (bologna, pepperoni, and salami), game meat, caviar, dried fish, and pickled herring.

Alcoholic Beverages. Beer, ale, red wine (especially Chianti), and Sherry.

Fruits/Vegetables. Avocado, yeast extracts, bananas, figs, raisins, and soy sauce.

Foods That Contain Other Vasopressors. Chocolate and caffeine.

Drugs To Avoid When On MAO Inhibitors

Amphetamines, caffeine, ephedrine, methyldopa, Neo-Synephrine, dopamine, reserpine and guanethidine.

Adverse Effects.

Common side effects include orthostatic hypotension, causing some individuals to fall; changes in cardia rate and rhythm; central nervous system effects, dizziness, vertigo, headache, overactivity, tremors, muscle twitching, mania, hypomania (the most severe psychological side effect), jitteriness, confusion, memory impairment, insomnia, weakness, fatigue, drowsiness, restlessness, and overstimulation including increased anxiety; gastrointestinal effects, constipation, nausea, diarrhea, abdominal pain; and miscellaneous effects such as dry mouth, edema, blurred vision, anorexia and weight changes, and minor skin reactions. In addition a long list of less common and rare side effects are known. The list is too long to list here.

ELECTROCONVULSIVE THERAPY (ECT)

Electroconvulsive Therapy (ECT) is generally considered as the major alternative to drug therapy for seriously depressed individuals. Although ECT does not fall into the scope of this text, its mention here seems important. The evidence does suggests that ECT has a better long and short term effect in treating very severe depression (Avery & Winokur, 1976). Most physicians prefer to begin treatment with drug therapy, unless the person is considered a suicidal risk. Some of the considerations for the use of drugs vs. ECT are as follows:

1. ECT is more effective in a higher percentage of depressed patients than drug therapy;

2. a general aversion exists to the use of ECT, while the use of medication is more acceptable;

3. treatments are very costly, requiring the presence of an anesthesiologist or other specially trained personnel prepared to deal with the individual who needs an endotrachela intubation due to the effects of the ECT and adjunctive drugs;

4. the use of ECT requires the use of potent adjunctive drugs, such as thiopental, atropine, and succinylcholine (a drug used to block the neuromuscular junctions);

5. under proper supervision, drugs are considered safer than ECT; and

6. ECT may be more convenient for the non-hospitalized patient; however, a course of treatment may require the individual to be brought to the clinic or hospital 6 to 12 times during a several week period.

Because of public opinion, cost, convenience, acceptability, and possible safety, the majority of physicians choose drugs to begin the treatment of depression.

SUMMARY

Chapter VII deals with depression and the antidepressant drugs. Depression may occur independent of other disorders (primary) or as a symptom of another psychological disorder (secondary). Depression is considered endogenous when it arises from internal causes and reactive or exogenous when it is the result of an interpersonal or psychological event. In DSM-III-R, depression is classified as a "Mood Disorder." Antidepressant drugs are of two types, the tricyclic antidepressants and the MAO inhibitors. The tricyclic antidepressants act at the synapse, while the MAO inhibitors act to inhibit the enzyme monoamine oxidase in the nerve cell ending. MAO inhibitors can cause a hypertensive crisis because of their effect on the amino acid, tyramine. Certain food restrictions are required to limit the intake of tryamine.

CHAPTER VIII

BIPOLAR DISORDERS AND LITHIUM

Lithium is an elemental substance readily found in nature. It is in the same chemical family as sodium and potassium. Although lithium is found in trace amounts in animal tissues, it has no known physiological role. Lithium first appeared in the practice of medicine in 1859, as a treatment for gout (Hollister, 1978). In the 1940s, the common practice was to substitute lithium chloride for sodium chloride in salt re-stricted diets. This practice led to serious consequences, including many deaths, due to lithium toxicity. By 1949, its use in the kitchen had become obsolete. During the same year, lithium was introduced into medicine for the treatment of mania but was not introduced into the United States for the treatment of mania until 1970.

John Cade (1970), of Australia, is given credit for intro-ducing lithium as a treatment for mania. He was doing research with manic patients, looking for toxic substances in their urine. Cade found that the uric acid of the manic patients would most often kill the rats. Thinking that uric acid might change the solubility of the toxic substance, he decided to give the rats lithium urate. The result was that both lithium urate and lithium carbonate protected the animal from the urine of the manic patients.

Lithium salts have two actions that make them effective in treating mania. First they are sedative, and second they protect against the toxic factors in the urine of manics (Hollister, 1978; Cade, 1970; Baldessarini, 1980).

The mechanism of action of lithium is not known. The most widely accepted theory has to do with ion distribution. Lithium alters sodium transport in the nerve and muscle cells. Lithium can replace sodium in the cells and substitutes for sodium in an action potential. In normal cell physiology, sodium ions enter the cells, and potassium ions leave. The effect, depolarization, occurs as the impulse travels along the nerve. Cells complete the cycle and recover by removing the sodium and taking in the potassium by means of a mechanism called the sodium-pump. Once in the cell, lithium can not be pumped out by the sodium-pump and is exchanged for sodium by a mechanism called the countertransport mechanism, which normally exchanges sodium for sodium. The net result of this activity is (1) a stabilizing effect on the nerve cell; (2) increased reuptake of the neurotransmitters dopamine, serotonin, and norepinephrine; (3) acceleration of the presynaptic destruction of catacholamines (an action that is opposite to the effects of MAO inhibitors); (4) an inhibiting of the release of neurotransmitters at the synapse; (5) possible effects to enzymatic activity; and (6) possible effects on the hormonal systems (Swonger & Constantine, 1983; Goldsmith, 1977; Kastrup, Olin, & Schwach, 1986; Hollister, 1978).

Lithium is useful in treating manic-depressive (bipolar) disorders. It also has shown value in preventing relapses of unipolar disorders. It is not considered a drug of choice for depressive disorders, even though it may have some use in individuals displaying a refractory response to the tricyclics (Bachmann, 1983). Studies have shown lithium to be superior to chlorpromazine in treating bipolar disorder. In fact, lithium was reported to have a faster onset of therapeutic effect with less side effects (Takahashi, Sakuma, Itoh, Kurihara, Saito, & Watanabe, 1975). Other research shows that lithium performed more effectively than imipramine or placebos in a two year follow-up of maintenance therapy (Prien, Klett, & Caffey, 1973). Lithium treatment has shown a 60 to 80% success rate for remission of mania states, and 60 to 70% effective as a maintenance regiment (Hollister, 1978). These effects seem to be independent of age, sex, and duration of illness (Bachmann & Sherman, 1983).

The major problem with lithium is its toxicity. Its toxic level is closely related to its therapeutic serum levels. Therefore, a very essential component of treatment is proper serum monitoring during treatment. Tolerance of lithium is greater during the acute manic phase, and decreases when manic symptoms subside (Kastrup, Olin, & Schwach, 1986). Acute manic dosage may be somewhat higher than maintenance dosages.

Therapeutic serum levels of lithium carbonate usually range from 0.6 to 1.5mEq/L. Maintenance treatment calls for 0.6 to 1.2mEq/L, and for acute mania the levels are 1.0 to 1.4mEq/L. Lithium toxicity is normally not experienced below a serum level of 1.5mEq/L. However, adverse effects do occur even at very low dosages. In Figure 8.1 are shown adverse effects at toxic levels.

Serum level	Toxic Effects
less than 1.5	Nausea; vomiting; diarrhea; thirst; polyuria (the passage of abnormally large amounts of normal urine); lethargy; slurred speech; muscle weakness; and hand tremor.
1.5 to 3.0	More persistent gastrointestinal upset; stumbling gait; more severe hand tremor; mental confusion; drowsiness; EKG changes; and incoordination.
2.0 to 4.0	muscle spasm and weakness; jerky eye movements; large output of dilute urine; tinnitus (a noise or ringing in the ears); convulsions; blurred vision; seizures; and stupor.
above 4.0	Serious complications involving irreversible kidney damage; pulmonary infection; or death.

Figure 8.1. Serum levels and toxic effects of lithium.

In looking at adverse reactions, some are related to serum levels, and some seem unrelated to dosage.

SERUM RELATED ADVERSE EFFECTS

Dose related side effects may be seen within the normal therapeutic dose range. The most common of these is tremor (seen in 30% of individuals and severe in 10%) (Kastrup, Olin, & Schwach, 1986). Thyroid abnormalities occur with significant frequency. Some 3 to 5% of individuals on lithium will become hypothyroid or have a euthyroid (a normal functioning thryoid) goiter. Milder forms of muscle spasm, twitching, and clonic movements of limbs also occurs. Central nervous effects include blackout; slurred speech; dizziness; incontinence of urine or feces; restlessness; confusion; fatigue; lethargy; and a tendency to sleep. Gastrointestinal effects may include nausea, vomiting, diarrhea, gastritis, pain, and excessive salivation. Dermatological effects found are dry or loss of hair, numbness of the skin, itching, and skin rashes. Autonomic effects are dry mouth and blurred vision.

NON-SERUM RELATED ADVERSE EFFECTS

Some side effects seem to be unrelated to dosage. The most common is weight gain (20 to 60% will gain 5 to 10 kg). Another problem area is in the mouth. Individuals often experience distorted taste, salty taste, swollen lips, and increase in dental caries.

Several important aspects need to be considered in determining a dose regimen for lithium. Prior to beginning treatment, a laboratory workup including a complete blood count, urinalysis, a battery of common biochemical tests, and a thyroid function test are usually performed. A baseline is important in assessing any impairment of thyroid function. Also an important evaluation is that of the renal function. Renal disease may counterindicate the use of lithium. Severe cardiac disease may be a counterindication, or may require the use of diuretics.

Age and sex are important. Older individuals are prone to have a decreased renal function. They also tend to have a lower percentage of water in their bodies. Females tend to have a higher percentage water in their bodies (55% as opposed to 50% for males). All this is important because the therapeutic dose is based upon a serum level with a very critical margin.

The ideal way of establishing a dose is to give one dose of 900 mg, and get a plasma concentration 24 hours later. The physician, pharmacist, or pharmacologist then can mathematically predict a dosage regimen that will allow for a specific therapeutic serum level. At the same time, the patient is monitored for therapeutic and adverse effects. When the case is such that a 24 hour waiting period is not feasible, then a dose regimen based upon body weight is begun, and corrections are made after a serum concentration is taken in 7 days. For example: a man weighs 80 kg, the initial dose is calculated at 0.5mEq/kg, or 40mEq, lithium carbonate is available in a 300mg or 8mEq dosage form, therefore 40/8 = 5 dose units or 1500 mg/day. After 7 days the serum concentration is obtained. According to toxicity and clinical response, the dose may be left the same, decreased or increased. With data available the dose can be predictably calculated. Serum levels are still necessary at weekly intervals for the first month, and then every 4 to 6 weeks. After remission of the acute state, the dose is lowered to a maintenance dose level—the average plasma concentration after 7 days of treatment with a dose calculated at 0.5mEq/kg is 0.91mEq/l (Stokes, Kocsis, & Arcuni, 1976).

Case

Mr. M. is a 54 year old caucasian male who has a long psychiatric history. Following the death of his mother, he experienced profound grief much beyond what is normal. After a year of depressive behavior, he was hospitalized and given electroconvulsive treatments (ECT). His response was brief and he began to suffer a relapse. After a mild depression that lasted only one week, he suddenly because agitated, began drinking, and staying awake days at a time. His behavior was described by his wife as "going until he dropped." He was diagnosed as suffering from anxiety and alcohol abuse. He was treated with an unknown drug, which kept him "knocked out all the time."

His first episode came twenty years ago, and has been followed by repeated episodes of profound depression. He was treated each time for alcohol abuse and acute depression. During this period, several brief periods of "religious intensity" occurred in which he stayed awake all night reading, preached to everyone, and felt like he was to save the world. He was treated and given diagnoses ranging from acute alcoholism to paranoid schizophrenia. After feeling "blue," and then as if his "head was going to explode," he became angry, grandiose, loud, belligerent, suspicious, and began drinking large quantities of alcohol. He ended in jail and was taken to the hospital where he was diagnosed as having bipolar disorder. His family history included his father, who was an alcoholic, and his mother and uncle who had an unidentified mental disorder. He was treated with lithium carbonate and chlorpromazine. In about five days his behavior became under control. He was discharged in two weeks and followed as an outpatient on lithium and chlorpromazine.

SUMMARY

Lithium carbonate is an effective treatment for the manic phase of "Bipolar Disorder." The major problem with lithium is its toxicity. It has a toxic level which is close to its therapeutic level. Close monitoring of patients on lithium is required.

PSYCHOSES AND ANTIPSYCHOTIC DRUGS

Three diagnostic categories are in the *Diagnostic and Statistical Manual, DSM-III-R,* of **psychoses,** excluding organic brain syndrome and the drug-induced psychoses. These are **schizophrenic disorders, paranoid disorders,** and **other psychotic disorders.** Schizophrenia is the most prevalent of these disorders, and the most frequently found diagnosis for admission into a mental hospital.

SCHIZOPHRENIC DISORDERS

One person in every hundred, or over two million Americans, will suffer from schizophrenia at some time during their life span. Researchers have found a higher incident of schizophrenia in the lower social classes. The theories to explain this phenomenon include (1) social and economic stresses as a causative factor; (2) the low social class is secondary to schizophrenia, due to the tendency of schizophrenic patients to move downward in social and economic levels (Mischler & Scotch, 1963); and (3) the reduced social network and social communication of the lower classes causes disruptions that may be linked to the prevalence of schizophrenia (Hammer, Makiesky-Barrow, & Gutwirth, 1978).

The issue of "nature versus nurture," in regard to etiology of the schizophrenic disorders, suggests the importance of organic versus psychological and interpersonal factors. A great deal of evidence is available to suggest that organic factors are predominant in schizophrenia. Studies of families and adoptions by American-Danish teams show that relatives of schizophrenics have a higher incidence of acquiring the disease. The closer the relationship, the greater the potential for becoming schizophrenic. Monozygotic twins, even when separated and raised apart, have a significantly better chance of becoming schizophrenic. The risk factor for the child of a schizophrenic is greater whether the child is reared by the parent or not (Kessler, 1980; Kety et al., 1975; Rosenthal et al., 1971; Wendler et al., 1974).

Hollister (1978) called schizophrenia, "a disorder of the brain, manifested primarily by a disturbance in logical sequencing, that produces abnormal thinking, behavior, and affect" (p. 132). He also stated that a "genetic predisposition is necessary for developing the disorder," (p. 132) and listed several factors that may be of significance. These are (1) the degree of genetic load, (2) the level of intelligence, (3) the presence of unfavorable developmental influences in prenatal life and childhood, and (4) the life experiences of the individual. The beliefs expressed by Hollister concur with other researchers. He also indicated that stress and environmental factors are involved in the clinical manifestation of the disorder.

No gross or cellular pathology has been discovered in the brain tissue of schizophrenics; however a number of biochemical changes do take place. These changes, however, may be a result of the disorder and not the cause. From these changes investigators have developed several theories of schizophrenic mechanisms.

Causal Hypothesis

The ***autoimmune hypothesis,*** originally suggested by Heath in 1954, is based upon the finding of fluorescent antibodies in areas of the brain of schizophrenics, but not in normal individuals. No further substantiation has occurred of this theory (Swonger & Constantine, 1983).

The **transmethylation theory** proposed by Osmond and Smythies (1952), some 30 years ago, is based upon the structural similarities between the catecholamine transmitters and certain psychedelic drugs, such as psilocybin, dimethyltryptamine (DMT), mescaline, and lysergic acid diethylamine (LSD). The theory speculates that the brain somehow creates a chemical reaction that changes the transmitters into their psychedelic counterpart. The bulk of the evidence tends not to support this hypothesis, because attempts to find enzyme systems capable of "methylating" the transmitters have been unsuccessful. Further evidence against this hypothesis includes (1) the endogenous methylated substance found in biological fluids is not different for schizophrenics and nonschizophrenics, and (2) pharmacological attempts to induce schizoid behavior by increasing or decreasing methylated amines have not been successful (Swonger & Constantine, 1983).

The **phenylethylamine hypothesis** proposes that biochemical abnormalities, resulting in increased levels of phenylethylamine, might be the cause of a psychosis, resembling an amphetamine-like psychotic reaction. A state of paranoid psychosis can be produced by doses of amphetamines (Wyatt, 1977). Phenylethylamine is a naturally occurring chemical in the body which is the by-product of phenylalanine. It is normally metabolized by MAO. The problem with this theory is that little evidence has been found to indicate a greater concentration of phenylethylamine in schizophrenics.

The most probable hypothesis for a mechanism of schizophrenia is the **dopamine hypothesis.** Support for the dopamine hypothesis comes from an understanding of the neuroleptic or antipsychotic drugs. These drugs have been well established as to not just sedate or calm individuals, but to have an actual "antischizophrenic" action. This is in juxtaposition to the many sedative and antianxiety drugs that have been tried on schizophrenics. These drugs have not shown any more success than placebos. The antipsychotic drugs are clearly more successful in treating schizophrenia. Symptoms that are specific to schizophrenia, such as thought disorder, respond to the antipsychotic drugs. The antipsychotic drugs, however, fare no better than the sedatives, antianxiety drugs, or placebos in treating anxiety, depression, or hostility.

Researchers have established that the antipsychotic drugs act by blocking the receptor sites of the neurotransmitter actions of dopamine in the brain. Dopamine is one of the two principal catecholamine neurotransmitters located in the brain. It serves as the precursor to norepinephrine in most areas of the brain, and is biochemically changed to norepinephrine by the enzyme, dopamine hydroxylase. Some neuron pathways lack the enzyme and, therefore, dopamine is not converted into norepinephrine.

One of these pathways is linked to Parkinson's disease. In Parkinson's disease, the body disrupts the dopamine pathway in the substantia nigra of the brain stem. Treatment consists of replacing dopamine, by administering its precursor levodopa. Another dopamine pathway is involved in hormonal release from the hypothalamus to the pituitary gland.

Arvid Carlsson in 1963, was the first to suggest that the antipsychotic drugs act by blocking dopamine receptors. The use of radioactive binding of antipsychotic drugs has substantiated that the blockade of dopamine receptors is responsible for the therapeutic effects of the antipsychotic drugs (Snyder, 1978).

Symptoms and Diagnosis

Schizophrenia is not a single disorder, but a complex variety of symptoms or syndromes. The DSM-III-R categorizes schizophrenia into **simple, disorganized, catatonic, paranoid, undifferentiated,** and **residual types.** The primary condition that is necessary for a diagnosis of schizophrenia is the presence of one or more of the following characteristics: delusions, hallucinations, incoherence, affective disturbances, catatonia, and disorganized behavior.

Schizophrenia is characterized with **thought disturbances.** Disturbed thinking may vary in severity, from illogical ideation in a single area, to a disorganization of total thought process. For example, a paranoid person may have normal intelligence and function well, with the exception of having delusions regarding specific subjects. Other schizophrenics may not make any sense because their thoughts follow no meaningful order. In schizophrenia a tendency is for "thought broadcasting" delusions; the thoughts of an individual are broadcasted from one's head to the external world where others hear the thoughts; "thought withdrawal"—thoughts have been removed from an individual's head; "thought insertion"—thoughts of another are inserted into an individual's head. Frequently a schizophrenic will have "delusions of being controlled," that is the experience of having thoughts, actions, impulses, or feelings that are not the individual's, but that of some imposing external force. Frequently, the schizophrenic has a disturbance in perception. This is referred to as a sensory hallucination. The most common is auditory, i.e., perceiving a voice from some outside source.

A second problem in schizophrenia is **inappropriate affect.** Individuals may not respond in a normal or recognized manner. Some individuals have a flat affect, while others may laugh and respond to no apparent stimuli.

The third characteristic of a schizophrenic is the tendency to be **withdrawn** into their inner world. Frequently, the schizophrenic pays no attention to the outer world and does not relate to other people.

The schizophrenic has a **decreased sense of self,** that is, little or no healthy feelings of individuality, uniqueness, and self-direction. Often the individual has trouble being self-initiating, and is unable to accomplish goal-directed activity.

Psychomotor disturbances lead to a withdrawal of activity or inappropriate excited movements. Rigid postures are not uncommon, as are unusual mannerisms.

Onset of schizophrenia is usually during adolescence or early adulthood. The active stage of the illness is almost always preceded by a **prodromal phase** in which a deterioration occurs of the previous level of functioning. The prodromal stage may vary in length with characteristic symptoms of withdrawal, impairment in role functioning, peculiar behavior, impairment in hygiene and grooming, inappropriate affect, personality change, bizarre ideation, and unusual perceptual experiences.

The prodromal phase is followed by the active phase with the characteristic symptoms (see below) having lasted for at least six months. The active phase is followed by a residual phase, with symptoms similar to the prodromal phase. A complete recovery is very rare.

DSM-III-R lists three sets of characteristic symptoms for diagnosing the active phase of Schizophrenia. The **active phase** is defined by having severe symptoms which must last for a period of one week or more. Symptoms may consist of one of the three following categories: (1) two of the following—dilusions, hallucinations that last for a considerable time, catatonic behavior, incoherence, or flat, grossly inappropriate affect; (2) the presence of bizarre delusions (content is absurd, and has no possible basis in fact), i.e., being controlled, thought broadcasting, thought insertion, or thought withdrawal; and (3) prominent hallucinations.

PARANOID DISORDERS

The paranoid disorders generally have their onset during middle or late adult life. They include four categories: (1) **paranoia,** having a chronic and stable persecutory delusional system of a least six months duration; (2) **shared paranoid** disorder, with a delusional system that develops as a result of a close relationship with another person or persons who have an established disorder with persecutory delusions; (3) **acute paranoid** disorder, with a duration of less than six months; and (4) **atypical paranoid disorder,** a catch-all category.

The diagnostic criteria of paranoid disorders excludes organic brain syndrome and a preceding full depressive or manic syndrome. It includes (1) persistent delusions with persecutory or jealous content; (2) no affective, associative, or behavioral disturbance, except in relation to the delusional system; (3) duration of at least one week; and (4) no prominent hallucinations.

OTHER PSYCHOTIC DISORDERS

Other psychotic disorders include schizophreniform disorder, brief reactive psychosis, schizoaffective disorder, and atypical psychosis. The first two disorders are categorized by duration. Schizophreniform disorder has a duration including prodromal, active, and residual phases, of at least two weeks and less than six months. Brief reactive psychosis lasts for less than two weeks, and usually for a few hours. Schizoaffective disorder is characterized by symptoms of schizophrenia, as well as pronounced symptoms of mania or depression. Whether the schizoid or affective symptomatology is secondary is not clear. The final category is *Atypical psychosis,* a residual category for conditions not meeting any other category.

ANTIPSYCHOTIC DRUGS

Six distinct chemical classes or types of antipsychotic drugs exist. All of the drugs have in common the ability to reduce the symptoms of schizophrenia and the ability to induce extrapyramidal side effects. The different classes, as well as the drugs within each class, exhibit a difference in antipsychotic potency, and in ability to produce extrapyramidal reactions. These two factors, the difference in antipsychotic potency and the ability to produce extrapyramidal effects, become the basis for selection of an antipsychotic drug for an individual.

The chemical types of antipsychotic drugs are

1. the phenothiazine, e.g., chlorpromazine (Thorazine);

2. the thioxanthenes, e.g., thiothixene (Navane);

3. the butyrophenones, e.g., haloperidol (Haldol);

4. the dibenzoxazepines, e.g., loxapine (Loxitane);

5. the dihydroindolones, e.g., molindone (Moban); and

6. the diphenylbutylpiperidine derivatives, e.g., pimozide (Orap), used as an orphan drug in treating Tourette's disorder. Gilles de la Tourette syndrome is a behavioral disorder characterized by tics, unpredicable barking, and aggressive behavior (usually non-violent).

The phenothiazine are further divided by the nature of the chemical substitution on the nitrogen atom of its middle ring (R_2) and carbon number two of the phenyl ring (R_1). The substitution may be of three groups: (1) An aliphatic or dimethylaminoalkyl group. These drugs are the most sedative and least potent antipsychotic. Examples are promazine, Sparine; chlorpromazine, Thorazine; and triflupromazine, Vesprin. (2) An alkyl piperidyl or piperidine group. These drugs have the least incidence of neurological side effects and are less sedative. Examples are thioridazine, Mellaril; and mesoridazine, Serentil. (3) A piperazine group. These drugs are the most potent antipsychotics, the least sedating, and have the highest incidence of neurological side effects. Examples are fluphenazine, Permitil or Prolixin; trifluoperazine, Stelazine; perphenazine, Trilafon; and prochlorperazine, Compazine.

Historically, the use of rauwolfia root for mental illness dates back many centuries. Hindu or Indian physicians reflect upon the sedative and hypotensive properties of the plant. In India, rauwolfia is called "pagal-kadawa," or insanity remedy. Dr. Nathan Kline (1958) of New York was one of the first to study rauwolfia and reserpine, the active constituent of the rauwolfia root. Reserpine is believed to work as an antipsychotic by depleting the monoamines from their storage sites in the neurons. Reserpine is a weak, but effective antipsychotic agent. It has severe side effects, including hypotension, excessive salivation, sedation, and diarrhea. Today it is used infrequently, only as an antihypertensive.

The phenothiazine compounds were first synthesized in the late nineteenth century in Europe. They were isolated in an attempt to develop the aniline dyes such as methylene blue. In 1890, Ehrlich suggested the use of methylene blue in the treatment of psychoses (Baldessarini, 1980). Not until the late 1930s was the first phenothiazine to be used in medicine, promethazine (Phenergan), compounded. Promethazine was found to have strong sedative and antihistaminic properties. Later, it was discovered that promethazine caused a marked prolongation of the effects of barbiturates on sleep. In 1949, the French surgeon Laborit (1952) introduced promethazine into clinical use as an anesthetic potentiator. This prompted a search for other phenothiazine derivatives. In 1949-1950,

Charpentier synthesized chlorpromazine (Thorazine). Laborit and others using this compound found it to produce an "artificial hibernation." Separately, chlorpromazine produced a state of waking consciousness that resembled sleep, with a lack of interest in what was going on around the individual (Baldessarini 1980).

Courvoisier (1953) attributed many medical possibilities to chlorpromazine. These included ganglion blocking, adrenolytic, antifibrillatory, antiedemic, antipyretic, antischock, anticonvulsant, and antiementic. It was also found to be capable of potentiating the activity of analgesics and central depressant drugs.

Chlorpromazine was first used as a supplement with general anesthetic agents. Its calming effect on these surgical patients led to its use in psychiatry. It was introduced in the United States in 1954 for use as an antipsychotic. In the first year of its use, the hospitalized psychiatric patient population began to decrease. Prior to the introduction of the antipsychotic drugs, mental hospitals were synonymous with Bedlam. They were noisy, confused, and violent places with locked wards and restraints were the rule. Today, the residential population in mental hospitals is one quarter of what it was thirty years ago. Most patients stay for weeks or months, rather than years. The antipsychotic drugs revolutionized the treatment of schizophrenia.

Mechanism of Action

The exact mechanism of action of the antipsychotic drugs is unknown. A safe statement to say is that a significant part of their activity is linked to the ability to inhibit the dopaminergic function. The antipsychotic drugs act in the central nervous system at the reticular activating system (RAS), the limbic system (amygdala and hippocampus), the hypothalamus, cortex, and the corpus striatum. The RAS and limbic systems are involved in filtering environmental stimuli, prior to their reaching the cortex. The belief is that the antipsychotic drugs act to stop schizophrenic symptoms in the cortex, RAS, and limbic system. The effect on the hypothalamus accounts for the endocrinal changes which are produced by these drugs. The activity at the striatum contributes to the extrapyramidal effects.

All the antipsychotic drugs appear to inhibit dopaminergic function; however, they do not all act in the same manner or at the same site. The phenothiazines act to inhibit the dopamine sensitive enzyme adenyl cyclase. This can be correlated by comparing the concentrations of phenothiazine required to inhibit adenyl cyclase and the clinical potencies of the phenothiazines. The butyrophenones are not good inhibitors of the adenyl cyclase enzyme; however, they are very potent antischizophrenic drugs. The butyrophenones are believed to act presynaptically by preventing the release of dopamine from the nerve terminal endings and by blocking dopamine receptors. The dibenzoxazepines are good inhibitors of adenyl cyclase. The thioxanthenes appear to act in the same manner as the phenothiazines. The precise mechanism of action of the specific antipsychotic drug is not clear; however, they can act in one or more of the following manners: (1) inhibition of the enzyme adenyl cyclase; (2) block post-synaptic dopamine receptors; and (3) act on the presynaptic dopaminergic fibers, inhibiting the release of dopamine from the nerve terminal endings. In all cases, the resultant effect is the inhibition of dopaminergic function (Bachmann & Sherman, 1983).

The antipsychotic drugs cause four general types of side effects including (1) extrapyramidal symptoms, (2) anticholinergic effects, (3) sedation, and (4) orthostatic hypotension. The principal side effect of the antipsychotic drugs is the extrapyramidal action of these drugs. This effect is due to the blockage of dopamine receptors in the corpus striatum of the brain, causing an action that mimics Parkinsonian symptoms. The second group of side effects is due to the anticholinergic action of the antipsychotic drugs. An inverse relationship exists between the anticholinergic potency and the ability to elicit extrapyramidal side effects (Snyder, 1978). Sedation and hypotension are believed to be caused by the affinity of antipsychotic agents for alpha-noradrenergic receptors in the brain stem. The alpha-noradrenergic receptors are blocked by the phenothiazines. These alpha-receptors cause blood vessels to contract. Beta-adrenergic receptors cause blood vessels to dialate. The phenothiazines cause a reverse epinephrine effect.

Epinephrine normally acts in the opposite manner. This is important to the physician treating a phenothiazine overdose. In selecting a vasoconstrictor, epinephrine must not be used. Norepinephrine or phenylephrine may be used. The blockage of alpha-receptors by phenothiazine allows the epinephrine to reach only beta-receptors, thereby resulting in an epinephrine induced dialation of blood vessels. This effects a lowering of blood pressure and the sedative and hypotensive symptoms. In most cases, the different drugs and classes of drugs have similar antischizophrenic action; however, the degree of side effects varies. In Figure 9.1 is shown the relative differences in side effects for the antipsychotic drugs. In Figure 9.2 are given the generic and trade names together with dosage.

The effects of the phenothiazine can be divided into two categories: the short term or immediate action, and the longer term action (from 2 to 21 days). Within minutes after an injection, or an hour for an oral dose, the patient becomes calmer and more sedate. His/her rage or agitation subsides. A decrease occurs in overall reactivity to sensory stimuli, and conditioned mental reflexes are blocked. Sometime, within 2 to 21 days, hallucinations, delusions, and paranoia are suppressed. Also, thinking is slowed down.

The phenothiazines are available as tablets, long acting capsules, oral liquids, suppositories, and injections. The injectables are of two types, the aqueous based ones that have a short duration of action, and the depot ones that are released up to a several week period. The use of injectable drugs has some advantages and disadvantages. Advantages include (1) very rapid onset of activity, (2) the assurance of compliance with dosage regimen, and (3) prolonged activity with an individual dosage. Disadvantages include (1) cost, (2) pain, (3) and the need for an experienced person to administer the dose.

The phenothiazines are well absorbed from the gastrointestinal tract. They are rapidly distributed to all body tissues. The phenothiazine are metabolized by hydroxylation and conjugation. Biotransformation occurs in the liver. The use of barbiturates, or meprobamate, for their enzyme inducing

(Continued on page 180)

Antipsychotic Agent	Sedation	Extra-Pyramidal	Anti-Cholinergic	Ortho-Hypotension
PHENOTHIAZINE				
Aliphatic				
Chlorpromazine	high	low to moderate	moderate	high
Promazine	moderate	high	moderate	moderate
Triflupromazine	moderate	high	moderate to high	moderate
Piperidine				
Thioridazine	high	low	high	high
Mesoridazine	high	low	moderate	moderate
Piperazine				
Acetophenazine	moderate	high	moderate	low
Perphenazine	low to moderate	high	low to moderate	low
Prochlorperazine	moderate	high	low	low
Fluphenazine	low	high	low	low
Trifluoperazine	low	high	low	low
THIOXANTHENES				
Chlorprothixene	high	moderate	moderate	moderate
Thiothixene	low to moderate	moderate to high	low	low
BUTYROPHENONE				
Haloperidol	low	high	low	low
DIHYDROINDOLONE				
Molindone	low to moderate	moderate	low to moderate	low to moderate
DIBENZOXAZEPINE				
Loxapine	low to moderate	moderate to high	low to moderate	low to moderate

Figure 9.1. Relative differences in side effects for antipsychotic drugs.

Lass Generic	Trade	DOSAGE Equivalent	DOSAGE Daily Range
PHENOTHIAZINE:			
Aliphatic			
Chlorpromazine	Thorazine	100 mg	30-800 mg/day
Promazine	Sparine	200 mg	40-1200 mg
Triflupromazine	Vesprin	25 mg	60-150 mg
Piperdine			
Thioridazine	Mellaril	50-100 mg	150-800 mg
Mesoridazine	Serentil	50-100 mg	30-400 mg
Piperazine			
Acetophenazine	Tindal	20 mg	60-120 mg
Perphenazine	Trilafon	8 mg	12-64 mg
Prochlorperazine	Compazine	15 mg	15-150 mg
Fluphenazine	Permitil Prolixin	2 mg	1-40 mg
Trifluoperazine	Stelazine	5 mg	2-40 mg
THIOXANTHENES			
Chlorprothixene	Taractan	100 mg	75-600 mg
Thiothixene	Navane	4 mg	8-30 mg
BUTYROPHENONE			
Haloperidol	Haldol	2-4 mg	1-15 mg
DIHYDROINDOLONE			
Molindone	Moban	10 mg	15-225 mg
DIBENZOXAZEPINE			
Loxapine	Loxitane	10 mg	20-250 mg

Figure 9.2. Generic and trade names with dosage for antipsychotic drugs.

effects, may enhance phenothiazine metabolism. Excretion is relatively slow, and divided equally through the kidneys and the gastrointestinal tract. Metabolites may show up in the urine 18 months after the drug has been terminated. Chlorpromazine has 168 possible metabolities which may be detected in the urine (Goldsmith, 1977).

Adverse Effects Of Antipsychotic Drugs

The antipsychotics have a large dosage range and, therefore are relatively safe in adults. Fatalities are somewhat common in children who ingest large overdoses of these drugs. The following discussion of adverse effects is general in nature. Most of the drugs are similar enough to consider them as a group. Individual exceptions to this do occur; however, they will not be taken up in this text. Readers with specific questions about an individual drug should consult one of the reference sources noted elsewhere in this text.

Autonomic Reactions. All the antipsychotic drugs have anticholinergic activity. Previously identified was the variance in the anticholinergic effects of the different antipsychotic drugs. The mechanism of these effects is the blockage of access of acetylcholine to its receptor sites in the parasympathetic division of the autonomic nervous system. This explains the mechanism of many of the side effects. Some of the side effects constituting autonomic reactions include dry mouth, perspiration, constipation, urinary retention, ejaculation inhibition, and male impotence. The last two effects are especially common with thioridazine (Mellaril). Other autonomic effects reported include diarrhea, nausea, vomiting, paresthesia, anorexia, flushed faces, salivation, priapism, enuresis, and polyuria.

Ocular. Ocular effects include blurred vision, photophobia, miosis, and mydriasis. Patients with a history of glaucoma are warned to use caution, as these drugs can bring on the disorder in susceptible individuals. These effects are mediated by parasympathetic blockade, due to the anticholinergic effect of the drugs.

Drowsiness. The belief is that the drowsiness experienced with these drugs is caused by the effects on the reticular activating system by their ability to relax muscles and by their ability to lower blood pressure. A tolerance to the drowsiness usually develops, and the symptoms go away in about a week. Some individuals will experience weakness or fatigue.

Allergic Reactions. Many of the adverse effects of drugs are known as "allergic" reactions. Oftentimes, a person taking a drug will report being "allergic"; however, he/she may be experiencing a normal or common side effect of the drug. For example, a person taking a phenothiazine drug may experience a dry mouth and believe that he/she is allergic.

Allergic reactions do manifest many adverse effects such as hives, itching, rash, swelling, and fainting. Allergies happen when the body reacts in an altered way to a specific stimulus. In order for a drug allergy to occur, the individual has had to have taken the drug into his/her body at some prior time. The absorbed drug then becomes an **antigen,** or a substance which stimulates the formation of **antibodies.** The antibody combines with the antigen to render the antigen inert, or to facilitate another body mechanism to destroy it. This antigen-antibody system is a vital part of the immunological system that the body uses to protect itself against disease-causing organisms.

As has been stated, the first dose of a drug will not cause an allergic response. However, a cross sensitivity can occur to a chemically related drug. After a drug enters circulation, it, and its metabolities, become attached to a plasma protein. A drug can become an antigen when it is in this protein-bound form. The drug-plasma protein antigen passes into the lymphatic circulation and the lymph nodes. White blood cells, known as **lymphocytes,** are found in the lymph nodes. These lymphocytes produce the antibodies. The newly formed antibodies enter into the blood circulation as part of the plasma protein. The allergic response is due to the combining of an antigen and an antibody. When an individual takes a dose of the antigenic drug, it attaches to plasma protein, and eventually to the antibody. If the antibody is attached to the cell surface, the antigen-antibody combination damages the cell membrane, resulting in the release of histamine. Histamine is responsible for many of the locally observed allergic responses.

A very severe and rapidly occurring allergic response is called ***anaphylactic shock.*** It is a systemic antibody response. Anaphylactic shock is characterized by a lowering of blood pressure, tissue swelling, or edema. It causes constriction of the muscles of the larynx and bronchials, resulting in wheezing and choking; and contraction of the muscles of the gut, resulting in diarrhea and vomiting. Anaphylaxis can be fatal.

The allergic or toxic effects of the antipsychotic drugs on the blood system include the following: (1) ***Agranulocytosis,*** in which a reduced or no bone marrow production occurs of the white blood cells, known as polymorphonuclear leukocytes. These cells function to destroy bacteria. In their absence, the individual is at risk of an infection. (2) ***Eosinophilia,*** a type of white blood cells, which have an affinity towards antigen-antibody reactions. An increase of eosinophils is indicative of an allergic condition. (3) ***Leukopenia*** is the suppression of all white blood cells. (4) ***Purpura*** is a discoloration of the skin. In addition to allergy as its cause, it may be the result of a severe infection or a bruise. Drug allergies may cause thrombocytes or platelets (small cells that are important in blood coagulation) to be destroyed, resulting in the skin discoloration. (5) ***Anemia*** is a reduction of hemoglobin. It can be caused by allergic bone marrow depression or the destruction of red blood cells by antigen-antibody reactions to the cell wall. Specific forms of anemia that are found with antipsychotic drugs are aplastic anemia (caused by underdeveloped bone marrow) and hemolytic anemia (due to active destruction of red cells within the circulation).

Cardiovascular Reactions. *Postural* or *orthostatic hypo-tension* are terms describing a condition which occurs when a person stands up after being in a reclined state. The symptoms include dizziness, unsteadiness, lightheadedness, and fainting. This condition is caused by a temporary insufficiency of blood to the brain. The body's mechanism to compensate for this effect includes an increase in heart rate, constriction of the blood vessels, and an increase in strength of heart contractions. The phenothiazines interfere with this mechanism by altering the vascular reflexes in the brain stem, and by their adrenergic effects on the heart and large blood vessels.

Other cardiovascular effects of the antipsychotics include hypertension, tachycardia (especially with a large increase in dosage), bradycardia, cardiac arrest, pulmonary edema, lightheadedness, faintness, and shock (a severe hypotensive reaction).

The phenothiazines can impose a direct myocardial depression, and may induce cardiomegaly (an enlargening or overgrowth of the heart, sometimes referred to as cardiac hypertrophy), congestive heart failure, and refractory arrhythmias.

Dermatologic Side Effects. The antipsychotic drugs may cause an effect known as photosensitivity. Two possible mechanisms for this reaction are (1) the circulating drug-protein complex which passes through the capillaries to the skin, and upon exposure to sunlight, a chemical reaction takes place, causing a severe sunburn; and (2) the antipsychotic drug may interfere with the production of melanin; the second is not an allergic effect. This photosensitivity reaction is reported in 3% of the users of chlorpromazine (Kastrup, Olin, & Schwach, 1986).

In rare instances, skin pigmentation changes have occurred, i.e., a darkening to a slate gray color. These changes occur mainly in female individuals who have been on long-term, high dosages. Other dermatological effects include rashes, often of a red or purple dot-like description; these are referred to as petechia. Urticaria, sometimes called hives, are elevated patch-like areas of the skin. This is an allergic reaction. Dry skin, edema, seborrhea, eczema, and hair loss are other reported dermatological effects of the antipsychotic drugs.

Extrapyramidal Effects. The extrapyramidal effects are often dose related, and can be divided into five categories:

1. *Akathisia*—a discomforting feeling of insomnia, restlessness, and compulsion to walk about with a marked inability to sit still. These symptoms are first observed in 2 to 4 weeks, with a peak in 6 to 10 weeks, and then a decline in 12 to 16 weeks.

2. **Akinesia**—diminished muscular movements, weakness, unusual numbness or tingling sensations. The symptoms are first seen in 0 to 2 weeks, with a peak in 1 week. They decline in 3 to 4 weeks.

3. **Dystonia**—uncoordinated jerking or spastic movements of the neck, face, eyes, tongue, torso, arm or leg muscles. The following are descriptions of the major dystonias:

   a. **Oculogyric Crisis.** The eyes roll backward in their sockets. The eye muscles become fixed, causing a painful upward gaze. The individual cannot control his/her eye movements.

   b. **Torticollis.** The neck twists sidewards, and the tongue protrudes from the mouth. The net result is the head is involuntarily turned to one side. The individual may have difficulty swallowing.

   c. **Opisthotonos.** The individual takes on a position in which his/her head and heels bend backwards, and the midsection bows forward. He/she drools and has spasms of the back muscles. Symptoms are seen in the first few days of taking the drug, with a peak in 1 week. They decline in 2 weeks.

4. **Rigidity**—The individual develops abnormally high muscle tone or tension, experienced as a "cogwheel" resistance to movement. He/she has unchanging blank facial expressions (called masked facies) and a stiff mechanical gait. The symptoms are first seen in ½ to 2 weeks, and peak in 2 to 4 weeks. They decline in 5 to 10 weeks.

5. **Tremor**—The individual experiences fine, quivering motions, caused by alternating rapid contractions, especially of the arm muscles. These symptoms are experienced within ½ to 2 weeks, and peak in 2 to 6 weeks. They decline in 8 to 16 weeks.

Extrapyramidal symptoms are managed through the use of barbiturates, antipsychotic dose reduction, and anticholinergic antiparkinsonian drugs. The most common drugs used are shown in Figure 9.3.

Generic Name	Trade Name	Average Daily Dose
Benztropine mesylate	Cogentin	0.5-6.0 mg
Diphenhydramine	Benadryl	50-200 mg
Trihexyphenidyl	Artane, Tremin	2-10 mg
Procyclidine	Kemadrin	10-20 mg
Biperidin	Akineton	2-8 mg

Figure 9.3. Drugs and dosage for treating extrapyramidal symptoms.

Tardive Dyskinesia. Tardive dyskinesia is a serious, often irreversible side effect, that may accompany the use of antipsychotic drugs. Estimates are that 56% of chronically hospitalized individuals and 43% of outpatients receiving moderate to high doses for over a year develop this syndrome. The term tardive means late onset, and the term dyskinesia refers to abnormal movements. Tardive dyskinesia is characterized by rhythmical involuntary movements of the tongue, face, mouth or jaw (i.e., protruded tongue, puffed cheeks, puckered mouth, chewing movements, and licking). Sometimes the individual also may experience involuntary movements of the extremities.

The mechanism of this side effect may help in understanding how the psychotropic drugs work. The antipsychotic drugs block dopamine. After a long period of dopamine blockade, the dopamine receptors become ultrasensitive and respond to lesser amounts of the neurotransmitters. In response, the dopamine receptors increase in number, with eventual, irreversible damage to the synaptic membranes of the dopaminergic neurons. Next, the dopamine tracts become even more sensitive, and begin to fire in an abnormal manner. This leads to the abnormal movements of tradive dyskinesia. The syndrome is most prevalent in the elderly, especially women. No known cure exists; however, sometimes the syndrome will totally or partially remit. The antipsychotic drug may actually mask the symptoms of tardive dyskinesia. The manifestations in Tardive dyskinesia are summarized in Figure 9.4.

Antipsychotic drugs should be prescribed in a conservative manner, with careful consideration of this serious side effect. The smallest dosage and the shortest duration of treatment may be helpful in safeguarding against tardive dyskinesia.

Adverse Behavioral Effects. In a few instances, an individual taking antipsychotic drugs may react to the drug by going into a psychotic state. Reasons for this are not clear. Other behavioral effects include exacerbation of the psychotic symptoms, including hallucinations; catatonic-like states; phobias; lethargy; restlessness; hyperactivity; agitation; nocturnal confusion; toxic confusional states; bizarre dreams; depression; despondency; euphoria; and excitement.

Respiratory Effects. Side effects of antipsychotic drugs include spasm of the larynx and bronchi. Sometimes, the individual experiences difficult or labored breathing, known as dyspnea.

Endocrine Effects. Endocrine effects include lactation and moderate breast engorgement in females; galactorrhea, an excessive or spontaneous flow of milk; mastalgia, pain in the mammary glands; amenorrhea, absence or abnormal stoppage of the menses; menstrual irregularities; gynecomastia, excessive development of the male mammary glands, even to the functional state; changes in libido; hypoglycemia or hyperglycemia, lowered or raised blood sugar; raised cholesterol levels; and pituitary tumors. Chlorpromazine has been known to block ovulation and suppress the estrogen cycle. It also causes infertility and a false pregnancy.

Other Adverse Effects. Cases of sudden death have been reported from the phenothiazines. The apparent cause of this phenomenon is believed to be cardiac arrest or asphyxia, due to failure of the cough reflex. Many individuals respond with increased or decreased appetite and weight. Eating excessively or craving all kinds of food, a disorder known as polyphagia, is sometimes manifested with the administration of these drugs.

Body Part/Muscle	Characteristic
Ocular	Blinking, spasms of lid or lash
Facial	Grimaces, tics
Oral	Cheek puffing, sucking, pouting, lips smacking, and puckering
Masticatory	Chewing, lateral jaw movements
Lingual	Tongue protruding, recurring involuntary irregular jerking movements
Pharyngeal	Involuntary swallowing, abnormal sounds
Neck	Tortocollis (wryneck, a contracted state of the cervical muscles, producing twisting of the neck and an unnatural position of the head); retrocollis (spasmodic wryneck in which the head is drawn directly backward)
Trunk	Shrugging, pelvic thrusting, rocking
Limbs	Recurring involuntary irregular jerking movements of the fingers and toes, flexing or torsion of the wrists and ankles, tapping

Figure 9.4. Manifestations in tardine thyskinesia.

Here the individual has developed a chemically induced bulimia. Some individuals, especially women, experience an abnormal growth of hair, known as hirsutism.

SUMMARY

Schizophrenia is a thought disorder. Many researchers point towards organic, rather than interpersonal or psychological factors in the etiology of schizophrenia; however, no pathology has been discovered in the brain tissue. The most probable hypothesis for a mechanism of schizophrenia is the dopamine hypothesis. The support for this hypothesis comes from an understanding of the neuroleptic drug mechanism. The antipsychotic drugs act by blocking the dopamine receptor sites in the brain. The use of the antipsychotic drugs has allowed the hospitalized psychiatric patient population to greatly decrease. Today, the residential population in mental hospitals is one-quarter of what it was thirty years ago. The antipsychotic drugs revolutionized the treatment of schizophrenia. The principle side effect of the antipsychotic drugs is the extrapyramidal action of these drugs. Tardive dyskinesia is a serious, often irreversible side effect of the antipsychotic drugs. It may effect as many as 56% of the hospitalized and 43% of the outpatients receiving moderate to high doses for over a year.

CHAPTER

PAIN AND
ANALGESIC DRUGS

Pain is the single most prevalent sensory symptom experienced by humankind. It is a warning that something is wrong or something needs attention. The body responds to pain through reflex actions, i.e., when something very hot touches the skin, the reflex response is to quickly remove the body part from heat source. This process happens so rapidly that the individual may not have conscious knowledge of the event until it has already happened. Pain is a necessary and important protective sensation.

Pain also can be a debilitating event. Chronic, malignant pain, such as is experienced in cancer, does not serve as a warning; the disease state is usually well advanced, prior to the sensation of severe pain. To reconcile the two different experiences of pain is difficult.

Pain and its treatment has plagued humanity since the beginning of recorded history. Early humans thought pain to be an evil spirit that had entered into the body. Attempts to remedy pain included boring holes in the afflicted individuals head or body and rituals to appease or scare away the evil spirits.

Pain is such an individual experience that it defies definition. Merskey and Spear in *Pain: Psychological and Psychiatric Aspects* (1967), suggested that pain was an unpleasant experience usually associated with tissue damage.

Sternbach (1974) offered the idea of pain being an abstract concept that is (1) a personal, private sensation of hurt; (2) a harmful stimulus which signals current or impending tissue damage; (3) a pattern of responses which operate to protect the organism from harm.

Swonger and Constantine (1983) stated that "pain, especially chronic pain and its management, play an important role in a person's psychological status." (p. 331).

What becomes clear is that pain is a personal and subjective experience. Merskey pointed out that "poena" in Latin, "poine" in Greek, "peine" in French are words suggesting punishment. The Greek and French word also indicates bodily or mental suffering.

Pain can be viewed as having both a physiological and emotional component. This accounts for the differing experience of pain by people based upon cause. For example, the athlete who is injured during an event may be unaware of the pain until a later time. Under emotional conditions, an individual may injure his/herself and not feel the pain. To illustrate this point, I relate the following incident. While meeting with my wife's attorney during a heated divorce settlement, I stood up and sprained my ankle. I walked to the elevator, then to my car, drove to my office, and got ready to see a client before I noticed my swollen ankle and pain associated with the injury. People also have differing thresholds of pain. Some seem to handle a great deal of pain, while others become extremely anxious at the thought of pain.

Some clinicians use the **PQRST approach** in organizing their evaluation of an individual's pain. The letter P representing the "precipitating" factors, i.e., emotions, stress, infection, posture, and exertion. The Q stands for the "quality" of the pain, i.e., sharpness, dullness, throbbing, prickling, burning, or pulsing. The letter R represents "region" or "radiation", i.e., lower back and radiating to the left leg. The S is for the individual's subjective evaluation of the "severity", i.e., can't sleep or became unconscious. The letter T represents the "temporal" nature of the pain, i.e., time of day, relationship to activities or meals, and acute or chronic.

Pain has a broad range, or spectrum. It might be the mild, acute pain of a cut or scratch, or the deep, agonizing pain of cancer. Pain can be acute or chronic. Acute pain usually infers that sudden sharp experience that subsides with the healing process. Chronic pain is associated with ongoing suffering, with emotional, physical, and economic stress of the individual and his/her family.

NEUROPHYSIOLOGY OF PAIN

Melzack and Wall (1965) proposed what has become known as the "gate-control" theory of pain. It includes elements from two earlier theories, the "specificity" theory and the "pattern" theory. The **specificity** theory proposes that a mosaic of specific pain receptors for sensations of cold, warmth, touch, and pain transmit impulses from the periphery to a pain center in the brain, the basis of pain being determined by the specific qualities of these cutaneous receptors.

The **pattern theory** opposes the idea of pain having a specific set of receptors. The theory proposes that the stimulus intensity and the central summation of the input, and not the peripheral stimulation, are the determining factors of pain. It also proposes that pain does not have a specific set of receptors.

In the **gate-control theory,** the proposal is that pain is controlled by a parallel set of fibers, the large fiber having an inhibitory effect of pain perception, and the small fiber having a facilitating effect. The substantia gelatinosa, a nerve center located in the spinal cord, and the root and nucleus of the 5th cranial nerve serve as gates which have the ability to open or close. The effect of the opening or closing increases or decreases the flow of nerve impulses from the stimulus to the brain. Two factors influence the amount of opening or closing of the gate. The amount of input from the peripheral nerves and the extent of the inhibitory influence from the brain. The thalamus serves as a second or upper gate to control the projection of pain. The chemical substances involved in the regulation of the gates of the pain pathways include peptides and amine transmitters. A peptide is a compound containing amino acids which is the product of hydrolyzing a protein. Somatic pain at the lower gate is controlled by the peptide enkephalin and the amine serotonin. A peptide known as substance P is released by incoming pain signals. Substance P in turn activates secondary impulses in the substantia gelatinosa. The release of substance P can be inhibited by enkephalin. Serotonin fibers descending from the brain control enkephalin release. Cranial pain is controlled by norepinephrine terminals.

The criteria of an ideal analgesic would include

1. effectiveness when administered orally,

2. causing rapid activity upon ingestion,

3. be effective in controlling pain,

4. not develop a tolerance,

5. not result in physical or psychological addiction,

6. not cause respiratory depression,

7. have few adverse or side effects, and

8. have an antidote available.

NARCOTIC ANALGESICS

The milky exudate of the incised, unripe seed capsules of the poppy plant, Papaver Somniferum, is known as opium. The word opium is derived from the Greek word meaning "juice." The effects of opium date back to the Sumerians. However, Theophastus, in the third century B.C., is acknowledged as the first to mention opium in writing (Jaffe & Martin, 1980). In 1803, the German chemist Serturner isolated and described an opium alkaloid that he named morphine, after the Greek god of dreams (Rodman, Karch, Boyd, & Smith, 1985). Morphine's chemical structure was not identified until 1925 by Gulland and Robinson (Feldman, 1984). Opium contains some twenty alkaloids. The isolation of codeine by Robiquet in 1832, and papaverine by Merck in 1848, led to the use of pure alkaloids by the mid-nineteenth century (Jaffe, 1980). The invention in 1853 of the hypodermic syringe by Pravaz, and the development of the hollow needle by Alexander Wood solved the problem of accurate administration of these drugs (Feldman & Quenzer, 1984). The early widespread use of opium in the United States is attributed to the influx of opium-smoking Chinese laborers, the extensive use of the drug during the Civil War, and the lack of restrictions of the drug during the early part of this century.

Mechanism Of Action

In 1974, two independent research teams identified a peptide in brain extracts that showed opiate-like activity. The family of **endogenous peptides** identified to have opiate-like activity is called **endorphins,** from "endo" denoting endogenous, and "orphin" from the suffix of the opiate alkaloids. These peptides have the same pharmacological effects as opium. They produce analgesia (Belluzi et al., 1976), inhibit electrical stilmulation induced muscle stimulation in laboratory animals (Kraulis et al., 1975), physical dependence (Wei & Loh, 1976a), and depress neuron firing in areas of the brain and spinal cord (Lamotte et al., 1976).

Opium alkaloids act as agonists, interacting with the receptors. The receptors have binding sites that are widely distributed throughout the central nervous system. The receptors are not evenly distributed; however, there seems to be a correlation between distribution site and analgesic effect. Furthermore, these sites show an affinity for the opium alkaloids which corresponds with their activity. In other words, codeine has less of an affinity for the receptor sites than morphine, which produces a more potent pharmacologic effect than codeine.

The opium receptor sites seem to be the normal sites of activity for the endorphin or endogenous morphine-like substances. A ligand is a molecule that donates the necessary electrons to form bonds. It usually is a neurotransmitter or drug molecule that is bound to a receptor molecule. The endogenous opiate receptor ligands include two pentapeptides called met-enkephalin and leu-enkephalin and a protein called beta-endorphin. These substances are highly concentrated along the pain pathways, the substantia gelatinosa, the hypothalamus, and the limbic system (Swonger & Constantine, 1983). Beta-endorphin is the most potent of the endogenous opium alkaloid substances found to date.

The discovery of the opium alkaloid receptors and the naturally-occurring polypeptides has helped researchers to understand the effects of the narcotics; however, a great deal is not known regarding the mechanism of pain modulation. Researchers have postulated that the exogenous opium alkaloids and the endogenous enkephalins have an effect of altering the release of neurotransmitters in neurons stimulated by pain (Chereson & Fudge, 1980; Feldman & Quenzer, 1984; Swonger & Constantine, 1983).

To date, five categories of opioid receptors are known. The actions of current narcotic analgesics can be defined by the activity of three of these receptor types. The first of these receptor types, known as Mu, is involved in analgesia, euphoria, respiratory effects, and physical dependence. The second receptor type, known as Kappa, mediates spinal analgesia, sedation, and miosis. The third receptor type, Sigma, is responsible for dysphoria (excessive pain, anguish, and agitation); psychotomimetic effects, i.e., hallucinations; and respiratory and vasomotor stimulation.

In Figure 10.1 are listed two selective opioid drugs together with their affinity and activity at three receptor types.

Morphine has its activity primarily at the Mu site, and to a lesser degree at the Kappa site. It is a narcotic agonist, being effective in producing analgesia, respiratory depression, euphoria, and physical dependence. It also causes some sedation and miosis. Pentazocine (Talwin) is an agonist-antagonist. It binds to the Mu site, competing with other substances for the sites. This makes it a competative antagonist

Drug	Mu	Kappa	Sigma
Morphine	High affinity High activity	Moderate affinity	No affinity High activity
Pentazocine (Talwin)	Moderate affinity No activity	High affinity High activity	High affinity High activity

Figure 10.1. Morphine and pentazocine together with their affinity and activity at three receptor types.

at the Mu site. It shows strong agonistic activity at the Kappa and Sigma receptor sites. Pentazocine was introduced in 1967 in an attempt to market an effective and potent analgesic with little or no addiction potential. It has been found to be effective in relieving moderate pain, but less effective against severe pain. Due to its antagonistic action at the Mu receptor, pentazocine is not used with other opioid analgesics, in order to avoid an acute withdrawal syndrome. Pentazocine's side effect include sedation and psychotomimetic effects, such as nightmares and hallucinations. Upon frequent and repeated use, tolerance to pentazocine has been reported; however, whether this tolerance is due to the degree of tolerance developed with the morphine-like narcotics is unclear.

The narcotic analgesic are readily absorbed from the gastronintestinal tract, and after subcutaneous or intramuscular injection. Their effectiveness is far greater after injection than after oral administration. Both codeine and levorphanol are about 60% as effective orally as by injection. Methadone and oxycodone are one-half as effective orally as by injection. The other narcotic analgesics are considerably less effective when administered orally, i.e., morphine and oxymorphone are 1/6th as effective, hydromorphone is 1/5th as effective, meperidine is 1/4th, and pentazocine is 1/3rd as effective. Orally administered doses have a slower onset, a lower peak effect, and a more prolonged duration of action than parenteral doses.

In classifying the narcotic drugs, a helpful procedure is to break them into groups as follows: the agonists, which show activity at the opiate receptors; the antagonists, which block the opiate receptor and inhibit the pharmacological activity of the agonist; and the third group which are both agonists and antagonists. Narcotics are divided three ways according to origin: naturally occurring, i.e., codeine and morphine; semi-synthetic analogues, i.e., hydromorphone and oxycodone; and synthetic compounds, i.e., meperidine and methadone. In Figure 10.2 are listed narcotic analgesics and antagonists.

Drug Dependence

An important aspect of narcotic use is drug dependence. Jaffe (1980) defined drug abuse as self-administered use of any drug in a way that digresses from the accepted medical or social standard within the culture. Feldman & Quenzer (1984) stated that drug abuse increases within a society during times of rapid social change. The most vulnerable members of the society are the groups that are most effected by these changes and, therefore, are the ones most likely to abuse drugs. This includes the adolescent population, children and adult children of alcoholics, children of drug abusers, people of the lowest socio-economic levels, and individual's who, for whatever reason, have an addictive tendency.

Three components involved in compulsive drug use are tolerance, physical dependence, and psychological dependence. *Tolerance* has been defined as being an ever-increasing resistance to the drug's desired effects, often, but not always, after prolonged administration. To continue the same effects, the drug has to be administered in larger and larger quantities. Tolerance develops with the natural and semisynthetic opium alkaloids after just a few days of use. Some of the tolerance to morphine is due to an increase in the rate of metabolism; however, the majority is of the pharmacodynamic type; that is, the cells of the body become accustomed to the drug.

Physical dependence is an adaptive or abnormal state produced by repeated drug administration, which results in the need for continued use of the drug in order to prevent a withdrawal syndrome. *Withdrawal syndrome* is a complex series of physiological and psychological symptoms charac-teristic of the specific drug.

Drug	Proprietary Name	Equivalent Dose (mg) IM	Equivalent Dose (mg) ORAL	T ½ (hours)	Dependence (compared to morphine)
Analgesics					
Morphine		10	60	2 to 3	—
Levorphanol	Levo-Dromoran	2	4	1.2	same
Hydromorphone	Dilaudid	1.5	8	4	same
Oxymorphone	Numorphan	1	6	—	same
Methadone	Dolophine	10	20	22	same
Meperidine	Demerol	75	300	3 to 4	same
Fentanyl	Sublimaze	0.1	—	—	same
Codeine	Codone	120	200	3 to 4	less
Oxycodone	Percodan* Percocet	—	30	—	same
Propoxyphene	Darvon Darvocet	—	300	6 to 12	less
Hydrocodone	Dicodid	—	5 to 10	3.8	less
Pentazocine	Talwin	60	180	2 to 3	less
Antagonists					
Buprenorphine	Buprenex	0.3	—	2.2	less
Nalbuphine	Nubain	10	—	5	less
Butorphanol	Stadol	2	—	3	less

* Active narcotic ingredient.

Figure 10.2. Narcotic analgesics and antagonists.

Physical dependence is characterized by craving or an intense drive for a drug that the person believes to be necessary for a sense of well-being. Jaffe (1980) called this state "psychic craving" or "compulsion," and others frequently refer to it as "habituation." *Addiction* or "true addiction" refers to the physical and psychological state that drives individuals to compulsive drug use. Psychological dependence is a state wherein a person takes drugs in an attempt to create a state of well-being. This person is unable to create a state of well-being from within due to early psychological injuries. Some people turn to drugs because they learned early in life that drugs can be used to cover up pain. This is often the case in the child of an alcoholic. In order for the individual to not feel the loss of well-being or the state of "fragmentation," he/she may turn to drugs. Drugs can effectively create a "pseudostate of well-being"; however, since a tolerance occurs with most of the drugs for this purpose, this state is not long lasting and requires increasing use of the drug to maintain it. A more indepth discussion of the psychological dynamics of substance abuse can be found in the chapter on substance abuse.

The belief is that tolerance to the opiates is a biochemical or neuronal compensation, and not a drug-receptor interaction. Morphine is thought to produce a blockade of dopamine receptors, a possible link to the early tolerance effect. After several days of morphine use, the dopamine turn-over returns to normal; this helps to explain long-term tolerance. With long term use, dopamine receptors become supersensitive and opiate receptors subsensitive (Swonger & Constantine, 1983).

The earliest hypothesis of the mechanism of tolerance and physical dependence of opiates was proposed by Himmelsbach in 1943. He suggested that acute administration of morphine disturbs the body's homeostasis." Then some adaptive mechanism causes a compensatory action that restores the "homeostasis." Tolerance occurs when the homeostasis has been restored. Therefore, the administration of the same size dosage no longer produces the same effects. The withdrawal of the drug stops all effects; however, the adaptive mechanism is still functioning. It overcompensates and produces a new disturbance in homeostasis that manifests, as withdrawal.

Several feasible mechanisms for the development of tolerance have been suggested. Collier (1968) and Jaffe and Sharpless (1968) proposed that a decrease in neurotransmission may lead to a "pharmacological denervation supersensitivity;" that is, more receptors are formed to offset the reduced activity.

Martin (1970) proposed a bypass or alternate nerve pathway that compensates for the inhibited one. When the drug is withdrawn, both pathways are active, thereby creating an overactivity that correlates to withdrawal.

Others have proposed mechanisms dealing with enzyme synthesis and neurotransmitter balance in the synaptic cleft (Feldman & Quenzer, 1984).

Adverse Effects Of Narcotic Analgesics

Central Nervous System. The most common symptoms are drowsiness and mental clouding or confusion. These effects may be desirable in certain situations, such as bed ridden individuals with severe pain. Other central nervous system effects include nausea and vomiting, cough suppression, euphoria, and respiratory depression. Nausea and vomiting are caused by the direct stimulation of the emetic chemoreceptor trigger zone in the medulla. The most dangerous effect of the narcotic analgesic is respiratory depression. Respiratory depression is brought on by a decreased responsiveness of the brain stem respiratory centers to increases in carbon dioxide.

Cardiovascular. The alpha-adrenergic receptors are depressed, producing peripheral vasodilation and a decreased capacity of the cardiovascular system to respond to changes in postural position; therefore, orthostatic hypotension and fainting occur.

Gastrointestinal Tract. The narcotic drugs cause an increase in the tone of the gastrointestinal tract, especially the sphincters. As a consequence, the motility is decreased, the evacuation time is increased, and secretions are decreased. Peristalsis is inhibited, causing more delay and allowing more water to be removed from the feces. This all leads up to constipation. Opium and its alkaloids are used to treat diarrhea.

Other Effects. Narcotics may cause an increased sphincter tone in the bladder, resulting in urinary retention and depression of the cough reflex, making them useful as antitussives.

The most common pharmacological effects of the common narcotics are their analgesic and antitussive effects. The common side effects include constipation, vomiting, physical dependence, respiratory depression, and sedation. In Figure 10.3 are listed pharmacological effects and side effects of the most frequently used narcotics.

	PHARMACOLOGICAL EFFECTS	
Drug	**Analgesic**	**Antitussive**
Morphine*		
Codeine	less	same
Meperidine	same	less
Propoxyphene	less	none

	SIDE EFFECTS				
Drug	**Consti-pation**	**Vomiting**	**Physical Depend**	**Respir. Depres.**	**Sedation**
Morphine*					
Codeine	less	less	less	less	less
Meperidine	less	same	same	same	same
Propoxyphene	less	less	less	less	less

* As the standard.

Figure 10.3. Pharmacological effects and side effects of the most frequently used narcotics (Adapted from Kastrup, Olin, & Schwach, 1986).

Drug Interactions. Several drug interactions are important to mention. The combination of meperidine and a monoamine oxidase inhibitor can precipitate an unpredictable, severe, and fatal reaction. Therefore, meperidine is not recommended if an individual is on or has received MAOIs, such as phenelzine (Nardil), in the last 14 days. In some individuals these reactions have been characterized by coma, severe respiratory depression, cyanosis, and hypotension. Other reactions include hyperexcitability, convulsions, tachycardia, and hypertension. Respiratory depression, hypotension, profound sedation, or coma have occurred with the concurrent administration of narcotics and general anesthetics, antihistamines, phenothiazines, barbiturates, tranquilizers, sedative-hypnotics, antidepressants, and other CNS depressants, including alcohol. These actions are often synergistic; caution and reduced doses should be used when these drugs are combined. Pentazocine, butorphanol, or nalbuphine may cause people addicted to heroin, or on methadone, to experience withdrawal symptoms. CNS toxicity (confusion, disorientation, respiratory depression, seizures, and apnea) have been reported when morphine is taken along with cimetidine (Tagamet).

NON-NARCOTIC ANALGESICS

The drugs categorized under the "umbrella heading" **non-narcotic analgesics** include several groups of compounds that are not chemically related. These drugs are classified as non-narcotic because they do not bind the opiate receptors and have a different mechanism of action than the narcotic analgesics. Many of the drugs discussed in this section have two pharmacological activities in common, other than the ability to produce analgesia. These are anti-inflammatory activity and antipyretic (fever-reducing) action. An **antipyretic,** aspirin-like drug reduces body temperature during a febrile state. The **anti-inflammatory** activity of these drugs makes them useful in treating musculoskeletal disorders, such as rheumatoid arthritis, osteorthritis, and ankylosing spondylitis. **Arthritis** is a general term to describe a condition involving inflammation of a joint. **Rheumatoid arthritis** is a chronic, systemic inflammatory disease. It usually affects the joint in the hands, legs, feet, wrists, or ankles. The synovial membrane becomes inflamed in rheumatoid arthritis, and with time a pannus or overgrowth of connective tissue forms over the membrane.

A *synovial joint* is one with freely movable parts. The bones in this type of joint, sometimes called diarthrosis, have a space between them, the joint cavity. The cavity is filled with a fluid called synovial fluid. Synovial joints perform four functions: (1) flexion, a bending motion that decreases the angle between bones; (2) extension, a straightening motion that increases the angle between bones; (3) abduction, a movement away from the midline of the body; and (4) adduction, a movement toward the midline of the body. Six types of synoval joints exist. They are (1) gliding joints, i.e., the wrists; (2) hinge joints, i.e., the elbow; (3) pivot joints, i.e., the joint at the proximal end of the radius and ulna; (4) condyloid joints, such as the joint between the wrist and the bones of the forearm; (5) saddle joints, like the joint between the wrist and the metacarpal bone of the thumb; and (6) ball-and-socket joints, such as the hip.

Osteoarthritis refers to a localized degenerative joint disease. The more correct terminology for this disorder is "degenerative joint disease" (DJD), as it is characterized by degeneration and eventual loss of cartilage and bone enlargement at the joint. Degenerative joint disease is divided into primary and secondary forms. *Primary DJD* has no known precipitating cause and symptoms show up when individuals are in their fifties or sixties. *Secondary DJD* results from an injury, such as a fracture, bad posture, overuse of a joint, or even chronic overweight. It manifests earlier in life.

Ankylosing spondylitis is a type of rheumatoid arthritis that attacks the spine. It is a rather rare disease that is six times more prevalent in females than males. Symptoms may occur between the ages of 15 and 40. Early symptoms include lower back pain, stiffness, and pain in the hips, buttocks and shoulders (Chereson & Fudge, 1980).

Mechanism of Action

Considerable progress has been made in the area of identifying the mechanism of action of the the non-narcotic analgesic drugs. The common link between these agents appears to be their ability to interfere with the biochemical synthesis of prostaglandins. In 1930 two American gynecologists, Kurzok and Lieb, discovered that upon exposure to human semen, strips of the human uterus relax or contract. Several years later, Goldblatt (1935) in England and von Euler (1936, 1973) in Sweden, independently described vasopressor activity and smooth-muscle-contracting in seminal fluid and the reproductive glands. Euler identified and named the active substance **prostaglandin.** More than 20 years was needed for the technological knowledge to identify a whole family of prostaglandin substances.

The prostaglandins are 20-carbon unsaturated fatty acids found in nearly all human and animal tissues. They appear to play an important role in cellular function and cellular metabolism. In humans, their precursor, arachidonic acid, can be found in the phospholipids of cell membranes. The arachidonic acid is either ingested from animal tissue or synthesized from dietary linoleic acid. The initiation of a trauma, stress, or excitement activates the release of the precursor from the phospholipids, with the help of the enzyme phospholipase A_2. After being released, the arachidonic acid is transformed into prostaglandin. The biosynthesis of prostaglandin is a complex step-by-step production enabled by a complex of enzymes: (1) starting with a trauma, the cell membrane releases the precursor from the phospholipids; (2) under the influence of the enzyme phospholipase A_2, arachidonic acid is formed; (3) then transformed into endoperoxides with the aid of the enzyme cyclooxygenase; and finally (4) in the presence of various enzymes, the endoperoxides are transformed into prostaglandin.

The analgesic mechanism of prostaglandin is best understood by looking at the role prostaglandin plays. During fever, inflammation, or pain, prostaglandin levels are increased. The prostaglandins cause chemical or mechanical stimulation by sensitizing the pain receptors, leading to the experience of pain.

Prostaglandins are involved in the mechanism of fever through their effect as endogenous pyrogens. The endogenous pyrogens are stimulated in the brain, especially the hypothalamus. The **hypothalamus** is the temperature control center or thermostat for the body. It establishes an alteration of the normal "set point" of body temperature called fever. **Fever** results from infections, inflammation, allergic reactions, tissue damage, malignancies, dehydration, and other disease states. These conditions cause the body temperature to rise by stimulating the release of endogenous pyrogens. The pyrogens travel to the hypothalamus via the circulation and trigger the release of prostaglandins. Prostaglandins cause a change in the set point. Aspirin-type drugs block the synthesis of prosta-glandin, therefore causing the set point to return to its normal value. Aspirin will not lower normal body temperature or hyperthermia related to environmental conditions or exercise.

Inflammation occurs as the result of a local tissue injury. Inflammation is an important part of the body's defense against invading microorganisms. During this process, several elements of blood pass into the surrounding tissues, and leukocytes migrate to the inflamed area. Three events are noticed during the inflammatory process—redness, flare, and wheal. The **redness** occurs because several chemical substances are released into local tissues. These substances include histamine and 5-hydroxytryptamine (5-HT), causing dilation of arterioles and constriction of venous capillaries. This results in a festering of blood at the injured site—flare. **Bradykinin** and prostaglandins are released, triggering pain impulses and increasing the inflammation. An autonomic reflex action that constricts vessels in the surrounding area accounts for the localization of the swelling. Plasma kinins were first observed in the urine in the 1920s. The discovery was that these substances could lower blood pressure when injected intra-venously. Later the finding was that these substances exit in the saliva, plasma, and a variety of other tissue. Bradykinin gets its name from its ability to "slowly" cause contraction in the gut. The plasma kinins are potent vasodilators, produce edema, evoke pain and reflexes by acting on nerve endings, contract or relax various smooth muscles, and effect other responses in the body (Douglas, 1980).

The third event is a **wheal.** A wheal is a flat edematous raised area of the shin usually accompanied by burning or itching which occurs when there is an influx of leukocytes that supplement the small pool of local phagocytic cells. The phagocytic cells engulf and encapsulate microorganisms or foreign particles at the infected or invaded tissue. Aspirin has no effect on histamine or 5-HT. Drugs that have antagonistic effect on 5-HT or histamine have little effect upon inflammation. The anti-inflammatory effect of the aspirin-like drugs is related to their ability to block the effects of prostaglandins.

Flower, Moncada, and Vane (1980) pointed out four important points that have been affirmed, with regard to the prostaglandins: (1) all mammalian cells studied have the necessary enzymes for the synthesis of prostaglandins, with the possible exception of erythrocytes; (2) when cells are damaged, prostaglandins are always released, and they have been found to increase in concentration in cases of inflammation; (3) all the aspirin type drugs (analgesic, antipyretic, anti-inflammatory drugs) inhibit the biosynthesis and release of prostaglandins in all cells tested; and (4) as a rule, other classes of drugs do not affect the biosynthesis of prostaglandins.

ASPIRIN AND THE SALICYLATES

Aspirin is the most widely used analgesic, antipyretic, and anti-inflammatory agent. Because it is recognized as a common household item, it is often underestimated as a potent pharmacological agent. The pharmacologist sees it as a highly effective agent, and at the same time one that causes serious toxicity and lethality among the young. Swonger and Constantine (1983) showed it to be one of the top five drugs causing drug-induced fatalities in the United States. The estimate is that approximately 200 people die of aspirin or salicylate poisoning annually. Approximately 15% of all fatal poisonings in children can be attributed to the salicylates. Approximately 50,000 cases of salicylate poisoning (accidental and associated with suicidal attempts) are reported annually. Four areas of symptoms are of note in salicylate poisoning: (1) vomiting, dehydration, and hyperthermia are all immediate life threatening symptoms; (2) mental confusion, tinnitus, delirium, and convulsions; (3) bleeding, anemia, and lung damage; and (4) acid-base imbalance.

The salicylates' pharmacological effects upon respiration are important in their ability to act as poisons. In large doses they cause respiratory stimulation, and in larger doses, respiratory depression. These effects on respiration play a role in the acid-base disturbances characteristic of salicylate poisoning. A mixed respiratory alkalosis and metabolic acidosis develops, which is intensified by respiratory depression.

Aspirin as an analgesic is effective in the treatment of low to moderate intensity pain, especially pain associated with inflammation. Some examples of the types of pain aspirin relieves include headache, neuralgia, arthralgia, and postoperative pain. Aspirin is ineffective against pain from the visceral organs. It does not develop tolerance or addiction.

As antipyretics, the salicylates are quite effective. Aspirin and the salicylates still remain the drugs of choice in the treatment of inflammation, such as rheumatoid arthritis, osteoarthritis, and ankylosing spondylitis. They do not stop the underlying disease; they only treat the symptoms of pain and inflammation.

Many studies have reported aspirin's use in preventing myocardial infarction. These reports suggest a once a day dosage of aspirin indicate a wide variety of success levels. In Figure 10.4 are listed generic names, proprietary names, manufacturers, usage, and dosage for salicylate analgesics. In Figure 10.5 are listed the adverse effects.

ACETAMINOPHEN AND RELATED ANALGESICS

Acetaminophen and phenacetin are both derivatives of paraaminophenol. Phenacetin was often used in combination with aspirin and caffeine. These three drugs make up the combination known as **APC.** Phenacetin was found to cause renal damage, especially after chronic use or high doses. Therefore, this combination is rarely used today.

Acetaminophen has similar analgesic and antipyretic effects to those of aspirin. It is unlike aspirin in its anti-inflammatory agent. It also has little effect on bleeding time and no effect on plasma urate levels. Therefore, it is preferred over

(Continued on page 208)

Generic Name	Proprietary Name and Manufacturer	Use and Dosage
Aspirin	Aspirin (various)	Minor aches and pains: 325 to 650 mg every 4 hours as needed.
		Arthritis and rheumatic conditions: 2.6 to 5.2 g/day in divided doses.
		Pediatric.
analgesic/antipyretic:		65 mg/kg/24 hours in 4 or 6 divided doses.
Aspirin Buffered	Bufferin (Bristol-Myers)	Same as aspirin[1]
Aspirin	Ecotrin (Smith Kline) Easprin (Parke-Davis)	Same as aspirin[2]
Salsalate (salicylsalicylic acid)	Disalcid (Riker)	Adult dose: 325 to 1000 mg 2 to 3 times a day.[3]
Sodium salicylate	Various	Adult dose: 325 to 650 mg 3 times a day
Choline salicylate	Arthropan (Purdue-Frederick)	870 mg up to 6 times a day.
Magnesium salicylate	Doan's Pills (DEP) Magan (Adria) Mobidin (Ascher)	Usual dose 600 mg 3 or 4 times a day. May increase to 3.6 to 4.8 g daily.[4]

[1] The small amount of antacid added to these products increases the dissolution and absorption rates of these products. These preparations do not contain enough antacid to protect the stomach.

[2] Enterinc coating allows the tablet to pass unharmed through the stomach and dissolve in the intestine.

[3] Insoluble in gastric secretions, it is not absorbed until reaching the small intestine.

[4] A sodium-free salicylate with a low incidence of gastrointestinal upset. Contraindicated in chronic renal insufficiency. Not used in children under 12 years.

Figure 10.4. Salicylate analgesics—generic name, proprietary names, manufacturers, usage, and dosage.

Figure 10.4. Continued.

Generic Name	Proprietary Name and Manufacturer	Use and Dosage
Calcium carbaspirin	Calurin (Dorsey)	Adults: 325 to 704 mg every 4 hours. [5] Children (6 to 12): 325 mg every 4 hours. Children (3 to 6): 176 mg every 4 hours.
Salicylamide	Uromide (Edwards)	Adults: 325 to 650 mg 3 or 4 times a day.
Sodium thiosalicylate	Thiocyl (Pasadena) Tusal (Hauck) Asproject (Mayrand) Rexolate (Hyrex)	Intramuscular use. Acute gout, 100 mg every 3 to 4 hours for 2 days then 100 mg per day. Muscular pain and musculoskeletal disturbances: 50 to 100 mg/day or alternate days.

[5] Complexation of calcium aspirin and urea said to be more soluble and less irritating than aspirin.

aspirin for individuals taking anticoagulants because of these effects. Acetaminophen does not cause gastrointestinal bleeding or ulceration. This makes it the analgesic of choice for those individuals who have a history of gastric bleeding or peptic ulcers.

Its extreme popularity can be attributed to the tremendous advertising campaign and its lack of some of the adverse effects found in aspirin.

Acetaminophen's primary adverse effect is its ability to cause hepatic damage, even to the point of death. A single high dose of 6 grams will probably cause hepatic damage in an adult. A dose of 20 to 25 grams is considered lethal. Toxic symptoms

	ADVERSE EFFECTS	
Serum concentration **Therapeutic effect**	**Side Effect**
100 mcg/ml Antiplatelet Analgesic Antipyretic	Gastric upset, ulceration, hypersensitivity.
150-300 mcg/ml Anti-inflammatory	Mild salicylism: dizziness, tinnitus, difficulty in hearing, nausea, vomiting, diarrhea, mental confusion.
250-400 mcg/ml Anti-Rheumatic fever	Salicylism, nausea, vomiting, hyperventilation, flushing, sweating, thirst, headache, diarrhea, tachycardia.
400+ mcg/ml Overdose	Respiratory alkalosis, hemorrhage, excitement, confusion, pulmonary edema, convulsions, tetany, metabolic acidosis, fever, coma, cardiovascular collapse, renal and respiratory failure.

Figure 10.5. Salicylate analgesics—adverse effects.

include diarrhea, nausea, vomiting, sweating, and abdominal pain. In normal dosage acetaminophen rarely causes adverse effects.

Acetaminophen is marketed by various companies under its generic name or using a trade name. The most well known of these is Tylenol. Two other common brand names are Phenaphen and Anacin-3.

NONSTEROIDAL ANTI-INFLAMMATORY DRUGS

Diflunisal is marketed as Dolobid (MSD). It is used for mild to moderate pain, osteoarthritis (OA), and rheumatoid arthritis (RA).

Ibuprofen is marketed as an over-the-counter drug in 200mg dosage units under the names of Advil (Whitehall), Haltran (Upjohn), Medipren (McNeil), Nuprin (Bristol-Myers), Midol 200 (Glenbrook), and Trendar (Whitehall). As a prescription product, it is marketed as Motrin (Upjohn) and Rufen (Boots). It is used for rheumatoid arthritis and osteoarthritis symptoms, relief of mild to moderate pain, treatment of primary dysmenorrhea, and the reduction of fever.

Suprofen is marketed as Suprol and used for the relief of mild to moderate pain, as well as for primary dysmenorrhea.

Ketoprofen is marketed by Wyeth Laboratories under the name Orudis. It is used for the acute or long-term treatment of symptoms and signs of rheumatoid arthritis and osteoarthritis.

Fenoprefen is sold under the trade name Nalfon by Dista. It is used for the signs and symptoms of rheumatoid arthritis and osteoarthritis, as well as for the relief of mild to moderate pain.

Naproxen is marketed by Syntex under the names Naprosyn and Anaprox. It is indicated for the relief of mild to moderate pain; treatment of primary dysmenorrhea, rheumatoid arthritis, osteoarthritis, ankylosing spondylitis, tendinitis, bursitis, and acute gout.

Sulindac is sold under the trade name Clinoril (MSD). Its applications include acute or long-term use in the relief of symptoms and signs of osteoarthritis, rheumatoid arthritis, ankylosing spondylitis, acute painful shoulder (bursitis/tendinitis), and acute gouty arthritis.

Indomethacin is sold by various companies under its generic name or by MSD as Indocin. It is indicated for rheumatoid arthritis, osteoarthritis, ankylosing spondylitis, tendinitis, bursitis, and acute gouty arthritis. This is a potent drug that is not to be used for simple analgesia. It has been used for several conditions not found on the product label, i.e., eye drops in treating a syndrome known as cystoid mascular edema (a swelling in the area of the retina).

Tolmetin sodium is manufactured and sold as Tolectin by McNeil Pharmaceuticals. It is prescribed for the long-term management of rheumatoid arthritis and osteoarthritis. It also is recommended for the treatment of juvenile rheumatoid arthritis.

Mefenamic acid is used for the treatment of primary dysmenorrhea and for moderate pain when the treatment is shorter than one week. Its proprietary name is Ponstel (Parke Davis).

Meclofenamate sodium is another product from Parke Davis. Sold as Meclomen, it is used for acute and chronic rheumatoid arthritis and osteoarthritis. Due to its GI side effects, it is not recommended as a first line treatment choice.

Piroxicam is marketed under the name Feldene (Pfizer). It is used for the signs and symptoms of osteoarthritis and rheumatoid arthritis.

Phenylbutazone and **Oxyphenbutazone** are mentioned together. They are manufactured by Geigy and USV under the proprietary names of Butazolidin (Geigy) and Azolid (USV) for phenylbutazone. Oxyphenbutazone is available under its generic name. They are used for rheumatoid arthritis, osteoarthritis, acute gouty arthritis, painful shoulder, and short-term treatment of degenerative joint disease of the knee and hip. These drugs can cause aplastic anemia and agranulocytosis. They are normally saved for cases in which the other drugs are not effective. Due to the severity of the side effects, careful consideration and monitoring are advised in choosing these drugs.

SUMMARY

Chapter X is focused on pain and its pharmacological treatment. Drugs used to treat pain are called analgesics. These drugs are usually classified as narcotic analgesics, such as morphine; and non-narcotic analgesics, such as aspirin. Pain is the single most prevalent sensory symptom experienced by humankind. It is a personal and subjective experience, having a physiological and a psychological component. According to the "gate-control" theory of pain, pain is controlled by a parallel set of fibers. One having an inhibitory effect and the other a facilitating effect. A nerve center, located in the spinal cord, has the ability to open and close, increasing or decreasing the flow of nerve impulses from the stimulus to the brain. In 1974, a peptide that showed opiate-like activity was identified in brain extracts. The discovery was that a family of these naturally occurring peptides exists. They are called endorphins. Endorphins have the same pharmacological effects as opium. The components that effect compulsive drug use are tolerance, psychological dependence, and physical dependence. Certain groups of people, such as adolescents, have a high vulnerability to drug abuse. This indicates that sociological and psychological issues are the precipitating factors. Sociologic factors include environment, such as urban living; economics, for example, lower income people have a high percentage of drug abuse; and ethnicity, i.e., the Native Americans have a very high rate of alcoholism. Psychological factors include (1) the level of stress and anxiety; (2) peer pressure, important especially among adolescents; (3) cultural and family beliefs, i.e., the child of an alcoholic is more prone to use alcohol or drugs to cover pain than a child of an non-alcoholic; (4) defensive style, the individual who is compliant is less likely to go against society's rules than one who is defiant; (5) the development of a healthy narcissism including: (a) emotional and psychological independence from parents, (b) the arrival at a self definition, resulting in a stable self concept, (c) the development of self determination and self motivation, (d) the establishment of self values, (e) the development of empathy and the integration of reciprocity within relationships, (f) the development of intellectual skills and capacities, (g) the ability to function with peers, and (h) developing the skills to function economically in the world; and (6) finally, having or learning other ways to feel good or be high without turning to drugs.

EPILEPSY AND
ANTIEPILEPTIC DRUGS

Epilepsy is derived from the Greek word meaning "to seize." The term epilepsy is used to classify a wide variety of disorders characterized by the occurrence of seizures. Hauser (1978) estimated that 0.3 to 0.6% of the population are epileptic. Rodman (1985) reported as many as 2% of the population are afflicted with the disorder. This disorder may vary in severity, with some individuals requiring prolonged hospitalization, while others live normal and productive lives. Many important individuals, including Mozart, Julius Caesar, Peter the Great, Alexander the Great, Mohammed, Dostoevsky, Balzac, and Handel suffered from epilepsy. The term primary idiopathic epilepsy is used to denote cases in which no cause for the seizure can be identified. Secondary, or symptomatic epilepsy, is used to designate those instances which factors such as trauma, infection, and developmental abnormalities precipitate or contribute to the disorder.

John Hughlings Jackson, nearly a century ago, proposed an hypothesis of the nature and mechanisms of epilepsy. He conceptualized that seizures were the result of "occasional, sudden, excessive, rapid and local discharges of gray matter," and that seizure activity was the result of normal brain tissue being invaded by the abnormal focus. Modern technology has confirmed Jackson's theory, the EEG has shown that seizures are electrical explosions in the brain (Gibbs & Gibbs, 1954, 1964).

The traditional classification of epilepsy includes **grand mal, petit mal, psychomotor,** and **jacksonian** type seizures.

Grand mal epilepsy is the most common form of epilepsy. It occurs alone, or in combination with other forms. The grand mal episode is usually preceded by a brief **aura,** a warning that may manifest as flashes of light, special sounds, or other visual, auditory, or sensorimotor phenomena, such as vertigo. Other forms of aura include "deja vu," gastric, gustatory, olfactory, nausea, dreamy states, or a "lump-in-the-throat" sensation. Following the aura, the individual becomes convulsive and falls into unconsciousness. The convulsive state includes a short phase in which muscles are strongly contracted. Legs extend, arms cross up over the chest, and the back arches. These tonic (continuous tension) spasms (lasting 3 to 15 seconds) are followed by a longer period of clonic jerking in which rigidity and relaxation alternate in rapid succession. During clonic jerking the limbs flail rapidly about and the individual is in risk of biting his/her tongue, of sustaining a concussion, and injuring his/her limbs. The clonic portion of the seizure is followed by a period of depression.

Status epilepticus is a condition in which attacks are continuous or in rapid succession. This serious situation requires prompt treatment with parenteral anticonvulsant drugs to avoid respiratory failure, exhaustion, and death.

Petit mal epilepsy is often referred to as "absence seizures" or "absences." This syndrome occurs mainly during childhood with symptoms disappearing as the individual matures. Attacks, usually short in duration (5 to 15 seconds), occur mostly in the female population and consist of brief lapses or clouding of consciousness without convulsions. Typically, the child suddenly stops what he/she is doing and stares blankly in a trance-like state for a few seconds. These attacks may happen many times during the day with the individual not being aware of the event. About 10% of "absence seizures" victims also experience psychiatric symptoms.

These "absences" symptoms are similar to a phenomenum called "splitting off" (Rosenberg et al., 1985). Splitting off is a defense used to avoid feelings of pain, by separating from one's body. This defensive tactic is in response to a very early childhood injury, i.e., not having the child's feelings honored and/or being expected to be the extension of the parent. Rosenberg et al. (1985) referred to this later injury as being a "solipsistic relationship." The split off individual may be experienced by the psychotherapist, as not being "there" or not being "present." Some symptoms of being "split off" include (1) having a fixed lack-luster gaze in his/her eyes; (2) not remembering much of his/her childhood; (3) frequent loss of memory in the present, such as continuously mislocating car keys; (4) excessive daydreaming; (5) staring blankly into space; (6) almost always referencing from his/her thinking and not feeling; and (7) not noticing objects and colors around him/her. The EEG of the "spit off" individual can be similar to that of the individual with "absences."

Psychomotor, or **temporal lobe,** epilepsy is characterized by behavioral changes. This disorder is of significant importance to the psychotherapist. Because of the similarity in behaviors found with the "psychopathic disorders" and psychomotor epilepsy, the possibility of a misdiagnosis exists. Ruling out the diagnosis of psychomotor epilepsy could save both the psychotherapist and the client considerable time and money. In psychomotor epilepsy, the individual may act out an automatic and repetitive pattern of movement. For example, he/she may continuously go through the motions of driving a car or smoking a cigarette. Other, more bizarre behavior may manifest, with the individual being unaware of what he/she has done. Swonger (1983) stated that 70% of the individuals convicted of motiveless crimes have abnormal EEGs. An abnormal discharge focus in the anterior temporal lobe can cause antisocial and bizarre behavior. Auras are frequent in psychomotor epilepsy, the most common being the gastric aura. During a psychomotor episode the individual may experience aggression, a lack of coordination, staring, swallowing, groping, chewing, laughing, crying, screaming, shouting, confused chatter, and undressing. Grand mal seizures are present in nearly 70% of psychomotor incidences. Behavioral or personality disturbances occur in approximately 20% of individuals. Other serious effects of psychomotor epilepsy include sleepiness, depression, anxiety, paranoia, hallucinations, and suicidal tendencies (Ginn, 1978; Swonger & Constantine, 1983).

Jacksonian or *"focal" seizures* have convulsive activity limited to a specific area of the body. The attack arises from a focal discharge, in a particular cortical area, that doesn't spread throughout the cortex. Jacksonian seizures begin as a focal discharge and manifest into a full grand mal episode.

Some individuals have seizures that are not classified as epilepsy. Convulsions may be manifested due to a brain tumor, some other brain disorder, or an extremely high fever. *Febrile seizures* are more common in very young children and can be prevented with aspirin and phenobarbital. Newborn infants have been known to convulse because of a Vitamin B-6 or calcium deficiency. These individuals are treated with proper diet and vitamin and mineral supplements.

Individuals who are physically dependent on drugs, such as alcohol and barbiturates may experience seizures when the drugs have been withdrawn.

Myoclonus is described as an isolated involuntary series of clonic muscular jerks. The muscle activity may be a twitch or a contraction, with a duration of one or more movements lasting up to 6 seconds. Myoclonia may be symptomatic of a neurologic disorder, a viral infection, a chemical intoxication, a degenerative disease, or a seizure disorder. The body therapist should be aware of this disorder, in that it may look similar to a releasing of fixed muscles. The body therapist or psychotherapist, through a history gathering and evaluation process, may send the client to a physician or neurologist for further evaluation. This experience along with a drug history may identify a serious chemical or substance intoxication. Success in the treatment of myoclonia has been reported with a combination of the amino acid L-5-hydroxytryptophan (L-5HTP) and the peripheral enzyme inhibitor carbidopa (Lodosyn). The only antiepiletic drugs known to be of use are clonazepam and valproic acid.

An *International Classification of Epileptic Seizures* was published by Gastaut in 1970. This classification is based upon the type of seizure experienced and is thought to be a more useful system for the purposes of drug treatment. In this classification, epileptic seizures are separated into categories of (1) partial seizures (local origin), (2) generalized seizures (no local onset and bilaterally symmetrical), (3) unilateral seizures (one-sided), and (4) unclassified seizures (data incomplete).

Partial seizures are broken down into those with elementary symptomatology (cortical focal) and those with complex symptomatology (temporal lobe, psychomotor). Symptoms of the first type include (1) motor symptoms including Jacksonian motor epilepsy, convulsions confined to a single limb or muscle group; (2) special sensory or somatosensory symptoms, characterized by specific and localized sensory disturbances, (Jacksonian sensory epilepsy); (3) autonomic symptoms; and (4) compound forms. The second type, also called temporal lobe or psychomotor seizures is characterized by the loss of consciousness, confused behavior, and a wide variety of manifestations.

Generalized seizures are subdivided into the following: (1) absences (petit mal), characterized by a brief and sudden loss of consciousness; (2) bilateral massive epileptic myoclonus, isolated clonic jerking; (3) infantile spasms, motor spasms or other convulsive signs; (4) clonic seizures (in young children), characterized by rhythmic clonic contractions of muscles and loss of consciousness with autonomic manifestations; (5) tonic seizures (in young children), characterized by opisthotonic (A form of tetanic spasm in which the head and the heels are bent backward and the body bowed forward.) movements, loss of consciousness, and marked autonomic manifestations; (6) tonic-clonic seizures (grand mal), manifestations of major convulsions with tonic spasms of the total body musculature followed by clonic jerking and a long depression of central functions; (7) atonic seizures, characterized by a loss of posture, sagging of the head and falling down; and (8) akinetic seizures, a complete relaxation of all the muscles and a loss of consciousness. For a more complete discussion on the types of seizures, readers may refer to Aird and Woodbury (1974) or Rall and Schleifer (1980).

Mechanism of Action

In general terms, two ways exist in which a drug may work to either eliminate or attenuate seizures. The first is to effect the responsible neuron by eliminating or reducing the excessive discharge that sets off the seizure. The second way is to control or reduce the spread of excitation from the focal point and prevent the disruption of functioning of other normal neurons. The exact mechanism of the antiepileptic agents is not known; however, the consensus is that they act in the second manner.

The antiepileptics or anticonvulsants are divided, in this text, into six groups for the purpose of discussing their use, pharmacology, and adverse reactions. These groups are the hydantoins, barbiturates, succinimides, oxazolidinediones, benzodiazepines, and miscellaneous.

HYDANTOINS

Phenytoin, the best-known and most widely used, least toxic agent of this category was first synthesized in 1908 by Biltz. Its anticonvulsant activity was noted in 1938 by Merritt and Putnam (1938a). It was introduced as a treatment of epilepsy in the same year (Merrit & Putnam 1938b). Apparently the primary site of activity of the hydantoins is the motor cortex where the spread of seizure activity is inhibited. Researchers believe the mechanism of action to be the stabilizing of nerve cells, created by the increase in the efflux of sodium ions from the cells.

Phenytoin is slowly absorbed from the small intestine. Absorption rate may vary from manufacturer to manufacturer depending upon the product formulation. This is one of the products for which a therapeutic difference may exist between bioavailability of different generic formulations. Phenytoin is available both in an oral and a parenteral dosage form. It is metabolized in the liver and eliminated in the urine. Its elimination is dose-dependent, that is its elimination half-life increases with increasing dosage.

Phenytoin is used as a primary drug of choice to control seizures other than petit mal. The hydantoins interact with quite a list of other drugs. They interact with the barbiturates and other drugs that are also metabolized in the liver. In the case of the barbiturates, since both drugs exhibit anticonvulsant activity, no clinical significance occurs. Salicylates displace the hydantoins from their plasma protein binding sites. This dose-dependent occurrence may decrease the total phenytoin plasma levels by 20 to 30%. Alcohol, cimetidine, diazepam, allopurinol, and several other commonly used drugs may increase the effects of the hydantoins by inhibiting their metabolism. Chlorpheniramine, ibuprofen, and imipramine increase the blood level of phenytoin, however the mechanism is not known.

Other drugs decrease the effects of the hydantoins. Some of these through blocking absorption, such as antacids and calcium. The hydantoins also have the ability to decrease the effect of several other drugs, i.e., oral contraceptive, estrogens. More details are available in the package insert, PDR, or other reference material.

Toxicity of the hydantoins is low in comparison to most of the other antiepileptic and psychotropic drugs. They are less sedative than the barbiturates and have virtually no abuse potential. On the other hand hypersensitivity is not uncommon with these drugs. Birth defects is a risk. This must be weighed against the risk that seizures in the mother hold for the fetus. Hyperplasia (softening and overgrowth of the gums) is common, occurring in approximately 20% of hydantoin users (Swonger & Constantine, 1983). Proper oral hygiene is said to reduce the chances of this occurrence.

Other adverse reactions include CNS effects (most common), such as slurred speech, mental confusion, dizziness, insomnia, motor twitching, fatigue, depression, numbness, tremor, and headache. Gastrointestinal effects include, nausea, vomiting, diarrhea, or constipation. Taking the drug immediately after a meal may lessen these effects.

The hydantoins may cause cardiovascular collapse, hypotension, liver toxicity or damage, dermatological manifestations,

Generic Name	Proprietary Name	Usage (Indications)
Phenytoin	Dilantin	Status epicepticus Tonic-clonic Psychomotor
Mephenytoin	Mesantoin	Tonic-clonic Psychomotor Focal Jacksonian
Ethotoin	Peganone	Tonic-clonic Psychomotor

Figure 11.1. Hydantoins—generic names, proprietary names, and usage or indications.

connective tissue syndromes (such as a coarsening of the facial features or enlargening of the lips), chest pain, weight gain, edema, fever, photophobia, and conjunctivitis.

BARBITURATES

Phenobarbital was the first effective organic antiepileptic agent (Rall 1980). It is still widely used due to its inexpensiveness, lower incidence of side effects, and birth defects. Phenobarbital is not contraindicated in any form of epilepsy. The limiting factors for the barbiturates are their abuse potential and greater degree of sedation. Tolerance is a factor, as is, the need for slow withdrawal to lessen the possibility of seizures.

Phenobarbital normally can control seizures in a dose range that has an acceptable sedative level. The mechanism of action of the barbiturates in affecting seizures is thought to be their effect on gamma-aminobutyric acid (GABA) transmission.

The long-acting barbiturates are used in treatment of epilepsy. Other than phenobarbital, this includes mephobarbital

(Mebaral), metharbital (Gemonil), and a drug that closely resembles the barbiturates, primidone (Mysoline). Primidone has no special advantages over phenobarbital. Phenobarbital has few side effects while primidone may cause nausea, headache, rash, and sexual impotence. The barbiturates are normally used in treating grand mal and psychomotor epilepsy.

SUCCINIMIDES

The succinimides are useful in the treatment of petite mal. Three drugs are in this category: ethosuximide (Zarontin), methsuximide (Celontin), and phensuximide (Milontin). These drugs are less toxic than the oxazolidinediones. Common side effects include the usual GI upsets (nausea, vomiting, cramps, anorexia, diarrhea, weight loss, and constipation), psychological symptoms (confusion, mental slowness, instability, depression, hypochondriacal behavior, sleep disturbances, night terrors, aggressiveness, the inability to concentrate), dermatological effects, CNS effects (drowsiness, dizziness, irritability, nervousness, headache, blurred vision, photophobia, hiccough, euphoria, lethargy, fatigue, and insomnia), urinary tract problems, vaginal bleeding with phensuximide, muscle weakness, swelling of the tongue, and gum hypertrophy.

OXAZOLIDINEDIONES

This group of drugs includes paramethadione (Paradione) and methadione (Tridione). They are used for the control of petit mal seizures. They can cause serious side effects and are contraindicated during pregnancy due to their potential to produce fetal malformations.

BENZODIAZEPINES

Clonazepam (Klonopin) has been marketed exclusively for treatment of epilepsy. It is indicated for the treatment of Lennox-Gastaut syndrome (petit mal variant), akinetic, and myoclonic seizures. It may be beneficial for individuals who have failed to respond to succinimides in the treatment of absence (petit mal). It is more toxic than diazepam (Valium) and more effective as an antiepileptic drug.

Diazepam (Valium) is indicated for parenteral use in managing status epilepticus and severe recurrent convulsive seizures.

MISCELLANEOUS

Valproic Acid (Depakene) is used in the treatment of petit mal. Its mechanism of action is presumed to be its ability to elevate GABA levels. Introduced in 1963, it was received with enthusiasm, based upon the belief that it had few adverse effects. The incident of occasionally fatal hepatic toxicity (15 to 30% of patients) (Swonger & Constantine, 1983) has limited its use. Other adverse effects are mild and not unlike the other antiepileptic agents.

Carbamazepine (Tegretol) was first employed to treat epilepsy in the United States in 1974. It has been available for the treatment of trigeminal neuralgia since the 1960s (Blom, 1963). The main drawback is carbamazepine's potential to produce fatal blood cell abnormalities (aplastic anemia, agranulocytosis, thrombocytopenia, and leukopenia). Carbamazepine is used for the treatment of grand mal and psychomotor epilepsy.

PSYCHOLOGICAL IMPLICATIONS

The body therapist and psychotherapist should take a medical history of the client prior to doing deep breathing, body work, or deep psychological work. The individual who has a history of a seizure disorder is a candidate to have a seizure during a therapy session. I recommend that breathing and body type therapy not be attempted with clients having such a history. The body psychotherapist should be aware of these disorders and prepared to deal with such an emergency. Doing deep breathing and body work is very potent and, although these problems do not come up often, the knowledge of proper first aid may be lifesaving.

The psychotherapist can gather a great deal of information about the client by taking both a medical and drug history. I recommend a technique of moving down or up the body and asking about any illness or injury to the particular body part. For example, I start with the head, and ask about any illnesses or injuries. If there are any I ask the client, "What was going on at the time?" This, not only gives me a medical history, but a way of gathering a great deal of psychological history in an orderly and non-threatening manner. I then will ask specific questions about the head, such as: "Do you get headaches?" "Do you have dizzy spells?" "Have you ever fainted?" "Have you or any one in your family every had a seizure?" I want to know when the client last had a physical and what the physician reported. If I have reasonable doubt about a diagnosis, I will ask the client to see a physician or specialist for an evaluation.

SUMMARY

Up to two percent of the population may be suffering from seizure disorders. These disorders are commonly referred to as epilepsy. Traditionally, epilepsy is classified into grand mal, petit mal, and psychomotor epilepsy. (1) Grand mal is the most prevalent and spectacular form of epileptic seizure. It is immediately preceded by an aura or warning, and during the attack the individual loses consciousness and breathing is suspended. His/her muscles become rigid (tonic), jaws clenched, arms extended, and legs outstretched, and he/she pitches forward or slumps to the ground. When breathing restarts, he/she begins jerking (clonic), muscle spasms begin, the head strikes the back, the arms repeatedly thrust outward, the legs jerk up and down, the jaws open and close, and the mouth foams. The seizure usually lasts for a minute. Jacksonian seizures are limited to a specific area of the body. (2) Petit mal is when the individual stops and stares blankly in a trance-like state for a few seconds. (3) Psychomotor or temporal lobe epilepsy is a psychic disturbance which varies from individual to individual, with a clouding of consciousness and, in some cases, a brief period of bizarre behavior. The psychotherapist may need to differentiate between psychomotor epilepsy and the psychopathic disorders. In 1970, an *International Classification of Epilepic Seizures* was published, based upon the type of seizure.

DRUGS AND SEX

In our culture, what has become the norm is to turn to drugs when faced with medical, psychological, or social problems. Throughout recorded history, people have looked for drugs that would enhance libido, and increase sexual performance and pleasure. Social drugs, such as alcohol, caffeine, and nicotine are portrayed to the public as "liberating" and even "promoting lechery." Illegal social drugs have developed mystiques about their sexual effects.

Many drugs affect sexuality. Drugs can either inhibit or stimulate sexual activity. The incidence of adverse effects, as well as the beneficial effects of drugs on various aspects of sexual function, including libido, performance, and pleasure, has been difficult to document. Most individuals are very private or embarrassed, and not likely to volunteer information regarding their sexual experience. Physicians, pharmacists, and psychotherapists have seemed reluctant to pursue this information.

Before discussing the various drugs known to alter sexual functioning, the anatomical, physiological, and endocrinological aspects of the male and female reproductive systems will be briefly reviewed.

MALE REPRODUCTIVE SYSTEM

The primary components of the male sexual act include the erection of the penis, enabling vaginal penetration, and ejaculation of semen containing sperm into the vagina (Guyton, 1976). The penis consists almost entirely of cylindrical cords of erectile tissue forming vascular chambers. During the flaccid state, the arterioles that normally supply the chambers are constricted, and therefore, contain little blood.

During sexual arousal, the arterioles become dilated, the chambers become engorged with blood, and the penis becomes erect. As the erectile tissue expands, the veins are compressed, minimizing the blood flow from the penis. An erectile reflex is initiated by receptors in the tip of the penis. Input from the brain can both inhibit or facilitate this reflex. In other words, an erection may be the response to thoughts or emotions without the direct mechanical stimulation to the penis. Therefore, the failure to have an erection may be the result of psychological or emotional disturbances.

The production of semen occurs in the seminiferous tubules of the testes. Normal males may manufacture several hundred million sperm per day. An average ejaculation contains approximately 300 million sperm in a volume of about 3 ml. The majority of the semen is made up of secretions from the prostate and seminal vesicles (Diem & Lentner, 1970; Guyton 1976).

Testosterone, the male sex hormone secreted by the interstitial cells of the testes, is responsible for spermatogenesis, the secondary sex characteristic in males, and growth. The testosterone and testosterone-like substances (*androgens*) normally found in women are produced primarily by the adrenal cortex. In females, androgens play an important role in the stimulation of general body growth, as well as maintaining sexual drive (Guyton, 1976).

The hormones of the anterior pituitary also are involved in the male reproductive system. The gonadotropins of the anterior pituitary, *follicle stimulation hormone* (FSH) and *luteinizing hormone* (LH), are secreted in both males and females. FSH and LH are essential for spermatogenesis and testosterone secretion. FSH directly stimulates spermatogenesis, while LH stimulates testosterone secretion. LH is indirectly involved in spermatogenesis, as testosterone is required in this process.

The release of LH and FSH is regulated by releasing factors in the hypothalamus. Testosterone is known to exert a negative-feedback inhibition of FSH and LH through the hypothalamus. The releasing factors are produced by nerve cells. These cells are believed to be controlled by both dopaminergic stimulatory and serotoninergic inhibitory mechanisms (Guyton, 1976). Consequently, drugs which influence the central nervous system may indirectly affect testicular functioning.

The *prostaglandins* are involved in the reproductive system, as well as practically every other organ system in the body of both males and females. Prostaglandins have been found in the seminal plasma, the prostrate gland, seminal vesicles, the ovary, fallopian tube, endometrium, myometrium, menstrual fluid, placenta, and in the amniotic fluid at the onset of labor (Gross, 1977). Prostaglandins stimulate and inhibit the release of hormones in the hypothalamus and pituitary. The prostaglandins directly stimulates LH release and indirectly is involved in the regulation of testosterone levels and the male reproductive system.

FEMALE REPRODUCTIVE SYSTEM

The female has no counterpart to male ejaculation. Two glands, Bartholin's and Skene's, secrete lubricating fluids. The two areas of sexual sensation in the female are the vagina and the external genitalia just above the vaginal opening, particularly the clitoris. The clitoris is made primarily of erectile tissue and contains numerous sensory nerve endings. It becomes erect during sexual excitement, and through mechanical stimulation constitutes a primary source of sexual tension (Guyton, 1976). Anatomically, the vagina is connected to the uterus, while the ovaries are associated with the uterus via the oviducts (uterine tubes or fallopian tubes). The female counterpart of the testes are the two ovaries. Like the testes, the ovaries have a dual function: (1) production of ova and (2) secretion of estrogen and progesterone (Guyton, 1976). These ovaries are made up of cell clusters called follicles, each containing one ovum surrounded by a single layer of cells. The development and growth of the follicles is controlled by estrogen, FSH and LH. Estrogen is secreted by follicle cells which are stimulated by FSH and LH. In 14 days, under the influence of estrogen, FSH, and LH, a single follicle and ovum reach maturity. During the second 14 days of the menstrual cycle, estrogen secretion is increased under the influence of FSH and LH.

Sometime in the middle of the 28 day menstrual cycle, LH production increases sharply through hypothalamic stimulation and regulation. FSH production is increased to a lesser extent. This induces a rupture of the follicle and the release of the ovum. The ruptured follicle is transformed into the corpus luteum, a gland-like structure which develops out of the follicular cells and secretes large quantities of both estrogen and progesterone. The elevated estrogen and progesterone cause the LH and FSH levels to decline. This lowered level of FSH and LH prevent the development of other follicles.

If the ovum is not fertilized, the corpus luteum begins to degrade during the last few days of the cycle. The mechanism of this activity is unknown. Consequently, the estrogen and progesterone levels fall, allowing FSH secretion to rise, and thereby a new follicle and ovum begin to develop (Guyton, 1976).

Prostaglandins stimulate LH release, which in turn regulates ovulation. Prostaglandins also have been shown to be involved in the transport of the ovum, termination of pregnancy, and the initiation of parturition (Labor, the act of giving birth) (Gross, 1977).

In the female, the neuronal control of sexual function is not well understood. The belief is that dopaminergic stimulation and serotoninergic inhibition are involved (Guyton, 1976).

SEXUAL DYSFUNCTIONS

Kaplan (1974) listed three types of sexual dysfunctions for males and four for females. These are for males (1) erectile dysfunction (impotence), (2) premature ejaculation, and (3) retarded ejaculation. For females the four are (1) general sexual dysfunction (frigidity), (2) orgastic dysfunction, (3) vaginismus, and (4) sexual anesthesia or conversion.

Erectile dysfunction, or impotence, is an "impairment of penile erection" (Kaplan, 1974 p. 256). It is the inability to achieve or maintain an erection. Some authors include in their definitions "sufficient for penetration" and/or "prior to ejaculation." The term "impotence" is widely used to describe this disorder; however, many professionals are moving away from it, due to the possible negative connotation. According to Kaplan (1974): erectile dysfunctions may be divided into two categories: (1) *primary impotence,* never having been potent with a woman, although attaining good erections by masturbating and being able to have spontaneous erections; (2) *secondary impotence,* functioned well for some period of time prior to the symptom. This author disagrees with Kaplan's definition, in that the occurrence of primary impotence ought not to be linked to the presence of a female partner. Primary impotence then is seen as the inability to achieve or maintain an erection in any sexually stimulating situation. Secondary impotence is defined as having acheived satisfactory erections in the past, and then developing the symptom. This definition not only accommodates homosexual relationships; it includes symptoms occurring without a partner. Since the belief of this author is that impotence is the symptomatic individual's problem, and not the partner's, this dysfunction needs to be defined in this way.

Premature ejaculation is normally thought to be the most common of the male sexual dysfunctions (Kaplan, 1974). Kaplan (1974) defined prematurity as a condition wherein "a man is unable to exert voluntary control over his ejaculatory reflex, with the result that once he is sexually aroused, he reaches orgasm very quickly". Masters and Johnson (1970) diagnose a man as premature if he reaches orgasm before his partner does,

50% of the time. Rosenberg (1985) defines premature ejaculation as "ejaculation before reaching a high enough level of excitement to allow for a true orgastic release" (p. 268). Stohs (1978, p. 55) pointed out three definitions for premature ejaculation: (1) "ejaculation during the process of foreplay understood by both partners to be leading toward intercourse;" (2) "ejaculation just before or during the act of penetration;" or (3) "ejaculation anytime during the first penile thrusts after intromission."

Masters and Johnson referred to **retarded ejaculation** as "ejaculatory incompetence." In this disorder, the ability to have an erection remains in tact. The male suffering from retarded ejaculation continues to respond to sexual stimuli, feel erotic feelings, and respond with a firm erection. He is unable to have an ejaculatory release, even though he experiences the urgent desire to do so. A wide variance exists in severity of this dysfunction. At one end of the scale is the male who has never experienced an ejaculation, and at the other, an individual who can respond through a fantasy, distraction, extra stimulation, or the use of a stressing position (Kaplan, 1974; Masters & Johnson, 1970; Rosenberg, 1985; Stohs, 1978).

General sexual dysfunction, or **frigidity,** are terms used to describe a condition characterized by the inhibition of general arousal of the sexual response. Psychologically, the individual may lack erotic feelings; while physiologically, she may not lubricate, her vagina does not expand, and she does not experience an orgasmic platform (Kaplan, 1974).

The impairment of the orgastic component of the female sexual response is the most common female sexual complaint (Kaplan, 1974). Sometimes called "anorgasmia", "preorgasmic", or "inorgastic," this **orgastic dysfunction** refers to the inability for a female to reach orgasm in situations judged to be appropriately stimulating.

Vaginismus refers to the involuntary "shutting tight" of the vagina, rendering penetration difficult or virtually impossible.

Sexual anesthesia, or **conversion,** is a condition in which females "feel nothing" on sexual stimulation. They may enjoy the closeness, warmth, and coziness, without having feelings in the genital area (Kaplan, 1974).

Nonspecific sexual withdrawal may be experienced by both males and females. It is called nonspecific because none of the above dysfunctions need be present. Psychologically, specific causes may exist for the withdrawal (Stohs, 1978).

DRUGS AND SEX

John Lust (1974), in *The Herb Book*, listed twenty-seven plants or plant parts that are said to have **aphrodisiac qualities,** the most popular of these being Ginseng. **Ginseng** comes from the Orient and a powder of the root is said to have aphrodisiac qualities. The drug is mildly stimulating to the central nervous system. Ginseng has collected moderate popularity in the United States, and is commonly found in pharmacies and "health food stores." Other common plants said to have sexual enhancing functions are clove, celery, coriander, jasmine, and onion. Most medical references state that the aphrodisiac action of these drugs is a placebo effect.

Farrington's Clinical Materia Medica of 1887 listed several preparations for the treatment of sexual disorders. Some of these include conium (poison hemlock), dioscorea (wild yam root), cinchona (the source of quinine and quinidine), nux vomica (the source of strychnine), gelsemium (yellow jasmine root), potassium bromide, cobalt, platinum, lime, phosphorus, and sulfur. For the treatment of **priapism** (prolonged erection of the penis), the author suggested agaric (a fungus), cantharides (Spanish fly), capsicum (red pepper), opium, physostigmine, parsley, picric acid, platinum, and phosphorus. A treatment offered for impotence was chlorine, conium, or phosphorus. Cannabis (marijuana) and digitalis were recommended for the treatment of gonorrhea.

Vecki in his book on impotence in 1915 concluded that "there is no such thing as an aphrodisiac." He went on to state that "anything which benefits a person's general system, also acts as an aphrodisiac."

Perhaps the best known aphrodisiac is cantharides (Spanish Fly). Cantharides is the dried and ground parts of a beetle, Cantharis vesicatoris. The active ingredient is can-tharidin, a rubefacient and vesicant. The drug is excreted through the kidneys and causes severe irritation of the urinary tract. The drug has been used in the cattle industry as an aphrodisiac. It is poisonous and considered very dangerous for humans. The only medical use for cantharides is in scalp tonics for its irritating action. Cantharides has been known to cause death and painful, prolonged priapism.

DRUGS THAT ENHANCE
SEXUAL FUNCTION

Hollister (1976) reported the use of **androgens** for men and **estrogens** for women as a treatment for declining sexual function during the middle and later years of life. Herbert Tanney (1986), in a paper entitled *The Good News About Estrogen*, suggested that women lose the function of their ovaries between the ages of 35 and 55.

Androgen exerts a significant influence on sexual behavior. When a male has low or almost no testosterone levels, due to castration, illness, or other cause, he loses his desire for, and interest in, sexuality and the ability to have an erection (Kaplan, 1974). A woman's sexual desire is also dependent upon androgens, or rather upon estrogens (Gross, 1977; Vander, et al., 1975). Androgen is a requisite for libido in women. Testosterone has an aphrodisiac effect for women, especially when the androgen level has been on the low side (Kaplan, 1974). Androgen has proven of some use in treating both men and women in the management of low **libido** (Kaplan, 1974). However, in the absence of advanced age or severe organic disease, impotence or decreased libido are most often associated with psychological or emotional disturbances (Thorn, 1977). In these cases, hormone therapy is of little use, except for the placebo effect (Stohs, 1978).

Levodopa (Dopar, Larodopa) has been shown to effect an increase in sexual function in 25 to 35% of individuals using the drug (Bowers, van Woert, & Davis, 1971). Increases in libido, sexual feelings and dreams, and sexual activity are reported in both males and females. Levodopa is metabolized into dopamine, and the mechanism of the aphrodisiac effect is thought to involve dopamine activation of the hypothalamic control center of hormone mediated sexual behavior (Gessa & Tagliamonte, 1974).

Alcohol and the barbiturates are centrally acting drugs which have been held, throughout time, as aphrodisiacs. These drugs are primarily depressants, working in a progressive, rather than a simultaneous manner. In low doses, these drugs may seem to increase sexual behavior by temporarily depressing the individual's inhibitions. In larger doses, they depress all behavior, including sexual (Kaplan, 1974).

Marijuana and the hallucinogens, such as LSD and MDA, are centrally acting substances also acclaimed for their aphrodisia effects. These drugs have not been found to directly act on sexual centers in the brain (Kaplan, 1974). Rosenberg, Rand and Asay (1985) suggested that these drugs enhance splitting off; therefore, the participant is less likely to be in touch with his/her emotional self. Individual reaction to hallucinogenic sexual experiences vary from "different" to "interesting"; however, they are not generally found to be intensely erotic (Kaplan, 1974). Kolodny (1974) reported that marijuana users have a lower level of testosterone than non-marijuana users. Mendelson (1974) was unable to reproduce and substantiate the reported effects of marijuana on testosterone, and Huang et al. (1978) found that it had no effect on testosterone; however, it did decrease spermatogenesis.

A little objective evidence is available to support the belief that amphetamines have a direct effect on sexuality (Masters & Johnson, 1970). Amphetamine users report a higher rate of promiscuity (Greaves, 1972). Angrist and Gershon (1976) suggested that amphetamine use leads to an increase in libido. Rosenberg, Rand, and Asay (1985) described the amphetamine user as one who can't contain or build excitement, is a premature ejaculator, or experiences diminished orgastic response. Hollister (1976) suggested that the chronic use of amphetamine is associated with diminished sexual performance in both males and females, as the drug becomes a substitute for sex.

The stimulant effects of cocaine are similar to those of the amphetamines; however, they have a shorter duration and are more intense. Kolb (1962) reported an increase in sexual activity among males using cocaine. Hollister (1976) stated that intranasal use of cocaine, in low dosage, may result in delayed ejaculation. Kolodny, Masters & Johnson (1979) reported that cocaine may possess sexually stimulating properties, such as increased desire, improved firmness and durability of erection, and an intensifying effect on orgasm in both males and females. Individuals who are addicted to cocaine usually lose interest in sex. Any possible transient aphrodisiac effects experienced with cocaine would seem to be overshadowed by the profound general toxic state which often leads to a state of psychosis (Kaplan, 1974).

Proponents of hallucinogenic drugs, such as LSD, indicate the positive sexual effect produced by these drugs (Stohs, 1978). These reports have had little verification. The hallucinogens can create a wide variety of sensations. Consequently, sexual feelings, thoughts, and attitudes may be enhanced or decreased. Hollister (1976) reported that the ability to participate in sexual activity is generally decreased by these drugs.

Caffeine and nicotine are frequently used social drugs. A single cup of coffee may supply up to 85mg of caffeine. Doses of 50 to 200mg of caffeine may result in increased alertness, decreased drowsiness, and less fatigue. Doses of 200 to 500mg may produce irritability, nervousness, tremors, and headache (Stephenson, 1977). Therefore, in the individual suffering from physical or mental fatigue, caffeine may be of some value in regard to sexual interest and performance. Nicotine has no direct effect on sexual function; however, it has been linked, through advertising, to liberation and sexual freedom (Stohs, 1978).

Amyl Nitrite is an agent used in the treatment of acute angina pectoris. It is supplied in a crushable capsule and is inhaled. The drug has been used during sexual encounters to intensify orgasm, by abruptly lowering blood pressure (Hollister, 1976). Amyl nitrite is dispensed only on prescription and is considered quite dangerous; coronary occlusions, possibly resulting in death, have been reported following the use of amyl nitrite during intercourse (Kaplan, 1974).

DRUGS HAVING AN ADVERSE EFFECT ON SEXUAL FUNCTION

The anticholinergic drugs, such as atropine, can cause erectile dysfunction (impotence) and failure to ejaculate. The mechanism of action for these responses involves the drug's ability to block the nerves which control the vascular response of the genitals. This group of drugs is often used for the treatment of ulcers and other stomach problems. Some medications used for glaucoma fall into this category. An important side effect of these drugs is their tendency to dry up secretions, including those that would normally lubricate the vagina. Giving this information to a client and recommending a lubricant may correct a serious physical and psychological problem (Kaplan, 1974, Kastrup, Olin, & Schwach, 1986).

The antihypertensive agents represent the most significant group of drugs having an adverse effect upon sexuality. In women, these drugs decrease the ability to have an orgasm, and in men, they cause impotence and retrograde ejaculation. For example, Kolodny et al. (1979) reported four different studies of methyldopa (Aldomet), in which 50% of the males, using 2gm daily, experienced significant disruptions in sexual function. Stohs (1978) quoted two studies in which 30% of the males involved showed symptoms of sexual dysfunction with methyldopa. The suggested mechanism of these sexual disruptions is the depletion of catecholamine neurotransmitters and the production of a "false" neurotransmitter (Page & Sidd, 1972), which may directly effect the peripheral nerves controlling erection and vaginal stimulation. Some of the sexual effects are due to the adverse effects of these drugs, i.e., drowsiness and fatigue.

Guanethidine (Ismelin), an antihypertensive agent that blocks release of norepinephrine from sympathetic nerve endings, is associated with impotence and retrograde ejaculation in males. The estimate is that up to 60% of males using this drug have experienced these effects (Riddiough, 1977).

Clonidine (Catapres), a drug used in the treatment of hypertension, shows effects similar to those found with methyldopa. The most common sexual problem reported is erection difficulties (Riddiough, 1977). Studies reported lower incidence of sexual dysfunction with clonidine than methyldopa; one reported 24% (Medical Letter 19, 1977), while another showed only 14% (Riddiough, 1977).

Propranolol is a beta-adrenergic blocking agent, often used for the treatment of cardiac arrhythmias and hypertension. Kolodny (1978) showed some cases of propranolol induced impotence.

A number of reports indicate that the diuretics, often used alone or in combination in the treatment of hypertension, may cause sexual dysfunctions (Kolodny, Masters, & Johnson, 1979). Spironolactone (Aldactone) has been indicated as causing decreased libido, impotence, and gynecomastia in men and menstrual irregularity and breast tenderness in women (Greenblatt & Koch-Weser, 1973, Levitt, 1970). The thiazide diuretics, furosemide (Lasix), and ethacrynic acid all have shown the ability to cause sexual dysfunction (Kastrup, Olin & Schwach, 1986).

The impairment of sexual function is a common effect found in individuals taking antipsychotic drugs. Stohs (1978) reported that males using thioridazine (Mellaril) have a high rate of sexual dysfunction. One report indicated that 60% of the males using this drug have problems (Greenblatt, 1973). Several other studies show thioridazine to block ejaculation (Segraves, 1977). The other antipsychotic drugs show less of a potential to inhibit sexual activity. The phenothiazines may cause decreased libido, impotence, and inhibited ejaculation. These drugs have a complex action, but some degree of adrenergic blockage occurs. In addition, cholinergic blockage occurs, due to atropine like action. The thioxanthenes, chlorprothixene (Taractan), and thiothixene (Navane) have effects on sexual response similar to the phenothiazines; however, difficulty in ejaculation is less common (Goldenberg, 1977).

The sedative-hypnotic drugs are almost all associated with some impairment of sexual function (Hollister, 1976). Some 90% of heroin addicts studied showed menstrual abnormalities (Stoffer, 1968), while another study showed that female opiate users have a greater degree of sexual dysfunction than males (Gossop, Stern, & Connell, 1974).

The tricyclic antidepressants, such as imipramine (Tofranil), desipramine (Norpramin), amitriptyline (Elavil), nortriptyline (Aventyl), and protriptyline (Vivactil) have central anticholinergic action. These drugs block the transport system for reuptake of norepinephrine after it has been released. Decreased libido, impotence, or inhibited ejaculation have been reported with these drugs (Segraves, 1977).

The monoamine oxidase inhibitors (MAOI), such as tranylcypromine (Parnate), phenelzine (Nardil), and isocarboxazid (Marplan), have been reported to cause impotence and delayed ejaculation, through their effects on norepinephrine metabolism (Goldenberg, 1977).

Other drug groups which adversely effect sexual function include (1) antineoplastics, such as the alkylating agents (i.e., nitrogen mustards and nitrosoureas), antimetabolites (i.e., Methotrexate and Fluorouracil), alkaloids, and antitumor antibiotics (i.e., Bleomycin and Doxorubicin), cause sterility or impotence in men; (2) steroids which cause decreased libido in males and females; and (3) other miscellaneous drugs which may cause impotence in males or decreased libido in females, such as disulfiram (Antabuse, an antialcoholic) and clofibrate (Atromid-S, used to lower cholesterol).

In my experience as both a pharmacist and psychotherapist, I have found that people do not voluntarily talk about sex, sex problems, and drugs. A highly skillful therapist colleague of mine tells about the client she treated for a reported eating disorder. After a year of food charts and failed therapeutic interventions, the client came forward and admitted to being a steady cocaine user. As a pharmacist, I have consulted with many males who had been put on antihypertension medication and were having difficulties with sexual function. Some would not discuss this with their physician, some were not following the prescribed dosage, some told me that their physician said there should not be any of the experienced side effects.

The psychotherapist, by being aware of the influence of the prescription, as well as the role that licit and illicit social drugs may be playing in the sexual activity of his/her client, can show a great deal of openness toward the subject(s) of sex and drugs, provide accurate and timely information to the client, and be comfortable and prepared to discuss problems with the client's physician, if the need should arise.

SUMMARY

In Chapter XII is reviewed the relationship drugs have with sex and sexuality. The male and female reproductive systems are discussed. Androgen is a requisite for libido in women. Certain drugs, such as levodopa, have been shown to have an increased effect on sexual function. The aphrodisia affects of the common drugs of abuse, such as marijuana and the hallucinogens, does not come from any direct involvement with the sexual centers of the brain. Any increase in sexual experience or functioning is either a placebo effect, or an indirect effect of the drugs' pharmacological effect. For example, a drink of alcohol may help an individual relax by depressing his/her inhibitions. Many drugs used for the treatment of hypertension, psychological disorders, and cancer have an adverse effect on sexuality.

COMMENTARY

I have chosen to include a commentary in this chapter. I am making these remarks under the heading of commentary because they are my personal beliefs, and come directly from my experience. These comments may be outside the scope of the book, and may differ from the generally excepted view point. Whenever possible, I have cited references for interested readers. I also invite the reader's thoughts, ideas, and comments.

In our Western world and way of being, we have almost an automatic response to look outside of ourselves for a solution to what is experienced as a problem. I have documented this historically, in terms of drugs and human sexuality. The problem I have with the use of drugs is that while they are altering the mind, they cause the user to not be present energetically. When a person is not present, he/she cannot make contact with his/her partner and cannot build a satisfactory charge to have a full orgastic release. Therefore, the "heightened" experience is not erotic, energetic, sexual, or even able to carry the individual over into a satisfying release. [See Kaplan's (1974) remarks in this chapter regarding the use of marijuana.]

Over the past several years an awakened interest has occurred in the Eastern practices of **Tantra.** The Eastern Tantra was a male-oriented experience and is not appropriate for our Western culture. However, several teachers and writers have incorporated the Tantric methods into practices that not only are very acceptable to the Westerner, but can open up a door to an expanded sexuality.

The AIDS epidemic is causing a great deal of change in our sexual practices. These include the curtailment of promiscuity, the entering of an age of committed relationships, and the cutting back of early and premarital sexual exploration. These changes are affecting both the heterosexual and homosexual community.

I predict that the psychotherapist in the next five years is going to have to deal with many more sexual issues and problems than ever before. Rosenberg and Rand, in their book *Body, Self, and Soul: Sustaining Integration* (1985), presented an excellent chapter on Sexuality and Sexual Counseling. The chapter is written for the psychotherapist and presents a model of sexuality that incorporates Eastern and Western ideation.

For those readers who are interested in further exploring, either for their personal growth, or for information to share with clients, I am including a bibliographic list.

BIBLIOGRAPHY FOR ADDITIONAL READING

Chang, Jolan (1977). *The tao of love and sex: The ancient Chinese way to ecstasy.* New York: E. P. Dutton.

Devi, Kamala (1977). *The eastern way of love: Tantric sex and erotic mysticism.* New York: Simon & Schuster.

Douglas, Nik, & Slinger, Penny (1979). *Sexual secrets: The alchemy of ecstasy.* New York: Destiny Books.

Kline-Graber, Georgia, & Graber, Benjamin (1975). *Woman's orgasm: A guide to sexual satisfaction.* Indianapolis: The Bobbs-Merrill Company.

Mandel, Gabriele (1979). *Tantra: Rites of love.* New York: Rizzoli International.

Ramsdale, D. A., & Dorfman, E. J. (1985). *Sexual energy ecstasy: A guide to the ultimate, intimate sexual experience.* Playa Del Rey: Peak Skill Publishing.

Rosenberg, J. L., Rand, M. L., & Asay, D. (1985). *Body, self, and soul: Sustaining integration.* Atlanta: Humanics.

Rosenberg, J. L. (1973). *Total orgasm: Advanced techniques for increasing sexual pleasure.* New York: Random House.

Thirleby, Ashley (1978). *Tantra: The key to sexual power and pleasure.* New York: Dell Publishing.

SUBSTANCE ABUSE

Substance abuse has become one of our society's most complex problems. The President of the United States has declared a "war on drugs." Psychotherapists are being given special training in the area of substance abuse. Police departments are sending educational teams into the schools to talk with young students, in the hope of getting the young child or teen to say "no to drugs."

Schaef (1987a) stated that we have become "a society of addicts," that "we live in an addictive system." A society having "all the characteristics" and "exibiting all the processes" of the "individual alcoholic or addict." Schaef is making the point that society is not bad and attempting to get good, but it is sick and needing to get well. As in all addictive systems, the first step to wellness comes with the end of the denial. In other words, wellness can only come when it is recognized that sickness exists.

ADDICTION

Addiction takes two general forms: addiction to substances, such as drugs, nicotine, alcohol, and food; and addictions to processes, such as work, money, and gambling. Religion and sex are two good processes in which some individuals attempt "quick fix" solutions to their problems. To these individuals, both religion and sex can be considered an addiction.

An addiction is defined by Schaef (1987a) as "any process over which we are powerless"—A force which "takes control of us, causing us to do and think things that are inconsistent with our personal values and leading us to become progressively more compulsive and obsessive" (p. 43). This force may be seen as a defense or even defensive style. Rosenberg (1985) defined three "defensive character styles" which are developed out of injuries to the "Emergent Self" (Stern, 1985) or "Self" (Rosenberg, 1985) during early childhood. In a psychological sense, addiction then can be seen as a defense against "fragmentation." The addicted substance or process, at least in the psychological sense, becomes the focus which keeps the individual from feeling the underlying pain. Addiction allows individuals not to deal with anger, pain, depression, confusion, or even joy and love. The addicted person is cut off from his/her own knowledge and senses. He/she begins to rely upon a set of confused perceptions. In time this lack of "internal awareness deadens the internal processes, which in turn allows the individual to remain addicted" (Schaef, 1987a).

To ask some questions at this time seems prudent. Why are people with healthy bodies and minds turning to drugs? What purpose does this serve? Why does it persist? Ray (1972) suggested that "drug-taking behavior" is "problem solving behavior." Like any other behavior, the assumption must be that drug-taking behavior persists either because it increases pleasure or reduces discomfort. By accepting this premise, then a reasonable statement to offer is that people do not randomly choose a drug or substance, but they select one that has a positive, satisfying, pleasurable effect, or one that causes a decrease in their discomfort.

To think that just one cause underlies a person's choice to take drugs is not reasonable. We know from the study of animals that susceptibility to narcotic addiction is, in part, genetically determined, and that some animals have been bred that are very easy or very difficult to addict (Nichols, 1967). Schuckit and Rayses (1979), psychotherapists and researchers at U. C. San Diego, have shown us that alcoholism is more common in families of alcoholics. In his studies of adopted twins, Goodman (1976) provided strong evidence that alcoholism is passed from parent to child.

Substance use (whether it is controlled by a genetic predisposition or not) is a complex interaction of past experiences and present environmental impact. By thinking of substance-use as a behavior, it become similar to any other behavior, and not a unique situation. Substance abuse can be viewed as a similar phenomenon to "neurotic behavior." Both "neurotic behavior" and substance abuse offer the individual benefits and disadvantages. The benefits are often of short term gain, such as a more positive feeling or a decrease in discomfort. The disadvantages are usually remote and decrease the individual's chance of a long-term, permanent solution to the underlying problem (Ray, 1972).

Drug use has a negative effect on the individual when it becomes the dominant mode of problem solving. Taking drugs can offer an immediate solution to an individual's problems. It offers the user short-term solutions. However, the use of drugs may have adverse long-term effects by causing new problems or by preventing a better solution to the precipitating problem.

CONSIDERATIONS IN PSYCHOACTIVE DRUGS

In dealing with the *psychoactive drugs*—those compounds that alter consciouness and affect mood—several basic points are worthy of consideration.

First, drugs are not "good" or "bad." In dealing with substance abuse, the behavior of the individual is the identified problem, and not the chemical substance itself. A good example of this is the drug diazepam (Valium). It is a useful and important drug that can be, and is, abused by some individuals. The labeling of a particular use of a drug is a reflection of the values of the society which tend to change over time. As an example, the use of alcohol during prohibition was not legal. Another example of this is society's attitude towards women smoking in the late 1800s, and then the change during the middle 1900s that made it "chic" and "sensuous."

Second, every drug, including those that are psychoactive, has multiple effects. The user may be focused upon a single effect, such as the alteration of consciousness, but the chemical acts on various parts of the body and brain, possibly causing adverse effects or side effects.

Third, all drugs have an effect that is dose related. This means that not only the magnitude, but the kind of effect can be changed with varying doses. Some effects of drugs may be intensified by increasing the dosage. In many drugs, the effects change with an alteration of the dosage. For example, at low dosage a barbiturate may act to stimulate the individual; however, as the dose increases, the drug acts as a depressant.

The fourth consideration is that the effect of psychoactive substances depends on the individual's history and expectations. Drugs have a multiple effect that will vary with the amount of drug used and the personality of the user, as well as his/her expectations about the effects of the drug.

A person's decision-making process when deciding whether or not to take drugs depends upon his/her background, present environment, and the availability of drugs. This last point about the availability of drugs is a minor one. If drugs were not available, then obviously no one would be using them. This, of course, is not the case. At the same time, if drugs were the only issue, then they could be cut off at the supply. The problem is with the people, and not the drugs. The people are looking for rapid solutions to problems, and drugs are simply one of the options available in our society.

Many reasons exist for people turning to drugs. In many cases the reason for taking illegal and legal drugs is the same. Some may turn to illegal drugs out of curiosity or defiance. Drugs are used to reduce tension and anxiety, to remove fatigue or boredom, to influence mood, to change activity level, to facilitate social interactions, and to feel good. There are many other legitimate medical uses of drugs such as infection control and pain management.

STAGES OF ABUSE

Drug abusers usually start with alcohol. At first they will have an occasional beer, or even try marijuana. This is usually done when someone else has the beer or drug. The drug use is probably an unplanned and convenient event. Some individuals start with glue or aerosol sniffing. This experimental, unplanned or convenient event is called "stage one use." Some substance abusers will never go beyond stage one.

During stage two, the abuser actively begins to seek out drugs. He/she begins to spend more time at parties where drugs are offered. The idea that "everyone is doing it" becomes prevalent. Oftentimes the individual has periods of passive withdrawal, lack of motivation, and loss of interest in school, work, other activities, hobbies and future goals. During stage one, the individual takes drugs to experiment. In stage two, the drug user begins to self-medicate, taking drugs when he/she feels bad, in order to make him/herself feel good again. One might look at stage one as denial of the use of drugs to others, and stage two as denial of drug use to one's self.

During stage three, getting high is the most important thing in life. It becomes a daily preoccupation. Drugs are used to feel good and to avoid feeling bad. Usually, alcohol and marijuana are the main drugs; however, at this point the tendency is to go on to harder drugs. This is the stage where the first overdose occurs, causing vomiting, blackout, numbness, unconsciousness, screaming, and sometimes death. No longer does any pretense of being drug-free exist. "Who cares what parents or anyone else thinks!" The stage three user begins to show physical signs such as constant cough, red eyes, sore throat, and fatigue. Stage three leads to loss of control of the drug use, and of everything else in life. A person in stage three often lies about his/her drug use, or hides his/her alcohol or drug supply.

Stage four is the final stage. Beyond this comes only death. During stage four, drugs are used all the time. Drugs are now used just to feel normal. Guilt feelings increase, questioning one's own use but being unable to control it. The abnormal becomes the normal, and the only choice is euphoria or pain (Nelson, 1978; Polson & Miller, 1984).

CASE EXAMPLES

Case I

An 18-year old male took several puffs of a marijuana cigarette and developed a serious depressive-paranoid reaction. The transitory and light intoxication, along with the drug being illegal, the fear of punishment, invoked a series of conflicting responses around guilt and shame. He experienced shame about his physical appearance, feelings regarding several homosexual adventures, about masturbation, guilt regarding his fantasy and wish to break away from an over protective family environment, and rebellion against his overly strict introjected control. This case points out a socially experimental, but not legally sanctioned incident of substance abuse. A response was triggered that was treatable with several hours of psychotherapy. The individual continued in treatment to deal with the causes underlying the manifested symptoms. He discovered that his mother had not wanted a son and that she was quite critical. He had grown up and taken her charac-teristics in the form of a negative introject. He began to realize that he was separate from his mother, that she had done the best she could, and that pain is part of life. He began to accept this as a part of his life process.

Case II

A 30-year old man used marijuana, cocaine, barbiturates, and several other drugs three or four times a week. The drugs were supplied to him and his wife by some friends. He had been arrested several times for being the middle man in trafficking, and his business was in serious trouble. He used the drugs socially and recreationally, to relax, to feel good, to enjoy life, but above all to cover up his frequent anxiety attacks. The courts referred him for psychotherapy. He attended the required sessions; however, he denied that he had any serious problem or need for treatment. This man used the drugs to support his defensive character style. He was invested in denying any possible underlying problems.

Case III

A 43-year old female psychotherapist indulged in several glasses of wine and/or vodka every day. She also took Tylenol with Codeine on an occasional basis. She said the wine or vodka "controlled her pain." As soon as she tried to stop, she went into "the shakes." She had a shallow marriage and refused psychotherapy; however, occasionally she entered a private hospital for withdrawal from her physical addiction. Upon return from the hospital she resumed to her previous pattern. This woman, the adult child of alcoholic parents, is a classical case.

Case IV

An unmarried female in her early twenties lived with a violent, drug-abusing boyfriend. She used diazepam (Valium) or barbiturates regularly in the morning to help her get through the day. She believed she was not addicted, just used enough of the drugs to handle her unpleasant, boring job and often frightening life. She often stayed at home, due to her over-sedated state. She spent her weekend time intoxicated, in bed with her boy friend. Once she was drug free, she experienced episodes of depression and anxiety, rendering her incapacitated. This is a case of a physical addiction, resulting in withdrawal symptoms. Underneath, she was using the drugs to covering her longing feelings and her fear of abandoment.

Case V

A 35-year old executive woman was very successful, had a caring relationship with a male attorney who lived with her and her teenage son. She was drinking a considerable amount of alcohol which she insisted she could handle. Her response, when confronted about her drinking, was that next time she would just have a few. However, each time she began to drink she got drunk, and several times passed out. Her male friend was encouraged to attend Al-Anon meetings, which he did. Through the Al-Anon process he was able to see how he contributed to her drinking. During a party at her home, she passed out from drinking, and her friend was able to get her to a substance abuse treatment facility. She did well with the treatment, became involved in A. A., and was able to live a normal life, as long as she remained free of alcohol and other chemical substances.

Discussion of Cases

In each of these cases, an inner need leads to substance abuse. The question is not of pathology, but of degree. For example, in Case I the young man needed to break away from his mother. When he took the marijuana, he was confronted with both the excitement, and his guilt and shame caused by his life-long dilemma. In several of the cases the need to use drugs becomes irresistibly intense—the individual seeking the drug at any and all costs, regardless of consequence. The substance abuse is more or less compulsive, depending upon the intensity and severity of the underlying unsolved inner conflicts, usually of an unconscious nature. In Case III and V an added factor of physical addiction was present. These individuals have a particular inability to process alcohol which leaves them with a highly toxic by-product in the system.

The unsolved inner conflicts begin to develop during early childhood. Each person goes through various developmental stages. When an insufficient or improper interpersonal relationship does not allow for a child to complete the task of a developmental stage, the resultant injury leads to fragmentation. Fragmentation is the loss of one's sense of identity or the sense of being annihilated (Rosenberg, 1985). The use of drugs is one way to defend against fragmentation or a loss of one's sense of identity.

IDEAL EARLY CHILDHOOD DEVELOPMENT

Rosenberg, Rand, and Asay (1985), Kaplan (1978), and Stern (1985) presented excellent material on the stages of early childhood development. A brief review of early childhood development is presented in the following paragraphs.

Attachment Stage

The first stage of ideal development is the "attachment" stage. It begins before birth and lasts until the fourth or fifth month. The child's task is to bond. This is a nonverbal, energetic, and physical experience. Kaplan (1978) described the task of the newborn and mother for the first six weeks as mending the rupture caused by the end of biological oneness.

The infant-mother merger is biological, and not psychological. The mother contributes her psychological experience to this early relationship. The infant at this stage is in "limbo." Both the child and mother together are needed to bridge the gap of the birth and the infant's new environment.

Stern (1985) described the infant prior to two months as being in a "presocial, precognitive, preorganized life phase" (p.37). The young infant, however, has begun to develop a sense of self. MacFarlane (1975) showed that three-day-old infants could identify their own mother's milk. In experiments using the infant's ability to turn his/her head from side to side, MacFarlane placed two breast pads soaked with milk on either side of the head. An infant would consistently turn toward the pad that had his/her mother's milk. Meltzoff and Borton's experiment (1979) with three-week-old infants showed that these children would visually choose a pacifier that they had sucked while blindfolded. (These experiments raise questions concerning the inner world of the very young infant.)

After four weeks, and continuing to five months, the baby leaves a state of limbo and enters into oneness. The infant-mother-complex is very strong. The infant experiences "being held" (Kaplan, 1978), as well as those moments of well-being and harmony that come from the inborn knowledge of sucking, holding on, and head-turning. As long as these events are happening according to the infant's urges or needs, the infant is emotionally satisfied. When this harmony is lost, the infant feels let down and emotionally falls apart. (This is the beginning of fragmentation.) In a healthy mother-infant relationship, empathy and pleasure giving and taking are mutually shared experiences.

At two months, the "lap baby," who has molded to mother's body, discovers the ability to stiffen his/her own body. This movement represents the first step of separation.

At two to four months the infant is sucking, grasping, looking, kicking, hand-waving, smelling and listening. The baby is beginning to educate his/her self.

> After four or five months of intense bonding with the mother, the baby develops the need, the strength and the perceptions to become an individual on his/her own. The process of development pulls him/her continually into life, away from the unity, the womb, the mother and toward a greater and greater individual sense of identity. (Rosenberg, Rand, & Asay, 1985, p. 148)

Reflection Stage

The infant enters the "reflection" stage at six months. Normally this stage lasts to one and one-half years. The task of this stage is mirroring. Mirroring can be defined as "the mother giving back to the child a picture of what he/she is" (Rosenberg, Rand, & Asay, 1985, p.150). To the five month old the notion that either he/she or his/her mother exists without the other is inconceivable (Kaplan, 1978).

This is not a selfish or possessive response on the part of the child. Simply the infant has had no other reason to experience the world in any other way. Mobility and curiosity begin the process of separateness. The infant begins to crawl and becomes quite dexterous.

Once again, the infant is in transition. Mother becomes divided into two roles: first, the "mother of oneness" and then, the "mother of separation."

The mother of oneness stays with the baby. The mother of separation comes and goes. The mother of oneness mirrors to the infant a sense of well-being and safety. The infant begins to hold on to these feelings. He/she can move away with confidence and a feeling of goodness and satisfaction.

During this period of experimentation, with mother's going and coming, checking and refueling, things will not always go well. The baby will look to mother for signs and clues. The mother will supply both verbal and nonverbal mirroring to the infant. Often, the world does not meet the expectations of the baby. He/she may be intolerant of the disappointments.

The baby shows protest, and often rage. "This rage derives from the panicky sense of ceasing to exist" (Kaplan, 1978, p.137). Stern (1985) pointed out that the period from nine to eighteen months is equally devoted to the baby's task of assuming independence, autonomy, individuation, and the seeking and creating of an intersubjective union with another person. In other words, the baby is separating and is discovering new ways of being with another person at the same time.

At eighteen months, the infant becomes aware of his/her mother's existence apart from himself/herself. This comes about developmentally with the thinking-mind joining the body-mind. As a result, the child is thrown into turmoil, as he/she begins a "second birth."

Healthy Introversion Stage

The baby moves into this third stage of ideal development at one and one-half years of age. This stage will last until age three. Rosenberg, Rand, and Asay, (1985) called this stage "healthy introversion." At this stage of development the child realizes that he/she is separate from mother and father. The child is now ready to begin the task of entering life as an individual. Rosenberg (1985) called this the task of "reinforcing self."

Alice Miller (1981) stated:

> For the majority of sensitive people, the true self remains deeply and thoroughly hidden . . . . . . so it is that many a gifted person lives without any notion of his or her true self. Such people are enamored of an idealized, conforming, false self. They will shun their hidden and lost true self, unless depression makes them aware of this loss . . . . or psychosis confronts them harshly with that true self. (p.ix)

She goes on to speak of "a healthy narcissism" . . . and she focuses on the ideal case of a person who is genuinely alive, with free access to the true self and his/her authentic feelings.

This "healthy narcissism" or "healthy introversion" is what the child will depend on to establish the inner resources that are necessary for him/her to handle failures as well as success in his/her trial-and-error interactions with the environment (Rosenberg, 1985). Miller (1984) told us that repressed traumatic experiences in childhood are stored up in the body and, although remaining unconscious, exert their influence even in adulthood. The individual "can turn to a place within his/her body for a grounding, supporting feeling of well being from which he/she can return, strengthened to the world. This is healthy narcissism" (Rosenberg, Rand, & Asay, 1985, p.163).

Rapprochement Stage

The fourth stage of ideal development is the "rapprochement stage" (Mahler & Furer, 1968; Mahler, Pine, & Bergman, 1975; Rosenberg, Rand, & Asay, 1985). It begins at one-and-one-half to three years and it continues throughout life. Here there is "reality testing," i. e., the individual's experimentation with taking his/her internal fantasy and bringing it into harmony with the outer world (external reality). In order for the individual to attempt this, he/she has had to develop a strong sense of Self by successfully moving through the "healthy narcissism" stage. The mother continues to mirror the child and contributes to the sense of Self.

DEFENSIVE STYLES

An individual, who lacks "healthy narcissism," emotionally falls apart during his/her attempts to test reality. Out of this early scenario each individual develops defensive styles (Rosenberg, Rand, & Asay, 1985).

Denial

Denial is one defense that the substance abuser often develops. Wurmser (1981) referred to drugs as pharmacologically reinforced denial. They are used to rid one's self of feelings blocking undesirable inner and outer reality. **Denial** may be defined as a failure to fully appreciate the significance or implications of what is perceived (Trunnell, 1974). Words of denial are common amongst substance abusers. "I can stop anytime I want." I take drugs only to have some fun, to feel relaxed, and to enjoy the company of my friends." "I don't have a problem."

Externalizing

Substance abuse may be considered a form of externalizing, a way of using external action to support the denial of inner conflict. In this way, the internal conflict is made into an external one.

FAMILY DYNAMICS

The family dynamics of the substance abuser have been studied with considerable interest. Many treatment facilities work with individuals and their families. The family therapist deals with an equilibrium in the family system called "homeostasis." The alcohol or chemical abuser sees the drug as serving the family balance. The actual drug abuse becomes a part of the family's system or equilibrium. Thus it becomes an investment in maintaining the specific drug abusing member's role in the family. Boszormenyi-Nagy (1974) saw the drug addict's life as one of overt breaking of all the rules and commitments, in order to show his/her independence and make a break away from the family. He/she ultimately attains the reverse: a "cementing" of his/her dependency on the family and a saving of the family cohesion. His/her addiction actually saves the family's cohesion. The addict fears separation from the family and the family feels likewise toward him/her. This is an interdependent process in which the addict's failure serves a protective function of maintaining family closeness (Wurmser, 1981). In these families what seems to exist are hidden loyalty conflicts. The overt behavior appears to be one of treason and breach of faith, while the covert behavior is one of hidden loyalty and dependency. These families may be divided into four categories: (1) those marked by severe and real external trauma, such as having had a mother who killed herself when she was pregnant, and therefore the child was taught that sex is bad; (2) those marked by intrusiveness, such as the abuse of the child for the parents' grandiose expectation, and the disregard for the child's age-appropriate needs [Rosenberg (1985) referred to this as the "solopsistic" relationship.]; (3) those marked by secretiveness and unavailability on the parent's part, living a "life lie" behind a facade of propriety and respectability; and (4) those families of utter inconsistency and unreliability, for example, one day something is good, and the next it is bad.

SOCIOLOGICAL VIEWPOINT

From the view point of the sociologist, substance abuse is a product of the society. Austin (1978) pointed out that thousands of substances may be seen as possible objects of abuse. The rationale for considering whether or not a substance is abused entails a social definition. It relates to the perceived negative consequences, of the compulsive use of a particular substance, at a particular point in time (Alksne, 1981), the criteria being that the norm violation be seen as a serious threat to the welfare of the society, community, and violator (preferably in that order). The individual who violates the norm in a manner that threatens society is labelled deviant, in this case "substance abuser." Thus, a definition of what is deviant, in this case substance abuse, depends on a perception that a problem exists and that in some way it negatively affects the social network that constitutes the main of the society. Some observers of substance abuse focus their perceptions on the basis of the "peculiar vantage points" from which they look at the phenomenon (Alksne, 1981). An example of this being the legal use of methadone, as opposed to the illegal use of heroin.

Within the society, certain rules are developed that make the question of substance abuse political. First, the society makes certain drugs available only upon the prescription of the medical practicioner. This means that the use of diazepam (Valium) may be considered licit by some and illicit by others. The dosage regimen or dose interval must be taken into consideration. The medically accepted use of a drug, say diazepam (Valium) might be to take one at bedtime. The individual who exceeds this norm is then a substance abuser. This could be the individual who has legally or illegally obtained the drug.

Other drugs are not legally obtainable in the society; therefore, all use becomes substance abuse, even though a large percentage of the society is using the drug, for example, marijuana. Over a period of time, society may change the "rules," such as the case of alcohol with Prohibition.

Zinberg (1981) suggested three factors or variables which are involved in the decision-making process that leads to whether an individual uses drugs, what the acute effects drugs have, and the ongoing social and psychological reaction to that use. These are (1) the pharmaceutical properties of the chemical or substance, (2) the attitudes and personality of the user, and (3) the physical and social setting in which use takes place. This theoretical position has been accepted (Huxley, 1954; Weil, 1972; Zinberg, 1972) stressing the importance of all three variables; however, the influence of setting and the way it interacts with the others has been least understood (Zinberg, 1974 & 1975).

A preoccupation seems to exist with the pharmaceutical properties, personal hazards of the drug, or with the personality deterioration of the substance abuser. One example of a setting that makes drug use okay is the hospital. In a hospital the use of narcotics, under a control, is a very acceptable practice. Another way of looking at the setting is driving an automobile. While it may be socially acceptable for someone to have a few glasses of alcohol while at home, this same practice is not acceptable prior to driving. Social controls (rituals and sanctions) apply to all drugs, not just alcohol. In certain social contexts the use of specific drugs is considered the norm. For example, a beer at a baseball game, a glass or two of wine with dinner, or a cocktail before dinner at a social function are considered the norm. Sometimes the norm includes acts which are not legal, but sanctioned by the society; for example, at a rock concert many listeners may be smoking marijuana, and the police will not arrest them.

Children are growing up in the 1980s with social learning that is different than any time in the past. They are aware of the wide range of behaviors associated with the use of alcohol, as well as other drugs. The most common source of their learning is the television. Television exposes children to drinking, smoking, and other drug use in a way that makes drug use glamourous. In addition to all the programs which glamourize drug use, the beer commercials lead them to believe that beer is the reward for a "hard day's work," or the most important aspect of socializing. Add the influence of the movies, magazines and newspapers, the observation of family and friends, and the youth of our society grow up being socially educated.

Out of this and the realization that a substance abuse epidemic does exist, new measures of education have been initiated. Famous actors and athletes appear on television, members of the police department talk at schools, and numerous television commercials for substance abuse programs are seen daily.

Other measures taken by society include attempts to restrict drug supplies and punishment for illegal drug use. These measures are only effective against a portion of the overall substance abusers.

SUMMARY

Addiction can be divided into two general forms, addiction to a substance and addiction to a process. Both healthy and unhealthy people may turn to drugs. I have suggested that individuals do not randomly choose their drug; they select one that will increase their pleasure or decrease their discomfort.

Psychoactive drugs themselves are not the problem. Drugs are neither good or bad. Drugs have multiple effects. The user selects a drug because of one or more desired effects; however, he/she also must experience various adverse or side effects. Drug effects are dose related. Effects of a drug can vary from individual to individual Four stages are commonly associated with drug abuse.

The psychotherapist or drug counselor needs an understanding of human developmental theory in order to understand the individual who turns to drugs. Successful treatment of a substance abuser must include both dealing with the addiction and treating the underlying injuries.

CHAPTER

LEGAL AND ILLEGAL DRUGS

All the drugs that are presented in this chapter have the potential for abuse. Weil (1972) make the point that the chemicals are not what "contain" the effects they cause, but that they enable the individual to experience his/her mind in a new way.

In order to make some attempt at classification, this text uses the idea of "effects" to classify the drugs covered. Four general terms of effect, borrowed from the "street" language, describe particular effects the drugs have. These are "downers," "uppers," "highlighters," and "hallucinogens."

Downers, refers to two general groups of drugs. The first group of downers are the sedative-hypnotic drugs, including alcohol, the barbiturates, the antianxiety drugs or "tranquilizers," and the antipsychotic drugs. These drugs primarily depress the central nervous system. They can cause death through the depression of the respiratory system and other vital centers that are essential for the maintenance of life.

Narcotics make up the second group of downers. Narcotic drugs include the opiates and narcotic analgesics. Opium and heroin are examples of opiates. The narcotic analgesics includes derivatives of opium, such as morphine and codeine and synthetic drugs, such as Percodan and Talwin. Narcotics act primarily on the central nervous system. Overdose can lead to coma, respiratory failure, and death.

Uppers, include the social drugs, caffeine and nicotine, the central nervous system stimulating amphetamines; cocaine, which gives a false sense of well-being and power (Rosenberg, 1985); and the antidepressants, sometimes falsely called "mood elevators."

Highlighters, including marijuana and MDA, appear to highlight awareness without a great deal of distortion, except for the sense of time, manifested as short-term memory changes. These drugs can heighten a person's awareness of the immediate moment. Rosenberg, Rand, and Asay (1985) described the effects of marijuana as "splitting-off." Thus, marijuana releases the drug user's inhibitions, but provides a means for him/her to build or hold a charge.[1]

The fourth category of effect drugs is **hallucinogens.** Examples of hallucinogens include LSD, STP, PCP, mushrooms, and peyote. These drugs can create states of consciousness that do not ordinarily exist in awareness; however, many of these states have been experienced by other means, such as "spiritual crisis," psychosis, and through various esoteric practices and disciplines which have "enlightenment" as their goal. These drugs do not create or introduce any new sensation, but disrupt the usual frames of reference. The hallucinogens cross sensory input, create changes in integration, modulation, sense of time, and creativity.

DOWNERS

Alcohol

Alcohol is a confusing and often misunderstood substance. It is thought of as a stimulant in small quantities, possibly due to its action of depressing centers in the brain. If ingested in

---

[1] The intensification and expansion of the individual's excitement in the body, coming from the free flow of energy.

larger amounts, it becomes a sedative, or even toxic. When ingested for long periods of time, it can cause severe damage to cells, tissues, and organs. Alcohol is addictive to only a minority of its users; most authorities estimate this to be about 10% in the United States.

Alcohol is the only drug that also can be classified as a food. It is rich in calories and can be a potent source of energy. Unfortunately, alcohol contains no vitamins or minerals. It, therefore, contributes little in the way of nutrients to the cells. Many drinkers who depend solely upon alcohol as a source of food will end up suffering from malnutrition. During the treatment phase of alcohol addiction, nutritional support is very important.

Alcohol has the ability to relieve the distress it creates. This is why an alcoholic will go into a state called withdrawal when he/she stops drinking. Drinking makes the alcoholic feel good. When the alcoholic stops drinking, he/she then becomes aware of the effects of the alcohol upon the body (Milam & Ketcham 1981).

The word alcohol is used to describe an entire class of organic chemicals. The substance referred to, when thinking of liquor, is ethanol or ethyl alcohol. Ethanol is produced in nature as the waste product or excrement of yeast, a fungus that lives in the body. Yeast have a healthy appetite for sweets. The yeast release an enzyme that converts sweets such as honey, fruit sugar (fructose), or sucrose (table sugar) into carbon dioxide and alcohol. This process is called fermentation. The yeast continue to feed on sugars until they die of acute alcohol intoxication. Yeast expire at a concentration of 13 to 14% alcohol. This is the way wine is made. The yeast are allowed to carry out their natural fermentation process, and the resultant wine contains between 10 and 14% alcohol. In the manufacturing of beer, the fermentation is artificially stopped between 3 and 6% alcohol.

The process of distillation was first used around the year A.D. 800. Hard liquor or fortified wines are made using this process. The alcohol content of distilled products is expressed in "proof." The word comes out of a seventeenth century

English tradition called "proving." In order to prove that the drink was strong enough, it was mixed with gun powder and then ignited. If it contained 49% alcohol it would ignite. A drink containing 50% alcohol is considered to be 100 proof. Proof is approximately double the percent alcohol (Milam & Ketchum, 1981).

When alcohol is consumed, it moves rapidly into the stomach. Approximate 20% goes directly into the blood stream through the stomach walls. The rest travels into the small intestine and is gradually absorbed into the blood stream.

The concentration of alcohol in the body is measured by **blood alcohol levels** (BAL). The BAL is the mathematical measurement of the percent alcohol in the blood. A 0.01 BAL indicates 1 part of alcohol in 10,000 parts of blood. The BAL raises when a person drinks more alcohol than the body can eliminate. The average person can eliminate approximately one-half ounce of alcohol per hour.

Many factors affect the rate at which the BAL raises. Some have to do with the drink and others with the individual. The first factor is how much the person has had to drink. For comparative purposes, 12 ounces of beer, 4 to 5 ounces of wine, or one mixed drink containing a shot of liquor (1 ½ ounces), all contain about the same amount of alcohol. The more concentrated the drink, the faster the alcohol is absorbed. The type of mixer is a factor. Water or fruit juice tend to slow the absorption while carbonation speeds it up. How fast one drinks is a factor. Food, particularly protein, in the stomach slows the absorption of alcohol. Many people believe that if they take vitamin B-1 they will not get drunk. No proof has been found to back up this claim. Temperature is a factor; a cold drink is absorbed more slowly than a warm one. Usually, very heavy people are less affected by alcohol. This is because the alcohol is diffused throughout the body, and heavy people have more body mass, blood, and water to dilute the alcohol. One's body condition is a factor in the way alcohol affects people. An ill person or a tired person is more strongly affected by alcohol. The presence of other drugs in the body is a very important factor. For example, the drug Valium is considered to be non-lethal, even in large overdoses; however, when ingested in conjunction with alcohol the combination is quite dangerous (Milam & Ketcham, 1981).

One's beliefs, thoughts, and feelings about drinking can be important factors in the effects of alcohol. Many experienced drinkers compensate for the expected effects of alcohol. They learn how alcohol affects them and then make adjustments in order to function. One's mood determines alcohol's effects. The setting in which one chooses to drink may affect his/her reaction to the alcohol. A person drinking at a party is more likely to have good feelings than a person drinking alone at home (Finn & O'Gorman, 1980).

Alcohol and the Body. To better understand what happens when we take a drink, let's look at what happens when alcohol is consumed. The alcohol travels rapidly into the stomach. From here, about one-fifth is absorbed into the blood through the stomach walls, and the rest makes its way out of the stomach and into the small intestine where it is absorbed into the blood stream. Aided by its small molecular structure, the alcohol can easily penetrate through the cell membranes and infiltrate into the brain, heart, lungs, liver, kidney, as well all the other organs and tissues of the body. The alcohol passes rapidly through the blood brain barrier. The blood brain barrier is an electrical chemical filtering system that protects the brain from chemicals. As a result, the alcohol has an immediate and profound effect upon the person's behavior. A drinker may become talkative, feel happy, energetic, and even euphoric at this early stage. He/she may perform better after one or two drinks. After two drinks, a normal drinker may begin to show signs of intoxication. Emotionally he/she may become joyful, sad, or angry. He/she may begin to show a lack of motor coordination. Walking may become difficult, speech slurred, and hands uncoordinated. After several more drinks, he/she may begin to experience blurred vision. Judgment and thought processes deteriorate. As the BAL rises in a normal person, he/she could experience respiratory failure, coma, or even death (Finn & O'Gorman 1980; Mann, 1981).

The human body is a very efficient machine. It works hard to eliminate alcohol as it enters the blood stream. Small amounts of alcohol are eliminated through sweating, breathing, and urination. The majority of work falls upon the liver, the organ responsible for the removal of the most drugs and chemicals from the blood stream. The liver begins its work immediately; an enzyme called **Alcohol Dehydrogenase** (ADH) causes the removal of two hydrogen atoms from the alcohol, turning it into a chemical called acetaldehyde. **Acetaldehyde** is a highly toxic substance that can produce rapid heart beats, dizziness, headache, nausea, and confusion. The drug Disulfiram (Antabuse), used sometimes to deter recovering alcoholics from drinking, blocks the liver's ability to eliminate acetaldehyde, causing an immediate and very severe reaction.

The liver releases another enzyme called Aldehyde-hydrogenase to transform the acetaldehyde into acetate, which then becomes converted into carbon dioxide and water in the blood stream. This process of alcohol oxidation supplies a great deal of energy to the liver. This energy contributes to the energy needs of the entire body. The majority of an individual's energy needs could be supplied by using alcohol for food. Many alcoholics don't eat food for long periods of time. One ounce of pure alcohol provides 170 calories. Alcohol calories are easily available to the body and require little work by the cells to release them. Remember, however, that nutritional problems can be encountered by heavy drinkers, because alcoholic beverages contain little or no vitamin or mineral contents. Alcohol also interferes with the absorption of many vitamins, minerals, and amino acids, and increases the loss of certain vitamins through the urine (Milam, 1981).

The alcohol conversion process is very efficient in most drinkers. At maximum efficiency, the liver converts approximately one-half ounce of alcohol per hour. The liver works very hard and gives the conversion of alcohol a priority. It neglects its other duties to keep up with the alcohol conversion process. When all of the alcohol is converted, the liver can return to its other duties.

When alcohol is present in the body in large quantities for an elongated period, a build up of toxins occur, and nutritional functions are disrupted. The liver's preoccupation with completing the alcohol conversion process eventually results in the loss of health, and the body's cells, tissues, and organs will suffer (Milam & Ketcham, 1981).

Effects of Alcohol. The most common effects of alcohol are listed in summary form under nine areas.

1. *Pleasure.* For most people alcohol heightens pleasure, helps people "let go," become more friendly and relaxed.

2. *Inhibitions.* Alcohol tends to loosen people's self control. Feelings may be released that are normally withheld. Sometimes people feel anger, hostility, inferiority, superiority, overconfidence, generosity, tenderness, jealousy, and love. Under the influence of alcohol, people who are ordinarily quiet can become loud or rude.

3. *Thinking.* Small amounts of alcohol normally have little effect upon thinking; however, larger amounts interfere with one's ability to make judgments.

4. *Performance.* In small amounts, alcohol can improve some people's performance. In larger amounts, most people lose the ability to perform even simple tasks.

5. *Body Temperature.* Most people feel warmer, even though the body temperature has remained the same or gone down.

6. *Energy.* Some people get energized, and some people find themselves feeling sleepy.

7. *Hangover.* The unpleasant feeling that one has the morning after. This effect is probably caused by the presence of toxic chemicals that have not been metabolized or eliminated. Some symptoms are nausea, fatigue, thirst, dizziness, and terrible headache.

8. *Physical Tolerance.* Over a period of time reduced effect occurs on the body.

9. *Diseases and Bodily Damage.*

   a. Liver: Cirrhosis (Scar tissue replaces liver cells.)

   b. Brain: Permanently destroys brain cells.

c. Delirium Tremens: Shaking, convulsions, auditory or visual hallucinations—a violent effect of withdrawal.

d. Fetal Alcohol Syndrome (FAS): A syndrome of birth defects found in children of alcoholic women. The main characteristics are a low birth weight and length, with failure of "catch up growth," small head circumference, midfacial anomalies resulting in micro-ophthalmia, poor development of the bridge of the nose, hypoplastic philtrum (the groove at the median line of the upper lip), a short up-turned nose, micrognathia (unusual or undue smallness of the lower jaw, with recession of the chin), and brain maldevelopment with mild to moderate mental retardation (Clarren & Smith, 1978). Other features found include skeletal and joint abnormalities, an abnormal crease in the hand, cardiac abnormalities, abnormalities of sexual organs and of the ears, and kidney abnormalitites (Seixas, 1979).

e. Death: Alcohol is the number two cause of death in the United States. Very few people die as a direct result of drinking alcohol. Most of these deaths are the result of automobile accidents (Finn & O'Gorman, 1980; Milam & Ketcham, 1981).

Alcoholism. For most people the consumption of alcohol is self regulating. A few beers or a couple of glasses of wine or several mixed drinks makes the average drinker uncomfortable enough to stop drinking. Most normal drinkers are influenced by the sedative effect and soon stop. Others can not tolerate the toxic effects such as nausea, dizziness, sweating, and vomiting.

For some people, a physical resistance or "tolerance" develops. This allows them to consume more alcohol without the unpleasant side effects (Milan & Ketcham, 1981).

The World Health Organization (WHO) has defined **addiction producing drugs,** "as those producing, in the great majority of users, an irresistible need for the drug, an increased tolerance to the effects of the drug, and physical dependence on the drug, manifested in severe, painful symptoms when the drug is withdrawn." Heroin, morphine and codeine are examples. Heroin is addictive in almost 100% of its users. Addiction usually occurs within four weeks of use.

Alcohol does not qualify as a addictive drug under the WHO definition. The percentage of users of alcohol who become addicted is small. Addiction to alcohol may take many years. Tolerance to alcohol is usually limited to three or four times the initial dose. Heroin addicts can tolerate up to 100 times the initial dose.

Alcohol doesn't fall into the WHO definition of **habit forming drugs.** The WHO describes habit forming drugs "as ones capable of causing an emotional or physiological dependence." The emphasis seems to be on the physiological dependence. This same belief is found in the medical model and in most pharmacological texts.

The WHO labels alcohol as an "intermediate in kind and degree" between the two categories of habituation and addiction. About 10% of alcohol users become addicted. For many others alcohol is habituating. Alcohol might be called a selectively addicting drug.

Milan (1981) and other authors have stated their belief that psychological, cultural, and social factors influence the alcoholic's drinking patterns and behavior. These psychological patterns have no effect upon whether or not the drinker becomes an alcoholic. Physiology, not psychology, determines whether or not a drinker becomes addicted. This is referring to the Delta or Gamma forms of alcoholism as described by Jellinek (1960). It deals only with the metabolic changes that the individual undergoes.

Evidence appears that some basic predisposing factor or factors lead to physical addiction. Factors that are identified include abnormal metabolism, preference, heredity, prenatal influences, and ethnic susceptibility. In normal metabolism, alcohol is converted to acetaldehyde, then to acetate, and then to carbon dioxide and water. In the alcoholic, unusual amounts of acetaldehyde build up. Charles Lieber (1976), chief of research on liver disease and nutrition at the Bronx Veteran's Administration Hospital, theorizes that this build up of acetaldehyde is caused partially by a malfunctioning of the liver's enzyme system.

Schuckit and Rayses (1979), psychotherapist and researcher at U. C. San Diego, take this acetaldehyde difference further. They showed that in alcoholics the breakdown of acetaldehyde into acetate is done at one-half the rate of the non-alcoholic. Their theory is that this slowing down in metabolism causes the acetaldehyde to accumulate.

Both Lieber's and Schuckit's research is oriented towards finding out if enzyme malfunction precedes heavy drinking or is caused by heavy drinking. Lieber discovered that alcoholics have abnormal liver mitochondria that are unable to change acetaldehyde into acetate at a normal rate. This "low capacity" is evident at the early stages of heavy drinking. This suggests that the cells are altered before heavy drinking begins. Shuckit's studies also indicate that metabolic abnormalities exist prior to heavy drinking. Children of alcoholics who had never consumed alcohol prior to the experiment were unable to convert acetaldehyde into acetate at the normal rate. This makes a very strong case for the belief that heredity is a factor in alcoholism (Milam,1981).

Alcoholics appear to have a liver cell malfunction which causes a buildup of acetaldehyde. Acetaldehyde is a dangerous substance that can cause harm to cells, inhibit protein synthesis, and compete with neurotransmitters in the brain. By tying up the neurotransmitters in the brain, the brain's amines interact with the abundant acetaldehyde to form the compounds known as "isoquinolines." These "isoquinolines" are similar to the opiates. The theory is that the "isoquinolines" react on the opiate centers in the brain, contributing to the addictive effect of alcohol (Milam, 1981).

Lieber, in 1968, gave rats a chemical to deplete the brain of serotonin. The rats decreased their intake of alcohol. Serotonin appears to increase animals' preference for alcohol. Alcohol-seeking animals have higher levels of serotonin than animals that avoid it. Drinking causes an increase in serotonin in animals that show preference for alcohol, but not in those that avoid it (Lieber, 1976).

The product of dopamine (a neurotransmitter found in the brain) and acetaldehyde is called tetrahydropapaveroline (THP). When THP is injected into rats' brains, it causes rats who normally reject alcohol to drink in excessive amounts (Meyers, 1977).

Goodman (1976) provided strong evidence that alcoholism is passed from parent to child. He studied children of alcoholics who had been removed from their parents at birth. He found that children of alcoholics showed a four-fold tendency to become alcoholic. Further, these children would develop alcoholism early in life. Children of non-alcoholic parents showed lower alcoholism rates, even when raised by an alcoholic foster parent. Goodman compared sons of alcoholics who were adopted and raised by an unrelated family with their brothers who had been raised by the alcoholic parent. He found that the brother raised by the alcoholic parent was no more likely to become alcoholic than the other brother. Goodman found psychological factors between the two groups, including depression, anxiety, neurosis, personality disturbance, psychopathology, criminality, and drug abuse to be "virtually indistinguishable." His conclusion is that psychological factors are not relevant to the onset of alcoholism. Goodman described conditions that fit the definition of the disease state of alcoholism. Approximately 10% of people who have drinking problems fall into this category.

A sharp difference seems to exist in alcoholism rates in different ethnic groups. Researchers attribute this factor to differing forms of the liver enzyme ADH. Native Americans and Eskimos have a very high rate of alcoholism, around 80 to 90%. Jews and Italians show a very low rate, approximately 1%. Some correlation appears between time of exposure to alcohol and a lower rate of alcoholism. Jews and Italians have been exposed for some 7000 years. Scandinavians, French, and Irish have been exposed for some 1,500 years. They show a medium rate. The Eskimos and Native Americans have been exposed to alcohol for 300 years (Finn & O'Gorman, 1980).

Jellinek (1960) stated, "Alcoholism is any use of alcoholic beverages that causes any damage to the individual or society or both." His organization of types of alcoholics gives a clear picture of the wide variety of problems falling under the umbrella of alcoholism. Jellinek categorized alcoholics as:

1. **Alpha Alcoholism.** A purely psychological continual dependence or reliance upon the effect of alcohol to relieve bodily or emotional pain. This is an undisciplined drinker who acts against sociologic rules such as time, place, occurrence, or amount. The "problem drinker" who doesn't lose control or the ability to abstain.

2. **Beta Alcoholism.** Complications such as polyneuropathy (a disease state involving several nerves that is often associated with chronic use of alcohol), gastritis (inflammation of the stomach with symptoms that include loss of appetite, nausea, pain, vomiting, and distention of the stomach), and cirrhosis (a disease of the liver marked by liver cell distruction and the manufacture of scar tissue) may occur without physical or psychological dependence. The dangers are nutritional deficiencies, lower productivity, and probable shortened life span.

3. **Gamma Alcoholism.** Symptoms include acquired increased tissue tolerance, adaptive cell metabolism, withdrawal symptoms, craving (physical dependence), and loss of control. A progression occurs from psychological to physical dependence. Both Alpha and Beta can develop into Gamma. Serious damage includes loss of control, impairment of interpersonal relationships, serious health problems, and serious financial and social problems. This is the predominant form of alcoholism in the United States. It fits the Alcoholics Anonymous definition of alcoholism.

4. **Delta Alcoholism.** Similar to Gamma Alcoholism, except that the person does not have loss of control. The inability to abstain remains. One day of abstinence brings on withdrawal symptoms. The ability to control

intake remains intact. This person is not found in A.A. since he/she does not go through distressing social and psychological experiences.

5. **Epsilon Alcoholism.** The periodic drinker. He/she can resist drinking for several months or years and then go on a heavy drinking period.

In Figure 14.1 is a summary of information about alcohol.

Barbiturates

Barbituric acid was first formulated in 1864 by Adolph von Bayer. Since that time, more than 2500 barbiturates have been synthesized, with about 50 compounds being marketed. These compounds are used medically for their effects as sedatives, hypnotics, anesthetics, and anticonvulsants.

In normal therapeutic use, the barbiturates are not particularly toxic; however, they have additive central nervous system effects with other depressants such as alcohol. Many reported cases of death caused by respiratory failure result from the use of barbiturates as a sleeping aid after an evening of drinking alcohol.

The effects of the barbiturates are similar to the effects of alcohol. Therefore, not surprisingly, the barbiturates are frequently misused. In fact, enough similarity exists between alcohol and barbiturate addiction that taking one drug can prevent the occurrence of withdrawal effects to the other agent.

As the dosage increases, the barbiturates can produce drowsiness, sleep, and intoxication similar to alcohol. These symptoms include euphoria, talkativeness, slurred speech, poor coordination, and faulty judgment.

To maintain euphoria with the barbiturates is difficult due to their sedative effect. A very thin window exists between the euphoric and sedative blood levels. For this reason young people tend to not use these drugs; they are most often abused by older users.

Generic Name	Chemical Name	Street Name	Usual Dose/ Duration of Action
Beer	Ethanol 2-6%	brew, suds	12 oz./2-4 hours
Wine	Ethanol 9-14%	grapes, vino	4 oz./2-4 hours
Fortified wines	Ethanol 20%	Sherry, Brandy	
Distilled spirits Hard liquor	Ethanol 35-50%	booze, juice, hooch, rum, gin, whiskey	1½ oz./2-4 hours
Sterno Canned heat	ethanol 96% methanol 4%*	gut rot	

Administration: Oral

Short Term Effects: Hangover; headache; dizziness; nausea; vomiting; dehydration; relaxation; sedation; impaired judgment, reaction time, coordination, and emotional control; automobile accidents.

Long Term Effects: Habituation; irreversible damage to brain and liver; accelerated aging process; increased incidence of heart attack and cancer; addiction with severe withdrawal; possible loss of job and family.

Potentional For:		
	Physical Dependence	yes
	Tolerance	yes
	Psychological Dependence	yes
	Overall Abuse	very high

Regulations and Controls: legally sold in all States at age twenty-one.

* Methanol is a highly toxic poison.

Figure 14.1. Summary of information about alcohol.

Barbiturate withdrawal can be a serious medical emergency. It is considered even more life-threatening than that of heroin. D'Andrea (1975) reported a 5 to 7% mortality rate in untreated withdrawal. In Figure 14.2 is a summary of information about barbiturates.

Antianxiety Drugs

The antianxiety drugs, sometimes referred to as the "minor tranquilizers," have drawn considerable public attention, as well as having been the topic of many government hearings and professional conferences and papers. These drugs are over-prescribed by the physician, overused by the public, lead to self-destructive behavior, and tolerance and physical dependence.

When the antianxiety drugs were first marketed, they were thought to be safe, and indeed are safer than the barbiturates they replaced. The literature makes claims for these drugs to be virtually "suicide-proof." This is true of the benzodiazepines, except when ingested along with alcohol or other depressants. The combination of alcohol and the benzodiazepines can be lethal.

Clinically, the benzodiapezines are used to treat anxiety, insomnia (flurazepam, temazepam, and triazolam), muscle relaxation (diazepam), and seizure disorders (clonazepam, clorazepate, and diazepam).

The physician is the one who is most frequently cited as being the major cause of the antianxiety drugs' misuse. This is, of course, based upon the fact that the physician is the "controller" or "gatekeeper" (Wesson, 1981) of the products of the pharmaceutical industry. This is an oversimplified view. These drugs are most commonly used for treating anxiety and insomnia, both common symptoms in our society. Wesson (1981) stated the view that the medical model believes that all symptoms, if "adequately treated," result in a "cure." This belief is also supported by some behavioralists. Others, including this author, believe anxiety to be a normal, and even healthy, experience of everyday life. The common practice by many physicians is to treat the slightest anxiety or insomnia with

(Continued on page 274)

Generic Name	Trade Name	Street Name	Usual Dose/ Duration of Action
Amobarbital	Amytal	Blues Blue Dolls Blue Bullets Blue Devils Blue Heavens	65-200 mg/ Intermediate*
Butabarbital	Butisol		15-30 mg/ Intermediate
Pentobarbital	Nembutal	Nembies Yellows Yellow Jackets Bullets	30-100 mg/ Short
Sodium thiopental	Pentothal	truth serum	varies/ short
Phenobarbital	Luminol	Phennies	10-100 mg/ Long
Secobarbital	Seconal	Reds Red Devils Red Birds Pinks Seggy Seccy F-40's Mexican Reds	30-100 mg/ Short
Amobarbital/ secobarbital	Tuinal	Rainbows Double Trouble	75-200 mg/ Short- Intermediate

* **Note:** Short = up to 4 hours
   Intermediate = 4 to 6 hours
   Long = 6 or more hours

Figure 14.2. Summary of information about barbiturates.

Figure 14.2. Continued.

Generic Name	Trade Name	Street Name	Usual Dose/ Duration of Action
Barbituate like drugs:			
Glutethimide	Doriden	Goofers Goofballs	500 mg/ Intermediate
Chloral hydrate	Noctec	Coral Jelly Beans Miki's Knockout Drops	500 mg/ Short
Methaqualone	Quaalude	Soppers Ludes Sopes	100-400 mg**/ Short
Methyprylon	Noludar	Noodlelars	100-200 mg/ Short

Administration: Oral.

Short Term Effects: CNS depression: sleep, relaxation, and sedation; euphoria; drowsiness; impaired judgment; relief of anxiety and tension; muscle relaxation; mood changes; and muscle control.

Long Term Effects: Irritability; weight loss; habituation and addiction with severe withdrawal sysmptoms; diversion of energy and money. Possible ulcers, nutritional problems, and infections.

Potentional For:	Physical Dependence	yes
	Tolerance	yes
	Psychological Dependence	yes
	Overall Abuse	high

Regulations and Controls: Included under the Federal Comprehensive Drug Abuse Prevention and Control Act of 1970 as Schedule III drugs. Available only by prescription which can be refilled up to five times within a six month period. Federal law prohibits any other manufacturing, sale, or possession. The penalties are moderate, and there is widespread illicit trafficing of this drugs.

**No longer legally obtained in the U.S. (Available through illicit sources).

pharmacological solutions. Many physicans state that they do in fact distinguish between incapacitating or morbid anxiety and "normal" anxiety (Wesson & Smith, 1981).

The pharmaceutical industry must be taken to task over the intense and often misleading advertising that is promoted in the direction of the physician. Medical journals and drug detail persons (two of the main sources of physicians' information on drugs) are used to sell the product.

These remarks address the supply and the supplier. Also an important person to consider is the "patient" or the individual representing the demand. Just over twenty years ago, the common practice in medicine was not to label or tell the patient what drugs they were receiving; this is no longer true. The patient population today is very much more knowledgeable and sophisticated. The informed patient of today, suffering from anxiety or insomnia, looks to the physician for treatment and to the prescription for relief.

Several possible physician-patient intractions can be thought of as drug abuse or misuse.

1. A very small number of physicians who, knowingly and for profit motive, initiate or maintain a patient's dependence upon antianxiety or other drugs without regard for the patient's welfare.

2. The physician who is misinformed or not very knowledge-able concerning the prescribing of the psychoactive drug.

3. The physician who unknowingly contributes to his/her patients' drug dependency through well intentioned and appropriate prescribing of drugs. Some patients go from physician to physician, getting drugs in this manner.

4. The patient who controls or manipulates the physician to prescribe whatever he/she wants, even when the physician is aware that this is not in the best interests of the patient.

5. The physician who underprescribes, to the detriment of the patient, by withholding a useful drug.

In Figure 14.3 in summary form is information related to current benzodiazepines marketed for anxiety.

Generic Name	Trade Name	Oral Dose[1]	$t\frac{1}{2}$[2]	Onset
Alprazolam	Xanax	0.75-4.0	12-15	
Chlordiazepoxide	Librium	15-100	5-30	intermed
Clorazepate	Tranxene	15-60	30-100	fast
Diazepam	Valium	6-40	20-50	very fast
Halazepam	Paxipam	60-160	14	
Lorazepam	Ativan	2-6	10-18	intermed
Oxazepam	Serax	30-120	5-13	slow
Prazepam	Centrax	20-60	30-100	very slow

Administration: oral, sometimes by injection.

Short Term Effects: Relief of anxiety, tension, and insomnia. CNS depression and muscle relaxation.

Long Term Effects: Sedation, lethargy, depression, and addiction.

Potentional For:
Physical Dependence	yes[3]
Tolerance	minimal
Psychological Dependence	yes
Overall Abuse	moderate

Regulations and Controls: Included under the Federal Comprehensive Drug Abuse Prevention and Control Act of 1970 as Schedule IV drugs.

---

[1] Defined in milligrams (mg) per 24 hours.

[2] Half-life information varies from reference to reference.

[3] A large population of individuals, more frequently women, have been given these drugs legally. They have not been able to stop because of withdrawal symptoms which may not appear for 5 to 10 days.

Figure 14.3. Summary of information related to current benzodiazepines marketed for anxiety.

Antipsychotic Drugs

The antipsychotic drugs have very little abuse potential. Most, if not all, have troublesome side effects. They also have unpleasant effects when taken by "normal" people. Information related to antipsychotic drugs has been summarized in Figure 14.4.

Narcotics

The Papaver somniferum (opium poppy) has caused both grief and joy. Opium has been employed by physicians for some 6000 years. It has stood alone, until the last century and a half, as the only medical substance that could be counted upon to relieve pain and suffering, induce sleep, and correct dysentery. It has long been thought of as an "aphrodisiac" which is said to prolong the male performance, probably because the user could not sustain, or release a charge (Ray, 1972; Rosenberg, Rand, & Asay, 1985).

Opium's ability to relieve anxiety and deliver pleasure makes it attractive as a recreational drug as well as an important medical tool.

The pharmacology and use of the narcotics is treated in Chapter X, Pain and Analgesic Drugs. An important characteristic of the opiates and narcotics is the ability of the user to rapidly develop a tolerance, so that addicts are able to take many times the usual lethal dose of heroin or morphine without much effect.

The following, taken from *Confessions of An English Opium-Eater* (DeQuincey, 1907) is included to give the reader some understanding of the contract between the feelings, effects, and experiences that result from alcohol and opium.

> .... "crude opium .... is incapable of producing any state of body at all resembling that which is produced by alcohol .... it is not in the quantity of its effects merely, but in the quality, that it differs altogether. The pleasure given by wine is always rapidly mounting, and tending to a crisis, after which as rapidly it declines: that from opium, when once generated, is stationary for eight or ten hours ... the one is a flickering flame, the other a steady and equable glow. But the main distinction lies in this-that, whereas wine disorders the mental faculties, opium, on the contrary (if taken in a proper manner), introduces amongst them the most exquisite order, legislation, and harmony. Wine robs a man of his self-possession; opium sustains and reinforces it. Wine unsettles the judgment ... opium, on the contrary, communicates serenity and equipoise to all the faculties ... "(p.179)

Class Name	Generic Name	Trade Name	Dosage
Phenothiazine: Aliphatic			
	Chlorpromazine	Thorazine	30-800 mg/day
	Promazine	Sparine	40-1200 mg/day
	Triflupromazine	Vesprin	60-150 mg/day
Phenothiazine: Piperidine			
	Thioridazine	Mellaril	150-800 mg/day
	Mesoridazine	Serentil	30-400 mg/day
Phenothiazine: Piperazine			
	Acetophenazine	Tindal	60-120 mg/day
	Perphenazine	Trilafon	12-64 mg/day
	Prochlorperazine	Compazine	15-150 mg/day
	Fluphenazine	Permitil/Prolixin	1-40 mg/day
	Trifluoperazine	Stelazine	2-40 mg/day
Thioxanthenes			
	Chlorprothixene	Taractan	75-600 mg/day
	Thiothixene	Navane	8-30 mg/day
Butyrophenone			
	Haloperidol	Haldol	1-15 mg/day
Dihydroindolone			
	Molindone	Moban	15-225 mg/day
Dibenzoxazepine			
	Loxapine	Loxitane	20-250 mg/day

Administration: oral, sometimes injected.

Short Term Effects: Relaxation, relief of anxiety and tension, suppression of hallucinations or delusions, improved function.

Long Term Effects: Many severe and often non-reversible side effects

Potentional For:		
	Physical Dependence	no
	Tolerance	no
	Psychological Dependence	minimal
	Overall Abuse	minimal

Regulations and Controls: Federal law requires prescription. Illict traffic is negligible.

Figure 14.4. Summary of information related to antipsychotic drugs.

Ray (1972) pointed out that in spite of all the good that DeQuincey found in opium, he suffered much from its use, finding long periods of his life in which he was unable to write as a result of his addiction.

The dangers of narcotics include (1) the induction of a rapid tolerance, which leads the user to an increase in dosage; (2) accidental overdosage, the margin between therapeutic or desired effect dose and lethal dose is small (tolerance plays an important factor in overdosing); (3) the high cost of procuring the needed drug causes many users to turn to criminal activities; and (4) the high incidence of illness resulting from personal and social deterioration as well as serious infection from non-sterile preparations and infections (D'Andrea, 1975).

The complications of using non-sterile intravenous injection sets include the possibility of acquiring AIDS, viral hepatitis, abscesses, or blood poisoning. Another serious problem with the use of opiates, as well as all other "street drugs" is the presence of adulterants. **Adulterants** or excipient ingredients are usually pharmacologically inactive ingredients added to a drug to give it bulk, or to act as a preservative, or as a binder or "glue" to hold other ingredients together. Other ingredients include coloring agents, sugar or wax coatings, or flavorings. Frequently, street drugs are cut or adulterated with unknown and sometimes dangerous additives.

Like alcohol, the use of narcotics by pregnant women can cause serious consequences for the fetus and newborn. About 80% of the newborns born to addicted mothers go through a withdrawal syndrome (Radcliffe, Sites, Rush, & Cruse, 1985). Symptoms typically begin in the first few days of life and include hyperactivity, irritability, tremors, regurgitation, poor feeding, and diarrhea. Convulsions may occur, being more common in methadone withdrawal. Apparently no significant birth deformity occurs with the newborn of addicted mothers. No studies were identified that evaluated the long-term effects of fetal addiction.

A high level of tolerance develops to the analgesic, euphoric, sedative, hypotensive, respiratory depressive, nausea and vomiting effects. A moderate degree of tolerance develops towards the slowed heart beat, with no tolerance to the pupillary constriction, constipation, and convulsive effects. Therefore, even the long-term user suffers from constipation and has the characteristic pin-point pupils (Radcliffe, Sites, Rush, & Cruse, 1985).

The usual cause of death is respiratory depression. Tolerance does develop to the effects of respiratory depression. The lethal dose level continues to rise as use increases. As long as the user is chronically "using," the tolerance seems to continue to rise. Then, when the user has even a brief period of abstinence and then he/she takes his/her usual dose, the tolerance has been lowered and the usual dose becomes lethal.

Narcotic use leads to a physical dependence and upon discontinuance of the substance, a narcotic withdrawal syndrome occurs. The particular narcotic used, the general health of the user, the amount, and the duration of use are factors that determine the extent of the withdrawal symptoms.

Generally, heroin and morphine withdrawal symptoms first occur in 8 to 12 hours after the last dose. These early symptoms include tearing, yawning, sweating, and runny nose. Between 12 and 14 hours, the withdrawing individual usually falls into a restless sleep, lasting several hours. When the person awakens, he/she tends to feel much worse. As the withdrawal progresses, the pupils become dilated, a loss of appetite occurs, and the person shows signs of restlessness, irritability, and shakiness. In about 48 to 72 hours, the withdrawal syndrome reaches full intensity, symptoms include increasing insomnia, irritability, violet yawning, marked loss of appetite, severe sneezing, tearing, and runny nose. Other common symptoms include nausea, vomiting, diarrhea, weakness, and depression. Excessive sweating begins and the individual undergoes a steady flow of "goosebumps," thought to be the origin of the term "cold turkey." The withdrawing individual has severe muscle and bone pain, also involuntary muscle jerks and kicks. After 7 to 10 days these symptoms stop, however the individual usually undergoes a period known as "protracted abstinence syndrome," which may last for several weeks. Symptoms include, low self-image, low threshold of discomfort, and a low tolerance for stress. During this critical time, many narcotics users have a relapse.

Withdrawal symptoms from meperidine begin in as little as 3 hours and reach a high intensity in 8 to 12 hours. Muscle twitching, irritability, and nervousness are often worse than with morphine withdrawal, however very little, if any, nausea, vomiting, and diarrhea occur, and the pupils do not become widely dilated. Symptoms disappear in 4 or 5 days.

Methadone withdrawal symptoms begin in 24 to 48 hours. Acute symptoms tend to peak during the third day and may not decrease for up to three weeks. Acute withdrawal often lasts for 6 or 7 weeks and the protracted withdrawal syndrome may may last as long as 24 weeks (D'Andrea, 1975; Radcliffe, 1985). A summary of information related to narcotics is in Figure 14.5.

UPPERS

Caffeine

Caffeine is one of three closely related alkaloids that occur in plants throughout the world. These drugs are chemically known as xanthines. **Xanthine** is a Greek word meaning yellow, which corresponds to the residue left when the xanthines are heated with nitric acid and dried.

Caffeine is the most significant of the three alkaloids. They share several pharmacological actions. They stimulate the central nervous system, act on the kidney to produce diuresis, stimulate cardiac muscle, and relax smooth muscle, especially the bronchial muscle (Rall, 1980).

A legend tells of a goatherder named Kaldi, who noted that his flock of goats after eating the berry of the coffee plant stayed awake and frisky throughout the night instead of sleeping. He tried the berries himself with similar results (Rall, 1980). Soon, some religious leaders were using Kaldi's berries to make a hot liquid beverage that allowed them to sustain a more lengthy prayer (Ellis, 1974). Coffee drinking was first popular in the Arabic world as a drink called "Qakwah" (Lemberger & Rubin, 1976) or "gawah" (Greden, 1981), which is a word meaning wine. The use of coffee became so widespread throughout the Mohammedan world that it became outlawed. It also was used

Trade Name	Generic Name	Street Name	Usual Dose (In mg)	Duration of Action
	Heroin (diacetylmorphine)	H, Horse, Harry, Hairy, Joy powder, Smack, Skag, Junk, Shit, Jive, Stuff, Blanco	3 mg	4 hours
	Opium	O, Op	15 mg	5 hours

The following analgesic are arranged in order of their decreasing potential for dependence

Trade Name	Generic Name	Street Name	Usual Dose (In mg)	Duration of Action
Dilaudid	Hydromorphone	Dillies	2 mg	4 to 6 hours
— — — —	Morphine (sulfate)	Miss Emma White Stuff MS	15 mg	4 to 6 hours
Demerol	Meperidine		50-100 mg	3 to 5 hours
Dolophine	Methadone	Dollies	2.5 - 10 mg	3 to 4 hours
Empirin & Codeine Tylenol & Codeine	Codeine	Number Fours	15 - 65 mg	4 hours
Percodan Percocet	Oxycodone		4.5 mg	4 to 6 hours
Darvon Darvon—N	Propoxyphene	N's, pinks	65 mg 100 mg	4 to 6 hours 4 to 6 hours
Talwin—NX*	Pentazocine		50 mg	3 to 4 hours

* Up until 1983, some heroin users substituted a mixture of pentazocine (Talwin) and tripelennamine (PBZ). They would obtain both tablets (requiring prescriptions) crush and inject the combination as a substitute for the heroin. A serious side effect known as "blue velvet lung," caused by the blue dye talc used in the PBZ, which became lodged in the small vessesl of the lungs. The makers of Talwin in order to stop the abuse of "Ts and blues" reformulated the Talwin with the addition of the narcotic agonist naloxone. When taken orally the naloxone is inactivated, however, when injected it acts to stop the effects of the pentazocine. It also can precipitate withdrawal.

Figure 14.5. Summary of information related to narcotics.

Figure 14.5. Continued.

Administration: opium, smoking; herion, IM or IV injection; other, injection or oral

Short Term Effects: CNS depression, sedation, euphoria, relief of pain, impaired intellectual function and coordination.

Long Term Effects: Constipation, weight loss, temporary impotency, habituation and addiction with severe withdrawal symptoms.

Potential for:	Physical Dependence:	yes
	Tolerance:	yes
	Psychological Dependence	high
	Overall Abuse:	high

Regulations and Controls: Included under the Federal Comprehensive Drug Abuse Prevention and Control Act of 1970 as Schedule I (heroin), II (opium, morphine, hydromorphone, methadone, meperidine, oxycodone), III (codeine and similar synthetic narcotic analgesics in combination with acetaminophen or aspirin), IV (propoxyphene), and V (cough and diarrhea mixtures).

---

medically as a cure for almost everything including measles and reducing lust. It first appeared in Europe as a medicine, but soon became a popular drink and coffeehouses sprung up throughout England and France during the seventeenth century. Charles II banned coffeehouses as hot-beds of seditious talk and slanderous attacks upon persons in high stations. The ban only lasted eleven days.

Although, coffee was the big drink in England, tea was the drink in the colonies across the Atlantic. Tea was cheaper and more available than coffee. The British act, taxing the colonists' tea, was among the acts that lead to the Revolution. To be a tea drinker was to be a "Tory." The drink of the new nation became coffee.

Daruma, the founder of Zen-Buddhism, was said to have fallen asleep during a 9 year meditation. Upon his awakening—out of shame—he proceeded to cut his eyelids off in a attempt to save his reputation. From the spot that his eye lids touched the earth came a new plant. From its leaves came a brew which could keep a person awake (Greden, 1981).

Tea has been cited as far back as 350 A.D. It was used medically, according to one Chinese manuscript. The fact that a tax was levied upon tea in 780 A.D. indicates its wide use for non-medical purposes. Tea came to Europe some eight centuries later as an herb that was used for tumors or abscesses, or for ailments of the bladder, to quench thirst, to lessen the desire for sleep, and to gladden or cheer the heart (Lemberger & Rubin, 1976).

The Aztec god of the air, Quetzalcoatl, is said to have presented man with the "chocolate tree." The cocoa tree is called Theobroma, food of the gods. Montezuma II, the emperor of Mexico in the early sixteenth century, is believed to have eaten only "chocolatl" every day. Chocolatl comes from the Mayan words "choco" (warm) and latl (beverage). Until the arrival of Cortez, in the early 1520s when he introduced sugar, the drink was quite bitter. Cortez took the Theobroma cacao bush back to Spain upon his return in 1528.

The active ingredient in chocolate is theobromine. It has physiological actions that closely parallel caffeine; however, it is much less potent as a central nervous system stimulant.

Greden (1981) suggested the clinical term "caffeinism" to describe a syndrome produced by acute or chronic overuse of caffeine. The predominant features of this syndrome are anxiety, mood changes, sleep disturbances, and psychophysiological complaints.

When caffeine use is discontinued by individuals who have developed a tolerance, a withdrawal syndrome generally appears within 18 to 24 hours (Greden, 1981). Symptoms include headaches, irritability, inability to work effectively, nervousness, restlessness, mild nausea, and lethargy. A summary of information related to caffeine is in Figure 14.6.

Source[1]	Amount of Caffeine (mg)	Quantity
Brewed coffee	100 to 150 mg	cup
Instant coffee	86 to 99 mg	cup
Decaffeinated coffee	2 to 30 mg	cup
Tea (leaf)	30 to 75 mg	cup
Tea (bag)	42 to 100 mg	cup
Cola drinks	25 to 60 mg	12 ounces
Coca-Cola	45 mg	
Pepsi-Cola	30 mg	
Cocoa	5 to 50 mg	cup
Chocolate bar	25 mg	1 ounce bar
No Doz and similar preparations	100 to 200 mg	tablet
OTC cold preparations	30 mg	

Administration: Oral

Short Term Effects: CNS stimulation, increased alertness, reduction of fatigue.

Long Term Effects: Insomnia, restlessness, habituation, and cafeinism.

Potential for:		
	Physical Dependence:	Yes
	Tolerance:	Yes
	Psychological Dependence	moderate
	Overall Abuse:	yes[2]

Regulations and Controls: Available and advertised without control or limits. No regulations for either adults or children.

---

[1] Data taken from Kastrup, Olin, & Schwach, 1986; Greden, 1981; Lemberger & Rubin, 1976; D'Andrea, 1975; and Rall, 1980.

[2] The use of caffeine may be of some concern to the psychotherapist, as the client may be using it to mask underlying feelings or cover symptoms. A psychotherapist needs to know whether or not the client's "sense of wellbeing" is coming from drinking 4 or 5 cups of coffee. The general medical and law enforcement establishment consider it to be of little problem.

Figure 14.6. Summary of information related to caffeine.

Nicotine

Tobacco is a native product of the Americas. The natives of San Salvador gave tobacco leaves to Christopher Columbus upon his arrival in 1492. It was introduced in Europe as an herb. The following quote from a 1591 book summarized the beliefs of that time about the substance: "To seek to tell the virtues and greatness of this holy herb, the ailments which can be cured by it, and have been, the evils from which it has saved thousands, would be to go on to infinity" (Ray, 1983, p.96). Others had differing opinions, including Dr. William Vaugh, who wrote in 1617:

> Tobacco that outlandish weede
> It spends the braine and spoiles the seede
> It dulls the spirite, it dims the sight
> It robs a woman of her right.
> (Quoted in Dunphy, 1969, p.573)

After much soul searching and debate, the authors of DSM-III included two headings: Tobacco Dependence" and "Tobacco Withdrawal." Much of the debate centered around how to avoid labeling approximately 30 million heavy smokers as having a "mental disorder." In the final version of DSM-III, the headings are Tobacco Dependence (which replaces Tobacco Use Disorder in DSM-II) and Tobacco Withdrawal. DSM-III-R changed the heading to Nicotine dependence.

Approximately 4000 compounds (Jaffe, 1980) are generated by the burning of tobacco, consisting of both gaseous and particulate phases. Some of the components of the gaseous phase that are known to be undesirable are carbon monoxide, carbon dioxide, nitrogen oxides, ammonia, volatile nitrosamines, hydrogen cyanide, volatile hydrocarbons, alcohols, aldehydes, and ketones. The particulate phase contains nicotine, water, and tar. The tar contains numerous compounds, including several radioactive ones.

Nicotine is well established as one the most toxic drugs known. A dose of 60 mgs is lethal to man. The average cigar contains twice this much nicotine; however, not all the nicotine is delivered or absorbed in a short enough period time to kill a person (Ray, 1983). Over the years, the amount of nicotine in cigarettes has been decreased. The typical filter cigarette contains between 20 to 30 mg of nicotine. Approximately 10 percent of that will be absorbed by the individual who inhales the smoke.

Nicotine acts on most cholinergic synapses, mimicking acetylcholine by acting at the cholinergic receptor site and stimulating the dendrite. Since nicotine is not rapidly deactivated, the continued action prevents incoming impulses from having an effect. Nicotine first stimulates then blocks the synapse. Within the central nervous system, the effects of nicotine are believed to be caused by its action on the cortex. The effects of nicotine after only one cigarette include inhibition of hunger, contractions in the stomach, a slight increase in blood sugar level, and a deadening of the taste buds. With regular smoking a decrease occurs in heart rate and oxygen consumption, a constriction of the blood vessels in the skin, a decrease in skin temperature, and an increase in blood pressure. Smoking during pregnancy results in lighter weight babies, a 200 to 300% increase in the number of premature babies, and twice as many aborted and stillborn babies (Public Health Services, 1967).

Some heavy smokers seem to adjust their plasma nicotine levels by titrating their smoking. That is, they reduce the number of cigarettes when their plasma level is high and increase the number when it is low. When the heavy smoker is given a cigarette with a lower nicotine concentration, he/she often smokes more and when given a cigarette with a higher nicotine concentration smokes less (Jaffe & Kanzler, 1981).

In 1984, a nicotine containing chewing gum was marketed in the United States under the trade name of "Nicorette." It contains a nicotine resin complex and is used for the temporary aid of cigarette smokers seeking to give up smoking. Individuals are instructed to chew up to 10 pieces of gum a day during the first month of treatment, to stop after 3 months of treatment, and to initiate a gradual withdrawal from the gum if it is still used after 6 months (Kastrup, Olin, & Schwach, 1986). A summary of information related to nicotine is in Figure 14.7.

Official Name	Slang Name	Usual Dose	Duration of Action
Cigarettes	Fags, Smokes,	3 to 9 mg	1-2 hours
Cigars	Stoggies	100 to 120 mg	
Pipe tobacco		100 mg	
Chewing tobacco	Cud, Chew, Bull		1-2 hours
Snuff			1-2 hours

Administration: Inhalation, smoked, or chewed.

Short Term Effects: CNS Stimulation, relaxation or distraction, increased blood pressure and heart rate, reduced appetite.

Long Term Effects: Lung and other cancer, heart and blood vessel disease, chronic cough, emphysema, habituation, diversion of energy and money, air pollution, fire, death.

Potential for:		
	Physical Dependence:	yes
	Tolerance:	yes
	Psychological Dependence	high
	Overall Abuse:	high

Regulations and Controls: Available and advertised with some limitations. Minimum age requirements, taxation, and cautionary package labeling: "SURGEON GENERAL'S WARNING: Quitting Smoking Now Greatly Reduces Serious Risks to Your Health!"

Figure 14.7. Summary of information related to nicotene.

Amphetamines

The use of amphetamine and its derivatives has only developed during this century. The major effects of the amphetamines were first discovered in the 1930s. An early use of amphetamine came out of its potent bronchial dialator effect. In 1932, the Benzedrine inhaler was introduced as an over-the-counter drug. The following excerpt from a popular national magazine article entitled *On a Bender with Benzedrine* illustrates its potential for abuse:

> . . . . . . after I bought an inhaler. Hal worked off the perforated cap and pulled out the medicated paper, folder accordion-wise . . . . "Like this—" Hal took the innocent looking scrap of paper he had torn away and held it between thumb and finger. He alternatedly dunked and squeezed this paper into his glass of beer" [Ray, 1983, from *Everybody's Digest 5* (2):50, 1946].

In 1949, Smith, Kline, and French Laboratories, the manufacturer of the Benzedrine inhaler, replaced it with a product called the Benzedrex inhaler. The Benzedrex inhaler still on the market, has equivalent nasal decongestant characteristics but not the stimulation of the Benzedrine inhalers. In 1959 the FDA banned all amphetamine inhalants; however, one company was able to sell their inhaler containing methamphetamine until 1965.

Up until mid-1970, amphetamines were being prescribed for a large number of medical conditions including fatigue, weight reduction, and depression. In 1970, the FDA restricted the use of the amphetamines to three types of conditions: narcolepsy, hyperkinetic behavior, and short-term weight reduction programs.

Methylphenidate (Ritalin) was first synthesized in 1944 and is chemically related to the amphetamines. It is thought to be the drug of choice in treatment of hyperactive children (Millichop & Fowler, 1967). It is a mild stimulant of the central nervous system that has a countering effect on physical and mental fatigue, while it has only a slight effect on blood pressure or respiration. Ray (1983) estimated that some 300,000 children have been treated with methylphenidate. This may be a low figure, and a great deal of controversy surrounds the "hyperactive" diagnosis of many of these young people. Frequently, those identified as hyperactive are responding to certain foods, such as sugar, with an allergic reaction. Others are bright children who get bored in the contained classroom style of most school systems. Oftentimes, the teacher or parents have the problem, that is, difficulty in dealing with the "active" or noncontained child.

The amphetamines gained a reputation during World War II for their ability to stop drowsiness or even keep individuals awake for long periods. A 1944 report in the Air Surgeon's Bulletin entitled "Benzedrine Alert" illustrates this point: ". . . . this drug is the most satisfactory of any available for temporarily postponing sleep, when the desire to sleep endangers the security of a mission." Astronaut Gordon Cooper was ordered to take an amphetamine prior to his manually controlled reentry in 1969 (Ray, 1983).

Amphetamine has been used for the treatment of narcolepsy. Its use in this disorder is infrequent, and cases have been reported of acute paranoid psychotic reactions developing (Ray, 1983).

The amphetamines gained a great deal of popularity because of their ability to decrease hunger. The mechanism of this action is not understood; however, amphetamines do not lower blood sugar levels and do decrease food intake. Some people believe that the euphoric effect of the amphetamines is the real basis for their widespread use in weight reduction programs. Two factors make the use of amphetamines questionable for weight control. First, a tolerance quickly develops to the appetite depressant characteristics. Second, the use of amphetamines ignores the psychological factors in weight reduction.

Federal government regulations in 1959, limiting the manufacture of the amphetamines, has cut the legal sale of these drugs; however, they are still in demand and are found on the "street." A summary of information related to amphetamines is in Figure 14.8.

(Continued on page 292)

Trade Name	Generic Name	Street Name	Usual Dose (In mg)	Duration of Action
	Amphetamine sulfate[1]	Bennies Beans Whites Crosstops Truck drivers Cartwheels	5-10 mg	4 - 6 hours[2]
Dexedrine	Dextroam-phetamine sulfate	Dex Dexies Oranges Hearts	2.5 - 15 mg	4 - 6 hours
Desoxyn	Methamphet-amine	Speed Crystal Crank Meth	5 - 15 mg	4 - 6 hours
Biphetamine	Amphetamine Complex		12.5 - 20 mg	10 - 14 hours
Obetrol	Amphetamine Mixture		10 - 20 mg	4 - 6 hours
Preludin	Phenmetra-zine		50-75 mg/day	4 - 6 hours
Didrex	Benzpheta-mine		25-150mg/day	4 - 6 hours
Ionamin	Phentermine		15-30 mg/day	8 - 10 hours
Tenuate Teparil	Diethylpro-prion		75 mg/day	8 - 10 hours
Sanorex Mezanor	Mazindol		2 mg/day	4 - 16 hours
Pondimin	Fenfluramine		NMT 120 mg	4 - 6 hours
Various	Phenylpro-panolamine		75 mg/day	4 - 6 hours

[1] Benzedrine (amphetamine sulfate) SKF and Dexamyl (a combination of dexedrine and amobarbital) have been taken off the market.

[2] Many come in timed release capsule or tablet form lasting 8 - 12 hours.

[3] A non-prescription diet aid that has little to no abuse potential.

Figure 14.8. Summary of information related to amphetamines.

Figure 14.8. Continued.

Administration: oral, sometimes injected.

Short Term Effects: CNS effects, euphoria, confidence, elation; relief from fatigue, increased mental alertness; appetite suppression; increased motor and speech activity; increased temperature due to an action of the temperature regulation center in the brain; restlessness; irritability, weight loss, toxic amphetamine psychosis, manifested as paranoid ideations; purposeless behavior, eventually not being able to differentiate between reality and dilusion, with eventual full blown paranoid schizophrenia; habituation; tolerance; peripheral effects, increased respiration rate; increased blood pressure and heart rate at high doeses; however, sometimes at low doses the heart rate is decreased and blood pressure is increased; decreased gastrointestinal activity which can cause constipation; urinary retention.

Long Term Effects: Diversion of energy and money, severe physical deterioration, high blood pressure; stroke; brain damage; senous infections.

Potential for:
Physical Dependence:	high
Tolerance:	yes
Psychological Dependence	high
Overall Abuse:	high

Regulations and Controls: Included under the Federal Comprehensive Drug Abuse Prevention and Control Act of 1970 as Schedule II. The Federal government has placed strick limits on the quantities that can be manufactured. Many of these drugs see only minimal legitimate use today, however, illicit use is still high. Other prescription diet-aids are controlled under Schedule III and IV.

Cocaine

Cocaine is the principle active alkaloid found in the leaves of the coca plant, Erythroxylon coca. The plant, a native of South America, grows on the slopes of the Andes Mountains in places unsuitable for growing almost anything else. It thrives at elevations of 2,000 to 8,000 feet where over 100 inches of rain falls a year.

The early natives chewed the leaves for religious purposes, and it was known as the divine plant of the Incas (Del Pozo, 1967). It is still common for the workers and natives in Peru and Bolivia to be constantly chewing a ball of coca leaves. Van Dyke (1981) estimated that over 4 million natives in Peru and Bolivia are chewing coca leaves on a regular basis. To bring out the alkaloid, the leave is chewed along with an alkaline material.

In 1855, Gardeke first extracted the active ingredient of the coca leave and called it erythroxylon. Five years later, Niemann isolated the alkaloid and gave it the name cocaine (Van Dyke, 1981). Cocaine, which makes up about 1% of the leaf's content, was used by Sigmund Freud. In 1885 he wrote a treatise, *On the General Effects of Cocaine*, in which he recommended that cocaine be utilized for the treatment of morphine dependence and withdrawal. Cocaine found its way into tonics, patent medicines, and beverages. Coca-cola originally contained this substance and is still flavored by decocainized coca leaves. Cocaine was taken out of the formula in 1903 (Musto, 1973). The Federal Harrison Narcotics Act of 1914 prohibited the use of cocaine in patent medicines and effectively outlawed the recreational use of cocaine by any other means. The law classified cocaine as a narcotic, a misconception that is still prevalent today (Van Dyke, 1981).

Cocaine is well absorbed from all mucous membranes. It is hydrolyzed in the stomach after oral administration to an inactive form. The cocaine that is absorbed from the gastrointestinal tract is metabolized on the first pass through the liver. In the United States the major route of administration of cocaine is insufflation ("snorting") which results in absorption through the nasal membranes. The drug enters the blood circulation immediately without having to pass through the liver. It also is common practice to take cocaine through the buccal, or cheek cavity, as is done in South America. Doses of cocaine administered intravenously produce "high" and pleasant feelings that persist for 30 to 40 minutes. A paste containing 40 to 85% cocaine sulfate called "pasta," which is often mixed with tobacco or marijuana and smoked rapidly, has become a practice of the urban youth of Peru. Van Dyke (1981) reported that excessive smoking of cocaine produces personality changes, depression, hallucinations (visual, auditory, and tactile), and paranoid psychosis, sometimes requiring the psychiatric hospitalization of the user. Cocaine is rapidly absorbed and central nervous system effects are seen within 15 minutes. The drug also may be found in the kidney, spleen, and pancreas.

Cocaine is a psychomotor stimulant with effects similar to those of amphetamine. Unlike the amphetamines, cocaine has an additional effect as a local anesthetic. This action and its ability to cause blood vessels to constrict make it a popular drug for surgeries of the nose.

The alkaloidal cocaine (free base) known as **Crack** is now widely found in the United States. This form of cocaine is suitable for smoking. The name "crack" refers to the sound made by the crystals popping when they are heated. It is sometimes called "rock" cocaine because of its physical appearance. Reports indicate that free base cocaine is in epidemic use, especially among adolescents. Overdose is frequent, many deaths have occurred, and a high percentage of its users become addicted.

The alkaloidal form of cocaine found naturally in coca leaves is self-limiting in that it causes vasoconstriction of the nasal mucous membranes, slowing the absorption and plasma concentration. Cocaine powder is usually diluted or "cut" before it is sold.

"Crack" is almost pure cocaine, made by preparing an aqueous solution of cocaine HC1 and adding ammonia, and sometimes baking soda, to alkalinize the solution and precipitate alkaloidal cocaine (Medical Letter #28, 1986). The resultant product is suitable for smoking ("freebasing") in what is called a "base pipe." The "rock" can also be crushed, mixed with tobacco, and smoked in a cigarette. Smoking freebase results in rapid and high concentrations of absorbed cocaine. In effect, freebasing is comparable to injecting cocaine intravenously. When cocaine is smoked or injected intravenously, the user gets an almost immediate intense euphoric experience. This is often followed within minutes by a "crash," leading to frequent use and to the suscetible individual, rapid addiction. "Freebasers" often use marijuana, alcohol, opiates, or other drugs to decrease the sense of irritability caused by the cocaine.

Some question exists as to the development of tolerance with cocaine. Many researchers believe that tolerance to cocaine does not occur. However, the chronic users tolerate extremely large doses that would be lethal to the new or not chronic user (Radcliffe, Sites, Rush, & Cruse, 1985). Cocaine, like the amphetamines, is a central nervous system stimulant that can increase the heart rate and blood pressure and may cause high fevers, seizures, and cardiac arrhythmias (Medical Letter # 28, 1986). Extreme anxiety, tactile hallucinations, loss of consciousness, and pneumonia occur with cocaine. Malnutrition, depression, and paranoid psychosis, similar to that experienced with the amphetamines, has been reported. Smoking cocaine may do damage to the lungs. Death may be the result of respiratory depression, possible brought on by seizures, (Radcliffe, Sites, Rush, & Cruse, 1985). A summary of information related to cocaine is in Figure 14.9.

Cannabinoids

Marijuana (also spelled marihuana) and hashish are among the oldest and most widely used drugs known to man. Their use was first described in 2737 B.C. by the Chinese Emperor, Shen Nung (Lemberger & Rubin, 1976). Shen Nung referred to the euphoric effects of Cannabis as the "Liberator of Sin" (Ray, 1983). Marijuana is a mixture of the dried leaves and flowering tops of the Indian hemp plant officially known as Cannabis sativa. Hashish is the resin derived from the flowering tops of the plant. Cannabis was recognized for its medical applications in the United States Pharmacopoeia as late as 1937.

Substance Name	Street Name	Method of Administration
Cocaine HCl	"C" Candy Coke Flake Snow Dust Bernice Charlie	Sniffing, oral, injection
Cocaine	Freebase Crack	Smoking or injection

Short Term Effects: CNS stimulation; increased alertness; false sense of well-being; notion of specialness; reduction of fatigue; loss of appetite; insomnia; euphoria.

Long Term Effects: Extreme irritability; extreme change to nasal tissue; psychosis; depression; addiction; some effects are not reversible.

Potential for:	Physical Dependence	yes
	Tolerance	yes*
	Psychological Dependence	very high
	Overall Abuse	extremely high

Regulations and Controls: The same as for narcotics.

Figure 14.9. Summary of information related to cocaine.

* Some researchers disagree.

The hemp plant has been cultivated widely for the use of its long fibers for making rope. It was first commercially grown in the United States in Jamestown, Virginia, in 1611. The early settlers knew nothing of its intoxicating properties (Grinspoon & Bakalar, 1981).

The Arabs claim the discovery of marijuana through the monk, Haider (Ray, 1983). Haider, a stoic, seclusive monk built a monastery in the desert and vowed to live life without enjoying any personal pleasures. The path of Haider changed when:

> One burning summer's day when the fiery sun glared angrily upon Mother Earth as if he wished to wither up her breasts. Haider stepped out from his cloister and walked alone to the fields. All around him lay the vegetation weary and without life, but one plant danced in the heat with joy. Haider plucked it, partook of it, and returned to the convent a happier man. The monks who saw him immediately noticed the change in their chief. He encouraged conversation, and acted boisterously. He then led his companions to the fields, and the holy men partook of the hasheesh, and were transformed from austere ascetics into jolly good fellows. (Robinson, 1925, p.29-30)

The history of cannabis in Western medicine is traced to W.B. O'Shaughnessy, a British physician, working in Calcutta. In 1839, he reported on the analgesic, anticonvulsant, and muscle relaxant propeties of the drug. This seemed to spark interest and some 100 papers appeared in the Western medical literature between 1840 and 1900 (Grinspoon & Bakalar, 1981). Cannabis was suggested for such diversant ailments as coughing, fatigue, rheumatism, asthma, delirium tremens, migraine headache, and painful menstruation.

Walter Bromberg (1934), a psychiatrist, described the effects of marijuana based upon his own experience:

> The intoxication is initiated by a period of anxiety within 10 to 30 minutes after smoking, in which the user sometimes . . . develops fears of death and anxieties of vague nature associated with restlessness and hyper-activity. Within a few minutes he begins to feel more calm and soon develops definite euphoria; he becomes talkative . . . is elated, exhilarated . . . begins to have . . . an astounding feeling of lightness of the limbs and body . . . laughs uncontrollably and explosively . . . without, at times, the slightest provocation . . . has the impression that his conversation is witty, brilliant . . . The rapid flow of ideas gives the

impression of brilliance of thought and observation . . . (but) confusion appears on trying to remember what was thought . . . he may begin to see visual hallucinations . . . flashes of light or amorphous forms of vivid color which evolve and develop into geometric figures, shapes, human faces, and pictures of great complexity . . . After a longer or shorter time, lasting up to two hours, the smoker becomes drowsy, falls into a dreamless sleep and awakens with no physiologic after-effects and with a clear memory of what happened during the intoxication. (p.303)

Bromberg's observations seem to be confirmed by most observers. The effects from smoking last from 2 to 4 hours, and the effects from ingestion 5 to 12 hours. Especially for the new user, an initial anxiety is often experienced. Most users report a heightened sensitivity to external stimuli, noting details ordinarily overlooked, with colors seeming brighter and richer, and bringing out meaning of value that would normally be of no interest to the viewer. The listener and the musician report enhanced appreciation of music.

Time is distorted and a splitting of consciousness occurs making the smoker both the intoxicant and the objective observer. For example, he/she may experience paranoid thoughts and at the same time be reasonably objective about them. Smokers often have a sense of thinking more clearly and having a deeper awareness of the meaning of things.

Several chemicals have been isolated from the hemp plant. Of these, one, delta-9-tetrahydrocannabionol (also called delta-9-THC or just THC), is believed to be responsible for most of the characteristic effects of marijuana. In fresh samples of cannabis, 95% of the THC present is in the form of its acid, a pharmacologically inactive compound. The active form of THC only develops upon storage or as the plant ages (Lemberger & Rubin, 1976).

Radcliffe, Sites, Rush, and Cruse (1985) estimated that over 50 million Americans have used marijuana. Also, 59.5% of the high school seniors graduating in 1981 had used marijuana at least once. (This excludes drop-outs who have an even higher rate of use.) In that same sample 34% of the high school seniors began smoking before entering high school. A summary of information related to cannabinoids is in Figure 14.10.

Forms	Location	Potency	Method	Duration	Content
Charas	India	Highest	smoked	6 - 8 hr	resin
Ganja	India	High	smoked beverage confections	4 - 6 hr	top leaves, resin
Bhang	India	Low	beverage	6 - 8 hr	top leaves, unculti- vated in- ferior plant
Hashish	Middle East	Highest	smoked	6 - 8 hr	powder of Charas
Kif	North Africa Morocco	High	smoked	4 - 8 hr	various
Dagga	South Africa	High	smoked	4 - 8 hr	various
Marijuana	North & South America	Potent	smoked	4 - 6 hr	dried leaves, flowers

Administration: usually smoked.

Short Term Effects: Relaxation; euphoria; slight tremors, increased heart rate and appetite; alteration of time perception, impairment of judgment and coordination; probably CNS depression; nausea, headache, vomiting, and dizziness; drop in body temperature; acute anxiety, frequently at onset; diminished performance.

Long Term Effects: Loss of interest in job, school, family, etc.; psychosis, characterized by confusion, delusions, hallucinations, emotional instability, excitement, disorientation, depersonalization, paranoid symptoms, and temporary amnesia (seen in India or with the use of the more potent varieties); sterility, marijuana has been reported to cause abnormal sperm, decreased motility of sperm, and a reduction of sperm count; tolerance and withdrawal. In laboratory animals, birth defects have been demonstrated and a decrease in the immune system—these have not been substantiated in humans.

Potential for:	Physical Dependence	yes
	Tolerance	moderate
	Psychological Dependence	high
	Overall Abuse	high

Regulations and Controls: Federal laws restrict its use or sale, may be obtained from the government for bonafide research. Extensive illicit traffic and home growth.

Figure 14.10. Summary of information related to cannabinoids.

HIGHLIGHTERS

MDA and MDMA

MDA (Methylene dioxyamphetamine) and MDMA (Methylene dioxymethamphetamine) are derivatives of amphetamine, sometimes referred to as the amphetamine psychedelics. These drugs are not considered psychedelics in the same sense as LSD.

Both drugs are similar to drugs derived from volatile oils found in certain plants, notably nutmeg and sassafras. These plants are psychoactive and have a long history of use. Both MDA and MDMA are synthetic and superior to their natural sources (Stafford, 1983).

MDA and MDMA were synthesized in 1910 and 1914, respectively. Little research was actually conducted until their popularization in the 1960s. MDA first appeared on the streets of the Haight-Ashbury area of San Francisco in 1967. MDA was placed on Schedule I in the Controlled Substances Act of 1970. MDMA was unknown in 1970 and was spared from inclusion in the act (Beck, 1986).

MDA produces a sense of physical well being, increased sensations of touch, and in some, an increased desire to be with other people. For these reasons, it has become known as the "love drug" and the "Mellow Drug of America." Its ability to induce calm and loving feelings as well, as its ability to reduce anxiety and depression, has made it popular in the drug culture.

Research and human experimentation with MDMA, commonly called "Ecstasy," first became reported in the late 1970s. Alexander Shulgin, long noted for his psychedelic drug research, said of MDMA: "It is a tool of communication that has shown, in recent years, an extraordinary utility in opening communication between individuals" (Shulgin, 1983).

Users having tried both MDA and MDMA mostly prefer MDMA. Beck (1986) proposed three reasons for this preference: (1) most users experience a greater euphoria and clarity with

MDMA, (2) MDMA has less stimulant side effect than MDA, and (3) the fact that until recently MDMA was not under Federal control, while MDA has been under Schedule I control.

Both drugs have attracted considerable interest as a psychotherapeutic tool. Using MDA increases the capacity to focus on specific items. Users could concentrate on inner process as well as outer perceptions (Zinberg, 1976). Reports say that MDMA causes positive changes in feelings and attitudes; as well as cognitive benefits, i.e., expanded mental perspective, insight into personal patterns or problems (Greer, 1983). A summary of information related to MDA and MDMA is in Figure 14.11.

Chemical Name	Street Name	Usual Dose	Duration of Action
Methylene dioxy- amphetamine	MDA Love Drug	100 - 150 mg	12 hours
Methylene dioxymeth- amphetamine	MDMA Ecstacy, ETC Adam MDM	100 - 150 mg	12 hours

Figure 14.11. Summary of information related to MDA and MDMA.

SCRAMBLERS/HALLUCINOGENS

The psychedelic or perceputal distorting drugs, sometimes called *scramblers,* are being discussed as a group. The focus is on lysergic acid diethylamide (LSD), the most common and well known drug of this group.

Rosenberg et al. (1985), in describing a body oriented psychotherapy session (referring to Integrated Body Psycho- therapy), suggested when a client releases the tensions of old traumas, the blockages to the energy flow in his/her body are dissolved. Then, through the breathing, he/she can attain altered states of consciousness not unlike those encountered with psychedelic drugs. This leads to the conclusion that occuring naturally are "endorphin-like" chemicals in the brain that can be stimulated to effect certain "archetypical trans-personal insights." The transpersonal experience can be trig-gered through the use of the hallucinogenic drugs, it might be triggered through a traumatic life experience, and, as Rosenberg pointed out it can be initiated through a process of "charged breathing." Naranjo (1973) is an example of a researcher who has advocated the use of drugs to explore these archetypical spaces. Rosenberg, Rand, and Asay (1985) pointed out the importance of being well grounded in order for the spiritual energy to be able to move in ones life. As Andrew Weil (1972) pointed out, chemicals do not contain the effects they cause, but enable people to experience their minds in a new way.

Lysergic Acid Diethylamide (LSD)

LSD belongs to a group of widely abused compounds that are derivatives of the amino acid tryptamine. Some of these indolealkylamine compounds occur in nature as plant alkaloids, such as in certain mushrooms and morning glory seeds. Others are chemically synthesized derivatives of the naturally occurring alkaloids. Some of these are similar in structure to the ergot alkaloids, a group of drugs finding many uses in medicine, such as treating migraine headaches, hypertension, and gynecologic dysfunctions. The indolealkylamines are chemically related to naturally occurring substances in the mammalian central nervous system such as the neurotransmitter, serotonin (5-hydroxytryptamine), and are believed to produce their effects by altering the functions of this and other neurotransmitters in the CNS.

Dr. Albert Hofmann, a researcher at the Switzerland location of the Sandoz Laboratories, first synthesized LSD in 1938. He was studying a series of compounds derived from ergot alkaloids obtained from Claviceps purpurea, the fungus that grows on various types of grains, especially rye. LSD also is known as LSD-25 because it was the 25th of the compounds worked with. The following extracts from Hofmann's laboratory notebook, recorded in 1943, illustrates the birth of LSD in the world of biochemical psychology, as well as giving a picture of its effects:

Last Friday, April 16, 1943, I was forced to stop my work in the laboratory in the middle of the afternoon and to go home, as I was seized by a peculiar restlessness associated with a sensation of mild dizziness. Having reached home, I lay down and sank in a kind of drunkeness which was not unpleasant and which was characterized by extreme activity of imagination. As I lay in a dazed condition with my eyes closed (I experienced daylight as disagreeably bright) there surged upon me an uninterrupted stream of fantastic images of extraordinary plasticity and vividness and accompanied by an intense kaleidoscope-like display of colors.

April 19, 1943: 4:20 P.M ingested orally (0.25mg LSD). The solution is tasteless . . . . 4:50 P.M. no trace of any effect . . . . . . 5:00 P.M. . . . . slight dizziness, unrest, difficulty in concentration, visual disturbances, marked desire to laugh . . . . I had a great deal of difficulty in speaking coherently, my field of vision swayed before me, and objects appeared distorted like images in curved mirrors . . . . . . I had the impression of being unable to move from the spot . . . .

By the time the doctor arrived, the peak of the crisis had already passed . . . . I remember the following symptoms . . . . . . vertigo, visual disturbances: the faces of those around me appeared as grotesque colored mask, marked motor unrest, alternating with paresis [slight or incomplete paralysis], an intermittent heavy feeling in the head, limbs, and the entire body, as if they were filled with metal, cramps in the legs, coldness and loss of feelings in the hands; a metallic taste on the tongue; dry, constricted alternating between clear recognition of my condition . . . .

Objects appeared in unpleasant, constantly changing colors, the predominant shades being sickly green and blue . . . . all acoustic perceptions were transformed into optical effects, every sound causing a corresponding colored hallucination constantly changing in shape and color like pictures in a kaleidoscope . . . . the next morning . . . . tired but . . . . feeling perfectly well." (Hofmann, pp.184-185, cited in Ray, 1983, p.233)

The story of LSD is not complete without including Timothy Leary. In the summer of 1960 in Mexico, Leary was introduced to "magic mushrooms" containing the hallucinogen, psilocybin. The mystical result of the trip as stated in the song by the Moody Blues, "Timothy Leary Is Dead," changed his life. Working at Harvard University, he collaborated with Dr. Richard

Alpert, later to become famous as Dam Rass. Leary and Alpert, during the 1960-1961 school year, began a series of experiments of graduate students using pure psilocybin. Leary and Alpert also studied other drugs. Leary's studies were far from scientific, and led to much controversy. He and Alpert were dismissed from their academic positions in 1963. By 1966, Leary started a religious order, the League of Spiritual Discovery, using LSD as the sacrament. The moto of the League was: "Turn On, Tune In, and Drop Out." Leary's efforts resulted in making LSD a household word.

A debate continues over the use of hallucinogenic drugs as a means of having a religious or personally meaningful experience. Some believe that:

> The self-denial, contemplation, and careful preparation that have characterized the lives of the great mystics of Eastern and Western civilizations are not likely to be replaced by the instant mysticism of a hullucinogenic trip. (Louria, 1967, p.92)

While others, such as Houston (1969) and Naranjo (1973), expressed opposing views in which they believed that the use of psychedelic chemicals can be of great value in providing access to the contents and process of the human mind.

LSD produces effects on the autonomic nervous system. The effects on the parasympathetic division such as salivation, tearing, and occasionally vomiting may occur. The more dominant effects act on the sympathetic division. These include dilation of the pupils, increased body temperature, sweating, and goosebumps. The blood pressure and heart rate can increase, and other physical effects such as tremor, muscle incoordination, and numbness or tingling are not unusual.

The psychic effects usually start an hour after ingestion, with perceptual alterations gradually appearing and eventually becoming more prominent. Of all the senses, the visual is the most affected. Colors and textures become more vivid and perception more detailed. Overlapping of objects is common as afterimages are greatly prolonged. True hallucinations are infrequent with ordinary doses, as are auditory hallucinations. Feelings of depersonalization, a loss of body image, and a loss of a sense of reality are prominent effects. Time perceptions are distorted, and the past, present, and future may be jumbled. Unpredictable emotional changes can occur, with shifts from euphoria to despair being brought on by little or no actual cause. Psychological dependency can occur; however, no evidence of physical dependency has been noted. Tolerance to the physical and psychic effect do occur; also, a cross tolerance exists among LSD, mescaline, and psilocybin (Radcliffe, Sites, Rush, & Cruse, 1985).

Phencyclidine (PCP)

Phencyclidine, commonly known as PCP, or **angel dust,** was synthesized and tested in the 1950s as a general anesthetic. It was found suitable for use in pediatrics; however, in adults it was found to cause extreme disorientation, agitation, and hallucinations. Legal use of PCP since 1965 has been limited to veterinary medicine. A drug similar to PCP, ketamine, is available as an anesthetic. It is used only in pediatrics because of its effect on adults being similar to PCP. This has given rise to some of its street names, e.g., "Hog," "Monkey," "Elephant," or "Horse Tranquilizer." Other street names include "Peace Pill" and "Rocket Fuel." PCP often finds its way to the unaware user as an adulterant in other drugs or as a substitute for other drugs of abuse. Neuropsychiatric effects of PCP include producing anesthesia, analgesia, delirium, schizophreniform psychosis, disinhibition, euphoria, violent behavior, intense depersonalization, and post-phencyclidine depression (Ungerleider & DeAngelis, 1981). The user, depending upon the dosage, may experience a pleasant disinhibition with a small dose, or with an overdose, death. A large percentage of the reported deaths come as a result of drowning.

Adverse reactions and effects of PCP differentiate it from other drugs of abuse. Initial effects are usually a pleasurable high or numbness. After larger doses the user can experience intense numbness, feelings of isolation, and the inability to move. Cramps, nausea, and vomiting have been reported, as well as confused and/or transient psychotic behavior, hallucinations, and coma or stupor. With larger doses a chronic organic brain syndrome can develop with loss of memory. Longer psycotic reactions may include bizarre behavior with agitation and confusion. Characteristics include being mute, staring, and a lack of response to pain. Some users become violent and aggressive, and often seem fearful. Chronic depression, lasting up to 4 months, has been observed (Ungerleider & DeAngelis, 1981).

PCP may itself be contaminated. The problem ingredient is called PCC (l-piperidine-cyclohexanecarbonile). It is quite unstable and takes on a fishy odor as it decomposes. PCC is a strong psychoactive drug with a high incidence of nausea, bloody vomiting, abdominal cramping, and deaths reported. It can be detected by the fishy odor, as PCP is odorless.

Psilocybin or Psilocin

The "sacred" or "magic" mushrooms of Mexico have a long history of religious and ceremonial use. The native name for these mushrooms is "teonanacatl," meaning "God's flesh." The mushrooms used were probably the Conocybe, Stropharia, and the Psilocybe. The active ingredient in these mushrooms are psilocybin and its derivative psilocin. Mushrooms are almost always taken orally with a very rapid hallucinogenic effect. Onset may occur within 10 to 15 minutes with peak effects in about 90 minutes. Total duration of action is usually 5 to 6 hours. Physiological and psychological activity is very similar to LSD; in fact, many people who believe that they are buying "Shrooms" on the streets are actually getting LSD. Tolerance develops with psilocybin and cross-tolerance occurs with LSD and mescaline.

Mescaline /Peyote

The "buttons" or buds of the peyote cactus have been used for centuries in northern Mexico for religious ceremonies. They are still legally used in certain church ceremonies today. The active ingredient in the peyote cactus is mescaline, which is also found in a number of other cactus varieties. The action of mescaline is similar to LSD; however, on a weight basis it is approximately 1/1000th as potent. Some 15 other active agents are in the peyote button and when it is ingested additional effects may occur.

The first effects of ingested mescaline are usually nausea and vomiting. After 1 or 2 hours the psychic phase begins and it may last up to 12 hours. Visual imagery is the most prominent psychic event, with only very rare experiences of true hallucinations.

Chemically, mescaline is similar to amphetamine and the neurotransmitters, epinephrine and norepinephrine. Its use causes tolerance, and a cross tolerance to LSD and psilocybin is experienced.

DMT (N,N Dimethyltryptamine)

DMT is used by South American Indians. It is inactive when taken orally, therefore it must be inhaled as a powder or smoked in a cigarette, marijuana, or in parsley which has been soaked in a solution of DMT. DMT is similar to psilocybin, as both are derivatives of tryptamine. Its action is similar to LSD, except that it has an extremely short duration of action— usually 30 to 60 minutes. Its short duration and quick onset has both brought it its street name, "business-man's lunch," and its main adverse effect—extreme panic reactions.

DOM (STP)

DOM is 2,5-dimethoxy-4-methyl-amphetamine, more often called STP—"serenity, tranquility, peace." It is structurally similar to mescaline. It is normally ingested orally and effects appear in approximately 1 to 1 ½ hours. Effects peak in about 4 hours and subside after 5 to 6 hours. Effects are similar to those of LSD, with physical symptoms including salivation, tearing, increased heart rate, blood pressure, respiration rate, and pupillary dilation. Psychic characteristics include vivid visual imagery and difficulty in controlling thoughts, expressions, and emotions. No cross tolerance exists with LSD mescaline, or psilocybin; however, tolerance does develop. LSD is, on a weight basis, 50 to 100 times as potent as DOM.

In Figure 14.12 is presented a summary of the drugs, hallucinogenic dosage, and duration of effects.

Drug	Hallucinogenic Dose	Duration of Effects
LSD	50 mcg	8 to 12 hours
Phencyclidine (PCP)	5 mg	4 to 6 hours
Psilocin	4 to 6 mg	4 to 6 hours
Mescaline	200 mg	8 to 12 hours*
DMT	50 mg	30 to 45 minutes
DOM	5 mg	16 to 24 hours

* **Note:** Very rare drug, often adulterated or substituted drug.

Figure 14.12. Hallucinogenic dose and duration of effects of the Hallucinogenic drugs.

MISCELLANEOUS DRUGS

Morning Glory Seeds/Ololiuqui

The Aztecs called the morning glory species Rivea corymbosa, Ololiuqui. The active ingredients are lysergic acid derivatives, and when eaten produce euphoria, sedation, and hallucination. Potency varies from plant to plant, and effects are not predictable.

Belladonna Alkaloids

Four plants in the nightshade family have been linked to religious rites, as well as accidental and deliberate poisonings. These are the deadly Nightshade (Atropa belladonna), Jimson weed (Datura strommonium), Henbane (Hyocyamus niger), and Angel's Trumpet (Datura sauveolens).

The active ingredients in these plants are known as the "belladonna alkaloids" and consist of atropine, scopalamine, and hyoscyamine. Ingestion of any plant part or the purified alkaloid can cause a state of delirium. The mental symptoms include wild delirium, disorientation, restlessness and irritability with loud hallucinations, or a state of stupor, confusion, uncoordination, and the lack of ability to concentrate or respond.

The belladonna alkaloids are anticholinegic agents; they inhibit the neurotransmitter acetylcholine. This action suppresses the parasympathetic division of the autonomic nervous system. This causes a decrease in parasympathetic activity and an increase in sympathetic activity. Characteristic symptoms include dilation of the pupil (possibly the origin of the name "belladonna" or "beautiful lady"), dry mouth and skin, flushing to compensate for decreased sweating, increased blood pressure, heart rate, and body temperature, urinary retention, and constipation. In pharmacy school, the saying about atropine went: "it would make one red as a beet, dry as a bone, blind as a bat, and mad as a hatter."

Inhalants

Three categories of inhalants are abused, mostly by young people. These are (1) anesthetics, drugs which induce sleep (i.e., nitrous oxide and chloroform); (2) volatile solvents, drugs which at normal temperatures can change from liquids to vapors (gases and glue); and (3) vasodilating nitrites, drugs that dialate blood vessels (amyl nitrite).

The anesthetic drugs, such as ether, chloroform, and nitrous oxide ("laughing gas") have long been used to induce intoxication. These drugs are usually inhaled; however, ether can be taken orally. To briefly understand the effects of these drugs, a helpful procedure is to review the stages of anesthesia. Stage I is the induction phase and is characterized by physical and neurological depression with possible euphoria. Stage II is excitatory and slurred speech, hallucinations, irritability, shouting, and vomiting. At this stage the effects are similar to the loss of inhibitions experienced with alcohol. Stage III is the beginning of anesthesia. Stage IV is deeper and can lead to respiratory arrest unless respiration is assisted. In Stage V cardiac arrest occurs and death results.

The most commonly used anesthetic for getting intoxicated is nitrous oxide. It is relatively nontoxic. Halothane (Fluothane), a synthethic anesthesic agent, has been the target of abuse, due to its easy accessibility in hospitals.

Commercial solvents such as paints, glues, cleaners and lacquer are highly volatile substances, abused by inhaling the hydrocarbon gas. Four types of hydrocarbons are the target of abuse. These are the straight-chained hydrocarbons, usually found in glues, the cyclic hydrocarbons or aromatic hydro-carbons, found in plastic cements, lacquers, paint remover, gasoline, and cleaning solutions; the chlorinated hydrocarbons, used in spot removers and cleaning substances; and the fluorinated compounds used as propellants in aerosols and coolants in refrigeration systems. These compounds are abused due to their ability to depress inhibitory functions. They are rapidly and readily absorbed in the brain due to their lipid solubility.

Amyl nitrite is manufactured in a crushable ampule for use in angina. It has been abused for its so-called aphrodisiac effect. Isobutyl nitrite has been sold in various places as "Locker Room," "Rush," "Kick," and "Jock Aroma." Its use is similar to amyl nitrite, except it does not require a prescription for purchase. The effect of these drugs on sexuality is said to be a lengthening of time and intensity of orgasm, possibly due to the dilation of genital arteries. As these drugs have no affinity for a particular blood vessel, they can be quite dangerous.

SUMMARY

Our clients and potential clients spend an estimated $110 billion dollars a year on illicit drugs alone (Bensinger, 1986). Some drugs have become more potent over the last 10 to 15 years, such as THC, tetrahydrocannabinol, which has shown an increase from one-half a percent to 5 or 6%. Other drugs, such as MDMA, which was readily available just a few years ago (it could be purchased in certain bars or pubs), is now under strict federal control.

Many substances are prone to be abused and are available to people. These substances are sought after and used or abused because they are effective. They can make people feel high (uppers), dampen feelings (downers), or help people forget about reality or their problems (highlighters and hallucinogens). They all also have side or adverse effects.

CHAPTER

TREATMENT OF THE SUBSTANCE ABUSER

An old saying is, "Once a drunk, always a drunk." This belief is still held by many, especially when we consider the typical "skid row" drunk. This attitude facilitated the use of jails, prisons, and mental institutions as the focus of many attempts to treat alcoholism.

In 1785, Dr. Benjamin Rush, a physician and teacher, wrote a paper entitled "An Inquiry Into the Effects of Ardent Spirits Upon the Human Body and Mind With an Account of the Means of Preventing and of the Remedies for Curing Them." This may have been the first medical paper to connect the idea of disease with the abuse of alcohol (Mann, 1981).

Thomas Trotter, an Edinburgh physician, took the disease concept of alcoholism even further. He wrote in his paper, *"An Essay, Medical, Philosophical, and Chemical, on Drunkenness and Its Effects on the Human Body,"* in 1804:

> "In medical language, I consider drunkenness, strictly speaking, to be a disease, produced by a remote cause, and giving birth to actions and movements in the living body that disorder the functions of health." (Milam & Ketcham, 1981, p.136)

Trotter's paper created a wrath of controversy that still lingers today. He challenged society's moral code, threatened a basic belief of the Christian church, and questioned the traditional medical position of lack of involvement. The strong position of both church and medical profession won out, and Trotter's "disease concept" ideas never took hold.

In 1806, a statement similar to Trotter's was issued by the Connecticut State Medical Society. Here too, the idea was dropped for lack of support. The temperance movement became noticeable in the 1830s. These people considered all alcohol to be evil and preached that only evil could come of its use. The Washington House, the first institution to treat alcoholics, was opened in Boston in the year 1841. By 1900, over fifty private and public facilities had been opened to treat "inebriates" (Milam & Ketcham, 1981).

The passage of the 18th Amendment to the Constitution, known as the Volstead Act, in 1919, began the experiment of prohibition. Prohibition was repealed in 1933.

In 1935 Will B. and Dr. Bob founded the organization known as **Alcoholics Anonymous.** Will B. and Dr. Bob did not use last names, initiating the anonymous tradition of A.A. The organization recognized alcoholism as an illness or condition beyond the control of the individual.

The next breakthrough in treating alcoholism came in 1958, with the founding of Synanon. **Synanon** was the prototype and grandfather of the therapeutic community. The methodology required a lifetime commitment and included 24 hour residential treatment using ex-addicts as facilitators.

Other community based treatment sprang up during the 1960s. Out of these experiences came the recognition of the need for re-education and a change in family environment for successful re-integration of the detoxified patient. Two of the important treatment concepts coming out of the therapeutic community were the use of ex-addicts as therapists, or counselors, and the long term (life time) expectation of remaining drug free.

MEDICAL ASPECTS OF TREATMENT

Although this book is not written for the physician, a brief and simplified review of the medical treatment for substance intoxication is included. The reasons for this are (1) to help the psychotherapist know when medical intervention is needed, (2) to have some understanding of the medical intervention, and (3) to have a better understanding of what a substance abuser may go through.

Alcohol Intoxication

Many alcoholics can withdraw without help; others are so severely dependent that they have to be supervised in going through a process called **detoxification.** The acute phase of alcohol withdrawal consists of four stages which can overlap and are unpredictable. Stage I includes symptoms of psycho-motor agitation; autonomic hyperactivity, such as tachycardia, hypertension, and excessive sweating (hyperhidrosis); loss of appetite (anorexia); and insomnia. During stage II the detox-ifying alcoholic experiences hallucinations, in the form of visual, auditory, or tactile perceptions, or sometimes a combination of all three. They are rarely of the olfactory type. These experiences are often quite frightening, and the individual frequently has little or no memory of the experience. In stage III, the subject experiences delusions, disorientation, and delirium, usually followed by amnesia. Stage IV consists of seizures. Stages III and IV combined are what is commonly called **Delirium Tremens.** Onset of major seizure activity usually occurs within 24 to 48 hours of withdrawal and is normally self limiting. Chlorpromazine, hydroxyzine, chloral hydrate, barbiturates, and paraldehyde have all found a use in the detoxification of the alcoholic. Today, clinicians tend to use two of the benzodia-zepines, diazepam and chlordiazepoxide. Both have the advan-tage of rapid intravenous injection. The phenothiazines and other major tranquilizers are effective in treating alcoholic hallucinations; however, they tend to lower the seizure threshold and can precipitate seizures in the withdrawing alcoholic. The clinician should monitor fluid and electrolyte levels to eliminate problems of overhydration or dehydration. An injection of thiamine (Vitamin B_1) is given to reverse any paresis (incomplete paralysis) of the sixth cranial nerve.

Three basic approaches are employed in treating the chronic phase of alcoholism. First, the **pharmaco-therapeutic** approach which utilizes drugs to offset the underlying anxiety or depression of the alcoholic. Second, the **pharmaco-aversion** technique, using a daily maintenance dose of disulfiram (Antabuse). If the individual ingests any alcohol when taking the disulfiram, he/she will experience some rather unpleasant effects. Disulfiram blocks the oxidation of alcohol at the acetaldehyde stage by inhibiting the enzyme, aldehyde dehydrogenase. This creates a concentration of acetaldehyde in the blood which may be ten times that of normal alcohol metabolism. The **disulfiram-alcohol reaction** is characterized by flushing, throbbing in the head and neck, throbbing headaches, nausea, copious vomiting, decreased blood pressure, thirst, respiratory difficulty, sweating, chest pain, palpitations, tachycardia, hypotension, weakness, vertigo, blurred vision, and confusion. More severe reactions can lead to respiratory depression, arrhythmias, myocardial infarction, acute congestive heart failure, unconsciousness, convulsions, and death. The disulfiram-alcohol reaction has been known to occur 14 days after the discontinuation of the disulfiram. The subject must be willing and informed, or he/she could suffer severe consequences. One problem is that many preparations, such as cough syrups, have alcohol in them. Individuals have even experienced serious Antabuse reactions due to the use of after shave lotions. The antibacterial agent metronidazole (Flagyl) causes a similar reaction with alcohol; however, it is less severe. The third approach is a non-drug group support method, almost always tied into a "Twelve Step" program, i.e., Alcoholics' Anonymous.

Hallucinogen Intoxication

Treatment for hallucinogen intoxication consists of psychological and emotional support until the drug effects have worn off. The intoxicated individual is placed in a semi-dark room and kept comfortable. It is best for someone who knows the individual or someone who can be warm, empathic, and reassuring, to be with and talk to him/her. **Talking the person** down from the effects of a hallucinogen may take from 2 to 12 hours. The physician may choose to administer a mild tranquilizer if the individual is very anxious. Antipsychotic agents are to be avoided, since the drug-induced psychosis will resolve itself. The use of the phenothiazines has been recommended in the past; however, this exacerbates the anxiety state, causes orthostatic hypotension, precipitates a post-psychotic depression, and increases the incidence of the "flashback" phenomenon. Also, if phencyclidine or some other drugs are present, the individual's condition can be worsened.

Individuals who have overdosed on LSD frequently seek medical help for drug-induced psychotic reactions. These reactions, commonly called the **bad trip,** often occur soon after taking the drug. Kleber (1967) described four categories of the "bad trip." These are (1) the prolonged "bad trip," an acute anxiety or panic reaction; (2) post-LSD depression; (3) long-term schizophrenic or psychotic depression; and (4) the "flashback" phenomenon. "Bad trips" includes three kinds. (1) **Body trips** are trips involving distorted perceptions of the individual's body, dealing with his/her physical appearance. (A predisposition of dirtiness or ugliness may precipitate this experience.) (2) **Environmental trips** are trips including distortions of the visual field surrounding the individual. This may include frightening illusions and hallucinations that cause the abuser to lose touch with reality and believe him/herself to be going insane. (3) **Mind trips** are trips involving subconscious material that surface during the "trip." Guilt feelings and identity crisis are common, and this leads the user to feelings of depression, failure, and suicide (Smith, 1970). Smart and Bateman (1967) have estimated the "bad trip" to resolve within 48 hours in approximately one-half the occurrences, with 25% lasting from 2 to 7 days, and the remaining 25% lasting longer periods, occasionally for more than a year.

The **flashback phenomenon,** sometimes referred to as the "free trip," is a spontaneous recurrence of a part of an earlier hallucinogenic drug trip. It is transient in nature, lasting for an unspecified period of time. This phenomenon can occur sporadically, or as much as several times a day. Each episode lasts for minutes or hours. Theories explaining "flashbacks" include LSD toxicity in the CNS, a psychoactive LSD metabolite, changes in retinal or optic pathway, and a learned mechanism similar to "war neuroses" experienced by soldiers (Kimble, 1973).

Central Nervous System
Stimulant Intoxication

Treatment of central nervous system stimulants, the amphetamines and related drugs, consists of **talking down** the individual. In cases of severe overdose, talking down can be a helpful technique to keep the person from panicking. The usual medical procedure is to keep the individual under observation and monitor the vital signs and electrical activity of the heart. When the person has "come down," an antidepressant with low cardiotoxic effects such as desipramine or nortriptyline can be administered. The urine is acidified with ammonium chloride, to accelerate the renal excretion, and a diuretic, such as furosemide (Lasix), is usually given intravenously. Ipecac syrup (an emetic) may be given to the conscious individual when some of the drug may still remain in the stomach. In the comatose person, gastric lavage (irrigating or washing out of the stomach) can be performed. Haloperidol is often used to combat aggressiveness, agitation, and hallucinations.

Barbiturate Intoxication

Barbiturate overdose can be quite difficult to handle. It is treated symptomatically and supportively. An adequate airway is maintained and oxygen or artificial respiration may be necessary. Emesis should be induced in the conscious individual. Diuretics are used to accelerate renal elimination of the drug. Treatment for hypotension and shock also may be necessary. In severe cases, hemodialysis (a procedure in which the blood is circulated through an artificial kidney machine to remove toxic elements) is useful when blood drug levels are very high. Since abrupt withdrawal may be fatal, an important procedure is to monitor the individual for symptoms, such as anxiety, arrhythmias, convulsions, delirium, fever, hypotension, tremor, and weakness. These may not be manifested until 72 hours after the cessation of the drug. Barbiturate withdrawal has a high mortality rate, and detoxification should be done in a hospital. Small doses of phenobarbital may be given orally during the withdrawal period. This is to prevent serious toxic withdrawal symptoms.

Benzodiazepine Intoxication

Individuals taking benzodiazepines should not stop abruptly. Gradual withdrawal over a 5 to 10 day period will normally prevent severe withdrawal symptoms such as convulsions or psychosis. Benzodiazepine withdrawal should be monitored by a physician. Withdrawal can be difficult. Often one or two delayed periods of withdrawal symptoms occur. Many times hospitalization is required to facilitate the process. A prolonged and very gradual withdrawal may work better for non-hospitalized individuals. The psychotherapist should not attempt to take away or initiate withdrawal. This can be dangerous, heading to severe complications.

Marijuana Intoxication

The key to treating marijuana intoxication is support and empathic understanding. The agitated individual should be placed in a dimly lit room with minimal external stimuli. Haloperidol can be used in case of hallucinations and delusions. Diazepam is used to control panic reactions. Because marijuana is often contaminated with PCP, a need exists to watch for signs of neurotoxicity or PCP intoxication.

Cocaine Intoxication

Acute cocaine intoxication is similar to that of amphetamine. Cocaine stimulates the heart rate and causes a rise in blood pressure. Other characteristics of cocaine intoxication include vasoconstriction, fever, mydriasis, cardiac arrhythmias, circulatory failure, convulsions, respiratory failure and coma. Psychological symptoms are not uncommon, including paranoia and hallucinations. A very common effect of acute cocaine use is the perforation of the nasal septum, caused by the irritation of snorting. Medical treatment consists of cardiac and vital sign monitoring, artificial respiration to support breathing, propranolol (Inderal) to reduce cardiotoxicity, and haloperidol (Haldol) to treat psychosis.

Narcotic Intoxication

Several different medical treatments are available for detoxifying narcotic (usually heroin) users. Over the years these have changed drastically. In the early 1900s treatment approaches included the **belladonna treatment:** A process in which scopolamine was administered every 30 to 60 minutes for 24 to 48 hours, or until scopolamine intoxication occurred. Patients had "constant diarrhea, but did not suffer" and had to be protected from injury or falls, as they were "uncoordinated and unable to stand." Added to this was the use of strychnine, nitroglycerine, digitalis, bromides, chloral hydrate, pilocarpine, atropine, and electricity. Cold baths were "thrown in" for good measure. As Kolb and Himmelshuch (1938) so gracefully put it, " . . . patients from whom morphine is taken get well in spite of the treatment." Another "cure," was the **bromide sleep treatment,** a process in which the patient received a substantial dose of sodium bromide every two hours and was revived by the use of oxygen, strychnine, etc. Kolb and Himmelshuch reported that two of ten patients died of the cure. Other cures included abrupt and rapid withdrawal, an immunity treatment, the use of endocrine hormone extracts, and the use of lipoid solutions.

From 1940 to 1970 treatment methods turned to the use of (1) **electroconvulsive therapy** (ECT); (2) an artificial "hibernation" produced by injections of sodium pentothal and rectal infusions of paraldehyde; (3) the substitution of methadone, a synthetic narcotic developed by German scientists during World War II, and then the methadone was gradually withdrawn (This is still considered by many to be the safest and most effective system.); and (4) the use of the phenothiazines, which was initially believed to work and later found to be of little value.

Current pharmacological treatment includes the use of (1) methadone (Kleber, 1981) and (2) a narcotic antagonist, such as naloxone (Narcan). Detoxification is further accomplished by the administering of clonidine (Catapres), a non-opiate drug originally marketed to lower blood pressure. Clonidine is effective in easing withdrawal because it acts at some of the same nerve endings as the opiates (Giannini, 1986).

Detoxification is not the main concern in treating the narcotic addict. Two out of three detoxified individuals go back to using narcotics within six months; the goal then, for treatment, is to lower the relapse rate. The therapeutic community, an idea that originated in the early 1960s, is one method that has a fairly impressive success rate; however, approximately 75% of the participants drop out within the first month of treatment. Treatment lasting for one or two years consists of a highly structured residential program. Today, these programs are directed by psychiatrists and facilitated by a milieu of professional and ex-addict counselors and therapists. The programs are quite restrictive and enable the individual to acquire gradual personal freedom. The use of drugs or alcohol is totally forbidden in these programs.

Many non-resident or short stay (usually 21 to 28 days) programs have come into their own in the last ten years. These programs are not effective for the "hard core" narcotic user. They can be helpful to many other types of drug abusers.

In the early 1960s, Vincent Dole and Marie Nyswander originated the concept of treating addicts by substituting the synthetic drug methadone for heroin or other illicit opiates. Methadone is taken orally. It has the advantage of lasting longer, being less intense in activity, and not producing the classical rush followed by the "letdown" syndrome that is experienced with heroin. The goal of the methadone programs is to stabilize the life of the opiate user by freeing him/her from the preoccupation of seeking drugs. The idea behind the early methadone treatment programs was to continuously maintain the addict on the substituted drug. Today, many clinics use methadone as a transitional aid, a step towards eliminating the use of drugs entirely. In these cases, methadone is withdrawn over an extended period, usually several months. The big advantage in the methadone programs is that patients do not drop out with the regularity of the therapeutic community. After one year, 65 to 90% of the participants continue to return for their daily dose (Mental Health Letter 3:8, 1987).

The British system for narcotic maintenance calls for the use of morphine or heroin. From 1924 to 1968, individual physicians were allowed to prescribe these opiates for addicts.

Since 1968, the registration of addicts has been mandatory, and only physicians at special clinics have been authorized to dispense these drugs. During the 1970s most of the clinics began to switch from heroin and morphine to oral methadone because of its safety factors.

Another new (to Western medicine) methodology in treating drug addiction and alcohol abuse is the use of acupuncture. Proponents make very positive claims for this process (Ny, 1981; Smith, 1979; Smith, Squires, Aponte, & Rabinowitz, 1982). Others have taken a critical view of this procedure, stating that studies did not include proper controls.

PSYCHOSIS OR SPIRITUAL AWAKENING

To make a statement in regard to the so-called *spiritual crisis* or *spiritual awakening* seems to be relevant, whether it is drug-related or not. "Spiritual crisis" refers to those experiences that can be classified, in a pure medical way, as psychotic, but to the individual involved it can be a very important life event, sometimes experienced as a "rebirthing" or "spiritual awakening." These experiences are frequently referred to as being "transpersonal," or beyond the "Self." Carl Jung, in talking about the kundalini, a word coming from yogic tradition, refers to it as an impersonal force, an autonomous process arising out of the unconscious that seems to use the individual as a vehicle (Sannella, 1981). Gopi Krishna (1971) said:

> This mechanism, known as Kundalini, is the real cause of all genuine spiritual and psychic phenomena, the biological basis of evolution and development of personality, the secret origin of all esoteric and occult doctrines, the master key to the unsolved mystery of creation, the inexhaustible source of philosophy, art and science, and the fountainhead of all religious faiths, past, present and future. (p.176)

Psychic experiences, whether triggered by known or unknown factors, acute anxiety, yogic or breathing practices, or drug ingestion can lead to, at least, a mini-version of this phenomena. The use of drug intervention can stop this process. Research has been done in this area; however, the findings are a long way from the mainstream of Western medicine.

Rosenberg (1985), refers to the **transpersonal experience,** as:

> ... one in which a person gains an awareness of his Self as something extending beyond his limits as an individual. It usually involves a realization or an insight or an understanding that he perceives as undeniably true. These truths come from within the individual and are verified intuitively (subjective validity) . . . . the concept is common throughout history and all over the world . . . . a person frees himself from his obsolete constraints and energy-blocking patterns, and starts to realize his Self. (p.274)

This material is being presented as a suggestion that at times allowing an individual to complete the cycle of the "psychotic" or "spiritual crisis" without interruption may be advantageous. From personal experience and from discoveries in the literature, probably, or at least possible percentage of these phenomenon is beyond what is recognized as psychosis. This is a field for which much needs to be learned. Interested readers may find more information in the following books:

Bentov, I. (1977). *Stalking the wild pendulum.* New York: E. P. Dutton.

White, J. (1979). *Kundalini, evolution and enlightenment.* Garden City: Anchor Books.

Sannella, L. (1981). *Kundalini: Psychosis or transcendence?* San Francisco: H. S. Dakin.

PSYCHOTHERAPIST'S ROLE

Recovery is an ongoing, life-long process for any individual who has been addicted to a chemical substance. This ongoing process is not unlike the recovery process of any individual coming out of a dysfunctional family. The process consists of stopping the behavior (the **primary care**) and treating the injured child (the **after care**). In order for any recovery program to work both primary and after care programs must be utilized. The psychotherapist may become involved with the primary care. However, because this aspect of treatment usually requires intense around the clock treatment, the psychotherapist becomes a part of a team approach to recovery. Successful recovery programs include **twelve step support groups.** The psychotherapist's role, beyond the primary care, can be in treating the injured child or working with the dysfunctional family members or family as a unit.

Many roads to recovery exist and many things can be done by parents, brothers, sisters, and the psychotherapist or others to help the substance abuser along the pathway of recovery. The psychotherapist must begin by becoming educated. Without the facts and knowing what to do and how to do it, the well-meaning psychotherapist will likely cause more harm than good. Several points are considered to be paramount to the psychotherapists: (1) Gain understanding of the role of feelings, attitudes, values, social environment, and family history that may influence the substance abuser to either use or abstain from using drugs. The therapist needs to understand his/her position on the subject. (2) Use factual and unbiased information concerning substance use and abuse. Understand the positive, as well as the negative, effects of drug use or nonuse. (3) Become aware of the conflicts in society regarding drug use. (4) Understand how peer pressure works and how it influences the decision-making process. (5) Understand how drug use creates social, health, and relationship problems. (6) Become familiar with organizations and agencies that are available to assist with substance abuse problems.

In treatment, the client and the therapist must identify and acknowledge that substance abuse is an issue. Not infrequently drug abusers feel ashamed and guilty, and as a result, deny the existence of any problem to themselves, as well as to the therapist. A helpful procedure is to think in terms of the substance abuse, or possible substance abuse, as a symptom of an underlying problem. (If the client presents himself/herself to this therapist as one having a substance abuse problem, then I proceed to treat that symptom and encourage him/her to look at the underlying issues. If he/she does not present substance abuse as an identified problem, then I look at the use of drugs as one of the places where underlying symptoms may be manifesting themselves.)

Since denial is an important defense to the substance abuser, more than likely the abuser, entering into therapy, is not going to mention his/her drug use or addiction. The gathering of a family and physical history, as well as a three or four day schedule of all foods, drinks, and drugs taken, can often help the psychotherapist find the hidden substance abuse problem. For example, if the client has alcoholic parents or reports a food intake that does not seem to coincide with the individual's personality then possibly the client has a substance abuse problem. Then the therapist needs to ask the client how often the marijuana is used or how many times a week does he/she drink and how many drinks are imbibed. Avoid asking if he/she drinks because the therapist will not usually get accurate information.

In our society, no clear-cut definition exists of what constitutes substance abuse. As a psychotherapist, I see part of my job as exploring the possibility with the client that he/she may be misusing or abusing drugs. Some questions that may help acknowledge the symptoms of substance abuse follow:

> Do you drink or use drugs after an argument or disappointment?
>
> When you are under pressure, do you increase your use of drugs or alcohol?
>
> Have you attempted any ways of controlling your alcohol or drug usage?
>
> Have these attempts been failures?
>
> Do you avoid your friends and family when using drugs or alcohol?

The following questions relate to how the individual feels about substance and alcohol abuse:

> Do you feel guilty when you use drugs or alcohol?
>
> Do you want to go on using drugs when your friends are ready to quit?
>
> Do you frequently regret what you have done while you are using drugs or alcohol?
>
> Does the way I and others are talking to you about drugs or alcohol annoy you?

Questions to ask other family members include the following:

> Does his/her drinking or drug use ever worry or embarrass you?
> Does it spoil family vacations or holidays?
> Do you lie to conceal it?
> Does he/she try to justify the use or avoid discussing it?
> Do others talk about his/her drinking?

Attempts to bring the client "to his/her senses" just do not work. If this is happening in therapy, the therapist is either "fixing" the client for another family member or is dealing with his/her own issue. Mann (1981) described a method frequently used by desperate and harassed families (and sometimes therapists) who are trying to bring their substance abuser to his/her senses. Many families or family members resort to these methods. There are two categories of these treatment methods: words and action, or talk and behavior. The talking comes first, and continues for some time before behavior is added. Early talking is usually very reasonable and even sweet. It often takes the form of a friendly discussion on what drinking is doing to the drinker. Perhaps pointing out his/her lack of judgment or forgetfulness. Next comes the, "What is it doing to the family?" speech. This can get more and more intense and eventually lead to out-and-out fighting. The pattern is to make this effort to discuss the problem over and over again. What happens is that the nagging (as heard from the substance abuser) backfires and actually gives him/her even more of an excuse to drink or use drugs. This is not to suggest that these discussions should be avoided, or even that it would be possible to do so. The point is that the repetitive efforts that are bringing no results (the key is *bringing no results*) are useless, and will, more than likely, make the situation more difficult. This method does not work; in fact, it will aggravate the condition it is meant to alleviate. The challenge for the psychotherapist is to not collude with the behavior. He/she should not get into a "tug-of-war" with the client about his/her drug or alcohol use. If the substance abuse is getting in the way of the treatment, which it probably is, since the use of drugs is a way of not being present or covering feelings, then the therapist should deal with that. It may be very appropriate to say to the client that you are not willing to work with him/her as long as drugs are being used. If this is stated, then the therapist should be prepared to mean it and to act on it. Idle threats are of little use and usually backfire. When I tell a client that I will only work with him/her if he/she attends A.A. or O.A. meetings, I make it very clear that these are my boundaries, and I do not do this to create guilt in client. This is just a way in which I take care of myself, and avoid colluding with the client's behavior. When I make this contract with a client I keep it.

If a family member brings, or comes in with the substance abuser and identifies the problem, then the therapist should urge him/her to attend Al-Anon or another 12 step support group and support him/her in dealing with his/her own problem. He/she needs to recognize how his/her behavior and/or needs are being taken care of in the relationship. The important point is for the therapist to not get caught in the middle of this struggle.

MILIEU TREATMENT AND OUTSIDE HELP

I believe that the psychotherapist treating substance abuse needs to call upon outside help. I am a very strong believer in the "Twelve Step" programs and their approach to substance abuse. A comment I often hear among my psychotherapist colleagues is that they do not like Alcoholics Anonymous (or one of the other "12 Step programs"). Some therapists voice their concern that they may lose their client to the process; they do not like the process; they object to the religious nature of it; they consider it to be another addiction, etc. This has not been my experience. I tell my clients that comment about the addictiveness of A.A. and that when they are well they can choose whether nor not to continue with the program. In fact, many people in the "Twelve Step Programs" welcome therapists that know, understand, and can support the program. A tradition of hard feelings have existed, back and forth, between A.A. and psychotherapists; in many cases this has given way to "mutual trust" (*Mental Health Letter*, Vol 3:12, 1987). My strong suggestion for any therapist interested in working with substance abuse is to go to A.A., Al-Anon, or other "Twelve Step" meetings and "work the program"; in this way the therapist will understand fully and be able to work with and support their client and the work done in the "Twelve Step" setting.

Food abuse is also a serious problem seen in therapy. I suggest that the therapist attend Overeaters' Anonymous (O.A.) meetings. This may be a more acceptable experience for some therapists. Meetings are held daily at noon and dinner time in many locations throughout the country.

Many people have a misconception of what Alcoholics Anonymous (A.A.) and the other Twelve Step programs really are all about. A.A. has been called a society, a movement, a fellowship, a semi-religious group, and a treatment method. None of these descriptions accurately depicts A.A. The outside world often sees it as a miracle. Friends and family of an alcoholic expect A.A. to be detective, nurse, and police. Alcoholics who have been drunk for years have become sober and have stayed sober through participation in A.A.

The Alcoholics Anonymous program functions for one purpose only. It has been described as a voluntary organization of alcoholics who gather solely for the purpose of helping themselves and other members to get sober and stay sober. A.A. has no affiliations with other groups or organizations. It supports no political causes or opinions. It does not operate or support any treatment facilities for alcoholics. Its only condition for membership is the honest desire to stop drinking. The organization will go to considerable lengths to help the committed member to become and stay sober.

When a newcomer comes to A.A., he/she learns that sobriety can be accomplished. He/she sees and hears others who have succeeded and that the members enjoy sobriety. The newcomer is taught the nature of his/her problem and is never told that he/she is an alcoholic. That fact is left to the individual to decide. Newcomers usually have a sponsor who may be either a stranger or a friend. The sponsor facilitates the newcomer's transition into the organization. A.A. uses many techniques to facilitate the person's process. One such procedure is the "twenty four hour plan." Members are taught to live in the present and his/her goal is to go without a drink *only for today.* This plan, as well as many of the A.A. methods, become useful in helping solve many other life problems. A.A. holds open and closed meetings. The open meeting is open to everyone who wants to come—alcoholics, family, friends, physicians, therapists, clergy, etc. The meeting usually have a leader and several speakers, each of whom identifies him/herself as an alcoholic and shares some of his/her personal experiences with drinking. The speaker's main desire is to personify hope to an alcoholic by being candid about his/her own past history. Meetings often end with coffee and refreshments. This becomes a time for meeting and talking with members. Newcomers are offered telephone numbers, and perhaps an invitation for coffee or lunch. Closed meetings are for alcoholics only. In this way, the closed meeting is a very important step for the newcomer. Attending his/her first closed meeting becomes the first step in the A.A. program, the admission that he/she is an alcoholic.

The backbone of the A.A. program is the "Twelve Steps." The Twelve Steps address the individual's need to make changes in his/her life. The individual takes inventory of his/her strengths and weaknesses and makes amends to those he/she has harmed and carries the message to others. The twelve step program has "spiritual" implications. This has been a problem to some people. When the word "God" is used, it is followed by "As we understood Him." This "spiritual" aspect of the A.A. program is very important in accepting and overcoming the individual's "powerlessness" over alcohol. Some substance abuse workers suggest that the word "Good" be substituted for "God" for those people who get hung up with the religious aspects of the program. A.A. becomes a support network for recovering users. It provides these people with a community of non-drinkers. It also gives them someone to reach out to in hard times or in time of trouble. What begins as the last place the denying alcoholic wants to go, becomes the foundation of a new and fulfilling way of life.

Many different "Twelve Step" programs today use the basic tools of A.A. **Al-Anon** and **Alateen** are the self-help recovery programs for friends and families of alcoholics. They are available whether or not the alcoholic seeks help.

If the substance abuser has reached stage three or four or dependency, the treatment probably requires a residency program. Many programs available today specialize in alcohol or chemical addiction or abuse. Many of these encourage and welcome the non-medical psychotherapist to participate in the treatment of their client. This can be an exciting and educational experience for the therapist. I have found, in the facilities that I have used, open-minded staff members who have helped me in this process. These facilities approach the treatment with a team of diversified professionals. Staff meetings are held where each individual patient is discussed and an individual treatment approach is developed.

In looking for a program, I recommend that it have the following:

1. Be a totally drug free environment (except for medically necessary drugs.)

2. Offer a qualified team of professionals; including ex-addict counselors.

3. Use the twelve step program and have on premises or make available A.A. or other "Twelve Step" meetings.

4. Association with peers who can identify with the pain and hurt of chemical use, both in the rehabilitation process and as counselors.

5. Emphasis on facing the past, acknowledging what drugs have done to the addict's life, and dealing with it.

6. Programs to rebuild the abuser's self worth.

7. Teach coping mechanisms for facing tomorrow drug-free.

8. Include family counseling.

9. Have support group meetings for family members.

10. Offer family education programs.

11. Be highly structured and long-term in format.

12. Develop a recovery plan for the individual and family.

I believe that two aspects to recovery exist. First is the addiction. Addictions can only be treated by acknowledging the addictive behavior and by stopping it. In my opinion, any treatment of an addiction other than, or less than, stopping the behavior is collusion. The second aspect of the recovery has to do with healing the injured child. In this aspect of recovery I look to the psychotherapist. He/she can be of considerable help. However, in order for the therapist to be properly attuned and empathic to the client, he/she needs to have knowledge and understanding of substance abuse and substance abusers.

SUMMARY

The following is from a New York State study of high school students comparing levels of substance abuse between 1971 and 1978, conducted by the State Division of Substance Abuse Services (1978):

. . . . lifetime and current use of marijuana have more than doubled.

. . . . the use of cocaine among 9th through 12th graders has tripled.

. . . . heroin use has remained the same.

. . . . inhalant use has almost tripled.

. . . . hallucinogenic use has slightly increased.

. . . . the use of tranquilizers shows the sharpest increase of both lifetime and current use.

The treatment of substance abuse is a major problem facing the health care practitioner in the 1990s. In California, the Board of Behavioral Science Examiners has recently required candidates for licensure to have received training in substance abuse. The current epidemic of drug abuse, which seems to include individuals of all ages, makes the probability of substance abuse a factor in the practice of psychotherapy more and more likely.

Substance abuse is one of our society's most complex problems. Significant evidence links narcotic and alcohol addiction to genetic factors. At the same time, the recognition needs to be made that situational and psychological factors influence the individual's choice of turning to drugs as a solution. Drugs of abuse may be classified by their effects, using street terminology: downers, uppers, highlighters, and scramblers. People choose drugs that have a positive, satisfying, pleasurable effect, or ones that cause a decrease in their discomfort. Many approaches are applicable to the treatment of substance abuse, for example the medical approach, the psyhological approach, the therapeutic community approach, the religious approach, and the punitive approach. In each approach, an important point is to identify that the use of drugs is an attempt to solve a problem. Drug taking behavior is problem-solving behavior. Therefore, in treating substance abuse, care must be taken to identify and treat the underlying problem and not stop at treating the drug taking behavior. Therapists and others must understand that underlying aspects to any behavior, including the use and abuse of drugs, are psychological.

BIBLIOGRAPHY

Abel, E. L. (1980). *Marihuana, the first twelve thousand years.* NY: Plenum.

Aird, R. B., & Woodbury, D. M. (1974). *Management of epilepsy* Springfield, IL: Charles C. Thomas.

Alcoholics Anonymous World Services. (1953). *Twelve steps and twelve traditions.* New York: The A. A. Grapevine.

Alford, G. S. (1983). Pharmacotherapy. In M. Hersen, A.E. Kazdin, & A.S. Bellack (Eds), *The clinical psychology handbook.* New York: Pergamon Press.

Alksne, H. (1981). The social bases of substance abuse. In J.H. Lowinson & P. Ruiz (Eds.), *Substance abuse: clinical problems and perspectives.* Baltimore: Williams and Wilkins.

Allbee, G. W. (1970). Notes toward a position paper opposing psychodiagnosis. In A. R. Maher (Ed.), *New approaches to personality classification.* New York: Columbia University Press.

American Psychiatric Association. (1980). *Diagnostic and statistical manual of mental disorders* (3rd ed.). Washington, DC: Author.

American Psychiatric Association. (1987). *Diagnostic and statistical manual of mental disorders* (3rd ed., revised). Washington, DC: Author.

Angrist, B., & Gershon, S. (1976). Clinical effects of amphetamine L-Dopa on sexuality and aggression. *Comprehensive Psychiatry 17:* 715-722.

Appenzeller, O. (1982). *The autonomic nervous system: An introduction to basic and clinical concepts.* New York: Elsevier Biomed Press.

Arey, L. B., Burrows, W., Greenhill, J. P., & Hewitt, R. M. (1957). *Dorland's illustrated medical dictionary, 23rd ed.* Philadelphia: W. B. Saunders.

Aserinsky, E, & Kleitman, N. (1955). Two types of ocular motility occurring in sleep. *Journal of Applied Physiology, 8,* 1-10.

Ashcroft, G. W. (1975). Psychological medicine: Management of depression. *British Medical Journal, 2,* 372-376.

Association of Sleep Disorders Center (1979). *Sleep disorders.* P.O. Box 2604, Del Mar, CA 92014.

Austin, G. A. (1978). *Prospectives on the history of psychoactive substances use.* NIDA Report #017-024-00879-6. Washington, DC: United States Government Printing Office.

Austin, G. A. (1984). *Drug use and abuse: A guide to research findings.* Santa Barbara: ABC-Clio Information Services.

Avery, D., & Winokur, G. (1976). Mortality in depressed patients treated with electroconvulsive therapy and antidepressants. *Archives of General Psychiatry, 33*, 1029-1037.

Bachmann, K. A., & Sherman, G. P. (1983). *Pharmacotherapeutic management of psychiatric problems, 2nd ed.* Columbus: Council of Ohio Colleges of Pharmacy.

Baldessarini, R. J., & Lipinsk, J. F. (1975) Lithium salts: 1970-1975. *Annals of Internal Medicine, 83*, 527-533.

Baldessarini, R. J.(1980). Drugs and the treatment of psychiatric disorders. In A.G. Gilman, L.S. Goodman, and A. Gilman (Eds.), *Goodman and Gillman's: The pharmacological basis of therapeutics, 6th ed.* New York: Macmillan Publishing.

Balter, M. B., Levine, J., & Manheimer, D. I. (1974). Cross national study of the extent of antianxiety/sedative drug use. *New England Journal of Medicine, 290*, 769-774.

Ban, T. A. (1969). *Psychopharmacology.* Baltimore: Williams & Wilkins.

Bancroft, J. (1983). *Human sexuality and its problems.* New York: Churchill Livingstone.

Baraldi, M., Guidotti, A., Schwartz, J.P., & Costa, E. (1979). GABA receptors in clonal cell lines: A model for study of benzodiazepine action at molecular level. *Science, 205*, 821-823.

Barchas, J.D., Berger, P., Ciaranello, R., & Elliot, G. (1977). *Psychopharmacology: From theory to practice.* New York: Oxford University Press.

Baum, L. F. (1944). *The new wizard of oz.* New York: Grosset and Dunlap.

Beck, J. (1986). MDMA: The popularization and resultant implications of a recently controlled psychoactive substance. *Contemporary Drug,* Spring.

Belluzzi, J. D., Grant, D., Gorsky, V., Sarantakis, D., Wise, C. D., & Stein, L. (1976). Analgesia induced in vivo by central administration of enkephalin in rat. *Nature, 260*, 625-626.

Bensinger, P. (1986). An inadequate war against drugs. *Newsweek,* July 28.

Bentov, I. (1977). *Stalking the wild pendulum.* New York: E.P. Dutton.

Benzedrine alert. (1944). *Air Surgeon's Bulletin* 1:2.

Bergersen, B. S., Krug, E. E., & Goth, A. (1966). *Pharmacology in Nursing.* St. Louis: C. V. Mosby Co.

Bhagat, B. (1979). *Mode of action of autonomic drugs.* New York: Graceway Publishing.

Black, C. (1982). *It will never happen to me.* Denver: MAC Publishing.

Blaine, J. D., & Julius, D. A. (1977). *Psychodynamics of drug dependence.* Rockville: U.S. Department of Health, Education, and Welfare, Public Health Service, Health Administration.

Blashfield, R. K., & Draguns, J. G. (1976). Evaluative criteria for psychiatric classification. *Journal of Abnormal Psychology, 85,* 140-150.

Bleuler, E. (1950). *Dementia praecox; or the group of schizophrenias.* New York: International Universities Press. Translated from the German edition published in 1911.

Blom, S. (1963). Tic douloureux treated with new anticonvulsant. *Archives of Neurology, 9,* 285-290.

Blum, R. H. (1969). *Society and drugs, Vol. 1.* San Francisco: Jossey-Bass.

Blum, K. (1984). *Handbook of abusable drugs.* New York: Gardner Press.

Bond, W. S. (1985). Psychopharmacotherapeutic agents (Part I). *American Druggist,* July.

Borraso, R. (1978). Cocaine: A review. *U.S. Pharmacist, 9.*

Borruk, E. L., Schoonover, S. C., & Gelenberg, A. J. (1983). *The practitioner's guide to psychoactive drugs.* New York: Plenum Medical Books.

Boszormenyi-Nagy, I., & Spark, G. M. (1974). *Invisible Loyalties.* Hagerstown, MD: Harper & Row.

Bower, E.M. (1969). Primary prevention of mental and emotional disorders. In A. V. Bindman & A. D. Spiegel (Eds.), *Perspectives in Community Mental Health.* Chicago: Aldine.

Bowers, M. B., van Woert, M., & Davis, L. (1971). Sexual behavior during L-Dopa treatment of parkinsonism. *American Journal of Psychiatry, 127,* 1691-1693.

Brecher, E. M.(1972). *Licit and illicit drugs.* Boston: Little, Brown.

Bromberg, W. (1934). A clinical study of cannabis sativa intoxication. *American Journal of Psychiatry, 91:*303.

Burn, J. H.(1971). *The autonomic nervous system for students of physiology & of pharmacology.* Oxford: Blackwell Scientific Publications.

Cade, J. F. (1970). The story of lithium. In F. J. Ayd & B. Blackwell (Eds.), *Biological psychiatry.* Philadelphia: Lippincott.

Calahan, D., & Cisin, T.H. (1969). *American drinking practices. Journal of Studies on Alcohol.* New Brunswick: Rutgers Center on Alcohol Studies.

Cannon, W. B. (1929) Organization for physiological homeostasis. *Physiology Review, 9*, 399-431.

Chang, J. (1977). *The tao of love and sex: The ancient Chinese way to ecstasy.* New York: E. P. Dutton.

Chereson, R. A., & Fudge, R. P. (1980). *Management of pain, 2nd ed.* Columbus, OH: Council of Ohio Colleges of Pharmacy.

Chess, S., Thomas, A., & Birch, H. G. (1978). *Your child is a person: A psychological approach to parenthood without guilt, the years from birth through first grade.* New York: Penguin Books.

Clark, M. (1979). Drugs and psychiatry: A new era. *Newsweek*, Nov. 12.

Clark, M., & Gelman, D. (1987). A user's guide to hormones. *Newsweek*, January.

Clarren, S. K., & Smith, D. W. (1978). The fetal alcohol syndrome. *New England Journal of Medicine, 298*: 1063.

Clouet, D. H., & Ratner, M. (1970). Catecholamine biosynthesis in brains of rats treated with morphine. *Science*, 168, 854-856.

Coleman, J. H. (1978). Affective disorders. In M.A. Koda-Kimble, B. S. Katcher, & L. Y. Young. (Eds.), *Applied therapeutics for clinical pharmacists, 2nd ed.* San Francisco: Applied Therapeutics.

Collier, H. O. J. (1968). Supersensitivity and dependence. *Nature*, 220, 228-231.

Collin, M. A. (1974). *Medical terminology and the body system.* Hagerstown, MD: Harper & Row.

Courvoisier, S., Fournel, J., Ducrot, R., Kolsky, M., & Koetschet, P. (1953). Proprieties pharmacodynamiques du chlorhydate de chloro-3 (diethylamino-3 propyl)-10 phenothiazine. *Archives Internations Pharmacodyn. Ther.*, 92-305-361.

D'Andrea, V. J. (1975). *Psychoactive drugs.* Palo Alto: Stanford University Press.

Damasio, A. (1979). The frontal lobes. In K. M. Heilman & E. Valenstein (Eds.), *Clinical neuropsychology.* New York: Oxford University Press.

Day, M. D. (1979). *Autonomic pharmacology: Experimental & clinical aspects.* New York: Churchill/Livingstone.

Deikman, A. J. (1971). Biomodal consciousness. In J. Kamiya & J. Stoyva (Ed.), *Biofeedback and Self-control.* Chicago: Aldine.

Del Pozo, E. C. (1967). Empiricism and magic in aztec pharmacology. In D. H. Efron (Ed.), *Ethano-pharacologic Search for Psychoactive Drugs.* Washington, DC: Public Health Series, Publications 1645.

Dement, W., & Kleitman, N. (1957). Cyclic variations in EEG during sleep and their relation to eye movements, body motility, and dreaming. *Electroenceph-alography and Clinical Neurophysiology, 9,* 673-690.

DeMyer, M. K., Shea, P. A., Hendrie, H. C., & Yoshimura, N. N. (1981). Plasma tryptophan and five other amino acids in depressed and normal subjects. *Archives of General Psychiatry, 38,* 642-646.

Depue, R. A., & Monroe, S. M. (1983). Psychopathology research. In M. Hersen, A. E. Kazdin, & A. S. Bellack, (Eds.), *The Clinical Psychology Handbook.* New York: Pergamon Press.

DeQuincey, T. (1907). *Confessions of an English opium-eater.* New York: E. P. Dutton.

Diagnostic and statistical manual of mental disorders. (1980, 1987). Washington, DC: American Psychiatric Association.

Devi, K. (1977). *The eastern way of love: Tantric sex and erotic mysticism.* New York: Simon & Schuster.

Diem, K., & Lentner, C., (1970). *Scientific tables, 7th ed.* Ardsley, NY: Ciba-Geigy Corporation.

Dorland's Medical Dictionary. (1957). Philadelphia: W.B. Saunders.

Douglas, N., & Slinger, P. (1979). *Sexual secrets: The alchemy of ecstasy.* New York: Destiny Books.

Douglas, W. W. (1980). Polypeptides-angiotensin, plasma kinins, and others. In A. G. Gilman, L. S. Goodman, & A. Gilman (Eds.), *Goodman and Gillman's: The Pharmacological Basis of Therapeutics, 6th ed.* New York: Macmillan.

Dowling, C. G. (1985). The trouble with ecstasy: The drug is seductive, controversial, dangerous—and now illegal. *Life,* Aug.

Dunphy, E. B. (1969). Alcohol and tobacco amblyopia: A historical survey. *American Journal of Ophthalmology,* 68:4.

Ellis, J. (1974). *A historical account of coffee.* London: Edward and Charles Dilly.

Erikson, E. (1963). *Childhood and society.* New York: Norton.

Erikson, E. (1964). *Insight and responsibility.* New York: Norton.

Evans, R. T., (1969). *Dialogue with Erik Erikson.* New York: E. P. Dutton.

Farrington E. A. (1887). *Clinical materia medica.* Philadelphia: Sherman.

Feldman, R. S., & Quenzer, L. F. (1984). *Fundamentals of neuropsychopharmacology.* Sunderland, MA: Sinauer Associates.

Finn, P. & O'Gorman, P. A. (1980). *Teaching about alcohol: Concepts, methods, & classroom activities.* Boston: Allyn and Bacon.

Flower, R. J., Moncada, S. & Vane, J. R. (1980). Analgesic-antipyretics and Anti-inflammatory agents; Drugs employed in the treatment of gout. In A. G. Gilman, L. S. Goodman, & A. Gilman (Eds.), *Goodman and Gillman's: The pharmacological basis of therapeutics, 6th ed.* New York: Macmillan.

Gardner, E. D. (1980). Human nervous system. In the *New Encyclopedia Britannica,* in 30 volumes. Chicago: Encyclopedia Britannica, Inc. Vol 12, pp. 994-1044.

Gaskell, W. H. (1916). *The involuntary nervous system.* London: Longmans, Green.

Gastaut, H. (1970). Clinical and electroencephalographical classification of epileptic seizures. *Epilepsia, 28,* 953-957.

Gernaro, A.R., Gibson, M.R., Harvey, S.C., Hutchison, A.S., Kowalick, W., Martin, A.N., Swinyard, E.A., Tice, L.F., & VanMeter, C.T. (Eds.). (1975). *Remington's pharmacentical sciences, 15th ed.* Easton, PA: Mack.

Gessa, G. L., & Tagliamonte, P. (1974). Role of brain monoamines in male sexual behavior. *Life Science, 14:* 425-436.

Giannini, A. J. (1986). Contemporary drugs of abuse. *American Family Physician,* 33:3.

Gibbs, F. A., & Gibbs, E. L. (1954). *Atlas of electroencephalography, Vol. 2.* Reading, MA: Addison-Wesley.

Gibbs, F. A., & Gibbs, E. L. (1964). *Atlas of electroencephalography, Vol. 3,* Reading, MA: Addison-Wesley.

Ginn, P. D. (1978). Epilepsy. In M. A. Koda-Kimble, B. S. Katcher, & L. Y. Young (Eds.), *Applied therapeutics for clinical pharmacists, 2nd ed.* San Francisco: Applied Therapeutics.

Giorgi, A. (1970). *Psychology as a human science.* New York: Harper Row.

Glynn, T. J. (1981). From family to peer: A review of transition of influence among drug using youth. *Journal of Youth and Adolescence, Vol. 10, No 5,* Plenum Publishing.

Goldblatt, M. W. (1935). Properties of human seminal fluid. *Journal Physiology* (London), *84*, 208-218.

Goldenberg, H. (1977). *Abnormal psychology: A social/community approach.* Monterey, CA: Brooks/Cole.

Goldenberg, M. M. (1977). *Drugs and sex.* Los Angeles: Unpublished.

Goldenberg, M. M. (1985). *Survey of psychotropic drug use.* Los Angeles: Unpublished.

Goldenberg, M. M.(1986). *Transcriptions of human sexuality classes taught by Jack L. Rosenberg.* Los Angeles: Unpublished.

Goldsmith, W. (1977). *Psychiatric drugs for the non-medical mental health worker.* Springfield IL: Charles C. Thomas.

Goodman, D. (1976). *Is alcoholism hereditary?* New York: Oxford Press.

Goodman, A. G., Goodman, L. S., & Gilman, A. (1980). *Goodman and Gilman's: The pharmacological basic of therapeutics, 6th ed.* New York: Macmillan.

Gossop, M. R., Stern, R., & Connell, P. H. (1974). Drug dependence and sexual function: A comparison of intravenous users of narcotics and oral users of amphetamines. *British Journal Psychiatry, 124:* 431-434.

Greaves, G. (1972). Sexual disturbances among chronic amphetamine users. *Journal of Nervous and Mental Disease, 155:* 363-365.

Greden, J. F. (1974). Anxiety or caffeinism: A diagnostic dilemma. *American Journal of Psychiatry, 131,* 1089-1092.

Greden, J. F. (1974). Caffeinism and caffeine withdrawal. *American Journal of Psychiatry, 131:*10, 1089-1092.

Greden, J.F. (1981). Caffeinism and caffeine withdrawal. In J.H. Lowinson & P. Ruiz (Eds.), *Substance abuse: Clinical problems and perspectives.* Baltimore: Williams & Wilkins.

Greenblatt, D. J., & Koch-Weser, J. (1973). Gynecomastia and impotence: Complications of spironolactone therapy. *Journal American Medical Association, 223:* 82.

Greer, G. (1983). *MDMA: A new psychotropic compound and its effects in humans.* Santa Fe: Self.

Griffith, H. W. (1983). *Complete guide to prescription and non-prescription drugs.* Tucson: H. P. Books.

Grinder, J., & Bandler, R. (1976). *The structure of magic II.* Palo Alto: Science and Behavior Books.

Grinspoon, L., & Bakalar, J. B. (1981). Marihuana. In J. H. Lowinson & P. Ruiz (Eds.), *Substance abuse: Clinical problems and perspectives.* Baltimore: Williams and Wilkins.

Grinspoon, L., & Bakalar, J. B. (1985). *Cocaine: a drug & its social evolution, rev. ed.* New York: Basic Books.

Gross, H. A. (1977). Prostaglandins. A review of neurophysiology and psychiatric implications. *Archives General Psychiatry, 34:* 1189-96.

Guilleminault, C., Eldridge, F. L., & Dement, W. C. (1973). Insomnia with sleep apnea: A new syndrome. *Science, 181,* 856-858.

Guyton, H. C. (1976). *Textbook of medical physiology, 5th ed.* Philadelphia: W. B. Saunders.

Hammer, M., Makiesky-Barrow, S., & Gutwirth, L. (1978) Social networks and schizophrenia. *Schizophrenia Bulletin, 4,* 522-545.

Harned, J. M. (1968). *Medical terminology made easy, 2nd. ed.* Berwyn IL: Physician's Record Co.

Hartmann, E. L. (1973). *The functions of sleep.* New Haven: Yale University Press.

Hauri, P.(1982). *The sleep disorders.* Kalamazoo, MI: The Upjohn Company.

Hauser, W. A. (1978). Epidemiology of epilepsy. *Adv. Neurol. 19,* 313-339.

Heilman, K. M., & Satz, P. (1983). *Neuropsychology of human emotion.* New York: Guilford Press.

Henderson, J. (1987). *The lover within: Opening to energy in sexual practice.* Barrytown, NY: Station Hill.

Hersen, M., Kazdin, A E., & Bellack, A. S. (1983). *The clinical psychology handbook.* New York: Pergamon Press.

Himmelsbach, C. K. (1943). Can the euphoric analgesic and physical dependence effects of drugs be separated? With reference to physical dependence. *Fed. Proc., 2,* 201-203.

Hollister, L. E. (1976). Drugs and sexual behavior in man. *Life Science 17:* 661-667.

Hollister, L. E. (1978). *Clinical pharmacology of psychotherapeutic drugs.* New York: Churchill Livingstone.

Holmes, T. H., & Rahe, R. H. (1967). The social readjustment rating scale. *Journal of Psychosomatic Research, 11*, 213-218.

Houston, J. (1969). Phenomenology of the psychedelic experience, In R. E. Hicks & P. J. Fink, (Eds.), *Psychedelic drugs.* New York: Grune and Stratton.

Huang, H. F., Nahas, G. G., & Hembree, W. C. (1978). Morphological changes of spermatozoa during marijuana induced depression of human spermatogenesis. *Federal Procedure 37:* 739.

Huba, G. J., & Bentler, P. M. (1980). The role of peer and adult models for drug taking at different stages in adolescence. *Journal of Youth and Adolescence, 9:*5.

Huba, G. J., Newcomb, M. D., & Bentler, P. M. (1986). Adverse drug experiences and drug use behaviors: A one year longitudinal study of adolescents. *Journal of Pediatric Psychology, 11:*2.

Huxley, A. (1954). *The doors of perception.* New York: Harper and Row.

Inaba, D. S., & Katcher, B. S. (1978). Drug Abuse. In M. A. Koda-Kimble, B. S. Katcher, & L. Y. Young (Eds.), *Applied therapeutics for clinical pharmacists, 2nd ed.* San Francisco: Applied Therapeutics.

Jaffe, J. H. (1980). Drug addiction and drug abuse. In A. G. Gilman, L. S. Goodman, & A. Gilman, (Eds.), *Goodman and Gilman's: The pharmacological basis of therapeutics, 6th ed.* New York: Macmillan.

Jaffe, J.H., & Kanzler, M. (1981). Nicotine: Tobacco use, abuse, and dependence. In J. H. Lowinson & P. Ruiz (Eds.), *Substance abuse: Clinical problems and perspectives.* Baltimore: Williams and Wilkins.

Jaffe, J. H., & Martin, W. R. (1980). Opioid analgesics and antagonists. In A. G. Gilman, L. S. Goodman, & A. Gilman (Eds.), *Goodman and Gillman's: The pharmacological basis of therapeutics, 6th ed.* New York: Macmillan.

Jaffe, J. H. & Sharpless, S. (1968). Pharmacological denervation supersensitivity in the central nervous system: A theory of physical dependence. *Proceedings of the Association for Research in Nervous and Mental Disease. 46:* 226-246. Baltimore: Williams & Wilkins.

Jakobovits, T. (1970). The treatment of impotence with methyltestosterone thyroid (100 patients-double-blind-study). *Fertility and Steroids, 21:* 32-35.

Jellinek, E. M. (1960). *The disease concept of alcoholism.* New Haven: College and University Press.

Johnson, C. D.(1983). Alcohol and sex. *Heart and Lung,* 12:1.

Johnson, C. W., Snibbe, J. R., & Evans, L. A. (1975). *Basic psychopathology: A programed text.* New York: Spectrum Publications.

Johnson, J. F. (1985). The narcotics we indulge in, Part I. *Journal of Psychoactive Drugs, 17*:3.

Johnson, J. F. (1986). The narcotics we indulge in, Part II. *Journal of Psychoactive Drugs, 18*:2.

Johnston, L. (1973). *Drugs and American youth.* Ann Arbor: Institute for Research, University of Michigan.

Jones, H. S., & Oswald, I. (1968). Two cases of healthy insomnia. *Electroencephalography and Clinical Neurophysiology, 24,* 378-380.

Judd, L. L. (1967). The normal psychological development of the American adolescent. *California Medicine, 107:6* pg. 465.

Kalat, J. W. (1984). *Biological psychology, 2nd ed.* Belmont, CA: Wadsworth Publishing.

Kaplan, H. S. (1974). *The new sex therapy: Active treatment of sexual dysfunctions.* New York: Brunner/Mazel.

Kaplan L. J. (1978). *Oneness & separateness: From infant to individual.* New York: Simon & Shuster.

Kaplan, L. J. (1984). *The farewell to childhood.* New York: Simon & Shuster.

Karadzic, V.T. (1973). Physiological changes resulting from total sleep deprivation. In W. P. Koella & P. Levin (Eds.), *Sleep: Physiology, biochemistry, psychology, pharmacology, clinical implications.* Basel: Karger.

Kastrup, E. K., Olin, B. R., & Schwach, G. H. (1986). *Facts and comparisons.* St. Louis: J. B. Lippincott.

Katchadourian, H. A., & Lunde, D. T. (1975). *Human sexuality, 2nd ed.* New York: Holt, Rinehart & Winston.

Kelly, J. S., & Beart, P. M. (1975). Amino acid receptors in CNS. GABA in supraspinal regions. In L. L. Iversen, S. D. Iversen, & S. H. Snyder (Eds.), *Handbook of psychopharmacology.* New York: Plenum Press.

Kessler, S. (1980). The genetics of schizophrenia: A review. *Schizophrenia Bulletin, 6,* 404-416.

Kety, S. S., Rosenthal, D., Wender, P.H., Schulsinger, F., & Jacobsen, B. (1975). Mental illness in the biological and adoptive families of adopted individuals who have become schizophrenic. In R. R. Feive, D. Rosenthal, & H. Brill (Eds.), *Genetic research in psychiatry.* Baltimore: Johns Hopkins University Press.

Kimble, D. D. (1973). *Psychology as a biological science.* Santa Monica: Goodyear.

Kleber, H. D. (1967). Prolonged adverse reactions from unsupervised use of hallucinogenic drugs. *Journal of Nervous and Mental Disorders, 144:* 308.

Kleber, H. D. (1981). Detoxification from narcotics. In J. H. Lowinson & P. Ruiz (Eds.), *Substance abuse: Clinical problems and perspectives.* Baltimore: Williams and Wilkins.

Kleitman, N. (1963). *Sleep and wakefulness.* Chicago: University of Chicago Press.

Klerman, G. L. (1978). The evolution of a scientific nosology. In J. C. Shershow (Ed.), *Schizophrenia: Science and practice.* Cambridge: Harvard University Press.

Kline, N. S. (1958). Clinical experience with iproniazid. *Journal Clinical Experimental Psychopathology, 19,* 72-78.

Kline-Graber, G., & Graber, B. (1975). *Woman's orgasm: A guide to sexual satisfaction.* Indianapolis: The Bobbs-Merrill.

Koda-Kimble, M. A., Katcher, B. S., & Young, L. Y. (1978). *Applied therapeutics for clinical pharmacists, 2nd ed.* San Francisco: Applied Therapeutics.

Kolb, L. (1962) *Drug addiction: A medical problem.* Springfield, IL: Charles C. Thomas.

Kolb, L., & Himmelbuch, C. K. (1938). Clinical studies of drug addiction: A critical review of the withdrawal treatments with methods of evaluating absence syndromes. *Public Health Report, 128:*1.

Kolodny, R. C. (1974). Depression of plasma testosterone levels after chronic intensive marijuana use. *New England Journal Medicine, 290:* 872-874.

Kolodny, R. C. (1978). Antihypertensive drugs and male sexual function. Presented at the Eleventh National Sex Institute, Washington, DC.

Kolodny, R. C., Masters, W. H., & Johnson, V. E.(1979). *Textbook of sexual medicine.* Boston: Little, Brown.

Korchin, S. J.(1976). *Modern clinical psychology.* New York: Basic Books.

Kovach, J. A., & Glickman, N. W. (1986). Levels and psychosocial correlates of adolescent drug use. *Journal of Youth and Adolescence, Vol. 15, No. 1,* Plenum Publishing.

Krantz, J. C., & Carr, J. C. (1961). *The pharmacologic principles of medical practice.* Baltimore: Williams & Wilkins.

Kraepelin, E. (1913). *Textbook of psychiatry.* Trans by R. M. Barclay. Edinborough: Livingston.

Kraulis, I., Foldes, G., Traikov, H., Dubrovsky, B., & Birmingham, M. K. (1975). Distribution, metabolism and biological activity of desoxycorticosterone in the central nervous system. *Brain Research, 88,* 1-14.

Kravitz, E. A., Kuffler, S. W., & Potter, D. D. (1963). Gamma-aminobutyric acid and other blocking compounds in crustacea. *Journal of Neurophysiology, 26,* 739-751.

Krishna, G. (1971). *The evolutionary energy in man.* Berkley: Shambhala.

Kubler-Ross, E. (1969). *On death and dying.* New York: Macmillan.

Kuhn, R. (1958). The treatment of depressive states with imipramine hydrochloride (G22355). *American Journal of Psychiatry, 115,* 459-464.

Kurzok, R., & Lieb, C. C. (1930). Biochemical studies of human semen, II. The action of semen on the human uterus. *Proc. Soc. Exp. Biol. Med, 28,* 268-272.

Laborit, H., Huguenard, P., & Alluame, R. (1952). Un nouveau stabilisateur vegetatif. *Presse Med., 60,* 206-208.

Lader, M. H. (1974). The peripheral and central role of the catecholamines in the mechanisms of anxiety. *International Pharmacopsychiatry, 9,* 125-137.

Laing, R. D. (1967). *The politics of experience.* New York: Pantheon.

Lamberg, L. (1984). *The American Medical Association: Guide to better sleep, revised and updated edition.* New York: Random House.

Lamotte, C., Perte, C. B., & Snyder, S. H. (1976). Opiate receptor binding in primate spinal cord: Distribution and changes after dorsal root section. *Brain Research, 112,* 407-412.

Langley, J. N. (1921). *The autonomic nervous system.* Cambridge: W. Heffer & Sons.

Lashley, K.S. (1929). *Brain mechanisms and intelligence.* Chicago: University of Chicago Press.

Laudeman, K. A., (1984). Seventeen ways to get parents involved in substance abuse education. *Journal Drug Education, Vol. 14, No. 4.* Baywood Publishing Co.

Lawson, G., & Ellis, D. C. (1984). *Essentials of chemical dependency counseling.* Rockville, MD: Aspen Systems.

Leiblum, S. R., & Pervin, L. A. (1980). *Principles and practice of sex therapy.* New York: Guilford Press.

Lemberger, L., & Rubin, A. (1976). *Physiologic disposition of drugs of abuse.* New York: Spectrum Publications.

Levitt, J. I. (1970). Spironolactone therapy and amenorrhea. *Journal of the American Medical Association, 211:* 2014-2015.

Lieber, C.S. (1976). The metabolism of alcohol. *Scientific American, March. 234 (3):* 25-33.

Lingeman, R. R. (1974). *Drugs from a to z.* New York: McGraw-Hill.

Lipton, M. A., Di Marcio, A., & Killam, K. F. (1978). *Psychopharmacology: A generation of progress.* New York: Raven Press.

Louria, D. B. (1967). LSD-medical overview. *Saturday Review,* 50-92.

Lowinson, J. H., & Ruiz, P.(1981). *Substance abuse: clinical problems and perspectives.* Baltimore: Williams and Williams.

L-tryptophan: A "natural" sedative. (1977). *The Medical Letter on Drugs and Therapeutics, 19,* 108.

Lust, J. (1974). *The herb book.* New York: Bantam.

MacFarlane, J. (1975). Olfaction in the development of social preferences in the human neonate. In M. Hofer (Ed.), *Parent-infant Interaction.* Amsterdam: Elsevier.

MacLean, P. D. (1949). Psychosomatic disease and the visceral brain: Recent developments bearing on the Papez theory of emotion. *Psychosomatic Medicine, 11,* 338-353.

MacLean, P. D. (1958). Contrasting functions of limbic and neocortical systems of the brain and their relevance to psychophysiological aspects of medicine. *American Journal of Medicine, 25,* 611-626.

MacLean, P.D. (1967). The brain in relation to empathy and medical education. *Journal of Nervous and Mental Disease, 144,* 374-382.

MacLean, P.D. (1970). The limbic brain in relation to psychoses. In P. Black, (Ed.), *Physiological Correlates of Emotion.* New York: Academic Press.

Maddux, J. F. (1981). *Careers of opioid users.* New York: Pralger.

Mahler, M. S., & Furer, M. (1968). *On human symbiosis & the vicissitudes of individuation.* New York: International Universities Press.

Mahler, M. S., Pine, F., & Bergman, A. (1975). *The psychological birth of the human infant.* New York: Basic Books.

Mandel, G. (1979). *Tantra: Rites of love.* New York: Rizzoli International.

Mann, M. (1981). *New primer on alcoholism: How people drink, how to recognize alcoholics, and what to do about them.* New York: Holt, Rinehart and Winston.

Martin, W. (1970). Pharmacological redundancy as an adaptive mechanism in the CNS. *Fed. Proc., 29,* 13-18.

Mason, J. L. (1980). *Guide to stress reduction.* Culver City, CA: Peace Press.

Masters, W. H., & Johnson, V. E. (1970). *Human sexual inadequacy.* Boston: Little, Brown.

Masters, W. H., Johnson, V. E., & Kolodny, R. C. (1986). *Masters and Johnson on sex and human loving.* Boston: Little, Brown.

Maxwell, G. (1964). *Psychopharmacological agents.* New York: Academic Press.

Medical Letter on Drugs & Therapeutics. (1977). *Clonicline (catapres) & other drugs causing sexual dysfunction.* Rochelle, NY: Medical Letter, 19:20.

Medical Letter on Drugs & Therapeutics. (1986). *Crack.* New Rochelle, NY: The Medical Letter, 28:69.

Meehan, B. (1984). *Beyond the yellow brick road: Our child and drugs.* Chicago: Contemporary Books.

Meltzoff, A. N. & Borton, W. (1979). Intermodal matching by human neonates. *Nature, 282,* 403-4.

Melzack, R., & Wall, P. D. (1965). Pain mechanisms: A new theory. *Science, 150:* 3699, 971-79.

Mendelson, J. H. (1974). Plasma testosterone levels before, during, and after chronic marijuana smoking. *New England Journal Medicine, 291:* 1051-1055.

Mental Health Letter. (1986). Care and treatment of schizophrenia-Part I and II. *The Harvard Medical School, Vol 2,* 12, and *Vol 3,1,* June and July.

Mental Health Letter. (1986). Why are children of alcoholics at high risk? *Harvard Medical School, 3:* 5 (Nov.)

Mental Health Letter. (1987). Opiate abuse Part II. *Harvard Medical School, 3:* 8 (Feb.).

Mental Health Letter. (1987). Treatment of alcoholism Part I. *Harvard Medical School, 3:12* (Jun.).

Merritt, H. H., & Putman, T. J. (1938a). A new series of anticonvulsant drugs tested by experiments on animals. *Archives of Neurological Psychiatry, 39,* 1003-1015.

Merritt, H. H., & Putman, T. J. (1938b). Sodium diphenyl hydantoinate in treatment of convulsive disorders. *Journal of the American Medical Association, 111,* 1068-1073.

Merskey, H., & Spear, F. G. (1967). *Pain: Psychological and psychiatric aspects.* London: Bailliere, Tindall, and Cassell.

Meyers, R. D., & Melchior A., (1977). Alcohol drinking: Abnormal intake caused by tetrahyropapaveroline in the brain. *Science, 196.*

Meyers, F. H., Jawetz, E., & Goldfein, A. (1980). *Review of medical pharmacology.* Los Altos, CA: Lange Medical Publications.

Milam, J. R., & Ketcham, K. (1981). *Under the influence: A guide to the myths and realities of alcoholism.* Seattle: Madrona Publishers.

Miller, A. (1981). *The drama of the gifted child.* New York: Basic Books.

Miller, A. (1983). *For your own good: Hidden cruelty in child rearing & the roots of violence.* New York: Farrar, Strauss, Giroux.

Miller, A. (1984). *Thou shalt not be aware.* New York: Farrar, Strauss, Giroux.

Miller, M. A., Drakonitedes, A. B., & Leavett, L. C. (1982). *Kimber Gray Stackpole's: Anatomy & physiology, 17th ed.* New York: Macmillan.

Millichop, J. G., & Fowler, G. W. (1967). Treatment of "minimal brain dysfunctions" syndrome selection of drugs for children with hyperactivity and learning disabilities. *Pediatric Clinics of North America, 14: 4.*

Mischler, E. G., & Scotch, N. A. (1963). Sociological factors in the epidemiology of schizophrenia. *Psychiatry, 26,* 315-343.

Moncada, S., Flower, R. J., & Vane, J. R. (1980). Prostaglandins, prostacyclin, and thromboxane A_2. In A. G. Gilman, L. S. Goodman, & A. Gilman (Eds.), *Goodman and Gillman's: The pharmacological basis of therapeutics, 6th ed.* New York: Macmillan.

Moriarty, K. M. (1984). Psychopharmacology: A historical perspective. *Psychiatric Clinician North America,* Sep. 7, (3), 411-33.

Mothner, I., & Weitz, A. (1984). *How to get off drugs.* New York: A Rolling Stone Press Book, Simon & Schuster.

Musto, D. F. (1973). *The American disease: Origins of narcotic control.* New Haven: Yale University Press.

Naranjo, C. (1973). *The healing journey: New approaches to conciousnes.* New York: Random House.

Nelson, D. D. (1978). *Frequently seen stages in adolescent chemical use.* Minneapolis: CompCare.

New York State Division of Substance Abuse Services. (1978). *Substance use among students grade 7 through 12.* Albany: Division of Substance Abuse Services.

Nicholi, A. M. (1983). The nontherapeutic use of psychoactive drugs, a modern epidemic. *New England Journal of Medicine, 308:* 16.

Nichols, J. R. (1967). Addiction liability of albino rats: Breeding for quantitive differences in mophine drinking. *Science 157:* 561-3. (4 Aug. 67).

Ny, L. K., & Wen, H. L. (1981). Acupuncture in substance abuse, In J. H. Lowinson & P. Ruiz (Eds.), *Substance abuse: Clinical problems and perspectives.* Baltimore: Williams and Wilkins.

Osmond, H., & Smythies, J. R. (1952). Schizophrenia: A new approach. *Journal Mental Science, 98,* 309-315.

Oswald, I. (1975) Psychological medicine. Sleep difficulties. *British Medical Journal, 1,* 557-558.

Otsuka, M. (1973). Gamma aminobutyric acid and some other transmitter candidates in the nervous system. In G. H. Acheson & F. E. Bloom (Eds.), *Pharmacology and the future of man: Proceedings of the fifth international congress of pharmacology, Vol. 4.* Basel: S. Karger.

Page, L. B., & Sidd, J. J. (1972). Medical management of primary hypertension: Part II. *New England Journal of Medicine, 287:* 1018-1023.

Papez, J. W. (1937). A proposed mechanism of emotion. *Archives of Neurology and Psychiatry, 38,* 725-743.

Parry H. J., Balter, M.B., & Mellinger, G. D. (1973). National patterns of psychotherapeutic drugs use. *Archives of General Psychiatry, 28,* 769-83.

Patterson, S. R., & Thompson, L. S. (1978). *Medical Terminology from Greek & Latin.* Troy, NY: Whitston Pub.

Physician's Desk Reference. (1983). Oradell, NJ: Medical Economics Company.

Pichot, P. (1986). Bases and theories of classification in psychiatry. In A.M. Freedman, R. Brotman, I. Silverman, & D. Hutson (Eds.), *Issues in psychiatry.* New York: Human Services Press Inc.

Pick, J. (1970). *The autonomic nervous system.* Philadelphia: J. B. Lippincott.

Piemme, T. E. (1976). Sex and illicit drugs. *Medical aspects of human sexuality,* 10-1:85-86.

Polson, B., & Miller, N. (1984). *Not my kid: A parent's guide to kids and drugs.* New York: Avon.

Ponterotto, J. G. (1985). A counselor's guide to psychopharmacology. *Journal of Counseling and Development,* 64:2.

Prien, R. F., Klett, C. J., & Caffey, E. M. (1973). Lithium carbonate and imipramine in prevention of affective episodes. A comparison in recurrent affective illness. *Archives of General Psychiatry, 29,* 342-425.

Public Health Services. (1967). *The health consequences of smoking.* Washington, DC: U.S. Government Printing Office, 1696.

Radcliffe, A. B., Sites, C.F., Rush, P. A., & Cruse, J. (1985). *The pharmer's almanac: A training manual on the pharmocology of psychoactive drugs.* Denver, CO: M.A.C.

Rahe, R. H. (1979). Life change events and mental illness: An overview. *Journal of Human Stress, 5,* 2-10.

Rall, T. W., & Schleifer, L. S. (1980). Drugs effective in the therapy of the epilepsies. In A. G. Gilman, L. S. Goodman, & A. Gilman (Eds.), *Goodman and Gillman's: The pharmacological basis of therapeutics, 6th ed.* New York: Macmillan.

Rall, T. W. (1980). Central nervous system stimulants. In A. G. Gilman, L. S. Goodman, & A. Gilman, (Eds.), *Goodman and Gilman's: The pharmacological basis of therapeutics, 6th ed.* New York: Macmillan.

Ramsdale, D. A., & Dorfman, E. J.(1985). *Sexual energy ecstasy: A guide to the ultimate, intimate sexual experience.* Playa Del Rey: Peak Skill Publishing.

Randall, L. O., Heise, G. A., Schallek, W., Bagdon, R. E., Banziger, R., Boris, A., Moe, R. A., & Abrams, W. B. (1961). Pharmacological and clinical studies on valium: A new psychotherapeutic agent of the benzodiazepine class. *Current Therapeutic Res. Clin. Exp, 3. No. 9,* 405-425.

Randall, L. O., & Kapell, B. (1973). Pharmacological activity of some benzodiazepines and their metabolites. In S. Garattini, E. Mussini, & L. O. Randall (Eds.), *The benzodiazepines.* New York: Raven Press.

Randall, L. O., Schallek, W., Heise, G. A., Keith, E. F., & Bagdon, R. E. (1960). The psychosedative properties of methaminodiazepoxide. *Journal Pharmacological Experimental Therapeutics, 129,* 163-171.

Ray, O. S. (1972). *Drugs, society, and human behavior.* St Louis: Mosby.

Ray, O. S. (1983). *Drugs, society, and human behavior, 3rd ed.* St. Louis: Mosby.

Rees, C. D., & Wilborn, B. L., (1983). Correlates of drug abuse in adolescents: A comparison of families of drug abusers with families of nondrug abusers. *Journal of Youth and Adolescence, 12:* 1.

Reeves, D. (1984). Parental power and adolescents' drinking. *Psychological Reports, 55.* pp. 161-62.

Reiter, T. (1963). Testosterone implantation: A clinical study of 240 implantations in aging males. *Journal American Geriatric Society, 11:* 540-550.

Riddiough, M. A. (1977). Preventing, detecting and managing adverse reactions of anti-hypertensive agents in the ambulant patient with essential hypertension. *Journal Hospital Pharmacy, 34:* 465-479.

Robin, H. S., & Michelson, J. B. (1988). *Illustrated handbook of drug abuse: Recognition and diagnosis.* Chicago: Year Book Medical Publishers.

Robinson, V. (1925). *An essay of hasheesh, 2nd ed.* New York: E. H. Ringer.

Rodman, M. J., Karch, A. M., Boyd, E. H, & Smith D. W. (1985). *Pharmacology & drug therapy in nursing.* Philadelphia: J. B. Lippincott.

Rosenberg, J. L. (1973). *Total orgasm: Advanced techniques for increasing sexual pleasure.* New York: Random House

Rosenberg, J. L., & Rand, M. L., & Asay, D. (1985). *Body, self, & soul: Sustaining integration.* Atlanta: Humanics Limited.

Rosenthal, D., Wender, P.H., Kety, S. S., & Welner, J. (1971). The adopted-away offspring of schizophrenics. *American Journal of Psychiatry, 128,* 307-311.

Routtenberg, A. (1968). The two-arousal hypothesis: Reticular formation and limbic system. *Psychological Review, 75,* 51-80.

Routtenberg, A. (1970). Stimulus processing and response execution: A neurobehavioral theory. *Physiological Behavior, 6,* 589-596.

Ryall, R. W. (1975). Amino acid receptors in CNS: GABA and glycine in spinal cord. In L. L. Iversen, S. D. Iversen, & S. H. Snyder (Eds.), *Handbook of psychopharmacology.* New York: Plenum Press.

Sannella, L. (1981). *Kundalini: Psychosis or transcendence?* San Francisco: H. S. Daskin.

Satir, V. (1964). *Conjoint family therapy.* Palo Alto: Science and Behavior Books.

Scarpitti, F. R., & Datesman, S. K. (1980). *Drugs and the youth culture.* Beverly Hills: Sage Publications.

Schaef, A. W. (1987a). We're a nation of addicts. *New Age Journal,* Mar/Apr.

Schaef, A. W. (1987b). *When society becomes an addict.* New York: Harper and Row.

Schecter, A., Alksne, H., & Kaufman, E. (1975). *Drug abuse: Modern trends issues, and perspectives.* New York: Marcel Dekker.

Schildkraut, J. J., & Kety, S. S. (1967). Biogenic amines and emotion. *Science, 156,* 21-30.

Schuckit, M. A., & Rayses, V. (1979). Ethanol ingestion: Differences in blood acetaldehyde concentration in relatives of alcoholics and control. *Science,* 203.

Scott, E. M. (1972). *The adolescent gap: Research findings on drug using and non-drug using teens.* Springfield, IL: Charles C. Thomas.

Segraves, R. T. (1977). Pharmacological agents causing sexual dysfunction. *Journal Sex and Marital Therapy, 3:* 157-176.

Seixas, F. A. (1979). Assessing emerging concepts. *Alcohol Clinical Experiences,* 1:281.

Shain, M., & Riddell, W. (1977). *Influence, choice, and drugs.* Lexington, MA: D. C. Heath.

Sharpless, S. K. (1970). Hypnotics and sedatives: 1. The barbiturates. In L. S. Goodman & A. Gilman (Eds.), *The pharmacological basis of therapeutics.* New York: Macmillan.

Shimoura, S. K. (1978). Parkinsonism. In M. A. Koda-Kimble, B. S. Katcher, & L. Y. Young (Eds.), *Applied therapeutics for clinical pharmacists, 2nd ed.* San Francisco: Applied Therapeutics.

Shulgin, A. T. (1983). *Drugs of perception.* Paper presented at U.C. Santa Barbara: Psychedelic Drugs Conference.

Skirboll, L. R., Grace, A. A., & Bunney, B. S. (1979). Dopamine auto- and postsynaptic receptors: Electrophysiological evidence for differential sensitivity to dopamine agonists. *Science, 206,* 80-82.

Small, L. (1973). *Neuropsychodiagnosis in psychotherapy.* New York: Brunner-Mazel.

Smart, R. G., & Bateman, K. (1967). Unfavorable reactions to LSD: A review and analysis of available case reports. *Canadian Medical Association Journal, 97:* 1214.

Smith, D. E. (1970). Editors notes. *Journal of Psychedelic Drugs, 3:* 5.

Smith, G. L., & Davis, P. E. (1976). *Medical terminology: A programmed text, 3rd ed.* New York: Wiley.

Smith, M. O. (1979). Acupuncture and natural healing in drug detoxification. *American Journal of Acupuncture, 2:* 7.

Smith, M. O., Squires, R., Aponte, J., & Rabinowitz, N. (1982). Acupuncture treatment of drug addiction and alcohol abuse. *American Journal of Acupuncture, 10:* 2.

Smith, S. (1984). How drugs act: How drugs are absorbed & reach their destination. *Nursing Times,* Nov. 28 to Dec. 4, 80(40):24.7.

Snyder, S. H. (1978). Antischizophrenic drugs and the dopamine receptor. *Drug Therapy (Hospital Edition),* May.

Spitzer, R. L., & Wilson, P. T. (1975). Nosology and the official psychiatric nomenclature. In A. Freedman, H. Kaplan, & B. Sadock (Eds.), *Comprehensive textbook of psychiatry.* Baltimore: Williams and Wilkins.

Sprock, J., & Blashfield, R.K. (1983). Classification and nosology. In M. Hersen, A. E. Kazdin, A. S. Bellack (Eds.), *The clinical psychology handbook*. New York: Pergamon Press.

Stafford, P. (1983). *Psychedelics encyclopedia, rev. ed.* Los Angeles: J. P. Tarcher.

Stanton, D. M. (1977). The addict as savior: Heroin, death, and the family. *Family Process, 16:* 191.

Stark, E. (1987). Forgotten victims: Children of alcoholics. *Psychology Today,* Jan.

Stein, L. (1968). Chemistry of reward & punishment. In D.H. Efson (Ed.), *Psychopharmacology: A review of progress, 1957-1967* (pp. 105-123). Washington, DC: U.S. Government Printing Office.

Stephenson, P. E. (1977). Physiologic and psychotropic effects of caffeine on man. *Journal American Diet Association, 71:* 240-247.

Stern, D. N. (1985). *The interpersonal world of the infant.* New York: Basic Books.

Stern, W. C., & Morgane, P. J. (1974). Theoretical view of REM sleep function: Maintenance of catecholamine systems in the central nervous system. *Behavioral Biology, 11,* 1-32.

Sternbach, R. A. (1974). *Pain patients: Traits and treatment.* New York: Academic Press.

Sternbach, L. H. (1973). Chemistry of 1,4-benzodiazepines and some aspects of the structure activity relationships. In S. Garattini, E. Mussini, & L. O. Randall (Eds), *The benzodiazepines.* New York: Raven Press.

Stimmel, G. L. (1978). Psychosis. In M. A. Koda-Kimble, B. S. Katcher, & L. Y. Young (Eds.), *Applied therapeutics for clinical pharmacists, 2nd ed.* San Francisco: Applied Therapeutics.

Stoffer, S. S. (1968). A gynecologic study of drug addicts. *American Journal Obstetrics & Gynecology, 101:* 779-783.

Stohs, S. J. (1978). Drugs and sexual function. *U. S. Pharmacist,* 3-10, 51-66.

Stokes, P. E., Kocsis, J. H., & Arcuni, O. J. (1976). Relationship of lithium chloride dose to treatment response in acute mania. Archives of General Psychiatry, 33, 1080-1084.

Sugrue, M. F. (1973). Effects of morphine and pentazocine on the turnover of noradrenaline and dopamine in various regions of the rat brain. *British Journal of Pharmacology, 47,* 644.

Swonger, A. K., & Constantine, L. (1976). *Drugs and therapy: A handbook of psychotropic drugs.* Boston: Little, Brown.

Swonger, A. K., & Constantine, L. L. (1983). *Drugs and therapy: A handbook of psychotropic drugs, 2nd ed.* Boston: Little, Brown.

Szasz, T. S. (1961). *The myth of mental illness.* New York: Harper.

Takahashi, R., Sakuma, A., Itoh, K., Kurihara, M., Saito, M., & Watanabe, M. (1975). Comparison of efficacy of lithium carbonate and chlorpromazine in mania: Report of collaborative study group on treatment of mania in Japan. *Archives of General Psychiatry, 32,* 1310-1318.

Tanney, H. (1986). *The good news about estrogen.* Century City, CA: Unpublished.

Temkin, O. (1965). The history of classification in the medical sciences. In M. Katz, J.O. Cole, & W.E. Barton (Eds). *The role and methodology of classication in psychiatry and psychopathology.* Maryland: U.S. Department of Health, Education & Welfare.

Thirleby, A. (1978). *Tantra: The key to sexual power and pleasure.* New York: Dell Publishing.

Thorn, G. W. (1977). Disturbances of sexual function, In G.W. Thorn (Ed.), *Harrison's principles of internal medicine, 8th ed.* New York: McGraw-Hill.

Tinklenberg, J. (1977). Antianxiety medications and the treatment of anxiety. In J. Barchas, P. Berger, R. Ciaranello, & G. Elliot (Eds.), *Psychopharmacology: From theory to practice.* New York: Oxford University Press.

Trotter, T. (1804). *An essay, medical, philosophical, & chemical, on drunkenness & its effects on the human body.* London: Longman, Hurst, Rees, & Orme.

Trunnell, E. E., & Holt, W. E. (1974). The concept of denial or disavowal. *Journal of the American Psychoanalytical Association, 22:* 769.

Tyrrell, W. B. (1979). *Medical terminology for medical students.* Springfield, IL: Charles Thomas.

Ungerleider, T. J., & DeAngelis, G. G. (1981). Hallucinogens. In J. H. Lowinson & P. Ruiz (Eds.), *Substance abuse: Clinical problems and perspectives.* Baltimore: Williams and Wilkins.

Van Dyke, C. (1981). Cocaine. In J. H. Lowinson & P. Ruiz (Eds.), *Substance abuse: Clinical problems and perspectives.* Baltimore: Williams and Wilkins.

Vander, A. J., Sherman, J. H., & Luciano, D. S. (1975). *Human physiology: The mechanisms of body function, 2nd ed.* New York: McGraw-Hill.

Vecki, V. G. (1915). *Sexual impotence, 5th ed.* Philadelphia: Saunders.

von Euler, U.S. (1936). On the specific vasodilating and plain muscle stimulating substance from accessory genital glands in man and certain animals (prostaglandin and vesiglandin). *Journal Physiology* (London), *88*, 213-234.

von Euler, U.S. (1973). Some aspects of the actions of prostaglandins. The First Heyman's Memorial Lecture. *Arch. Int. Pharmacodyn Ther., 202*, 295-307.

Webb, W. B. (1974). Sleep as an adaptive response. *Perceptual and Motor Skills, 38*, 1023-1027.

Wei, E., & Loh, H. (1976a). Physical dependence on opiate-like peptides. *Science, 193*, 1262-1263.

Wei, E. & Loh, H. (1976b). Chronic intracerebral infusion of morphine and peptides with osmotic minipumps, and the development of physical dependence. In H.W. Kosterlitz (Ed.), *Opiates and endogenous opioid peptides*. Amsterdam: Elsevier/North Holland.

Weil, A. T. (1972). *The natural mind.* Boston: Houghton Mifflin.

Weil-Malherbe, H. (1967). The biochemistry of the functional psychoses. *Adv. Enzymol, 29*, 479-553.

Wender, P. H., Rosenthal, D., Kety, S. S., Schulsinger, F., & Welner, J. (1974). Cross-fostering: A research strategy for clarifying the role of genetic and experimental factors in the etiology of schizophrenia. *Archives of General Psychiatry, 30*, 121-128.

Wesson, D. R., & Smith, D. E. (1981). Abuse of sedative-hypnotics. In J. H. Lowinson & P. Ruiz (Eds.), *Substance abuse: Clinical problems and perspectives*. Baltimore: Williams and Wilkins.

White, J. (1979). *Kundalini, evolution and enlightenment.* Garden City: Anchor Books.

White, J. C. (1952). *The autonomic nervous system, anatomy, physiology & surgical application.* New York: Macmillan.

Wilford, B. B. (1981). *Drug abuse, a guide for the primary care physician.* Chicago: American Medical Association.

Willis, J. H. (1974). *Drug dependence: A study for nurses and social workers, 2nd ed.* London: Farber.

Winokur, A., Amsterdam, J., Caroff, S., Snyder, P. J., & Brunswick, D. (1982). Variability of hormonal responses to a series of neuroendocrine challenges in depressed patients. *American Journal of Psychiatry, 139*, 39-44.

World Health Organizations (1955). Alcohol & alcoholism—report of an expert committee. *Technical Report, 94*, Geneva: WHO.

Wurmser, L. (1981). Psychodynamics of substance abuse. In J. H. Lowinson & P. Ruiz (Eds.), *Substance abuse: Clinical problems and perspectives*. Baltimore: Williams and Wilkins.

Wyatt, R. J. (1977). B-phenylethylamine and the neuropsychiatric disturbances. In E. Usdin & J. Barchas (Eds.), *Neuroregulators and psychiatric disorders*. New York: Oxford University Press.

Young, C. G., & Austrin, M. G. (1979). *Learning medical terminology, step by step*. St. Louis: C. V. Mosby.

Zinberg, N. E. (1976). Observations on the phenomenology of consciousness change. *Journal of Psychedelic Drugs, 8:* 1.

Zinberg, N. E. (1981). Social interactions, drug use, and drug research. In J. H. Lowinson & P. Ruiz (Eds.), *Substance Abuse: Clinical Problems and Perspectives*. Baltimore: Williams and Wilkins.

Zinberg, N. E., & DeLong, J. V. (1974). Research and the drug issue. *Contemporary Drug Problems, 3:* 71.

Zinberg, N. E., Jacobson, R. C., & Harding, W. M. (1975). Social sanctions and rituals as a basis for drug abuse prevention. *American Journal of Drug Alcohol Abuse, 2:* 165.

Zinberg, N. E., & Robertson, J. A. (1972). *Drugs and the public*. New York: Simon and Schuster.

INDEX

Barbiturate-like hypnotics 137-8, 142
Barbiturates 132, 134-7, 142, 220-1, 233, 257, 269-71, 272-3
Barchas, J.D. 332, 351
Bartholin's gland 227
Basal ganglia 63
Base pipe 294
Bateman, K. 315, 349
Baum, L. F. 332
Beans (amphetamine sulfate) 290
Beart, P.M. 118, 340
Beck, J. 299, 332
Beer 270
Behavior, *Figure* 127
Bellack, A.S. 94, 97, 98, 331, 335, 337
Belladonna
    alkaloids 307-8
    treatment 318
Belluzzi, J.D. 193, 332
Benadryl (diphenhydramine) 185
Bennies (amphetamine sulfate) 290
Bensinger, P. 309, 332
Bentler, P.M. 339
Bentov, I. 321, 332
Benzedrex inhaler 288
Benzedrine
    alert 332
    inhaler 288
Benzodiazepine intoxication 317
Benzodiazepine 116-21, 122, 138-40, 142, 221-2, 271, *Figure* 118
    anxiety 275
    intoxication 317
Benzphentamine (Didrex) 290
Benztropine mesylate (Cogentin) 185
Berger, P. 332, 351
Bergersen, B. S. 332
Bergman, A. 252, 343
Bernice (cocaine HCl) 294
Beta alcoholism 268
Beta-adrenergic receptors 176
Beta-endorphin 194
Bethanechol (Urecholine) 151
Bhagat, B. 332
Bianco (heroin/diacetylmorphine) 281
Bindman, A.V. 333

Biotransformation 45-7
Biperidin (Akineton) 185
Biphetamine (amphetamine complex) 290
Bipolar disorders 145-6, 147-50, 161-6
    cyclothymia 147
    depressed 148
    manic 148
    mixed 148
Birch, H.G. 334
Birmingham, M.K. 193, 342
Black, C. 333
Blackwell, B. 333
Blaine, J.D. 333
Blashfield, R.K. 95, 333, 350
Bleomycin 237
Bleuler, E. 98, 333
Blitz 218
Blom, S. 222, 333
Blood
    alcohol levels (BAL) 260-1
    supply 64
    vessels in the head 77
Blum, K. 333
Blum, R.H. 114, 333
Board of Behavioral Science Examiners in California 10, 329
Body surface area (BSA) 29
Body trips 315
Bond, W.S. 333
Borderline, personality disorder 104
Boris, A. 347
Borraso, R. 333
Borruk, E.L. 333
Borton, W. 249, 344
Boszormenyi-Nagy, I. 253, 333
Bower, E.M. 93, 333
Bowers, M.B. 232, 333
Boyd, E.H. 348
Bradykinin 204
Brain 50, 62-70
    blood supply 64
    membranes 63
    stem 50
    structure 62-3
    ventricles 64
Brecher, E. M. 333

Ecstacy, ETC, (methylene dioxyam-phetamine MDMA) 299, 300
ECT (Electroconvulsive therapy) 158, 318
Edinger-Westphal nucleus 77
EEG (electroencephalograph) 125-8, 141-2, 214, 215
EENT (eye, ear, nose, throat) 121
benzodiazepine effects 121
Effector sites 53
Efron, D.H. 335, 350
Ejaculation
failure 235
incompetence 230
premature 229-30, 233
retarded 230
Elavil (amitriptyline) 154, 237
Eldridge, F.L. 129, 338
Electroconvulsive therapy (ECT) 158, 318
Electroencephalograph (EEG) 125-8, 141-2, 214, 215
Elephant (phencyclidine, PCP) 304
Elimination
drug 47
Elixirs 27
Elliot, G. 332, 351
Ellis, D.C. 342
Ellis, J. 280, 335
Empirin & Codeine (codeine) 281
Emulsions 27
Encopresis 101
Encyclopedia Britannica 62
Endep (amitriptyline) 154
Endocrine effects
antipsychotic drugs 186
benzodiazepines 120
tricyclic antidepressant 153
Endocrine system   83, 87, Figure 88-90
Endogenous
depression 144
peptides 193
Endoplasmic reticulum 52
Endorphins 193, 212
Enkephalin 192
Enuresis 101
Environment
factors determining dose 32
Environmental trips 315

Enzyme interactions
drug 37-8
Enzymes 46
Eosinophilia 182
Epilepsy
primary idiopathic 213
secondary idiopathic 213
symptomatic idiopathic 213
Epilepsy seizures 213-32
absence 214-5
febrile 216
focal 216
generalized 217
grand mal 214, 223
jacksonian type 214, 216, 223
myoclonus 216
partial 217
petit mal 214-5, 223
psychomotor 214, 215-6, 223
temporal lobe 215-6, 223
Epinephrine effect 176-7
Epsilon Alcoholism 269
EPSP (Excitatory postsynaptic potential) 59, 135
Erectile dysfunction 229, 235
Erection, penis 226
Erikson, E. 335
Esophagus 78
Estrogen 228, 232, Figure 90
Ethacrynic acid 236
Ethanol 270
Ethchlorvynol (Placidyl) 138, 142
Ethosuximide (Zarontin) 221
Ethotoin (Peganone) 220
Evans, L. 339
Evans, R. T. 336
Excipient ingredients 278
Excitatory postsynaptic potential (EPSP) 59, 135
Extrapyramidal effects
antipsychotic drugs 183-5
Extrapyramidal symptoms 176, 184-5
Extrapyramidal system 68
Eye 77, Figure 84

F

Factitious disorders 103
Facts and Comparisons book 19

Generalized 217
    epilepsy seizures 217
Genetics
    factors determining dose 31
Genitalia 227
Genitourinary effects
    anxiety 111
    benzodiazepines 121
Gernaro, A.R. 336
Gershon, S. 233, 331
Gessa, G.L. 233, 336
GH (growth hormone) 88
GI (gastrointestional) 115, 221
Giannini, A.J. 318, 336
Gibbs, E.L. 214, 336
Gibbs, F.A. 214, 336
Gibson, M.R. 336
Gilles de la Tourette syndrome 173
Gilman, A. 332, 335, 337
Ginn, P.D. 216, 336
Ginseng 231
Giorgi, A. 336
Glands
    exocrine 83, *Figure* 88-90
    lachrymal 77, *Figure* 84-5
    salivary 77, *Figure* 84-5
Glia cells 54
Glickman, N. W. 341
Glossopharyngeal nerves 77
Glucagon, *Figure* 90
Glucocorticoid (Cortisol), *Figure* 89
Glutethimide (Doriden) 21, 138,
    142, 273
Glycosides 24
Glynn, T.J. 336
Goldblatt, M.W. 203, 337
Goldenberg, H. 337
Goldenberg, M.M. 94, 236, 237, 337
Goldsmith, W. 162, 180, 337
Golgi 52
Goodman, A.G. 117, 337
Goodman, D. 243, 267
Goodman, L. S. 117, 335, 332, 337
Gorsky, V. 193, 332
Gossop, M.R. 236, 337
Goth, A. 332
Graber, B. 240, 341
Grace, A.A. 147, 349
Grand mal
    epilepsy seizures 214, 223

Grant, D. 193, 332
Greaves, G. 233, 337
Greden, J. F. 113, 283, 336, 337
Greenblatt, D.J. 236, 337
Greenhill, J.P. 331
Greer, G. 300, 337
Griffith, H. W. 337
Grinder, J. 68, 338
Grinspoon, L. 296, 338
Gross, H.A. 227, 228, 232, 338
Growth hormone (GH), *Figure* 88
Guidotti, A. 118, 332
Guilleminault, C. 129, 338
Gulland 193
Gums 24
Gutwirth, L. 167, 338
Guyton, H.C. 226, 227, 228, 338
Gyri 66

H

H, Horse (Heroin/Diacetylmorphine)
    281
Habit forming drugs 265
Habituation 40
Haider 296
Hairy (Heroin/Diacetylmorphine)
    281
Halazepam (Paxipam) 275
Halcion (triazolam) 139
Haldol (Butyrophenone/haloperidol)
    173, 178, 179, 277, 316, 317
Half-life 33
Hallucinations 140, 177, 313
Hallocinogen intoxication 314-5
    talking the person down 314,
    316
Hallucinogens 233, 238, 300-1, 310
    LDS 258
    PCP 258
    STP 258
    mushrooms 258
    peyote 258
Haloperdol (Haldol) 173, 178, 179,
    316, 317
Haloperidol (Butyrophenenone) 277
Haltran (Ibuprofen) 210
Halucinogens 258
Hammer, M. 167, 338

K

Kalat, J.W. 56, 64, 69, 128, 146, 147, 340
Kamiya, J. 334
Kantzler, M. 286, 339
Kapell, B. 117, 347
Kaplan, H.S. 229, 230, 231, 232, 233, 234, 239, 340
Kaplan, L. J. 235, 248, 249, 250, 251, 340
Karadzic, V.T. 124, 340
Karch, A.M. 348
Kastsrup, E.K. 118, 120, 134, 136, 137, 141, 152, 162, 163, 164, 200, 235, 236, 284, 286, 340
Katchadourian, H.A. 340
Katcher, B.S. 334, 339, 341
Kaufman, E. 348
Kazdin, A. 94, 97, 98, 331, 335, 338
Kefauver-Harris Drug Amendment 21
Keith, E.F. 117, 347
Kelly, J.S. 118, 340
Kemadrin (Procyclidine) 185
Kessler, S. 168, 340
Ketcham, K. 345
Ketoprefen (Orudis) 210
Kety, S. S. 146, 168, 340, 348, 351
Kidneys 79
Killam, K. 343
Kimble, D.D. 315, 340
Kleber, H.D. 315, 318, 341
Kleitman N. 124, 128, 331, 335, 341
Kleptomania 103
Klerman, G.L. 99, 341
Klett, C.J. 162, 346
Kline, N.S. 174, 341
Kline-Graber, G. 240, 341
Klonopin (Catapres) 318
Koch-Weser, J. 236, 337
Kocsis, J. H. 165, 350
Koda-Kimble, M.A. 334, 341
Koetschet, P. 334
Kolb, L. 234, 318, 341
Kolodny, R.C. 233, 235, 236, 341, 344
Kolsky, M. 334
Korchin, S.J. 94, 99, 341

Kovach, J.A. 341
Kowalick, W. 336
Kraepelin, E. 98, 99, 341
Krantz, J.C. 133, 341
Kraulis, I. 193, 342
Kravitz, E. 117, 342
Krishna, G. 320, 342
Krug, E.E. 332
Kubler-Ross, E. 143, 342
Kuffler S.W. 117, 342
Kuhn, R. 150, 342
Kundalini 320
Kurihara, M. 162, 351
Kurzok, R. 203, 342

L

l-tryptophan 140-1, 142
l-5-hydroxytryptophan (l-5HTP) 216
Laborit, H. 174, 342
Lachrymal
    glands 77, *Figure* 84-5
Lader, M.H. 113, 342
Laing, R.D. 94, 342
Lamberg, L. 130, 131, 342
Lamotte, C. 193, 342
Langley, J.N. 74, 342
Larodopa (Levodopa) 232-3
Lashley, K.S. 66, 342
Lasix (furosemide) 236, 316
Lateral ventricles 66
Laudeman, K.A. 342
Lawson, G. 342
League of Spiritual Discovery 303
Leary, T. 302-3
Leavett, L.C. 345
Legal drugs 257-310
Leiblum, S.R. 342
Lemberger, L. 280, 283, 284, 294, 297, 342
Letner, C. 226, 335
Leukopenia 182
Levine J. 16, 113, 332
Levitt, J.I. 236, 343
Levo-Dromoran (Levorphanol) 197
Levodopa (Dopar/Larodopa) 232-3, 238
Levorphanol (Levo-Dromoran) 197

Mayrand (asproject) 208
Mazindol
    Mezanor 290
    Sanorex 290
MDA (Methylene dioxyamphe-
    tamine) 233, 258, 299-300
Mead 114
Mebaral
    mephobarbital 137, 221
Mechanisms of sleep 125-8
Meclofenamate sodium (Meclomen)
    211
Meclomen (meclofenamate sodium)
    211
Medical aspects
    treatment 313-20
Medical Letter on Drugs and Ther-
    apeutics 236, 293, 294, 344
Medical treatment
    See intoxication
Medipren (Ibuprofen) 210
Medulla Oblongata 64
Meehan, B. 344
Mefenamic acid (Ponstel) 211
Mehyprylon (Noludar) 138, 142
Melancholia 97, 148
Melchior, A. 267, 345
Mellaril
    phenothiazine/piperidine 277
    thioridazine 174, 178,179, 236
Mellinger, G.D. 346
Meltzoff, A. N. 249, 344
Melzack, R. 191, 344
Membrane
    arachnoid 63
    dura mater 63
    pia mater 63
    postsynaptic 58
    presynaptic 58
Memory 66
Mendelson, J.H. 233, 344
Mental health
    letter 319, 325, 344
    primary componenets 93-4
Mental retardation 100
Meperidine (Demerol) 197, 200,
    201, 280, 281
Mephenytoin (Mesantoin) 220
Mephobarbital (Mebaral) 137, 221
Meprobamate 114-6, 122

Merck 193
Merritt, H.H. 218, 344
Merskey, H. 190, 345
Mesantoin (Mephenytoin) 220
Mescaline 305-6, 307
Mesoridazine (phenothiazine/
    piperidine/Serentil) 174, 178, 179
Metabolism
    conjugation 46
    dehalogenation 46
    desulfuration 46
    drug 45-6
    hydrolysis 46
    methylation 46
    oxidation 46
    reduction 46
Metencephalon 63
Meth (Methamphetamine) 290
Methadione (Tridione) 221
Methadone (Dolophine) 197, 280,
    281, 318, 319
Methamphetamine (Desoxyn) 290
Methanol 270
Methaqualone (Quaalude) 273
Metharbital (Gemonil) 221
Methohexital (Brevital) 135
Methotrexate 237
Methprylon (Noludar) 273
Methsuximide (Celontin) 221
Methylene dioxyamphetamine (Love
drug/MDA) 300
    adam 300
    MDA 300
Methylene dioxymethamphetamine
    ecstacy ETC 300
    MDMA 300
Methylphenidate (Ritalin) 288
Metronidazole (Flagyl) 314
Meyers, R.D. 267, 345
Mezanor (Mazindol) 290
MI (Myocardial infarction) 152-3,
    206
Michelson, J.B. 348
Midbrain 63, 64-5
Midol (Ibuprofen) 210
Milam, J.R. 259, 260, 262, 264, 266,
    311, 312, 345
Miller, A. 251, 252, 345
Miller, N. 245, 346
Millichop, J.G. 288, 345

Milontin (Phensuximide) 221
Mind trips 315
Mineralocorticoid (Aldosterone),
   Figure 89
Minor tranquilizers 271
Miosis 77
Miscellaneous drugs 307
Mischler, E.G. 167, 345
Miss Emma (Morphine sulfate) 281
Mitochondria 51
Moban
   dihydroindolone 277
   molindone 173, 178, 179
Mobidin (Magnesium salicylate)
   207
Molindone (Moban/Dihydroin-
   dolone) 173, 178, 179, 277
Moncada, S. 205, 336, 345
Monkey (Phencyclidine) 304
Monoamine oxidase (MAO) 37, 52,
   62, 156
   inhibitors (MAOI) 237
Monroe, S. M. 335
Mood disorders 102, 145-6, 147,
   159
   biological basis 146-7
   bipolar 145-6
   unipolar 145
Mood elevators 258
Morgane, P.J. 124, 350
Moriarty, K.M. 84 269, 345
Morning Glory Seeds/Ololiuqui 307
Morphine Sulfate 193, 194-5, 197,
   198, 200, 257, 279, 281
Mose, R.A. 347
Mothner, I. 345
Motrin (Ibuprofen) 210
Muscle relaxation (Diazepam) 271
Muscular effects
   anxiety 111
Mushrooms 258
Mussini, E. 350
Musto, D.F. 292, 345
Myocardial infarction (MI) 152-3,
   206
Myoclonus
   epilepsy seizures 216
Mysoline (primidone) 221

N

N's (Darvon) 281
Nahas, G.G. 233, 339

Nalbuphine (Nubain) 197
Nalfon (fenoprefen) 210
Naloxone (Narcan) 318
Name
   brand 23
   chemical 22
   generic 22
   official 22
   trademark 23
Naproxen (Anaprox) 210
Naranjo, C. 301, 303, 345
Narcan (naloxone) 318
Narcissistic 104
Narcotic analgesic 257
   adverse affects of 199-201
   mechanism of action 193-6
Narcotic drugs 257, 276-81, 281
   agonists 195
   antagonists 196
   dangers 278
   drug dependence 196, 198-9
   drug interactions 201
   intoxication 318-20
   naturally occurring 196
   pharmacological effects 200
   semi-synthetic analogues 196
   side effects 200
   synthetic compounds 196
Nardil (phenelzine) 156, 201, 237
National Formulary (NF) 20
Navane (thiothixene) 173, 178, 179,
   277
Nelson, D.D. 245, 345
Nembutal (pentobarbital) 137, 272
Nerve impulse 54-8
Nerves
   abducens 72
   accessory 73
   cervical 73
   coccygeal 73
   cranial 71-3
   cranial 72, 77
   dorsal 73
   facial 72, 77
   glossopharyngeal 73, 77
   hypoglossal 73
   lumbar 73
   oculomotor 72
   olfactory 72
   optic 72

Olin, B.R. 340
Oloiuqui 307
Opiates 236, 257, 276
Opioid receptors 193-4
 Kappa 194-5
 Mu 194-5
 Sigma 194-5
Opisthotonos 184
Opium (O. Op) 19, 257, 281
Opium alkaloids 193-4
Opium poppy 276
Oranges (Dextroamphetamine sul-
 fate) 290
Orap (Pimozide) 173
Organic mental disorders 101-2
Organs
 skin 78, *Figure* 86
Orgastic dysfunction 230
Orthostatic hypotension 176, 182
Orudis (Ketoprofen) 210
Osmond, H. 169, 346
Osteorthritis (OA) 202, 210
Oswald, I. 124, 340, 346
Otsuka, M. 346
Ovaries 227
Ovary glands, *Figure* 90
Overeaters' Anonymous (OA) 326
Oxazepam (Serax) 275
Oxazolidinediones 221
 adverse effects 221
Oxidation
 metabolism 46
Oxycodone (Percocet/Percodan)
 197, 281
Oxymorphone (Numorphan) 197
Oxyphenbutazone 211

P

Package inserts 17-8
Page, L.B. 235, 346
Pain 189-212
 gate-control theory 191-2, 212
 neurophysiology 191-2
 pattern theory 191
 PQRST 190-1
 specificity theory 191
Pancreas gland, *Figure* 90
Pancreas 79, *Figure* 84

Papaver somniferum 276
Papez, J.W. 69, 346
Paradione (Paramethadione) 221
Paradoxical sleep 127
Paramethadione (Paradione) 221
Paranoia 104, 177
Paranoid disorders 167, 172
 acute paranoid 172
 atypical paranoid disorder 172
 paranoia 172
 shared paranoid 172
 symptoms 172
Parasomnias 103
Parasympathetic system 65, 76-7
Parathyroid glands, *Figure* 89
Parathyroid hormone, *Figure* 89
Parietal lobe 66
Parkinson's disease 170
Parkinsonian symptoms 176
Parnate (Tranylcypromine) 156, 237
Parry, H.J. 16, 113, 346
Partial, epilepsy seizures 217
Pasadena (thiocyl) 208
Passive aggressive 104
Pastes, physical state 28
Patches 26
Pathological gambling 103
Pathology
 factors determining dose 30
Pattern theory
 pain 191
Patterson, S.R. 346
Paxipam (Halazepam) 275
PCC 305
PCP (Phencyclidine) 258, 304, 317
 intoxication 317
Peace pill, phencyclidine (PCP) 304
Peganone (Ethotoin) 220
Penis, erection 226
Pentazocine (Talwin) 95, 197, 281
Pentobarbital (Nembutal) 137, 272
Pentothal (Sodium thiopental) 135,
 272
Peptides 60
Percocet (Oxycodone) 197, 281
Peripheral nervous system 71-4
Permitil
 fluphenazine 174, 178, 179
 phenothiazine 277
 piperazine 277
 prolixin 277

R

RA (Rheumatoid arthritis) 201, 210, 211
Rabinowitz, N. 320, 349
Radcliffe, A.B. 278, 279, 280, 294, 297, 304, 347
Rahe, R.H. 109, 339, 347
Rall, T.W. 217, 347
Ramsdale, D.A. 240, 347
Rand, M.L. 348
Randall, L.O. 117, 347, 350
Rapid eye movement (REM) 134
    sleep 127-8, 135-6, 138, 142
Rapprochement stage 252
RAS (Reticular activating system) 113, 125-6, 127, 138, 141, 175
Rass, D. 303
Ratner, M. 334
Ray, O.S. 242, 243, 276, 278, 285, 286, 288, 289, 294, 296, 302, 347
Rayses, V. 242, 266, 348
Reactive depression 144
Rebirthing 320-1
Receptor theory 36-7
Reduction, metabolism 46
Rees, C. D. 347
Reeves, D. 347
Reflection stage 250-1
Reiter, T. 347
Release, sustained 25
REM (Rapid eye movement) sleep 127-8, 134, 135-6, 138, 142
Replacement 38
Reproductive system
    female 227-8
    male 226-7
Resin 24
Respiratory effects
    antipsychotic drugs 186
    anxiety 111
    barbiturates 137
Restoril (temazepam) 139
Retarded ejaculation 230
Reticular activating system (RAS) 113, 125-6, 127, 138, 141, 175
Reticular formation 69
Rexolate (hyrex) 208
Rheumatoid arthritis (RA) 201, 210, 211

Ribosomes 52
Richter, C. 146
Riddell, W. 349
Riddiough, M.A. 235, 236, 347
Rigidity 184
Ritalin (methylphenidate) 288
RNA 52
Robertson, J.A. 255, 353
Robin, H.S. 348
Robinson, V. 193, 296, 348
Robiquet 193
Roche Laboratories 116-7
Rocket fuel (Phencyclidine/PCP) 304
Rodman, M. 42, 62, 193, 213, 348
Root 15-6
Rosenberg, J.L. 80, 215, 230, 233, 239, 240, 242, 248, 250, 251, 252, 253, 258, 276, 300, 301, 321
Rosenthal, D. 168, 169, 340, 348, 351
Routtenberg, A. 125, 348
Rubin, A. 280, 283, 284, 294, 297, 342
Rufen (ibuprofin) 210
Ruiz, P. 331, 336, 343, 351
Rumination 101
Rush, B. 311
Rush, P.A. 278, 279, 280, 294, 297, 304, 347
Ryall, R.W. 117, 348

S

Saito, M. 162, 351
Sakuma, A. 162, 351
Salicylamide (Uromide) 208
Salicylates
    pharmacological effects 205
Salivary
    glands 77, *Figure* 84-5
Salsalate (Salicylsalicylic acid/ Disalcid) 207
Saltatory conduction 57-8
San Salvador 285
Sannella, L. 320, 321, 348
Sanorex (mazindol) 290
Sarantakis, D. 193, 332

thioridazine (Mellaril) 236
thioxanthenes 236
tranylcypromine (Parnate) 237
tricyclic antidepressants 237
Sex and Drugs 225-40
Sex hormones, *Figure* 89
Sexual
dysfunctions 229-31
Sexual disorders 102-3
Sexual enhancement
alcohol 233
amphetamines 233
amyl nitrite 234
anticholinergic 235
atropine 235
barbiturates 233
caffeine 234
chlorprothixene (Taractian) 236
clonidine (Catapres) 235-6
guanethidine (Ismelin) 235
hallucinogens 233-4
Larodopa 232
levodopa 232
marijuana 233
methyldopa (Aldomet) 235
nicotine 234
papar 232
taractian, chlorprothixene 236
thiothixene (Navane) 236
Shain, M. 349
Sharples, S.K. 349
Shea, P.A. 146, 335
Sherman, G. P. 332
Sherman, J.H. 232, 351
Sherrington, S.C. 58
Shimoura, S.K. 349
Shit (Heroin/Diacetylmorphine)
281
Shulgin, A.T. 299, 349
Sidd, J. 235, 346
Side effect 39
Silverman, I. 346
Sinequan (Adapin/Doxepin HCl)
121
Sites, C.F. 278, 279, 280, 294, 297,
304, 347
Skag (Heroin/Diacetylmorphine)
281
Skene's gland 227

Skin
organs 78, *Figure* 86
Skin effects
anxiety 111
benzodiazepines 121
Skirbol, L.R. 147, 349
Sleep 123-5
See disorders
See waves
apnea myoclonus 129
definition 123
disorders 128-30
enuresis 129
insomnia 128-9, 133
mechanisms 125-8
narcolepsy 130
non-rapid eye movement 134
pharmacology of 132-3
rapid eye movement (REM)
128, 134
sedative-hypnotics 132-3
stages 126-8
states 127
walking 129
Sleep disorders 103
dyssomnias 103
parasomnias 103
Slinger, P. 239, 335
Slow-wave sleep (SWS) 127
Smack (Heroin/Diacetylmorphine)
281
Small, L. 96, 349
Smart, R.G. 315, 349
Smith D. E. 271, 274, 351
Smith, D.E. 315, 349
Smith, D.W. 264, 334, 348
Smith, Kline, and French
Laboratories 288
Smith, M.O. 320, 349
Smith, S. 84, 349
Smythies, J.R. 169, 346
Snibbe, J.R. 339
Snow (Cocaine HCl) 294
Snyder, P.J. 146, 351
Snyder, S.H. 170, 176, 193, 342,
349
Social drugs 258
Sociological viewpoint
substance abuse 254-6
Sodium thiosalicylate (Thiocyl) 208

Sodium salicylate 207
Sodium thiopental (Pentothal) 272
Solar plexus
    celiac ganglia 75
Solid, physical state 25-6
Solutions 26
Somatoform disorders 102
Spanish Fly (Cantharides) 231-2
Sparine
    phenothiazine 277
    aliphatic 277
    promazine 174, 178, 179
Spark, G.M. 333
Spear, F.G. 190, 345
Specific developmental disorders
    101
Specificity theory
    pain 191
Speed (Methamphetamine) 290
Spermatogenesis 233
Spiegel, A.D. 333
Spinal cord 50, 70-1
Spinal nerves 73-4
Spinal reflex 50
Spiritual awakening 320-1
Spironolactone (Aldactone) 236
Spirtual crisis 320-1
Spitzer, R.L. 94, 97, 349
Spleen 79
Splitting off 215, 233, 258
Sprock, J. 350
Squires, R. 320, 349
Stadol, butorphanol 197
Stafford, P. 350
Stages
    attachment 248-50
    healthy introversion 251-2
    intoxification 313, 327
    rapprochement 252
    reflection 250-1
Stages of abuse 245
Standard Classified Nomenclature
    of Disease, The 99
Stanton, D.M. 350
Stark, E. 350
State Division of Substance Abuse
    Services 329
Steady state 33
Stein L. 146, 193, 332, 350

Stelazine
    phenothiazine 277
    piperazine 277
    trifluoperazine 174, 178, 179
Stephenson, P.E. 234, 350
Stern, D.N. 242, 248, 249, 251, 350
Stern, R. 236, 337
Stern, W.C. 124, 350
Sternbach, L.H. 116, 117, 350
Sternbach, R.A. 190, 350
Sterno 270
Steroids 87
Stimulation 38
Stimuli
    emotional 49
    external 49
    internal 49
Stoffer, S.S. 236, 350
Stohs, S.J. 230, 231, 232, 234, 235,
    236, 350
Stokes, P.E. 165, 350
Stomach 78-9
Stoyva, J. 334
STP 258, 306
Stress, sources 109
Stuff (Heroin/Diacetylmorphine)
    281
Styles
    defensive 252-3
    denial 252
    externalizing 253
Subcutaneously 34
Sublimaze, fentanyl 197
Substance abuse 9-10, 241-56,
    311-30
    case examples 246-8
    family dynamics 253
    sociological viewpoint 254-6
    stages 245
    treatment of 10, 311-30
Substance abuser of
    alcohol 313-4
    barbiturate 316
    benzodiazepine 317
    cocaine 317
    CNS stimulants 316
    hallucinogen 314-5
    marijuana 317
    medical treatment 313-20
    narcotic 318-20

Substance P 192
Substantia gelatinosa 194
Succinimides 221
    adverse effects 221
Suffix 14-5
Sugrue, M.F. 350
Sulci 66
Sulindac (Clinoril) 210
Support groups 322
Suppositores 26
Suprofen (Suprol) 210
Suprol (suprofen) 210
Surmontil (trimipramine) 154
Suspensions 27
Swinyard, E.A. 336
Swonger, A.K. 93, 95, 125, 131, 132,
    133, 144, 146, 147, 162, 168,
    169, 190, 194, 198, 205, 215,
    216, 219, 222, 351
SWS (slow-wave sleep) 127
Sympathetic systems 65, 76-7
Symptoms
    autonomic nervous system 11
    fluid 202
    types 202
Synthetic drugs 258
Syrups 26
System
    ascending riticular activition
        69
    endocrine 83, 87-90, *Figure*
        88-90
    extrapyramidal 68
    limbic 69-70
    pyramidal 68
Systems, psychopathological
    interpersonal systemic process
        97
Szasz, T.S. 94, 351

T

Tablets 25-6
Tachycardia 152
Tagamet, cimetidine 201
Tagliamonte, P. 233, 336
Takahashi, R. 162, 351
Talbutal (Lotusate) 137

Talwin (pentazocine) 195, 197, 258,
    281
Tanney, H. 232, 351
Tantra 239
Taractan
    chlorprothixene 178, 179
    thioxanthenes 277
Tardive dyskinesia 185-7, 188
Tegretol (carbamazepine) 222
Telencephalon 63
Temazepam (Restoril) 139, 271
Temporal lobe 67
    epilepsy seizures 215-6, 223
Tenuate (diethylproprion) 290
Teratogenic effect 39
Terminal buttons 53
Terminology
    derivation 12-6
    Greek 11-6
    Latin 11-6
    medical 11-6
    prefix 12-14
    root 14-5
    suffix 15-6
Testes 226
Testosterone 226, 232, 233
Tetracyclic 152
Tetrahydropapaveroline (THP) 267
Thalamic system, *Figure* 127
Thalamus 63, 65
Thalidamide 21
THC (Tetrahydrocannabinol) 297,
    309
Therapeutic
    community 39, 312, 319
    index 40
Therapy
    affect 96
    behavioral 96
    behavior modification 96
    insight 96
    psychoanalyist 96
    supportive psychotherapies 96
Thiamine (Vitamin B1) 313
Thiocyl sodium thiosalicylate 208
Thiopental (Pentothal) 135
Thioridazine (Mellaril) 174, 178,
    179, 236
    phenothiazine 277
    piperine 277

Trip 315
Troches 26
Trotter, T. 311-2, 351
Truck drivers (Amphetamine sulfate) 290
Trunnell, E.E. 252, 351
Tryptophan 146-7
TSH (thyroid-stimulating hormone) 88
Tuinal (amobarbital/secobarbital) 272
Tusal (hauck) 208
Twelve step support group 322, 314, 325-9
Tylenol 209
    acetaminophen 136
    codeine 281
Tyramine containing foods 157
Tyrrell, W.B. 351

U

Ungerleider, T.J. 304, 305, 351
Uppers 258, 280-98, 310
    cocaine 258
    antidepressants 258
    mood elevators 258
    xanthine 280
    nicotine 258
    amphetamines 258
    social drugs 258
    caffeine 258, 280-4
Urecholine (bethanechol) 151
Urinary bladder 79, *Figure* 85
Uromide (salicylamide) 208
USP (Pharmacopeia of the United States of America) 19

V

V Codes 104
Vagina 227
Vaginismus 230
Valenstein, E. 67, 334
Valium 19
    diazepam 116-7, 122, 139, 222, 243, 254, 275
Valproic acid (Depakene) 222
    adverse effect 222

Van Dyke, C. 292, 293, 351
van Woert, M. 232, 333
Vander, A.J. 232, 351
Vane, J.R. 205, 336, 345
VanMeter, C.T. 336
Vaugh, W. 285
Vecki, V.G. 231, 351
Ventricles 63, 64
Ventricles 64
Veronal 134
Vesprin
    phenothiazine 277
    aliphatic 277
    triflupromazine 174, 178, 179
Vitamin B 1
    thiamine 313
Vivactil (protriptyline) 154, 237
Volstead Act 312
von Baeyer, A. 134
von Euler, U.S. 203, 352

W

Wall, P.D. 191, 344
Wallace Laboratories 114
War neuroses 315
Warfarin (Coumadin) 136
Washington House 312
Watanabe, M. 162, 351
Waves
    alpha 126
    beta 126
    delta 126
    theta 126
Webb, W.B. 124, 352
Wei, E. 352
Weight
    factors determining doses 28-9
Weil, A.T. 255, 257, 301, 352
Weil-Malherbe, H. 156, 352
Welner, J. 168, 348, 351
Wen, H.L. 320, 346
Wender, P. H. 168, 340, 348, 352
Wernicke's area 67
Wesson, D.R. 271, 274, 351
Wheal 204-5
White matter 63
White Stuff (Morphine sulfate) 281
White, J. 321, 351

ABOUT THE AUTHOR

Myron M. Goldenberg, adjacent to the state park, in Topanga, California, where he lives with his wife Linda and daughter, Lara.

Myron M. Goldenberg

His formal education includes doctorates in Pharmacy and Psychology. He is a graduate of the University of Southern California, Azusa Pacific University, and Sierra University. He is a teacher at the Rosenberg-Rand Institute in Venice, California.

Beyond his formal training, he has studied and been in supervision in Integrated Body Psychotherapy, Family Therapy, Reichian Therapy, Object Relations, Self Psychology, Acupressure, Metaphysics, and Esoteric Healing. The diversity of his training ranges from teachers such as Bruno Bettelhein to Brugh Joy.

His professional evolution includes being a community pharmacist, a hospital pharmacy director, an army officer including a tour in Vietnam, and is currently in private practice in psychotherapy in Santa Monica, CA. He has led workshops both in the United States and Canada. His writings and teachings have been both in the area of physical and mental health. For the past four years he has published a newsletter for the Rosenberg-Rand Institute.

His outdoor interests including hiking, biking, carpentry, running, golf, and tennis. On the artistic front, he enjoys painting and music.